Collar And Daniell's First Year Latin

A ROMAN CITIZEN SPEAKS

COLLAR AND DANIELL'S
FIRST YEAR LATIN

REVISED BY

THORNTON JENKINS

HEAD MASTER, HIGH SCHOOL, MALDEN, MASSACHUSETTS

GINN AND COMPANY
BOSTON · NEW YORK · CHICAGO · LONDON
ATLANTA · DALLAS · COLUMBUS · SAN FRANCISCO

COPYRIGHT, 1901, BY WILLIAM C. COLLAR AND M. GRANT DANIELL
COPYRIGHT, 1918, BY GINN AND COMPANY
ENTERED AT STATIONERS' HALL
ALL RIGHTS RESERVED

422.12

HARVARD UNIVERSITY
LIBRARY OF GRADUATE SCHOOL
OF EDUCATION

TRANSFERRED TO
HARVARD COLLEGE LIBRARY

The Athenæum Press
GINN AND COMPANY · PRO-
PRIETORS · BOSTON · U.S.A.

PREFACE

The book that is placed in the hands of a pupil during his first year of the study of Latin should be simple and clear and interesting in its treatment of the language; it should teach with the utmost thoroughness those principles that it attempts to teach, but it should not attempt to teach to-day what may be taught more properly to-morrow; it should get the pupil into the reading of easy connected Latin as soon as possible, and for this purpose should supply a generous amount of material graded to his attainment; and it should never allow the pupil to leave the classroom without a reminder of the extent to which Latin is a part of his own language.

With these convictions the revision of Collar and Daniell's "First Year Latin" was undertaken. All these principles underlay the plan of "First Year Latin," but the unanimity with which they have been accepted since the publication of that text has made it possible in the revision so to extend their application as to produce what is in effect a new book.

The vocabulary has been made briefer and more Cæsarian. From the vocabularies of the lessons the pupil is asked to learn the meanings of some five hundred and seventy words. About ninety per cent of these words are included in the list of one thousand words which Professor Lodge[1] suggests should be learned before the end of the second year of the study of Latin. Over sixty per cent occur more than ten times in Cæsar. In the Selections for Reading the pupil has a chance to become acquainted casually with a wider vocabulary.

[1] Vocabulary of High School Latin.

A number of constructions which were taught in the original book have been omitted. With three exceptions the constructions included in the revision are those which Byrne[1] recommends for the first year. Similarly, the pupil is no longer required to learn uncommon forms which are not necessary for his second-year reading.

Increased attention has been given to derivatives. Related English words are often placed after the Latin words in the vocabularies of the lessons as well as in the general vocabulary. Everywhere in the reviews this important part of the study of Latin is kept constantly before the pupil. Suggestions are offered for the keeping of notebooks of English derivatives. The force of certain common prefixes and suffixes in the formation and meaning of Latin words is also explained.

Interspersed throughout the book there are ten Review Lessons, which take up the words and constructions previously taught. The machinery for drill has been further strengthened by a summary of the uses of nouns and of verbs, and by review questions touching upon the syntax, forms, derivatives, and principles of each lesson. These questions have been placed after the Selections for Reading, that they may be somewhat removed from the lessons they concern.

The treatment of the Essentials of Grammar has been made more useful by a comparison of English grammar with Latin grammar, and by the inclusion of Latin equivalents for the English illustrative words and phrases.

The material for reading has been somewhat changed, particularly by the omission of the Fables and Stories, and by the introduction of the Story of Perseus, of the simplified narrative of Cæsar's Campaign against the Helvetians, and of a number of pages from Eutropius. In all the selections the

[1] The Syntax of High School Latin.

syntax has been made to conform with that taught in the lessons, so that the pupil may not be bothered or discouraged by unfamiliar constructions.

As an aid to the pupil's pronunciation, a mark of accent has been placed on the words in the vocabularies of the first eighteen lessons, and on declensions and conjugations, both in the text and in the Appendix.

Teachers who are familiar with "First Year Latin" will find that none of its well-known excellences have been sacrificed in the revision. There are, for example, the same short lessons, usually less than two pages in length. In the exercises the sentences for translation remain simple. Nowhere are many constructions brought within the limits of a single sentence. The exercises for translation from English into Latin are relatively shorter than those from Latin into English. The order in which the verb is developed and in which the various constructions are presented will be found the same, with a few exceptions. In the study of syntax the pupil is still led from the observation of model sentences to the deduction of usages and principles. Passages of connected Latin are introduced early and are of frequent occurrence throughout the lessons, and there is ample material for reading after the lessons have been completed. The content of the book is still such that it is possible for high-school classes to go through the lessons within thirty weeks.

The "Teacher's Manual," in addition to general directions and notes on each lesson, contains carefully graded sentences for sight reading and for the practice of the "direct method," as well as material for drill on English derivatives of the Latin words of the vocabularies.

It is hoped that teachers will find the numerous illustrations a help to them in familiarizing pupils with the life of the

Romans. The four plates in colors were made especially for this book by Mr. Arthur E. Becher after a careful study of all the phases of Roman life that they represent. As for the other pictures, half tones have been used where the subject could be made more realistic if reproduced directly from a photograph. In cases where line engravings seemed more suitable, drawings in the style of the early Italian engravings were made for the purpose by Mr. Thomas M. Cleland, Mr. W. A. Dwiggins, and Mr. Adrian J. Iorio. As a whole the illustrations are believed to be of a quality unexcelled in schoolbooks.

The reviser wishes to acknowledge his indebtedness to the suggestions received from Mr. Collar himself, who, before his death, had given considerable thought to the aim and scope of the revision. Indebtedness is also gratefully acknowledged to Professor Charles Knapp, of Barnard College, New York; to Mr. Herbert F. Hancox, of Lewis Institute, Chicago; and to Miss Grace I. Bridge and Miss Grace E. Jackson, of the Hyde Park High School, Chicago, for their helpful criticisms.

T. J.

CONTENTS

	PAGE
ESSENTIALS OF GRAMMAR	1
TO THE BEGINNER IN LATIN: WHAT LATIN IS, AND WHY IT IS STUDIED. HOW TO STUDY LATIN	15
INTRODUCTION: ALPHABET, SOUNDS OF THE LETTERS, SYLLABLES, QUANTITY, ACCENT	19

LESSON

I. THE SINGULAR AND PLURAL OF NOUNS AND VERBS. THE NOMINATIVE CASE USED AS SUBJECT 24

II. THE ACCUSATIVE CASE USED AS THE DIRECT OBJECT . . 26

III. THE PRESENT INDICATIVE ACTIVE OF THE FIRST CONJUGATION 28

IV. THE GENITIVE CASE USED TO DENOTE POSSESSION . . . 30

V. THE PRESENT INDICATIVE ACTIVE OF THE SECOND CONJUGATION. CAUSAL CLAUSE WITH **Quod** 32

VI. THE DATIVE CASE USED AS THE INDIRECT OBJECT. THE ABLATIVE USED IN PREPOSITIONAL PHRASES TO SHOW PLACE WHERE 34

VII. THE FIRST DECLENSION. GENDER 36
    FIRST REVIEW LESSON 38

VIII. THE SECOND DECLENSION 40

IX. ADJECTIVES OF THE FIRST AND SECOND DECLENSIONS . . 42

X. THE PRESENT INDICATIVE OF **Sum**. PREDICATE NOUN AND PREDICATE ADJECTIVE 44

XI. APPOSITION. **Cornēlia et Iūlia** 46

XII. THE SECOND DECLENSION: NOUNS IN -er, -ir, -ius, AND -ium 48

XIII. ADJECTIVES OF THE FIRST AND SECOND DECLENSIONS ENDING IN -er. **Dē Graeciā** 50

LESSON		PAGE
XIV.	THE IMPERFECT AND FUTURE INDICATIVE OF **Sum**. THE DATIVE WITH ADJECTIVES	52
	SECOND REVIEW LESSON	54
XV.	THE IMPERFECT INDICATIVE ACTIVE, FIRST AND SECOND CONJUGATIONS. THE ABLATIVE OF MEANS	56
XVI.	THE FUTURE INDICATIVE ACTIVE, FIRST AND SECOND CONJUGATIONS. THE ABLATIVE OF MANNER	58
XVII.	PRINCIPAL PARTS. THE PERFECT STEM. THE PERFECT INDICATIVE ACTIVE, FIRST CONJUGATION. **Dē Sabīnīs**	60
XVIII.	THE PERFECT INDICATIVE ACTIVE, SECOND CONJUGATION. THE ABLATIVE OF ACCOMPANIMENT	62
XIX.	THE DEMONSTRATIVE **Is**. THE PERFECT INDICATIVE OF **Sum**	64
XX.	THE INTERROGATIVE **Quis**. **Dē Deīs Rōmānōrum**	66
XXI.	THE PRESENT, IMPERFECT, FUTURE, AND PERFECT INDICATIVE ACTIVE OF THE THIRD CONJUGATION	68
	THIRD REVIEW LESSON	70
XXII.	READING LESSON. **Dē Īcarō. Rōmānī prō Sociīs pugnant**	72
XXIII.	THE THIRD DECLENSION	74
XXIV.	THE THIRD CONJUGATION: VERBS IN -iō. THE ABLATIVE OF PLACE FROM WHICH. THE ACCUSATIVE OF PLACE TO WHICH	76
XXV.	THE ABLATIVE OF CAUSE. PREPOSITIONAL PHRASES EXPRESSING CAUSE	78
XXVI.	THE THIRD DECLENSION: i-STEMS	80
XXVII.	THE ACCUSATIVE AND THE ABLATIVE WITH PREPOSITIONS. ADJECTIVES USED AS NOUNS	82
XXVIII.	READING LESSON. **Horātius Pontem dēfendit. Dē Nātiōnibus Eurōpae**	84
	FOURTH REVIEW LESSON	86
XXIX.	ADJECTIVES OF THE THIRD DECLENSION	88
XXX.	THE FOURTH CONJUGATION. **Conloquium**	90
XXXI.	THE ABLATIVE OF TIME. *Laconic Speeches*	92

CONTENTS

LESSON		PAGE
XXXII.	The Pluperfect and Future Perfect Indicative Active of All Conjugations	94
XXXIII.	The Demonstratives **Hic** and **Ille**. Place from Which and to Which, in Names of Towns	96
XXXIV.	Reading Lesson. **Victōria Caesaris. Dē Caesare et Britannīs**	98
XXXV.	The Present, Imperfect, and Future Indicative Passive of the First and Second Conjugations. The Ablative of Agent	100
XXXVI.	The Relative **Quī**	102
	Fifth Review Lesson	104
XXXVII.	The Present, Imperfect, and Future Indicative Passive of **Regō** and **Capiō**	106
XXXVIII.	The Personal and Reflexive Pronouns	108
XXXIX.	The Present, Imperfect, and Future Indicative Passive of the Fourth Conjugation. **Veturia, Māter Coriolānī. Dē Perseō**	110
XL.	The Possessive Adjectives. The Ablative of Separation	112
XLI.	The Perfect, Pluperfect, and Future Perfect Indicative Passive of All Conjugations. **Iuppiter Perseum servat**	114
XLII.	The Fourth Declension	116
XLIII.	The Comparison of Adjectives	118
	Sixth Review Lesson	120
XLIV.	The Comparison of Adjectives ending in -er or -lis. The Partitive Genitive	122
XLV.	Reading Lesson. **Scīpiō et Hannibal. Perseus Medūsam quaerit**	124
XLVI.	The Irregular Comparison of Adjectives. The Ablative of Degree of Difference	126
XLVII.	The Formation and the Comparison of Adverbs	128
XLVIII.	The Fifth Declension. The Accusative of Extent	130

LESSON	PAGE
XLIX. READING LESSON. *A Letter from Pompeii.* **Perseus Medūsam interficit**	132
L. THE SUBJUNCTIVE MOOD. THE PRESENT SUBJUNCTIVE. PURPOSE CLAUSES WITH **Ut** AND **Nē**	134
LI. THE IMPERFECT SUBJUNCTIVE. SEQUENCE OF TENSES	136
LII. SUBSTANTIVE CLAUSES OF PURPOSE. RESULT CLAUSES	138
SEVENTH REVIEW LESSON	140
LIII. READING LESSON. **Caesar Hostīs vincit. Andromeda Fīlia Cēpheī**	142
LIV. THE PERFECT AND THE PLUPERFECT SUBJUNCTIVE. INDIRECT QUESTIONS	144
LV. NUMERAL ADJECTIVES. THE OBJECTIVE GENITIVE	146
LVI. ADJECTIVES HAVING THE GENITIVE IN -īus. **Mōnstrum appropinquat**	148
LVII. THE INFINITIVE AS SUBJECT AND AS COMPLEMENT	150
LVIII. THE INFINITIVE AS OBJECT. THE ACCUSATIVE AS SUBJECT OF THE INFINITIVE. INDIRECT STATEMENTS	152
LIX. READING LESSON. **Caesar in Conciliō dīcit. Perseus Cēpheō Andromedam reddit**	156
LX. THE DEMONSTRATIVES **Īdem, Ipse, Iste.** THE IRREGULAR VERB **Possum**	158
EIGHTH REVIEW LESSON	160
LXI. THE INDEFINITE PRONOUNS. *The Nations of Gaul*	162
LXII. THE DATIVE WITH COMPOUNDS. THE DATIVES OF PURPOSE AND REFERENCE	164
LXIII. THE DATIVE WITH SPECIAL INTRANSITIVE VERBS. THE IRREGULAR VERBS **Volō, Nōlō, Mālō**	166
LXIV. READING LESSON. *Belling the Cat. Nasica and Ennius. Orgetorix and the Helvetians*	168
LXV. PARTICIPLES	170
LXVI. READING LESSON. **Dicta Antīquōrum.** *Orgetorix and the Helvetians* (CONTINUED)	173
LXVII. THE ABLATIVE ABSOLUTE	175

CONTENTS

LESSON		PAGE
LXVIII.	The Gerund. The Irregular Verb Eō	178
	Ninth Review Lesson	180
LXIX.	The Gerundive. The Irregular Verb Ferō	182
LXX.	Reading Lesson. *The Helvetians leave their Territory*	184
LXXI.	The Ablative of Specification. Deponent Verbs	186
LXXII.	Temporal Clauses with Cum. The Irregular Verb Fīō	188
LXXIII.	Reading Lesson. *Cæsar refuses the Helvetians Permission to go through the Roman Province*	190
LXXIV.	Substantive Clauses of Fact introduced by Quod. The Indicative in Adverbial Clauses	192
LXXV.	Subordinate Clauses in Indirect Statements	194
	Tenth Review Lesson	196
	Summary: The Uses of Nouns and Verbs	198

Selections for Reading:
  Cæsar: The Campaign against the Helvetians 201
  Cæsar: The Story of the Aduatuci 206
  Stories of Hercules 208
  Stories of Ulysses 213
  Eutropius: History of Rome 218
  Stories from Roman History 223

Review Questions 227

Appendix I:
  Rules of Syntax 245
  Formation of Latin Words 249
  English Derivatives 251

Appendix II:
  Declensions and Conjugations 253

Latin-English Vocabulary 287

English-Latin Vocabulary 331

Index 341

FIRST YEAR LATIN

ESSENTIALS OF GRAMMAR

THE PARTS OF SPEECH

Nouns

I. *a.* A *noun* is the name of a person, place, or thing: *boy, London, ship*; **puer, Londīnium, nāvis**.

b. A *proper noun* is the name of a particular person, place, or thing: *Cornelia, Rome, Rhone*; **Cornēlia, Rōma, Rhodanus**.

c. A *common noun* is a name that may be applied to any one of a class of objects: *boy, city, day*; **puer, urbs, diēs**.

d. A *collective noun* is a name that may be applied to a group of objects, though itself in the singular number (XXIII): *crowd, family*; **multitūdō, gēns**.

e. A *verbal noun* is the name of an action: *seeing, writing, to see, to write*; **videndī** (459), **scrībendī, vidēre, scrībere**.

f. An *abstract noun* is the name of a quality or condition: *goodness, truth, poverty*; **bonitās, vēritās, paupertās**.

Pronouns

II. *a.* A *pronoun* is a word used to take the place of a noun or of another pronoun: *I, you, him, this, who*; **ego, tū, eum, hoc, quī**.

b. The noun (or pronoun) for which a pronoun stands is called its *antecedent* (from **antecēdere**, *to go before*). Thus, in the sentence *John goes to school, but he does not study*, the noun *John* is the antecedent of *he*. The antecedent is especially common with a relative pronoun (II, *d*). Neither in Latin nor in English does the antecedent necessarily stand in advance of its pronoun: *What he says, he believes,* **quod dīcit,** *id* **crēdit.**

c. A *personal pronoun* shows by its form whether it stands (1) for the speaker: *I, we;* **ego, nōs,** that is, the *first person;* (2) for the person spoken to: *thou, you;* **tū, vōs,** that is, the *second person;* or (3) for the person or thing spoken of: *he, she, it, they;* **is, ea, id, eī,** that is, the *third person*.

d. A *relative pronoun* connects a subordinate clause, in which it stands, with the antecedent: *The book* **that** *you have is mine,* **liber** *quem* **habēs meus est.** The relative pronouns in English are *who, which, that,* and *as;* in Latin the relative is **quī.**

e. An *interrogative pronoun* is used to ask a question: *Who is walking in the garden?* **Quis in hortō ambulat?** The interrogative pronouns in English are *who, which,* and *what;* in Latin, **quis** and **uter.**

f. A *demonstrative pronoun* points out an object definitely: *this, that, these, those;* **hic, ille, hī, illī.**

g. An *indefinite pronoun* refers to an object indefinitely: *some, some one, any, any one;* **aliquis, quis.**

h. A *reflexive pronoun* refers back to the subject: *He blamed himself,* **sē culpāvit.**

ADJECTIVES

III. *a*. An *adjective* is a word used to qualify or limit a noun or a pronoun: *good book, beautiful moon, five girls;* **liber** *bonus,* **lūna** *pulchra,* **quīnque puellae.**

b. *A, an,* and *the,* really limiting adjectives, are sometimes called *articles*. *The* is the *definite article, a* or *an* the *indefinite article*. These articles are not used in Latin.

c. Numeral adjectives denote how many persons or things are under consideration. They are either *cardinal*, denoting how many: *one, two, three, four*; **ūnus, duo, trēs, quattuor**; or *ordinal*, denoting which in order: *first, second, third, fourth*; **prīmus, secundus, tertius, quārtus.**

d. Possessive adjectives denote ownership: **my friend, our house**; **meus amīcus, nostra domus.** Possessive adjectives are frequently used as possessive pronouns.

e. The demonstrative pronouns, the indefinite pronouns, and the interrogative pronouns *which* and *what* may be used as adjectives, and are then called respectively *demonstrative adjectives*: **this book, that house; hic liber, illa domus**; *indefinite adjectives*: **some boys, aliquī puerī**; and *interrogative adjectives*: **Which way shall we go? Quā viā ībimus?**

f. Adjectives are often used as nouns: "*The land of the free,*" **patria līberōrum.**

Verbs

IV. *a.* A *verb* is a word which can declare or assert something about a person, a place, or a thing: *The man laughs*, **vir rīdet**; *the town is captured*, **oppidum captum est**; *the leaf falls*, **folium cadit.**

b. A verb which has an object (xiv, *a*) to complete its meaning is said to be *transitive*, or to be *used transitively*: *The girl has a rose*, **puella rosam habet.**

c. A verb which does not have an object (xiv, *a*) to complete its meaning is said to be *intransitive*, or to be *used intransitively*: *Birds fly*, **avēs volant**; *I walk*, **ambulō.**

Note. Thus certain verbs may at one time be transitive and at another intransitive: *The wind blew the snow into our faces; the wind blew furiously.*

d. Verbs are classified as *regular* or *irregular*. This distinction is made merely for convenience. A *regular verb* in English forms its imperfect (past) tense (XXXIII, *a*) and past participle (XXXIV, *b*) by the addition of *d* or *ed* to the present: present, *love*; past, *loved*; past participle, *loved*. For Latin regular verbs see 658–662.

e. An *irregular verb* in English does not form its imperfect (past) tense by the addition of *d* or *ed* to the present: present, *give*; past, *gave*; past participle, *given*. For Latin irregular verbs see 663–668.

f. An *auxiliary verb* is used in the conjugation of other verbs: *I am loved, he has given*. In Latin the verb **esse**, *to be* (663), is so used: **missus est**, *he has been sent*.

Adverbs

V. *a.* An *adverb* is used to modify a verb, an adjective, or another adverb: *He walks swiftly,* **celeriter ambulat**.

b. An *adverb* of *place* answers the question *where?* — *here, there, hence*; **hīc, illīc, hinc**.

c. An *adverb* of *time* answers the question *when?* — *then, now, often*; **tum, nunc, saepe**.

d. An *adverb* of *manner* answers the question *how?* — *so, well, ill*; **sīc, bene, male**.

e. An *adverb* of *degree* answers the question *how much?* — *little, almost, enough*; **paulō, paene, satis**.

f. A *modal adverb* expresses affirmation or negation, or the degree of confidence with which a statement is made: *yes, no, certainly, perhaps*; **certē, forsitan**.

Prepositions

VI. A preposition is used before a noun or pronoun to show its relation to another word in the sentence. Usually the relation shown is position, direction, or time: *He sent a legion against the enemy,* in **hostēs legiōnem mīsit**. In Latin certain phrases which would be introduced in English by a preposition are expressed by the use of one of the cases (XXIV, *b*) without a preposition: *At dawn he sent a legion,* **primā lūce legiōnem mīsit**.

Conjunctions

VII. *a.* A *conjunction* connects words, phrases (XVI), clauses (XX), and sentences (XVIII): *boys and girls,* **puerī et puellae**; *they fought bravely but were conquered,* **fortiter pugnāvērunt sed victī sunt**.

b. A *coördinate conjunction* connects words, phrases, clauses, and sentences of equal order or rank. The conjunctions in the examples in VII, *a* are coördinate.

c. A *subordinate conjunction* connects a subordinate clause (XX, *a*) with a principal clause (XX, *a*): *The boy was praised because he was industrious,* **puer laudātus est quod impiger erat**.

Interjections

VIII. An *interjection* is used to express strong feeling. It is not grammatically related to any other word in the sentence: *oh! ah! alas! hurrah!* **ēheu! ecce!**

NOTE. The following couplets have often proved useful to young persons in identifying the parts of speech:

>Three little words we often see
>Are Articles, *a*, *an*, and *the*.
>
>A Noun's the name of anything;
>As *school* or *garden*, *hoop* or *swing*.

Adjectives tell the kind of noun;
As *great, small, pretty, white,* or *brown.*

Instead of nouns the Pronouns stand;
I come, *you* go, as *they* command.

Verbs tell of something being done;
As *read, write, spell, sing, jump,* or *run.*

How things are done the Adverbs tell;
As *slowly, quickly, ill,* or *well.*

They also tell us where and when;
As *here* and *there* and *now* and *then.*

A Preposition stands before
A noun; as *in* or *through* a door.

Conjunctions join the words together;
As rain *and* sunshine, wind *or* weather.

Conjunctions sentences unite;
As kittens scratch *and* puppies bite.

An Interjection shows surprise;
As *Oh!* how pretty! *Ah!* how wise!

THE SENTENCE

IX. A *sentence* is a word or a group of words expressing a thought: *Stars shine; he walks;* **stellae lūcent; ambulat.**

X. *a.* A *declarative sentence* declares or asserts something: *The farmers are plowing the fields,* **agricolae agrōs arant.**

b. An *interrogative sentence* asks a question: *Why are the farmers plowing the fields?* **Cūr agricolae agrōs arant?**

c. An *imperative sentence* expresses a command, a request, or an entreaty: *Plow the fields to-day,* **hodiē agrōs arāte.**

d. An *exclamatory sentence* expresses strong feeling or emotion: *Would that he had remained!* **Utinam mānsisset!**

XI. *a.* A sentence is made up of two parts, one called the *subject* and the other the *predicate*.

b. The *subject* represents the person, place, or thing about which something is declared or asserted: **Birds sing, avēs cantant.**

c. The *predicate* declares or asserts something about the person, place, or thing which the subject represents: *Birds sing,* **avēs** *cantant.*

NOTE. In English and in Latin either the subject or the predicate, or both, may be enlarged to any extent by the addition of qualifying words and expressions called modifiers: **My sister's small birds | sing sweetly in the morning.**

XII. The *simple subject* is the noun or pronoun which signifies the person, place, or thing about which the assertion is made. The *simple predicate* is the verb that makes the assertion. *Birds* is the simple subject, and *sing* the simple predicate, in the note under XI, *c.*

XIII. The *complete subject* is the simple subject with all its modifiers. The *complete predicate* is the simple predicate with all its modifiers. Thus, in the example in the note under XI, *c* the complete subject is all that precedes the vertical line, and the complete predicate all that follows it.

XIV. *a.* The *object* of a verb is a word or an expression that completes the meaning of the verb, and signifies that which is affected by the action: *He sent messengers,* **nūntiōs mīsit**; *he wished me to go to Italy,* **mē in Italiam īre voluit.**

b. The *direct object* represents that which is immediately affected by the action of the verb; the *indirect object* that to or for which the action is performed. Thus, in *He gave me a book,* **mihi librum dedit,** *book* is the direct object, and *me* the indirect.

XV. *a.* A *predicate noun* or a *predicate adjective* is used after certain intransitive or passive verbs to complete their meaning, and to describe or define the subject: *Marcus is a sailor*; *the sailor is brave*; **Mārcus nauta est**; **nauta fortis est**.

b. The predicate noun or adjective is called the *complement* of the verb. Intransitive verbs that require a complement are called *copulative verbs*. The verb *be* (Latin **esse**) in its various forms (*am, was, has been*, etc.) is often called the *copula*.

c. The predicate noun or adjective has the same case as the subject; hence the term *predicate nominative*.

XVI. *a.* A *phrase* is a combination of words (not subject and predicate) used as a single part of speech.

b. An *adjective phrase* modifies a noun: *A man of great valor*, **vir magnae virtūtis**.

c. An *adverbial phrase* modifies a verb: *They work with great diligence*, **magnā cum dīligentiā labōrant**. In Latin certain cases of nouns are used to express what in English would be prepositional phrases of an adverbial nature (VI).

XVII. A *simple sentence* contains but one statement, that is, one subject and one predicate: *Cæsar drew up a line of battle*, **Caesar aciem īnstrūxit**.

XVIII. A *compound sentence* contains two or more independent statements: *Cæsar drew up a line of battle, but the enemy fled*, **Caesar aciem īnstrūxit, sed hostēs fūgērunt**.

NOTE. An independent statement is one that can stand alone; it does not depend on (qualify or limit) another statement.

XIX. A *complex sentence* contains one independent (principal) statement and one or more dependent (subordinate) statements: *When the messenger had replied, the lieutenant spoke as follows,* **cum nūntius respondisset, lēgātus haec dīxit.**

NOTE. A dependent, or subordinate, statement is one that qualifies or limits another in some way; thus, the dependent statement *when the messenger had replied* limits the verb *spoke*, telling when the lieutenant spoke.

XX. *a.* The separate statements in a compound or a complex sentence are called *clauses*, and, as has already been seen, they may be either *independent (principal)* or *dependent (subordinate)*.

b. When dependent (subordinate) clauses modify nouns or pronouns they are called *adjective clauses*: *The girls whom we praised were good*, **puellae quās laudāvimus bonae erant.**

c. When dependent (subordinate) clauses modify verbs they are called *adverbial clauses*: **When the messenger had replied, the lieutenant spoke as follows,** **cum nūntius respondisset, lēgātus haec dīxit.**

d. When dependent (subordinate) clauses are used as nouns they are called *substantive clauses*: **That you are here pleases us,** **quod ades nōs dēlectat.**

e. Dependent (subordinate) clauses introduced by *when* (Latin **cum, ubi,** etc.) are called *temporal clauses*; introduced by *because* (Latin **quod** etc.), they are called *causal clauses*; introduced by *if* (Latin **sī**), they are called *conditional clauses*; introduced by *although* (Latin **cum, etsī,** etc.), they are called *concessive clauses*; introduced by a relative pronoun (Latin **quī**), they are called *relative clauses*.

f. The independent clause of a complex sentence is called the *principal clause*. Connected clauses that are of the same rank, both independent or both dependent, are said to be *coördinate*.

INFLECTION

XXI. *Inflection* is a change in the form of a word to indicate a change in its meaning or use: *man, men, boy, boy's, love, loved*; **vir, virī, puer, puerī, amant, amābant.**

DECLENSION

XXII. The inflection of a noun or pronoun is called its *declension*. Nouns and pronouns in English are declined to show number and case, and a few nouns to show gender. In Latin the nouns and pronouns are declined; adjectives also are declined in gender, number, and case to agree with the nouns which they modify.

Number

XXIII. A noun or pronoun is in the *singular number* when it means one person, place, or thing: *town, city, I*; **oppidum, urbs, ego**; in the *plural number* when it means more than one person, place, or thing: *towns, cities, we*; **oppida, urbēs, nōs.**

Case

XXIV. *a.* The several forms taken by words that are declined are called *cases*. In English there are the following cases, to indicate the uses of nouns and pronouns:

1. The *nominative*, primarily used as the subject of a sentence: **He** *throws the ball.*

2. The *possessive* (genitive), used to denote possession or ownership: *John throws his ball; see the* **queen's** *crown.*

3. The *objective* (accusative), used as the object of a transitive verb or of a preposition: *John throws the ball to him.*

4. The *dative*, used to express the indirect object of the verb: *John throws him the ball.* Only personal pronouns and the pronoun *who* have separate forms for these cases in English.

Nouns have the nominative, objective, and dative alike, with a separate form for the possessive.

b. In Latin there are seven cases: *nominative, genitive, dative, accusative, ablative, vocative,* and *locative*; but a single form sometimes does duty for several cases (cf. **agricola**, 63). The nominative, genitive, and accusative cases are used much like the same cases in English. The dative expresses in general that relation of words to other words which is expressed in English by prepositional phrases beginning with *to* or *for*: *to the farmer, for the man.* The ablative expresses in general that relation of words to other words which is expressed in English by prepositional phrases beginning with *from, with, by, in*: *with a spear, by a story.*

c. The direct object of a verb in Latin is in the accusative case, but sometimes the direct object in English is expressed in Latin by the dative (425, 433).

Gender

XXV. *a.* The gender of English nouns is what is called *natural gender,* and hence has very little to do with grammar. Thus, a noun denoting a male is in the *masculine gender*: *man, boy, father*; a noun denoting a female is in the *feminine gender*: *woman, girl, mother*; one denoting either male or female is in the *common gender*: *cat, dog, parent*; one denoting a sexless object is in the *neuter gender*: *river, wind, mountain.*

b. In Latin only nouns that denote persons and some animals have natural gender: **nauta**, *sailor* (masc.); **māter**, *mother* (fem.). All others have an arbitrary gender, called *grammatical gender,* determined chiefly by the ending: **flūmen**, *river* (neut.); **ventus**, *wind* (masc.); **nūbēs**, *cloud* (fem.).

Comparison

XXVI. *a.* English adjectives and adverbs are inflected to show degree. This is called *comparison*. There are three degrees of comparison, the *positive*, the *comparative*, and the *superlative*: positive *wise*, comparative *wiser*, superlative *wisest*; positive *good*, comparative *better*, superlative *best*; positive *often*, comparative *oftener*, superlative *oftenest*.

b. Adjectives and adverbs are also compared in English by prefixing the adverbs *more* and *most*: *beautiful, more beautiful, most beautiful*.

c. Comparison in Latin is indicated exactly as in English: **sapiēns, sapientior, sapientissimus ; bonus, melior, optimus ; idōneus, magis idōneus, maximē idōneus ; saepe, saepius, saepissimē.**

Conjugation

XXVII. *a.* The inflection of a verb is called *conjugation*. Verbs are conjugated to show voice, mood, and tense, and the number and person of the subject.

b. The English verb has but few changes of form. Thus the verb *love* has in common use only the forms *love, loves, loving,* and *loved*. Most of the conjugation of the verb is made up of verb phrases formed by the use of auxiliaries (IV, *f*): *I am loved, I shall love, I shall have been loved,* etc.

c. The Latin verb has many changes in form to show voice, mood, tense, number, and person: **amor**, *I am loved*; **amābō**, *I shall love*; **amātus erō**, *I shall have been loved*.

Voice

XXVIII. A verb is in the *active voice* when it represents the subject as acting (or being): *The man praised the boy,* **vir puerum laudāvit**. A verb is in the *passive voice* when it represents the subject as acted on: *The boy was praised by the man,* **puer ā virō laudātus est**.

Mood

XXIX. A verb is in the *indicative mood* when it is used in stating a fact or in asking a question: *The citizens are assembling*, **cīvēs conveniunt**; *why do they carry arms?* **cūr arma portant?**

XXX. *a.* In English a verb is in the *subjunctive mood* when it asserts something doubtfully or conditionally. It is used in subordinate clauses, and is usually introduced by *if*, *though*, and the like: *If he were here, I should be glad*; "*Though he slay me, yet will I trust in him.*"

NOTE. The subjunctive is very little used in modern English, its place being taken by the indicative.

b. In Latin the subjunctive has a great variety of uses, in independent as well as in dependent clauses (344, 358, 373, etc.).

XXXI. *a.* A verb is in the *imperative mood* when it expresses command, request, or entreaty: **Fortify the city**, **urbem mūnīte**.

b. Unless emphatic the subject of the imperative (*thou* or *you*) is not expressed either in English or in Latin.

The Infinitive

XXXII. *a.* The *infinitive* in English (*to love, to have loved*, etc.) is a verbal noun. It has neither person nor number. Like a noun it may be the subject or the object or the complement of a verb: *To see is to believe*; *he wishes to go home*. Like a verb it may have a subject, an object, and adverbial modifiers: *We wish you to begin your work early*.

b. The Latin infinitive is used in the same way that the English infinitive is used. It differs, however, from the English infinitive in not being used in prose in expressions of purpose (*They came to see me*), and in being used constantly for the verb of a statement that is given indirectly: *He said that he would come*, **dīxit sē ventūrum esse.**

c. The verbal noun in *-ing* is sometimes called an infinitive: **Seeing is believing** = *to see is to believe.* This verbal noun has its counterpart in the Latin gerund (459).

Tense

XXXIII. *a.* A verb is in the *present, past (imperfect)*, or *future* tense according as it represents an action as taking place in present, past, or future time: *I love, I loved (was loving), I shall love*; **amō, amābam, amābō.**

b. The *present perfect (perfect)* tense represents an action completed in the present: *I have loved*, **amāvī**; the *past perfect (pluperfect)* an action completed in the past before some other past action or state: *I had loved*, **amāveram**; and the *future perfect* an action completed in the future before some other future action or state: *I shall have loved*, **amāverō.**

The Participle

XXXIV. *a.* The *participle* is a verbal adjective. Like an adjective it may qualify a noun: **struggling soldiers, mīlitēs labōrantēs.** Like a verb it may have an object and adverbial modifiers: *Fearing danger they remained in the camp*, **perīculum veritī in castrīs mānsērunt.**

b. There are in English three participles in the active voice: present, *loving*; past, *loved*; perfect, *having loved*; and three in the passive voice: present, *(being) loved*; past, *loved*; perfect, *having been loved*. In Latin the past and perfect active and the present passive participles are wanting, but there is a future participle.

c. The participle in *-ing* is used with the auxiliary *be* to make the progressive form of the verb: *you are loving, he was loving, they will be loving.* Latin has no special tenses for the progressive forms.

TO THE BEGINNER IN LATIN

What Latin is. Latin is the language that was used by the ancient Romans. It gets its name from the *Lati'ni*, a little tribe living in western Italy more than twenty-five hundred years ago. The Latini, and their successors, the Romans, slowly extended their lands and their power until they gained control of all Italy, and finally of all the civilized world of those days. Their dominions reached from the Atlantic Ocean to Persia and from the Baltic Sea to the deserts of Africa, and their language was spoken wherever they ruled. For about six hundred years the Romans were the most powerful nation on the earth. Their history covers in all a period of twelve centuries; no nation has had a longer history.

Why Latin is studied. And now why is it that it is worth your while to study a language that is so many centuries old?

First, a knowledge of Latin helps you to use English more correctly. As more than half the words in the English language are of Latin origin, you yourself in a sense speak Latin to-day. There are the words of your everyday talk, like *animal*; there are the learned words, like *emancipate*; there are the terms of law, of medicine, and of the sciences, like *mandamus*, *delirium*, and *antennae*; and there are the words which are newly come into use, like *tractor*. If you study Latin, you will be helped to know the meaning of many of these words, how to spell them, and how to use them correctly; all of which is quite worth your while, particularly if you are intending to enter one of the professions.

Again, the study of Latin will train your mind. Latin is somewhat unlike English in the form of its words and much unlike English in the order of the words in its sentences. You will therefore be obliged to look carefully, and to think carefully, and to speak carefully whenever you try to read and to translate anything written in Latin. But this close attention will do good to your mind: it will train your powers of observation, of clear thinking, and of clear expression; in fact, no other subject that you study in school can do as much for you as can Latin toward developing these desirable powers.

Furthermore, the reading of Latin will add to your information. If you are to be a well-informed person, you will need to know something about Rome and the Romans, and what they have meant in the history of the world; and in no other way can you better come to know and to appreciate the literature, the life, the customs, and the civilization of the Romans than by the faithful study of their language and of the things written in that language.

How to study Latin. 1. Never allow yourself to think that Latin is not worth your best efforts or that it is too hard for you. Industry and confidence will bring you success in this study.

2. Have a fixed hour each day for the study of your Latin. If possible, prepare your lesson for to-morrow immediately after reciting the lesson of to-day. Your interest will then be greater and your mind better fitted to grasp the subject.

3. Learn each day's lesson with thoroughness. Neglect no part of the lesson even if it seems to you unimportant.

4. Before beginning a new lesson recall what you have already learned about the subject to be taught in the new lesson. For example, if you are about to study a new use of one of the cases, recall all the uses of that case which you have previously learned.

5. Review the vocabularies regularly. A knowledge of the meanings of the words will be a great saving of time to you, as well as a constant encouragement. Aim to know every word

you have met, and to this end keep lists of words about the meaning of which you are doubtful.

6. Recite the declensions and the conjugations by yourself aloud. It will help you to remember them, and you will make better recitations. Read the Latin sentences aloud each day.

7. Go over the new lesson slowly, and thus avoid mistakes in the spelling of words, in their endings, and in the explanation of Latin constructions.

8. Recall your English grammar when you are learning Latin constructions; most of the Latin usages that you will learn in your first year are like English usages.

9. Study the lessons as a whole. Then go back to special difficulties. Go over the lesson again just before the recitation and consider the troublesome parts.

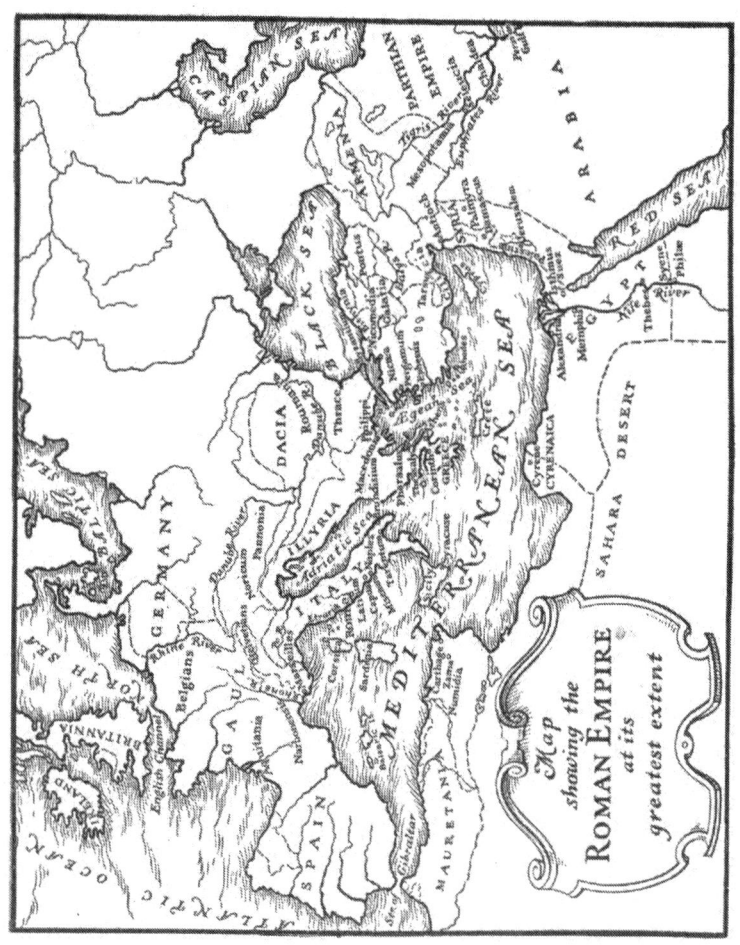

INTRODUCTION

ALPHABET

1. The Latin alphabet has no *j* or *w*. Otherwise it is the same as the English.

2. The vowels are **a, e, i, o, u**. The other letters are consonants.

3. The letter **i** is used both as a vowel and as a consonant. Before a vowel in the same syllable it has the force of a consonant and is called **i**-*consonant*. Thus in **iaciō**, *I throw*, the first **i** is a consonant, and the second a vowel.

SOUNDS OF THE LETTERS[1]

4. The vowels are either long or short. In this book the long vowels are marked (-); unmarked vowels are to be regarded as short. The vowels are sounded as follows:

ā like the last *a* in *aha'*	ă like the first *a* in *aha'*
ē like *e* in *they*	ĕ like *e* in *met*
ī like *i* in *machine*	ĭ like *i* in *pin*
ō like *o* in *note*	ŏ like *o* in *obey*
ū like *oo* in *boot*	ŭ like *oo* in *foot*

5. The diphthongs are sounded as follows:

ae like *ai* in *aisle*	**eu** like *eu* in *feud*
au like *ou* in *our*	**oe** like *oi* in *boil*
ei like *ei* in *eight*	**ui** like *we*

---

[1] Latin is pronounced to-day substantially as it was pronounced by the Romans at the beginning of the Christian era.

6. The consonants generally have the same sound as the corresponding consonants in English. But there are the following exceptions:

c is like *c* in *come*	bs and bt are like *ps* and *pt*
g is like *g* in *get*	ch is like *k* in *kite*
i-consonant is like *y* in *yet*	gu, qu, and sometimes su before a
s is like *s* in *sun*	vowel are like *gw*, *qw*, and *sw* (*u* is
t is like *t* in *time*	not counted as a vowel)
v is like *w* in *wine*	ph is like *p*
x is like *x* in *extra*	th is like *t*

When a consonant is doubled (as ll), it should be pronounced twice.

EXERCISE IN PRONUNCIATION

7. 1. sum, tum. 2. cum, dum. 3. ad, id. 4. in, an. 5. at, et, ut. 6. hic, hīc, hāc. 7. hŏc, hūc. 8. hoc, num. 9. is, bis, īs. 10. dīc, dūc. 11. fac, fer. 12. aut, hae. 13. ē, ā, ī. 14. ex, ab, ob. 15. dō, dā, dē. 16. pāx, dux. 17. nox, vŏx. 18. pars, sōl. 19. trēs, mōs. 20. quō, quā. 21. iūs, quī. 22. quae, quin. 23. quis, sē. 24. mē, tē. 25. gēns, sīc. 26. vel, vir, iam.

SYLLABLES

8. A syllable consists of a vowel or a diphthong with or without one or more consonants. Hence a word has as many syllables as it has vowels and diphthongs: ŏ-ce′-a-nus, *ocean*.

9. When a word is divided into syllables, a single consonant between two vowels is joined with the vowel following: lă-ti-tū′-dŏ, *width*.

10. If there are two or more consonants between two vowels, the first is pronounced with the preceding vowel: im-mor-tā′-lis, *immortal*.

But a consonant followed by l or r is pronounced with the l or r, except in ll and rr: pū'-bli-cus, *public*; when ll or rr occurs, one l or one r is joined to the preceding syllable, and the other to the following syllable: ter'-ra, *land*.

Compound words are divided in such a way as to show the component parts: ab'-est (ab, *away*, + est, *he is*), *he is away*.

11. The last syllable of a word is called the *ultima*; the one next to the last, the *penult*; the one before the penult, the *antepenult*.

12. A vowel is generally short before another vowel or h: pŏ-ĕ'-ma, *poem*; nĭ'-hĭl, *nothing*.

13. A vowel is generally short before nt or nd, and before final m or final t: vo'-cănt, *they call*; vo-cā'-băm, *I was calling*.

14. A vowel is long before nf or ns: a'-māns, *loving*.

15. A vowel resulting from the contraction of two vowels is long: cō'-gŏ (co-agŏ), *I bring together*.

16. The quantity of vowels other than those mentioned in the preceding sections must be learned by observation.

QUANTITY OF SYLLABLES

17. A syllable is *long by nature* when it contains a long vowel or a diphthong: **vic-tō'-ri-a**, *victory*; **prae'-mi-um**, *reward*.

18. A syllable is *short by nature* when it does not contain a long vowel or a diphthong: **o-pī'-ni-ŏ**, *opinion*.

19. A syllable is *long by position* when it has a short vowel followed by x or z, or by two or more consonants, unless these two consonants are p, b, t, d, c, g, followed by l or r; but the short vowel is still pronounced short: dĕ-trĭ-men'-tum, *loss*.

ACCENT

20. Words of two syllables have the accent on the first syllable: pa′-ter, *father*.

21. Words of more than two syllables have the accent on the penult when it is long, otherwise on the antepenult: dē-mōn-strā′-re, *to point out*; ce-le′-ri-tās, *swiftness*; ē-ven′-tus, *outcome* (cf. 19).

22. Several words, of which the commonest are -ne, the sign of a question, and -que, *and*, are appended to other words. The words so appended are known as enclitics. The words to which they are appended are accented on the syllable preceding the enclitic, whether that syllable is long or short: a-mat′-ne? *does he love?* ar-mă′-que, *and arms*.

EXERCISE IN ACCENT AND PRONUNCIATION

23. Divide the following words into syllables, state the rule for the accent, and then pronounce:

1. dīvidunt, appellāre
2. īnstitūtīs, differēbāmus
3. hūmānitāte, prōvinciā
4. longus, animōs
5. importābunt, bellum
6. causīs, praecēdō
7. fīnis, prohibitus
8. initiō, persuāserāmus
9. tempora, magistrātuum
10. frāternus, conloquium

24. The following Latin version of "Twinkle, Twinkle, Little Star" may be used for practice in pronunciation, and for illustration of the preceding statements about syllables, accent, etc.:

MICĀ, MICĀ

Micā, micā, parva stella!
Mīror quaenam sīs, tam bella!
Splendēns ēminus in illō,
Alba velut gemma, caelō.

INTRODUCTION 23

Quandō fervēns Sōl discessit,
Nec calōre prāta pāscit,
Mox ostendis lūmen pūrum,
Micāns, micāns per obscūrum.

Tibi noctū qui vagātur
Ob scintillulam grātātur;
Nī micārēs tū, nōn scīret
Quās per viās errāns īret.

Meum saepe thalamum lūce
Speculāris cūriōsā;
Neque carpseris sopōrem
Dōnec vēnit Sōl per auram.

THE ARCH OF TITUS, SHOWING A ROMAN INSCRIPTION

LESSON I

THE SINGULAR AND PLURAL OF NOUNS AND VERBS
THE NOMINATIVE CASE USED AS SUBJECT

25. The Singular and Plural of Nouns and Verbs.

NOUN	VERB
Nom. Sing. agricol**a**, *farmer*	*3d Pers. Sing.* labōra**t**, *works, is working, does work*
Nom. Plur. agricol**ae**, *farmers*	*3d Pers. Plur.* labōra**nt**, *work, are working, do work*

a. Observe that the distinction between the singular and the plural is shown by the final letters of the noun and of the verb. These final letters of a noun are called *case endings*; the final letters of a verb are called *personal endings*.

b. Form the nominative plural of the nouns in the vocabulary, and the third person plural of the verbs.

26.   ·   **VOCABULARY**

agri'cola, farmer (*agriculture*)
Cornē'lia, Cornelia
Iū'lia, Julia
nau'ta, sailor (*nautical*)
puel'la, girl
et, *conj.*, and
-ne, *enclitic, sign of a question*
am'bulat, walks (*perambulate*)

appropin'quat, approaches, draws near (*propinquity*)
can'tat, sings (*incantation*)
labō'rat, works, labors, suffers (*laboratory*)
na'tat, swims (*natatorium*)
quis, *interrog. pron.*, who?
quid, *interrog. pron.*, what?

27. The Nominative Case used as Subject.

1. **Puella cantat,** *the girl sings (is singing, does sing).*
2. **Puellae cantant,** *the girls sing (are singing, do sing).*
3. **Cantatne puella,** *does the girl sing (is the girl singing)?*
4. **Cantantne puellae,** *do the girls sing (are the girls singing)?*

a. In Latin there is no article (III, *b*): **puella** may be translated *girl, a girl,* or *the girl*; and **puellae**, *girls* or *the girls*.

b. What is the subject (XI, *b*) of each of the model sentences, and what is the predicate (XI, *c*)? In what case is the subject of a Latin verb (XXIV)?

c. Observe that the verbs agree with their subjects in number.

d. Observe that **-ne** is not separately translated. Usually it is attached to the emphatic word in the sentence, and the emphasized word is placed first. When an interrogative word is used, **-ne** is omitted: see sentence 11 below. In English **-ne** is represented on the printed page by the question mark, and in oral translation by the inflection of the voice.

28. *Rule for the Nominative Case as Subject.* *The subject of a verb is in the nominative case.*

29. *Rule for the Agreement of the Verb with its Subject.* *A verb agrees with its subject in person and number.*

EXERCISES

30. 1. Nauta cantat. 2. Nautae cantant. 3. Agricola labōrat. 4. Agricolae labōrant. 5. Puella natat. 6. Puellae natant. 7. Cornēlia appropinquat. 8. Puellaene appropinquant? 9. Cornēlia et puellae cantant. 10. Iūlia labōrat et cantat. 11. Quid appropinquat? 12. Labōrantne nautae? 13. Quis ambulat?

31. 1. The sailor is swimming. 2. The girls are singing. 3. Who approaches? 4. Are the sailors approaching? 5. Does Cornelia sing? 6. Cornelia and Julia are walking and singing. 7. The girl sings, and the farmer works. 8. Sailors and farmers are working.

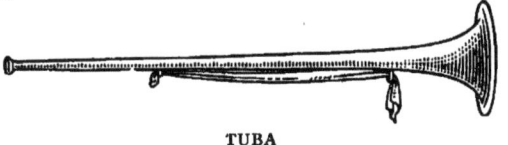

TUBA

LESSON II

THE ACCUSATIVE CASE USED AS THE DIRECT OBJECT

32. The Accusative Case used as the Direct Object.
   1. **Nauta puellam vocat,** *the sailor calls the girl.*
   2. **Nautae puellās vocant,** *the sailors call the girls.*

a. Observe that **puellam** is the object (xiv, *a*) of **vocat**, and **puellās** of **vocant**; and that when a Latin noun is used as the object, the case ending is not the same as when it is the subject and so in the nominative. The case of the object in Latin is called *accusative* (xxiv) and not objective, as in English.

b. Form the accusative singular and plural of the nouns in sections 26 and 34.

33. *Rule for the Accusative as the Direct Object.* *The object of a verb is in the accusative case.*

34.   VOCABULARY

a′qua, water (*aquatic*)
Gal′ba, Galba
lit′tera, letter (of the alphabet);
   plur., a letter, epistle (*literary*)
ter′ra, land (*terrace*)
tu′ba, trumpet (*tuba*)
a′mat, loves, likes (*amateur*)

con′vocat, calls together (*convoke*)
ha′bet, has, holds (*habit*)
lau′dat, praises (*laud*)
vi′det, sees (*provide*)
quem, *acc. of* quis, whom?
quid, *acc. of* quid, what?
nunc, *adv.*, now

35. Order of Words. Observe that in the model sentences (32) the order of Latin words is unlike the order of the words in the English sentences. The normal position of the subject of a Latin sentence is at the beginning; that of the verb is at the end. Variations from this order put emphasis on the word moved toward the beginning of the sentence; thus, **puellam nauta vocat** means that the sailor calls *a girl*. In translating Latin sentences put the emphasis where it belongs.

ACCUSATIVE AS DIRECT OBJECT

EXERCISES

36. 1. Galba tubam habet. 2. Tubāsne habet Galba? 3. Puellae Cornēliam et Iūliam laudant. 4. Litterās nauta videt. 5. Nautās Galba convocat. 6. Quis Galbam videt? 7. Quem videt Galba? 8. Agricola puellās nunc convocat. 9. Videntne nautae terram? 10. Cornēliam puellae amant.

37. 1. Who is approaching? 2. The sailor and Galba are approaching. 3. What has the farmer? 4. The farmer has land. 5. Does Galba praise the farmers? 6. The girl sees the water and the land. 7. The sailors call together the farmers. 8. Julia now has the letter.

A SCENE IN A ROMAN STREET

LESSON III

THE PRESENT INDICATIVE ACTIVE OF THE FIRST CONJUGATION

38. The Four Conjugations. Regular verbs in Latin are divided into four classes, or conjugations (XXVII), distinguished from one another by the stem vowel before the ending -re of the present infinitive active.

	PRESENT INFINITIVE	PRESENT STEM	DISTINGUISHING VOWEL
First Conj.	amā're	amā-	ā
Second Conj.	monē're	monē-	ē
Third Conj.	re'gere	rege-	ĕ
Fourth Conj.	audī're	audī-	ī

39. The Present Indicative Active of the First Conjugation.

SINGULAR		PERSONAL ENDINGS
1st Pers.	a'mō, *I love, am loving, do love*	-ō, *I*
2d Pers.	a'mās, *you love, are loving, do love*	-s, *you*
3d Pers.	a'mat, *he, she, it loves, is loving, does love*	-t, *he, she, it*

PLURAL		
1st Pers.	amā'mus, *we love, are loving, do love*	-mus, *we*
2d Pers.	amā'tis, *you love, are loving, do love*	-tis, *you*
3d Pers.	a'mant, *they love, are loving, do love*	-nt, *they*

a. Observe that in **amō** the final **a** of the stem disappears, giving **amō** instead of **amaō**. In what forms is this **a** of the stem not long (13)?

b. When the subject of a verb is a personal pronoun, it is seldom expressed in Latin unless emphatic. Why is the omission of the subject possible? Translate **puellās convocātis** and **nautam vident**.

c. Inflect like **amō** the present indicative active of **ambulō, appropinquō, cantō, convocō, labōrō, laudō,** and **natō**.

40.   VOCABULARY

dō, *pres. stem* dă- (*the a of* dō *is regularly short, but long in* dās), give (*dative*)

in'cola, inhabitant

sae'pe, *adv.*, often

sed, *conj.*, but

spec'tō, *pres. stem* spectā-, look at (*spectator*)

EXERCISES

41. 1. Ambulat, convocat, cantat. 2. Convocantne? cantantne? laudantne? 3. Natās, labōrās, ambulās. 4. Amāmus, appropinquāmus, ambulāmus. 5. Convocātis, cantātis, amātis. 6. Amant, dat, laudāmus. 7. Quem spectās? 8. Incolās laudō. 9. Iūliam saepe laudātis. 10. Sed litterās laudāmus. 11. Quid nunc datis?

42. 1. I swim, he swims, I am swimming. 2. Are you working? we sing, does she praise? 3. They are approaching, they give, you walk. 4. You are praising, they swim, he does labor. 5. We call together the inhabitants, but you call together the sailors. 6. The girls are now looking at the water.

RUINS OF A ROMAN AQUEDUCT

LESSON IV

THE GENITIVE CASE USED TO DENOTE POSSESSION

43. The Genitive Case used to denote Possession.

1. **Fīliae Galbae cantant,** *the daughters of Galba sing*, or *Galba's daughters sing.*
2. **Fīliās nautārum laudāmus,** *we praise the daughters of the sailors*, or *we praise the sailors' daughters.*

a. Observe that **Galbae** modifies **fīliae** and tells whose daughters are singing. In the same way **nautārum** modifies **fīliās** and tells whose daughters we are praising. This usage of **Galbae** and of **nautārum** is like that of the English possessive case (XXIV, *a*, 2). In Latin the case thus used is called the *genitive* (XXIV, *b*), and this usage of that case is called the *Genitive of Possession.*

b. Observe the case endings of the genitive. Form the genitive singular and the genitive plural of the nouns in sections 26, 34, and 45.

c. Note the translations given to the genitives in the model sentences. Translate **fīlia agricolae** and **fīliae agricolārum.**

d. The genitive normally stands after the word it modifies.

44. *Rule for the Genitive of Possession. The word denoting the owner or possessor is in the genitive case.*

45. VOCABULARY

fē′mina, woman (*feminine*)
fī′lia, daughter (*filial*)
fortū′na, fortune (*fortunate*)
poē′ta, poet (*poetic*)
rēgī′na, queen
cu′ius, *gen. of* quis *and of* quid, of whom? whose? of what?
dēlec′tō, *pres. stem* dēlectā-, delight, please (*delectable*)
exspec′tō, *pres. stem* exspectā-, wait, wait for (*expect*)
fu′gō, *pres. stem* fugā-, put to flight, rout
lī′berō, *pres. stem* līberā-, set free, free (*liberate*)
por′tō, *pres. stem* portā-, carry, bring (*portable*)
et′iam, *adv.*, even

GENITIVE OF POSSESSION

EXERCISES

46. 1. Dēlectat, fugāmus, līberās. 2. Exspectāmus, portant, dēlectās. 3. Dēlectāmus, fugātis, līberant. 4. Līberatne? līberō, portāmus. 5. Fīliās incolārum līberant. 6. Poētae fortūna rēgīnam dēlectat. 7. Spectāmus fīliās fēminae. 8. Fīliane Galbae litterās exspectat? 9. Etiam tubae nautārum incolās fugant. 10. Cuius litterās portās?

47. 1. I am calling together the sailors of the queen. 2. The poets' daughters love the land. 3. Whose daughter are you setting free? 4. Do they praise Galba's daughters? 5. We are now waiting for the farmers. 6. Whom does the fortune of the farmers delight?

A STREET IN POMPEII TO-DAY

LESSON V

THE PRESENT INDICATIVE ACTIVE OF THE SECOND CONJUGATION · CAUSAL CLAUSE WITH *QUOD*

48. **The Present Indicative Active of the Second Conjugation.**

SINGULAR

1st Pers. mo'neō, *I advise, am advising, do advise*
2d Pers. mo'nēs, *you advise, are advising, do advise*
3d Pers. mo'net, *he, she, it advises, is advising, does advise*

PLURAL

1st Pers. monē'mus, *we advise, are advising, do advise*
2d Pers. monē'tis, *you advise, are advising, do advise*
3d Pers. mo'nent, *they advise, are advising, do advise*

a. What verbs belong to the second conjugation (38)?

b. Observe that to the stem **monē-** the same personal endings are added to inflect **moneō** that were added to the stem **amā-** to inflect **amō**. Observe the three forms in which the present tense has the **e** of the stem not marked long. Compare the forms of the present tense of **amō** (39).

c. To the stems **docē-, habē-, terrē-,** and **vidē-** add the personal endings and thus inflect their present indicative active.

49. VOCABULARY

pecū'nia, money (*pecuniary*)
pīrā'ta, pirate (*piratical*)
prae'da, booty, plunder (*predatory*)
cūr, *adv.*, why?
do'ceō, docēre, teach, show (*docile*)
ha'beō, habēre, have, hold (*habit*)

mo'neō, monēre, advise, warn (*admonition*)
ter'reō, terrēre, scare, frighten (*terror*)
vi'deō, vidēre, see (*improvident*)
quod, *conj.*, because

a. The infinitive will hereafter be given with each verb in the vocabulary. Of what help will this be to you (38)?

PRESENT INDICATIVE, SECOND CONJUGATION

50. Causal Clause. For the kinds of clauses in a complex sentence see XIX, XX.

Incolās monet quod pīrātae appropinquant, *he warns the inhabitants because the pirates are approaching.*

a. Observe that **quod** introduces a dependent clause, which tells the reason, or cause, of what is stated in the independent part of the sentence. Such a **quod** clause is called a *causal clause.*

51. *Rule for a Causal Clause with* **Quod.** *The cause of an action may be expressed by a dependent clause introduced by* **quod.**

EXERCISES

52. 1. Pecūniam habēs. 2. Iūliam doceō. 3. Incolās saepe monēs. 4. Puellāsne terrent? 5. Quem vident? 6. Monēmus et docēmus. 7. Quid habēmus? 8. Praedam nunc videō. 9. Tubam vidētis. 10. Agricolāsne monētis? 11. Litterās habent. 12. Iūlia fīliās poētae docet. 13. Etiam pecūniam agricolārum habent pīrātae. 14. Fīliārum fortūna fēminam dēlectat. 15. Cūr Iūliam et Cornēliam monet? 16. Quem docēs et monēs? 17. Fēminae puellās laudant quod labōrant.

53. 1. They are advising. 2. They have. 3. I am warning. 4. You frighten. 5. We see. 6. Does he teach the girls? 7. Do Cornelia and Julia look at the pirate? 8. Why do the pirates frighten the inhabitants? 9. They have the money and the booty. 10. We praise the woman because she teaches the girls. 11. What do you see? What are you looking at?

A ROMAN COIN

LESSON VI

THE DATIVE CASE USED AS THE INDIRECT OBJECT · THE ABLATIVE USED IN PREPOSITIONAL PHRASES TO SHOW PLACE WHERE

54. The Dative and Ablative Cases. Besides the three cases that you have already studied, there are in Latin in common use two other cases, the *dative* and the *ablative*. For the general character of these cases see XXIV, *a*, 4; *b*.

55.   VOCABULARY

do'mina, lady, mistress (of slaves) (*dominant*)
fā'bula, story (*fable*)
īn'sula, island (*peninsula*)
vi'a, way, road, street (*viaduct*)
in, *prep. with abl.*, in, on
dēmōn'strō, dēmōnstrāre, point out, show (*demonstrate*)

ha'bitō, habitāre, dwell, live (*inhabitant*)
ma'neō, manēre, remain (*mansion*)
nār'rō, nārrāre, tell, relate (*narrator*)
cui, *dat. of* quis *and of* quid, to whom? for whom? to what? for what?

56. The Dative used as Indirect Object.

    Cornēliae et puellīs fābulam nārrō, *I am telling a story to Cornelia and the girls*, or *I am telling Cornelia and the girls a story.*

   a. Observe that what is being told is a story, **fābulam**, the direct object; and that the *persons to whom* the story is told are *Cornelia* and the *girls*. **Cornēliae** and **puellīs**, therefore, are in the dative case, as this is the case which expresses the relation of *to* or *for* (XXIV, *b*). This usage, which is like the English (XXIV, *a*, 4), is called the *Dative of the Indirect Object.*

   b. The case endings of the dative are **-ae**, singular, and **-īs**, plural. Form the dative, singular and plural, of the nouns in sections 26, 34, and 55.

DATIVE AS INDIRECT OBJECT

57. Rule for the Dative of the Indirect Object. *The indirect object of a verb is in the dative case.*

58. The Ablative used in Prepositional Phrases to show Place Where.

> In terrā et in īnsulīs habitant, *they live on the land and on the islands.*

a. Observe that the phrases (XVI, *a*) *on the land,* **in terrā,** and *on the islands,* **in īnsulīs,** show *place where.* **Terrā** and **īnsulīs** are in the ablative case (XXIV, *b*).

b. The case endings of the ablative are **-ā,** singular, and **-īs,** plural.

c. Form the ablative, singular and plural, of the nouns in sections 26, 34, and 55.

59. Rule for the Ablative of Place Where. *Place where is commonly expressed by a phrase consisting of a preposition, usually* **in,** *with the ablative case.*

60. Order of Words. The indirect object normally stands before the direct object. An ablative normally stands before the direct object. Variations from this order give emphasis to the word removed from its normal position.

EXERCISES

61. 1. Agricola dominae viam dēmōnstrat. 2. Puellīs etiam Cornēlia fābulam nārrat. 3. In īnsulā habitāmus. 4. Quis poētīs īnsulam dēmōnstrat? 5. Cūr pīrātae in aquā manent? 6. Cui pecūniam dās? 7. Nautae agricolīs praedam dēmōnstrant. 8. Incolae in viīs appropinquant et rēgīnam spectant. 9. Dominam amant quod fābulās nārrat.

62. 1. To whom are you pointing out the lady? 2. I am pointing out the letter to Julia. 3. They are telling stories to the queen. 4. Galba's daughter gives money to the sailors. 5. Do the pirates live on the island? 6. Whose daughters are approaching in the street?

LESSON VII

THE FIRST DECLENSION · GENDER

63. The First Declension. There are five declensions (XXII) of Latin nouns. Those nouns which end in **-a** in the nominative singular and in **-ae** in the genitive singular are said to belong to the *first declension*. Learn the complete inflection of the noun **agricola**:

	SINGULAR	CASE ENDINGS
Nom.	agri'col**a**	-a
Gen.	agri'col**ae**	-ae
Dat.	agri'col**ae**	-ae
Acc.	agri'col**am**	-am
Abl.	agri'col**ā**	-ā
	PLURAL	
Nom.	agri'col**ae**	-ae
Gen.	agricol**ā'rum**	-ārum
Dat.	agri'col**īs**	-īs
Acc.	agri'col**ās**	-ās
Abl.	agri'col**īs**	-īs

a. Observe that the inflection of a noun consists merely in adding the case endings to an unchangeable part of the word. This unchangeable part is called the *base*. Decline like **agricola** the nouns in section 55.

64. Gender. Latin nouns are masculine, feminine, or neuter in gender (XXV, *a*, *b*).

a. Nouns of the first declension are feminine unless they denote males. **Nauta, agricola, Galba, poēta,** and **pīrāta** are the masculine nouns you have learned. Hereafter the gender of nouns will be shown in the vocabularies by the letters *m.*, *f.*, or *n.*

THE FIRST DECLENSION

65.   **VOCABULARY**

dīligen'tia, -ae, *f.*, diligence (*diligent*)
fu'ga, -ae, *f.*, flight, rout (*refuge*)
Germā'nia, -ae, *f.*, Germany (*Germanic*)
Grae'cia, -ae, *f.*, Greece (*Grecian*)
Ita'lia, -ae, *f.*, Italy (*Italian*)
por'ta, -ae, *f.*, gate (*portal*)
prŏvin'cia, -ae, *f.*, province (*provincial*)
pug'na, -ae, *f.*, fight (*pugnacious*)
sil'va, -ae, *f.*, woods, forest (*silvan*)
victō'ria, -ae, *f.*, victory (*victorious*)

a. The ending -ae of the genitive singular is placed after the nouns in the vocabulary to indicate that these nouns belong to the first declension.

EXERCISES

66. 1. Cūr poētae in silvīs manent? 2. Cui victōriam rēgīnae nārrās? 3. In portā Iūliam et Cornēliam videō. 4. In Germāniā et in Graeciā saepe agricolās convocant. 5. Habitantne in prōvinciā? 6. Victōria nautārum agricolās terret. 7. Dīligentia puellārum fēminam dēlectat. 8. In pugnā pīrātās Italiae fugāmus. 9. Galba fugam pīrātārum nārrat.

67. 1. I am living in a province of Greece. 2. The forests of the provinces delight the poets. 3. He gives money to Julia's daughter. 4. To whom do you give water? 5. Whose diligence do you praise? 6. They are waiting in the road and looking at the woods.

A WALL DRAWING. PROBABLY THE WORK OF A ROMAN SCHOOLBOY

FIRST REVIEW LESSON

LESSONS I-VII

68. Give the English meanings of the following words:

agricola	dō	habitō	-ne	quis
ambulō	doceō	in	nunc	quod
amō	domina	incola	pecūnia	rēgīna
appropinquō	et	īnsula	pīrāta	saepe
aqua	etiam	labōrō	poēta	sed
cantō	exspectō	laudō	porta	silva
convocō	fābula	līberō	portō	spectō
cui	fēmina	littera	praeda	terra
cuius	fīlia	maneō	prōvincia	terreō
cūr	fortūna	moneō	puella	tuba
dēlectō	fuga	nārrō	pugna	via
dēmōnstrō	fugō	natō	quem	victōria
dīligentia	habeō	nauta	quid	videō

69. Give the Latin meanings of the following words:

often	sing	approach, draw near
to whom? to what?	walk	give
labor, work, suffer	farmer	booty, plunder
whom?	call together	island
wait, wait for, expect	flight, rout	poet
put to flight, rout	land	trumpet
love, like	forest, woods	teach, show
girl	diligence	lady, mistress
gate	delight, please	remain
and	who?	way, road, street
water	but	inhabitant
have, hold	in, on	advise, warn
dwell, live	look at	sailor
story	because	province

FIRST REVIEW LESSON

point out, show	fight	tell, relate, narrate
daughter	victory	letter
set free, free, liberate	see	praise
queen	fortune	what?
why?	carry, bring	scare, frighten
money	woman	whose?
even	pirate	swim
now		

70. Decline the nouns and conjugate the verbs in 68. Give the genitive singular of each noun; give the other cases, in the singular and in the plural. Give the third person, singular and plural, of the present indicative of each verb in 68.

71. Following the suggestions in 634, give English words derived from the Latin words in 68. Define these derivatives, and illustrate each by an English sentence.

72. Give the rule, if there is one, for the following constructions, and illustrate each by a brief sentence in Latin:

1. Nominative as the subject
2. Agreement of the verb with its subject
3. Accusative as the object
4. Genitive of possession
5. Causal clause with **quod**
6. Dative of the indirect object
7. Ablative of place where
8. Questions

ROMAN WRITING MATERIALS

LESSON VIII

THE SECOND DECLENSION

73. The Second Declension. Most nouns of the second declension end in -us or -um. Those ending in -us are generally masculine; those in -um are neuter. **Hortus,** *garden,* and **dōnum,** *gift,* are inflected as follows:

SINGULAR

		Case Endings		Case Endings
Nom.	hor'tus	-us	dō'num	-um
Gen.	hor'tī	-ī	dō'nī	-ī
Dat.	hor'tō	-ō	dō'nō	-ō
Acc.	hor'tum	-um	dō'num	-um
Abl.	hor'tō	-ō	dō'nō	-ō

PLURAL

Nom.	hor'tī	-ī	dō'na	-a
Gen.	hortō'rum	-ōrum	dōnō'rum	-ōrum
Dat.	hor'tīs	-īs	dō'nīs	-īs
Acc.	hor'tōs	-ōs	dō'na	-a
Abl.	hor'tīs	-īs	dō'nīs	-īs

a. Learn the case endings first. Then learn the inflection by adding the case endings to the base of each noun. Then practice the inflection of the nouns in section 74.

b. What do you notice about the dative and the ablative plural of the first and second declensions? What cases are alike in the second declension?

74.   **VOCABULARY**

amī'cus, -ī, *m.,* friend (*amicable*)
do'minus, -ī, *m.,* master (of slaves) (*domineer*)
dō'num, -ī, *n.,* gift, present (*donor*)
e'quus, -ī, *m.,* horse (*equine*)
frūmen'tum, -ī, *n.,* grain
hor'tus, -ī, *m.,* garden (*horticulture*)
Mār'cus, -ī, *m.,* Marcus
op'pidum, -ī, *n.,* town
ser'vus, -ī, *m.,* slave (*servile*)
tribū'nus, -ī, *m.,* tribune (*tribunal*)

THE SECOND DECLENSION

EXERCISES

75. 1. Oppidum videō. 2. Oppida vidēmus. 3. Dominusne servum monet? 4. Equum tribūnus spectat. 5. Equī dominōrum servōs dēlectant. 6. Mārcus amīcō fābulam nārrat. 7. Dominī amīcīs praedam dant. 8. In oppidīs amīcōs saepe convocāmus. 9. Servī appropinquant et frūmentum et aquam portant.

76. 1. Who has the tribune's horse? 2. The servants now have the gifts of the masters. 3. Have you friends in the garden? 4. A servant carries the grain of the tribune. 5. Whose gift are they showing to Marcus? 6. We see the town and the gardens of the town.

RUINS OF AN AMPHITHEATER

LESSON IX

ADJECTIVES OF THE FIRST AND SECOND DECLENSIONS

77. Adjectives in Latin. Latin adjectives, unlike English adjectives, are declined (xxii). There are two declensions of adjectives.

78. Adjectives of the First and Second Declensions. One class of adjectives has in its masculine and neuter forms the case endings of the second declension, and in its feminine forms the case endings of the first declension: as, **bonus** (masc.), **bona** (fem.), **bonum** (neut.), *good.* Learn the full declension of **bonus** (643).

79. *Rule for the Agreement of Adjectives.* *Adjectives agree with their nouns in gender, number, and case.*

	MASCULINE	FEMININE	NEUTER
Nom.	hortus bonus	puella bona	dōnum bonum
Gen.	hortī bonī	puellae bonae	dōnī bonī
Dat.	hortō bonō	puellae bonae	dōnō bonō
	etc.	etc.	etc.

a. Complete the declension of the expressions given above. Decline together **amīcus bonus**, *good friend*; **fābula grāta**, *pleasing story*; **oppidum magnum**, *large town*.

80. The rule given in 79 does not mean that adjectives must have the same case endings as the nouns they modify. An adjective modifying a masculine noun of the first declension will not have the same case endings as the noun. Thus,

	SINGULAR	PLURAL
Nom.	nauta bonus	nautae bonī
Gen.	nautae bonī	nautārum bonōrum
Dat.	nautae bonō	nautīs bonīs
	etc.	etc.

ADJECTIVES, FIRST AND SECOND DECLENSIONS

a. Complete the declension of **nauta bonus**. Decline **poëta grātus**, *pleasing poet*.

81. Order of Words. An adjective normally follows the noun which it modifies.

82.   VOCABULARY

car'rus, -ī, *m.*, wagon, cart (*car*)
ci'bus, -ī, *m.*, food
pī'lum, -ī, *n.*, javelin
rē'mus, -ī, *m.*, oar (*trireme*)
ven'tus, -ī, *m.*, wind (*ventilate*)
pro'bō, probāre, approve, approve of (*approbation*)
bo'nus, bo'na, bo'num, good, kind (*bonus*)

grā'tus, grā'ta, grā'tum, pleasing, welcome (*gratitude*)
mag'nus, mag'na, mag'num, great, large (*magnitude*)
va'lidus, va'lida, va'lidum, strong, robust (*valid*)
at'que, *conj.*, and also
nōn, *adv.*, not (*nonexistent*)
ubi, *adv.*, where? (*ubiquitous*)

EXERCISES

83. 1. Equōs magnōs spectāmus atque probāmus. 2. Tribūnus amīcō bonō pīlum dat. 3. Dōnum grātum nautae Iūliam dēlectat. 4. Nauta validus rēmōs validōs habet. 5. Servōs bonōs videt puella. 6. Nautās ventī magnī nōn terrent. 7. Ubi frūmentum agricolārum validōrum vidētis? 8. In carrō magnō frūmentum portant. 9. Pīrātae agricolās terrent quod pīla habent.

84. 1. I have a large wagon. 2. The good master has a good slave. 3. And he also gives the good slave a welcome gift. 4. Does the slave approve of the gift? 5. They do not live in a large town of Greece. 6. He is not calling together the good sailors. 7. Where do you see a large forest?

LESSON X

THE PRESENT INDICATIVE OF *SUM* · PREDICATE NOUN AND PREDICATE ADJECTIVE

85. The Present Indicative of *Sum*. The irregular verb **sum**, *I am*, is conjugated in the present indicative as follows:

	SINGULAR	PLURAL
1st Pers.	sum, *I am*	su'mus, *we are*
2d Pers.	es, *you are*	es'tis, *you are*
3d Pers.	est, *he, she, it is*	sunt, *they are*

86. Predicate Noun and Predicate Adjective. For the definition of a predicate noun and of a predicate adjective, see xv.

1. **Mārcus est agricola**, *Marcus is a farmer.*
2. **Nautae sunt amīcī**, *the sailors are friends.*
3. **Hortus est magnus**, *the garden is large.*
4. **Puellae sunt grātae**, *the girls are welcome.*

a. Observe the case of **agricola, amīcī, magnus**, and **grātae** (xv, *c*).

87. Rule for the Agreement of a Predicate Noun. *A predicate noun agrees in case with the subject of the verb.*

88. Rule for the Agreement of a Predicate Adjective. *A predicate adjective agrees in gender, number, and case with the subject of the verb.*

89. Order of Words. The verb **sum** generally has no emphasis (unless it begins the sentence), and it is placed in the sentence where it sounds best or where it adds clearness.

In Latin phrases consisting of a monosyllabic preposition, adjective, and noun the order of words is often adjective, preposition, noun: as, **magnō in oppidō**, *in the large town.*

WITHIN A ROMAN HOUSE

90. VOCABULARY

bel′lum, -ī, n., war (*belligerent*)
Britan′nia, -ae, f., Britain (*Britannic*)
de′a, -ae, f., goddess (*deity*)
de′us, -ī, m., god (*deify*)
Eurō′pa, -ae, f., Europe (*European*)
Rō′ma, -ae, f., Rome
Rōmā′nus, -ī, m., a Roman (*Roman*)
Ves′ta, -ae, f., Vesta (*vestal*)
lā′tus, lā′ta, lā′tum, wide, broad (*latitude*)
lon′gus, lon′ga, lon′gum, long (*longitude*)
me′us, me′a, me′um, my, mine
no′vus, no′va, no′vum, new (*novelty*)
par′vus, par′va, par′vum, small, little
tu′us, tu′a, tu′um, your, yours (referring to one owner)
e′rat, he, she, it was
e′rant, they were

EXERCISES

91. 1. Galba agricola est. 2. Galba est validus. 3. Iūlia et Cornēlia sunt fīliae meae. 4. Fīlia mea est parva. 5. Estne oppidum tuum magnum? 6. Britannia est īnsula Eurōpae. 7. Vesta erat dea Rōmae. 8. Carrī Rōmānōrum bonī et validī erant. 9. Nōn grātum est bellum. 10. Bella nōn grāta sunt. 11. Graecia est terra parva Eurōpae. 12. Sumus amīcī tribūnī. 13. Magnō in oppidō viās lātās vidēmus.

92. 1. The streets of the town are long. 2. The streets of Rome were not broad. 3. The roads of Britain are broad and long. 4. Where are you? 5. The new gifts of the tribune are pleasing. 6. We praise the gods because they give gifts. 7. We are Romans, but we are living in Britain.

PUERI PUELLAEQUE

LESSON XI

APPOSITION
93. Apposition.
1. **Galba, tribūnus, pīlum habet,** *Galba, the tribune, has a javelin.*
2. **Mārcum amīcum amō,** *I love (my) friend Marcus.*

a. Observe that **tribūnus** denotes the same person as **Galba**, and is joined to **Galba** as a descriptive or explanatory noun; and that **amīcum** is related in the same way to **Mārcum**. Such words are called *appositives*.

94. Rule for Apposition. *An appositive agrees in case with the noun which it explains.*

95. VOCABULARY

clā′rus, -a, -um, famous, clear (*clarify*)
dē, *prep. with abl.*, from, concerning (*depend*)
ōce′anus, -ī, *m.*, ocean (*oceanic*)
pa′rō, parāre, prepare, get ready (*prepare*)
pa′tria, -ae, *f.*, native land, country (*patriotism*)
tem′plum, -ī, *n.*, temple

CORNELIA ET IULIA

96. Cornēlia et Iūlia puellae parvae sunt. Ubi habitant? Nōn in Graeciā, sed clārō in oppidō Italiae habitant. Incolae Rōmae sunt. Italia patria Rōmānōrum est. Rōma viās lātās et templa magna habet. Rōmānī bella amant et probant.

Poētae fīlia est Cornēlia. Poēta lātīs in hortīs saepe ambulat. Atque dē bellō longō et fugā incolārum Germāniae cantat, quod victōriam Rōmānōrum probat.

Iūlia fīlia agricolae validī est. Agricola equōs et carrōs novōs habet. Cibum et frūmentum equī agricolae portant.

APPOSITION

TEMPLUM

Servī agricolae equīs aquam dant. Iūlia equōs amat et servōs laudat. Bonus dominus est agricola.

Mārcus et Galba, tribūnī, amīcī puellārum sunt. Mārcus poētae amīcus est et fābulās grātās Cornēliae nārrat. Galba Iūliae silvās et īnsulās ōceanī dēmōnstrat.

Fēmina bona puellās docet. Dīligentia Cornēliae fēminam dēlectat. In hortō poētae puellās convocat et fābulās nārrat. Fābulae dē bellō puellās parvās terrent.

Saepe Vestae dōna parant. Quis est Vesta? Vesta dea Rōmānōrum est et templum habet. Saepe in viīs Rōmae puellae ambulant et praedam Germāniae et Britanniae spectant.

LESSON XII

**THE SECOND DECLENSION: NOUNS IN −*ER*, −*IR*, −*IUS*, AND −*IUM*

97. Nouns of the Second Declension in -*er* and -*ir*. Some nouns of the second declension end in -er and -ir. They are slightly different from **hortus** in their inflection:

SINGULAR

Nom.	pu'er	a'ger	vir
Gen.	pu'erī	a'grī	vi'rī
Dat.	pu'erō	a'grō	vi'rō
Acc.	pu'er**um**	a'gr**um**	vi'r**um**
Abl.	pu'erō	a'grō	vi'rō

PLURAL

Nom.	pu'erī	a'grī	vi'rī
Gen.	puerō'rum	agrō'rum	virō'rum
Dat.	pu'erīs	a'grīs	vi'rīs
Acc.	pu'erōs	a'grōs	vi'rōs
Abl.	pu'erīs	a'grīs	vi'rīs

a. Observe that these nouns are declined in the same way as **hortus** except that they lack the ending -**us** in the nominative singular. **Ager** is like **puer** except that **e** before **r** occurs only in the nominative singular.

98. Nouns of the Second Declension in -*ius* and -*ium*. Nouns of the second declension ending in -ius and -ium contract the genitive ending -iī to -ī. The accent remains on the same syllable as in the nominative: **auxi'lium**, gen. **auxi'lī**. Learn the declension of **fīlius** and **proelium** (637).

99. Gender of Nouns of the Second Declension. Nouns of the second declension ending in -**um** are neuter; most others are masculine.

THE SECOND DECLENSION

100. VOCABULARY

a'ger, agrī, *m.*, field (*agriculture*)[1]
auxi'lium, auxi'lī, *n.*, aid, help (*auxiliary*)
fī'lius, fīlī, *m.*, son (*filial*)
gla'dius, gladī, *m.*, sword (*gladiator*)
nūn'tius, nūntī, *m.*, messenger (*pronunciation*)

prae'mium, praemī, *n.*, reward (*premium*)
proe'lium, proelī, *n.*, battle
pu'er, puerī, *m.*, boy (*puerile*)
so'cius, socī, *m.*, comrade, ally (*associate*)
vir, virī, *m.*, man (*virile*)

EXERCISES

101. 1. Fīliī virōrum in Britanniā sunt. 2. Virī erant sociī. 3. Nūntius sociōrum sum. 4. Puerōs parvōs, fīliōs tribūnī, exspectāmus. 5. Puerī gladium et pīlum Mārcī habent. 6. Quis virō viam dēmōnstrat? 7. Proelium est longum et sociī auxilium exspectant. 8. In agrō labōrant vir et fīliī nūntī. 9. Cūr virīs praemia nunc datis?

102. 1. The son of the messenger is a small boy. 2. We see your sword, but we have not your javelin. 3. They frighten the little boys and the woman. 4. The men are putting the allies to flight. 5. Where do the messengers live? 6. I have my son's sword. 7. Wars and battles delight the Romans.

---

[1] The spelling of the English derivatives *agriculture, puerile,* and *virile* will help you to recall the spelling of the genitives of **ager, puer,** and **vir.**.

LESSON XIII

ADJECTIVES OF THE FIRST AND SECOND DECLENSIONS ENDING IN -ER

103. Adjectives of the First and Second Declensions in -er. Some adjectives of the first and second declensions end in -er in the nominative singular masculine. Their inflection resembles that of **puer** and of **ager**.

a. Learn the declension of **līber** and **noster** (643).

b. Observe that **līber** retains the **e** in all forms, as **puer** does, while **noster**, like **ager**, has no **e** after the nominative.

c. Decline **miser**, *wretched*, like **līber**. The other adjectives in this book that end in -er are declined like **noster**.

d. Decline together **vir līber**, *free man*; **fēmina misera**, *poor woman*; **bellum miserum**, *wretched war*; **poēta līber**, *free poet*; **amīcus noster**, *our friend*.

104. VOCABULARY

lī′ber, lī′bera, lī′berum, free (*liberal*)
mi′ser, mi′sera, mi′serum, poor, unhappy, wretched (*miserable*)
mul′tus, mul′ta, mul′tum, much (*multitude*)
mul′tī, mul′tae, mul′ta, many

nos′ter, nos′tra, nos′trum, our (*nostrum*)
su′perō, superāre, surpass, defeat, overcome, conquer (*insuperable*)
ves′ter, ves′tra, ves′trum, your (of more than one owner)
vo′cō, vocāre, call (*vocation*)

EXERCISES

105. 1. Equōs in agrō Mārcī amīcī videō. 2. Nūntius miser fābulam miseram dē fugā sociōrum nārrat. 3. Vestrīs amīcīs praemia dant. 4. Pecūnia, dōnum Cornēliae, fīlium nostrum dēlectat. 5. Sumus virī līberī in oppidō līberō. 6. Deae Graeciae multae erant. 7. Socius noster est miser, quod gladium

ADJECTIVES ENDING IN -ER

nōn habet. 8. Rōmānōs in proeliō superant. 9. Vocatne fīlius tuus? 10. Dominō servus miser cibum parat.

106. 1. Our friends, Marcus and Galba, are wretched. 2. There are many carts in the streets of our town. 3. She calls together the unhappy sons of the messengers. 4. Where do you see your horse? 5. The winds do not frighten the sailors. 6. We are sons of free men. 7. I have a javelin, the gift of a friend.

DE GRAECIA

107. Graecia, terra parva, prōvincia Rōmānōrum erat. Athēnae, Sparta, Thēbae, Corinthus clāra oppida Graeciae erant. In oppidīs erant templa multa deōrum et deārum. In viīs oppidōrum statuae (*statues*) multae virōrum clārōrum erant. Incolae nōn erant miserī. Quis incolās Graeciae nōn laudat?

A RESTORATION OF THE ROMAN FORUM

LESSON XIV

THE IMPERFECT AND FUTURE INDICATIVE OF *SUM* · THE DATIVE WITH ADJECTIVES

108. The Imperfect Indicative of *Sum*. The imperfect indicative of **sum** is inflected as follows:

Singular	Plural
1. e'ram, *I was*	erā'mus, *we were*
2. e'rās, *you were*	erā'tis, *you were*
3. e'rat, *he, she, it was*	e'rant, *they were*

109. The Future Indicative of *Sum*. The future indicative of **sum** is inflected as follows:

Singular	Plural
1. e'rō, *I shall be*	e'rimus, *we shall be*
2. e'ris, *you will be*	e'ritis, *you will be*
3. e'rit, *he, she, it will be*	e'runt, *they will be*

110. The Dative with Adjectives.

Dōnum puerō erit grātum, *the gift will be pleasing to the boy.*

a. Observe that **puerō** is translated with the adjective **grātum**, *pleasing to the boy*. Certain Latin adjectives, particularly those meaning *near, fit, friendly, pleasing, like*, and their opposites, are thus followed by the case expressing *to* or *for*, exactly as they are followed in English by a phrase beginning with *to* or *for*: as, *fit for war, unfriendly to us*. This usage is known as the *Dative with Adjectives*.

**111. *Rule for the Dative with Adjectives. Certain adjectives meaning* near, fit, friendly, pleasing, like, *and their opposites, may be accompanied by a dative to show the person or the thing toward which the quality of the adjective is directed.*

THE IMPERFECT AND FUTURE OF *SUM*

112.   **VOCABULARY**

amī'cus, -a, -um, friendly
cer'tē, *adv.*, certainly
fīnī'timus, -a, -um, neighboring, near (*affinity*)
idō'neus, -a, -um, fit, suitable
inimī'cus, -a, -um, unfriendly, hostile (*inimical*)
iniū'ria, -ae, *f.*, injustice, wrong (*injury*)

in'terim, *adv.*, meanwhile (*interim*)
lī'ber, librī, *m.*, book (*library*)
propin'quus, -a, -um, near (*propinquity*)
pro'ximus, -a, -um, nearest, next, very near (*proximity*)

EXERCISES

113. 1. Est, erat, erit. 2. Sunt, erant, erunt. 3. Sumus, erāmus, erimus. 4. Sum, eram, erō. 5. Es, erās, eris. 6. Estis, erātis, eritis. 7. Certē erāmus inimīcī Mārcō, vestrō fīliō. 8. Proximī oppidō erant multī agrī. 9. Iniūriae sociōrum multae erunt. 10. Īnsulam terrae propinquam videō. 11. Ventī nautīs nōn erunt grātī. 12. Agricolae bellō longō idōneī nōn erant. 13. Interim vestrīs fīliīs erimus amīcī. 14. Gladiī atque pīla proeliō idōnea[1] sunt.

114. 1. I am, we are. 2. Where were we? I was in the town. 3. I shall be, we shall be. 4. Is he a tribune? They are allies. 5. Meanwhile you will be a free man. 6. Our towns are near Greece. 7. In our towns the men are unfriendly to Rome. 8. There will be[2] a great battle in Britain. 9. The books will certainly be welcome to my friend Marcus.

[1] The predicate adjective **idōnea** is neuter because the two subjects are things without life.
[2] Express *there will be* by **erit**, and place **erit** at the beginning of the sentence. How do you say *there are? there is? there were?*

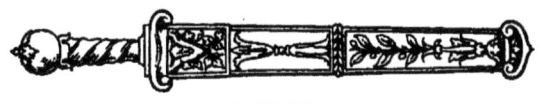

GLADIUS

SECOND REVIEW LESSON

LESSONS VIII-XIV

115. Give the English meanings of the following words:

ager	deus	interim	nūntius	rēmus
amīcus, *noun*	dominus	lātus	ōceanus	servus
amīcus, *adj.*	dōnum	liber	oppidum	socius
atque	equus	līber	parō	superō
auxilium	fīlius	longus	parvus	templum
bellum	fīnitimus	magnus	patria	tribūnus
bonus	frūmentum	meus	pīlum	tuus
carrus	gladius	miser	praemium	ubi
certē	grātus	multus	probō	validus
cibus	hortus	multī	proelium	ventus
clārus	idōneus	nōn	propinquus	vester
dē	inimīcus	noster	proximus	vir
dea	iniūria	novus	puer	vocō

116. Give the Latin meanings of the following words:

garden	from, concerning	strong, robust
many	where?	native land, country
oar	son	great, large
man	war	your (*sing.*)
call	comrade, ally	slave
god	meanwhile	aid, help
long	horse	near
sword	wind	nearest, next
goddess	boy	javelin
food	good, kind	unfriendly
much	not	new
grain	messenger	battle
approve, approve of	famous	get ready
injustice, wrong	friendly	certainly

SECOND REVIEW LESSON

friend	field	book
tribune	small, little	fit, suitable
your (*plur.*)	gift	free
temple	pleasing, welcome	our
my, mine	surpass, defeat, overcome, conquer	town
master	wide, broad	reward
cart	neighboring, near	ocean
and also	poor, unhappy, wretched	

117. Decline each noun and adjective in 115. Conjugate each verb in the present indicative active. Give the genitive singular of each noun; give the other cases, in the singular and the plural. Conjugate **sum** in the imperfect and future indicative.

118. Following the suggestions in 634, give English words derived from the Latin words in 115. Define these derivatives, and illustrate each by an English sentence.

119. Give the rule for the following constructions, and illustrate each by a sentence in Latin:

1. Agreement of adjectives
2. Predicate noun
3. Predicate adjective
4. Apposition
5. Dative with adjectives

A ROMAN BOY   A ROMAN GIRL

LESSON XV

THE IMPERFECT INDICATIVE ACTIVE, FIRST AND SECOND CONJUGATIONS · THE ABLATIVE OF MEANS

120. The Imperfect Indicative Active, First and Second Conjugations. The imperfect indicative active of the first and second conjugations is inflected as follows:

Singular	Plural
1. amā'ba m, *I was loving*	amābā'mus, *we were loving*
2. amā'bā s, *you were loving*	amābā'tis, *you were loving*
3. amā'ba t, *he was loving*	amā'ba nt, *they were loving*

Singular	Plural
1. monē'ba m, *I was advising*	monēbā'mus, *we were advising*
2. monē'bā s, *you were advising*	monēbā'tis, *you were advising*
3. monē'ba t, *he was advising*	monē'ba nt, *they were advising*

a. Observe that in this tense the personal ending of the first person singular is -m, not -ō.

b. Observe that **amābam** is formed by adding to the stem **amā-** the tense sign -bā-, and to that tense sign the personal endings: **amā-ba-m** etc. Divide **monēbam** into three parts in the same way.

c. Inflect the imperfect of the verbs in 68 and 115.

d. The imperfect tense expresses action going on in past time.

121. The Ablative of Means.

Rōmānī gladiīs et pīlīs pugnābant, *the Romans were fighting with swords and javelins.*

a. Observe that **gladiīs** and **pīlīs** are in the ablative, since they express the relations of *with* and *by*. They answer the questions *with what? by means of what?* The ablative so used is called the *Ablative of Means.* It is limited to nouns that denote things, and is translated by a phrase beginning with *by*, *with*, or *by means of.*

THE IMPERFECT INDICATIVE ACTIVE

122. Rule for the Ablative of Means. *The means by which an action is accomplished is expressed by the ablative without a preposition* (XXIV, *b*).

123. VOCABULARY

ar'mō, armāre, arm, equip (*armor*)
com'pleō, complēre, fill (*complete*)
dĕfes'sus, -a, -um, tired out, weary
Helvē'tiī, -ōrum, *m. plur.*, Helvetians
lēgā'tus, -ī, *m.*, lieutenant, ambassador (*legation*)
pug'nō, pugnāre, fight (*pugilist*)
scū'tum, -ī, *n.*, shield (*escutcheon*)
vī'cus, -ī, *m.*, village (*vicinity*)

EXERCISES

124. 1. Dēmōnstrābant, parābat, complēbātis. 2. Nārrābam, vidēbās, habitābāmus. 3. Superābās, habēbātis, probābat. 4. Cantābās, līberābam, manēbātis. 5. Terrēbam, vocābat, dēlectābātis. 6. Lēgātōs convocābam. 7. Agricolae frūmentum et cibum carrīs parvīs portābant. 8. Interim gladiīs in silvīs pugnābant. 9. Scūtīs amīcōs nostrōs armābāmus. 10. Lēgātum, amīcum meum, vocābam. 11. Pīlīs tribūnum et lēgātum in pugnā superābant. 12. Deīs dōna vestra erunt grāta. 13. Vīcus proximus ōceanō erat.

125. 1. I was walking, but you (*sing.*) were waiting in the field. 2. We were arming, they were remaining. 3. You (*plur.*) were approaching, and they were fighting. 4. He was working in the village. 5. We were teaching by means of stories and books. 6. With your swords you were liberating your friends. 7. Food was welcome to the tired Helvetians. 8. The men were fighting with long javelins. 9. The lieutenant was filling the village with food and grain.

LESSON XVI

THE FUTURE INDICATIVE ACTIVE, FIRST AND SECOND CONJUGATIONS · THE ABLATIVE OF MANNER

126. The Future Indicative Active, First and Second Conjugations. The future indicative active of the first and second conjugations is inflected as follows:

Singular	Plural
1. amā'bō, *I shall love*	amā'bimus, *we shall love*
2. amā'bis, *you will love*	amā'bitis, *you will love*
3. amā'bit, *he will love*	amā'bunt, *they will love*

Singular	Plural
1. monē'bō, *I shall advise*	monē'bimus, *we shall advise*
2. monē'bis, *you will advise*	monē'bitis, *you will advise*
3. monē'bit, *he will advise*	monē'bunt, *they will advise*

a. Observe that the future of **amō** is formed by adding to the stem **amā-** the tense sign **-bi-**, and to the tense sign the personal endings; but the **i** is dropped in the first person, and in the third person plural is changed to **u**.

1. How is the future of **moneō** formed?

b. Inflect the future of the verbs in 68 and 115.

127.   **VOCABULARY**

aedi'ficō, aedificāre, build (*edifice*)
ae'ger, ae'gra, ae'grum, sick
cum, *prep. with abl.*, with
cū'ra, -ae, *f.*, care, anxiety (*curator*)
in, *prep. with acc.*, into, to

nāvi'gium, nāvi'gī, *n.*, boat
pro'perō, properāre, hasten
quō, *adv.*, whither?
stu'dium, studī, *n.*, zeal, eagerness (*study*)
te'neō, tenēre, hold, keep (*tenant*)

128. The Ablative of Manner.

1. Mārcus cum studiō labōrat, *Marcus works with zeal (zealously).*
2. Mārcus magnō cum studiō labōrat, *Marcus works with great zeal.*
3. Mārcus magnō studiō labōrat, *Marcus works with great zeal.*

a. Observe that *manner* is expressed in these sentences by the use of the ablative case. Observe that 2 and 3 are translated in the same way, and that **cum** may be omitted when there is an adjective in the phrase. The ablative thus used answers the questions *how ? in what way ? in what manner ?* and is called the *Ablative of Manner.* The ablative of manner may often be translated by an adverb: **cum studiō**, *zealously.*

129. *Rule for the Ablative of Manner.* The ablative with **cum** *is used with abstract nouns* (1, *f*) *to denote the manner of an action; but* **cum** *may be omitted if an adjective modifies the noun of the phrase.*

EXERCISES

130. 1. Vocābunt, complēbunt, properābunt. 2. Armābitne? superābit, tenēbimus. 3. Manēbuntne? dēmōnstrābimus, terrēbō. 4. Labōrābis, docēbitis, habēbō. 5. Quō properābit agricola validus? 6. In agrōs properābunt agricola et puerī. 7. In agrīs labōrābunt magnō cum studiō. 8. Cum cūrā frūmentum in vīcum portābunt. 9. Magnā dīligentiā nāvigium aedificābitis. 10. Servī aegrī parvō studiō labōrant.

131. 1. You (*sing.*) will build. 2. He will hasten. 3. Who will not remain? 4. You (*plur.*) will hold. 5. We shall carry the sick men with great care. 6. Whither will the lieutenant hasten? 7. He will hasten into Greece and also will arm the inhabitants. 8. Where will our friends fight zealously? 9. The men were diligently filling the boats.

LESSON XVII

PRINCIPAL PARTS · THE PERFECT STEM · THE PERFECT INDICATIVE ACTIVE, FIRST CONJUGATION

132. Principal Parts. The principal parts of the verb **amō** are as follows:

PRES. IND. ACT.	PRES. INF. ACT.	PERF. IND. ACT.	PERF. PASS. PART.
amō	amāre	amāvī	amātus

a. The principal parts of the verb are so called because all forms of the verb can be made from them, or from the three stems shown in the principal parts. These three stems are as follows:

1. Present stem: **amā-**, found by dropping the **-re** of the present infinitive active.
2. Perfect stem: **amāv-**, found by dropping the personal ending **-ī** of the first person singular of the perfect indicative active.
3. Participial stem: **amāt-**, found by dropping the nominative ending **-us** of the perfect passive participle.

133. The Perfect Stem. By the use of the present stem you have conjugated the present, imperfect, and future tenses. By the use of the perfect stem **amāv-** the perfect, pluperfect, and future perfect tenses are conjugated.

134. The Perfect Indicative Active of the First Conjugation. The perfect indicative active of **amō** is inflected as follows:

SINGULAR	PERSONAL ENDINGS OF PERFECT TENSE
1. amā′vī, *I have loved, I loved*	-ī
2. amāvis′tī, *you have loved*, etc.	-istī
3. amā′vit, *he has loved*, etc.	-it
PLURAL	
1. amā′vimus, *we have loved*, etc.	-imus
2. amāvis′tis, *you have loved*, etc.	-istis
3. amāvē′runt, *they have loved*, etc.	-ērunt

PERFECT INDICATIVE, FIRST CONJUGATION

a. Observe that the perfect tense has two meanings: *I have loved* and *I loved*. Both express completed action. *I have loved* indicates that the action is completed at the present time; and the perfect tense so used is known as the *perfect definite*. *I loved* indicates merely that the action was completed at some indefinite time in the past; and the perfect tense so used is known as the *perfect indefinite*. The imperfect tense, in contrast with the perfect, expresses an action going on in the past (120, *d*).

b. Give the principal parts of each verb of the first conjugation in 68 and 115; they are formed in the same way as those of **amō** (except **dō, dare, dedī, datus**). Inflect the perfect tense of each.

EXERCISES

135. 1. Vocāvitne? convocāvit, superāvit. 2. Pugnāvērunt, exspectāvērunt, labōrāvērunt. 3. Properāvimus, aedificāvimus, armāvimus. 4. Laudāvīne? vocāvistī, properāvistis. 5. Portāvit, dēlectāvit, dedit.

136. 1. You have praised, you showed, you related. 2. I have given, I brought, I set free. 3. They approved, they have sung, they swam. 4. We gave, we dwelt, we showed.

137.   VOCABULARY

ar'ma, -ōrum, *n. plur.*, arms
di'ū, *adv.*, for a long time, long
prō, *prep. with abl.*, before, for, in defense of (*proceed*)
Rŏ'mulus, -ī, *m.*, Romulus
Sabī'nī, -ōrum, *m. plur.*, the Sabines
vul'nerō, vulnerāre, vulnerāvī, vulnerātus, wound (*vulnerable*)

DE SABINIS

138. Rōmulus Rōmam, clārum oppidum Italiae, aedificāvit. Validī virī erant Rōmānī et patriam amābant. Saepe prō patriā pugnābant et saepe Sabīnōs armīs in bellō superābant. Sabīnī bona arma habēbant et magnō cum studiō pīlīs longīs diū pugnāvērunt. Sed Rōmānī Sabīnōs fugāvērunt et multōs virōs gladiīs vulnerāvērunt.

LESSON XVIII

**THE PERFECT INDICATIVE ACTIVE, SECOND CONJUGATION
THE ABLATIVE OF ACCOMPANIMENT**

139. Principal Parts of Verbs of the Second Conjugation.
The principal parts of verbs of the second conjugation are not so regular as those of the first conjugation. You have already had some verbs of the second conjugation. Their principal parts are as follows:

Pres. Ind.	Pres. Inf.	Perf. Ind.	Perf. Part.
compleō	complēre	complēvī	complētus
doceō	docēre	docuī	doctus
habeō	habēre	habuī	habitus
maneō	manēre	mānsī	mānsūrus
moneō	monēre	monuī	monitus
teneō	tenēre	tenuī	———
terreō	terrēre	terruī	territus
videō	vidēre	vīdī	vīsus

a. Learn the principal parts of these verbs. What is the perfect stem of each?

b. Learn the inflection of the perfect tense of **moneō** (659), and practice the inflection of the perfect tense of the other verbs.

EXERCISES

140. 1. Monuit, monuērunt, docuit. 2. Docuērunt, habuit, habuērunt. 3. Terruistī, terruistis, tenuistīne? 4. Vīdī. vīdēruntne? mānsimus. 5. Tenuit, tenuērunt, terruērunt.

141. 1. I have filled, you have seen, we have held. 2. He frightened, it had, they have filled. 3. She has remained, I have taught, you (*plur.*) have warned.

PERFECT INDICATIVE, SECOND CONJUGATION

142. The Ablative of Accompaniment.

Cum fīliō meō ambulābat, *he was walking with my son.*

a. Observe that the phrase **cum fīliō** answers the questions *with whom? in whose company?* This use of the ablative with the preposition **cum** is called the *Ablative of Accompaniment.*

143. *Rule for the Ablative of Accompaniment.* The ablative with **cum** *is used to show accompaniment.*

144. VOCABULARY

captī′vus, -ī, *m.*, captive (*captivate*)
cau′sa, -ae, *f.*, cause, reason
hi′emō, hiemāre, hiemāvī, hiemā-tūrus,[1] spend the winter
lo′cus, -ī, *m.* (*plur.* loca, *n.*), place (*location*)
perī′culum, -ī, *n.*, peril, danger (*peril*)

EXERCISES

145. 1. Puerī carrum nostrum frūmentō complēvērunt. 2. Cum cūrā puellam aegram certē portāvērunt. 3. Scūta et gladiōs captīvōrum prō portīs vīdī. 4. Locus proeliō idōneus nōn erat. 5. Lēgātus cum multīs virīs in Germāniam properāvit. 6. Causam bellī dēmōnstrābit. 7. In Graeciā cum amīcīs vestrīs hiemāvī. 8. Magnō cum perīculō mānsērunt.

146. 1. The swords and the javelins frightened the captives. 2. They fought with the tribune in the long war. 3. The women were spending the winter in Italy. 4. Who will tell the lieutenant the cause of the war? 5. They have filled the place with arms. 6. The Romans have fought with the allies in defense of Rome.

---

[1] Future active participle (441, *a*). This form, if it occurs, is given in the principal parts where the perfect passive participle is not in use.

LESSON XIX

THE DEMONSTRATIVE *IS* · THE PERFECT INDICATIVE OF *SUM*

147. The Demonstrative *Is*. The demonstrative is, *this, that,* plur. *these, those,* is declined as follows:

	SINGULAR			PLURAL		
	MASC.	FEM.	NEUT.	MASC.	FEM.	NEUT.
Nom.	is	e'a	id	iĭ (e'ī)	e'ae	e'a
Gen.	e'ius	e'ius	e'ius	eō'rum	eā'rum	eō'rum
Dat.	e'ī	e'ī	e'ī	iīs (e'īs)	iīs (e'īs)	iīs (e'īs)
Acc.	e'um	e'am	id	e'ōs	e'ās	e'a
Abl.	e'ō	e'ā	e'ō	iīs (e'īs)	iīs (e'īs)	iīs (e'īs)

a. Iĭ and iīs are pronounced as monosyllables, ī and īs.

148. The Uses of *Is*. There is no word in English like is. Although it is a demonstrative pronoun (II, *f*) and means *this* and *that*, it does not point emphatically to what is near, as does hic, or to what is remote, as does ille (228). Generally it refers to somebody or to something that has just been mentioned. Sometimes it approaches in meaning the English definite article *the*. It is translated by *this* or *that* as the meaning of the sentence may require.

    1. **Is agricolās convocāvit,** *this* (or *that*) *man called the farmers together.*
    2. **Is servus cum dīligentiā labōrat,** *this* (or *that*) *slave works diligently.*

    a. Observe that is is used in the first sentence as a pronoun, and in the second sentence as an adjective (III, *e*). Is, when an adjective, usually precedes its noun.

    b. Decline together **id dōnum ; is nūntius ; ea patria.**

THE DEMONSTRATIVE *IS*

149. The Perfect Indicative of *Sum*. The perfect indicative of sum is conjugated as follows:

Singular	Plural
1. fu′ī, *I have been, was*	fu′imus, *we have been, were*
2. fuis′tī, *you have been, were*	fuis′tis, *you have been, were*
3. fu′it, *he has been, was*	fuē′runt, *they have been, were*

EXERCISES

150. 1. Id scūtum vīdī. 2. Is gladius est meus. 3. Ea pugna erit longa. 4. Eō gladiō pugnābō. 5. Eī captīvō cibum dedit. 6. Id erat tuum. 7. Perīculum eōrum lēgātōrum dēmōnstrābat. 8. In Germāniā et in terrā Helvētiōrum fuimus. 9. Fuitne tua fīlia aegra? 10. Dominus eius servī fuit dēfessus. 11. Ea victōria Rōmānōs dēlectāvit. 12. Cum eō amīcō in Britanniam properābam. 13. Ubi fuistis?

151. 1. By means of these arms we shall overcome the pirates on the ocean. 2. That help is pleasing to the Romans. 3. I have often been in those woods. 4. I have taught the sons of these farmers. 5. You have seen and praised these allies because they fought with zeal. 6. Whither were you hastening with this boy? 7. The causes of this war have been many.

SCUTA

LESSON XX

THE INTERROGATIVE *QUIS*

152. The Uses of the Interrogative *Quis*. The interrogative **quis (quī)**, *who? which? what?* may be used as a pronoun or as an adjective (II, *e*; III, *e*): **quis vocat?** *who calls?* **quod dōnum habēs?** *what gift have you?*

153. The Declension of the Interrogative Pronoun. The interrogative pronoun **quis** is declined as follows:

	SINGULAR		PLURAL		
	MASC. AND FEM.	NEUT.	MASC.	FEM.	NEUT.
Nom.	quis	quid	quī	quae	quae
Gen.	cu'ius	cu'ius	quō'rum	quā'rum	quō'rum
Dat.	cui	cui	qui'bus	qui'bus	qui'bus
Acc.	quem	quid	quōs	quās	quae
Abl.	quō	quō	qui'bus	qui'bus	qui'bus

a. Which forms have you already learned?

154. The Declension of the Interrogative Adjective. The interrogative adjective **quī** is declined as follows in the singular (the plural is the same as that of **quis**):

	SINGULAR		
	MASC.	FEM.	NEUT.
Nom.	quī	quae	quod
Gen.	cu'ius	cu'ius	cu'ius
Dat.	cui	cui	cui
Acc.	quem	quam	quod
Abl.	quō	quā	quō

a. Decline together **quī captīvus**; **quae causa**; **quod perīculum**.

EXERCISES

155. 1. Quī id templum aedificāvērunt? 2. Quī lēgātī eōs virōs armāvērunt? 3. Quid in eō agrō est? 4. Cui dat Mārcus id praemium? 5. Quibus terrīs est Britannia proxima? 6. Quem laudātis? 7. Quem librum laudāvit Cornēlia? 8. Quō gladiō captīvum vulnerāvērunt? 9. Quod perīculum nārrās?

MARS

156. 1. Who was the messenger of the gods? 2. What gift did he give to this boy? 3. Whose shield did that slave have? 4. To whom have they shown the causes of this war? 5. Whom have you overcome? 6. With what arms have they overcome the Helvetians? 7. In which village did they live?

157. VOCABULARY

adōrō, adōrāre, adōrāvī, adōrātus, pray to, worship (*adoration*)
animus, -ī, *m.*, feeling, mind (*animus*)
imperium, impe′rī, *n.*, command, power (*imperial*)
i′taque, *conj.*, and so, therefore

DE DEIS ROMANORUM

158. Mars, prōavus (*the ancestor*) Rōmānōrum, arma et proelia et bella amābat. Rōmulus et Remus, fīliī deī armōrum, Rōmam aedificāvērunt. Itaque proelia et bella animōs Rōmānōrum dēlectāvērunt. Mercurium et Neptūnum et Vestam Rōmānī adōrābant. Mercurius, nūntius deōrum, imperia deōrum incolīs terrārum (*the earth*) nārrābat. Neptūnum, deum aquārum et ōceanī, nautae adōrābant. Fēminae Vestam, deam focī (*hearth*), adōrābant et eī deae multa dōna parābant.

LESSON XXI

THE PRESENT, IMPERFECT, FUTURE, AND PERFECT INDICATIVE ACTIVE OF THE THIRD CONJUGATION

159. The Present, Imperfect, Future, and Perfect Indicative Active of the Third Conjugation. Learn the present, imperfect, future, and perfect indicative active of the verb **regō** (660). What are the present and perfect stems?

a. Observe that the personal endings, except in the first person singular of the future, are the same as in the first and second conjugations.

b. Observe that the differences between this conjugation and the first and second conjugations are in the present and future tenses.

c. Observe that in the present tense the **e** of the present stem **rege-** disappears before **ō** in the first person, just as happened in **ama-ō**; and that it becomes **u** in the third person plural, while in the other persons it is **i**. The inflection is like that of **erō**, future of **sum**.

d. Observe that the future does not use -bi- as a tense sign, but has -a- in the first person singular, and -e- in the other persons.

e. Give heed to the quantities and the accents. Inflect like **regō** the verbs in the following vocabulary.

160.   **VOCABULARY**

bene, *adv.*, well (*benevolent*)
hodiē, *adv.*, to-day
ōlim, *adv.*, once, formerly
tum, *adv.*, then
dūcō, dūcere, dūxī, ductus, lead (*conduct*)

emō, emere, ēmī, ēmptus, buy (*preëmption*)
mittō, mittere, mīsī, missus, send (*remit*)
regō, regere, rēxī, rēctus, rule, manage (*regent*)

EXERCISES

161. 1. Regit, regēbat, reget. 2. Emō, emēbam, emam. 3. Dūcunt, dūcent, dūcēbat. 4. Rēxit, rēxērunt, dūxit. 5. Dūxērunt, ēmistī, ēmistis. 6. Mīsī, mīsimus, mīsit. 7. Mittimus, mittunt, mittent. 8. Is agricola multōs agrōs habet. 9. Frūmentum in oppidum magnum nāvigiīs mittet. 10. Frūmentum in vīcum equīs validīs mittet. 11. Quis eōs equōs in viā dūcet? 12. Fīliī agricolae, Mārcus et Galba, equōs dūxērunt et hodiē dūcent. 13. Tum arma nova ement. 14. Ōlim Rōmānī Italiam bene rēxērunt.

162. 1. They rule, they were ruling, they will rule. 2. He leads, he was leading, he will lead. 3. I have bought, we bought, they bought. 4. I am sending, I shall send, I have sent. 5. You send, you will send, you have sent. 6. The Romans once had many lands. 7. Often they did not rule these lands well. 8. Then the allies sent assistance. 9. What girls spent the winter in Italy? 10. I shall send a lieutenant with these captives into Italy.

GLADIATORS ENTERING THE ARENA

THIRD REVIEW LESSON

LESSONS XV-XXI

163. Give the English meanings of the following words:

adōrō	causa	hiemō	mittō	regō
aedificō	compleō	hodiē	nāvigium	scūtum
aeger	cum	imperium	ōlim	studium
animus	cūra	in	perīculum	teneō
arma	dēfessus	is	prō	tum
armō	diū	itaque	properō	vīcus
bene	dūcō	lēgātus	pugnō	vulnerō
captīvus	emō	locus	quō	

164. Give the Latin meanings of the following words:

lead	rule	zeal, eagerness
once, formerly	place	care, anxiety
peril	equip, arm	arms
with	sick	pray to, worship
before, for, in defense of	shield	hold, keep
then	spend the winter	hasten
whither?	this, that	captive
village	into, to	to-day
tired out, weary	send	cause, reason
feeling, mind	well	buy
fight	lieutenant, envoy	command, power
wound	fill	and so, therefore
for a long time, long	build	boat

165. Decline each noun and each adjective in 163. Conjugate each verb in the present, imperfect, and future indicative active. Give the principal parts of each verb in 68, 115, and 163. Conjugate each verb in 163 in the perfect indicative active. Decline **is** and **quis**.

THIRD REVIEW LESSON 71

166. Following the suggestions in 634, give English words derived from the Latin words in 163. Define these derivatives, and illustrate each by an English sentence.

167. Give the rule for the following constructions, and illustrate each by a sentence in Latin:

1. Ablative of means
2. Ablative of manner
3. Ablative of accompaniment

A RACE IN THE CIRCUS MAXIMUS

LESSON XXII

READING LESSON

168. VOCABULARY

āla, -ae, *f.*, wing
cēra, -ae, *f.*, wax
Crēta, -ae, *f.*, Crete
Daedalus, -ī, *m.*, Dædalus, father of Icarus
iam, *adv.*, now, already
Īcarus, -ī, *m.*, Icarus
-que, *conj.*, *enclitic* (22), and
quoque, *adv.*, also, too
aptō, aptāre, aptāvī, aptātus, fit, fit to, adjust (*adapt*)
cōnfirmō, cōnfirmāre, cōnfirmāvī, cōnfirmātus, strengthen, encourage (*confirmation*)
dēcidō, dēcidere, dēcidī, ——, fall off, fall down (*deciduous*)
fingō, fingere, fīnxī, fictus, fashion, devise (*fiction*)
postulō, postulāre, postulāvī, postulātus, demand (*postulate*)
solvō, solvere, solvī, solūtus, loose (*solve*)
volō, volāre, volāvī, volātūrus, fly (*volatile*)

169. DE ICARO

MĀRCUS. Fābulam bonam amīcus meus hodiē nārrāvit.
IŪLIA. Dē quō nārrāvit amīcus tuus?
MĀRCUS. Dē Īcarō, Daedalī fīliō, puerō miserō.
IŪLIA. Ubi habitābat Īcarus? In Britanniā?
MĀRCUS. Nōn in Britanniā habitābat, sed in Crētā, īnsulā magnā et clārā. Daedalus fīliō ālās fīnxit et parāvit. Eās ālās Īcarō magnā cum cūrā cērā aptāvit. Ālae Īcarō grātae erant. Tum Daedalus puerum volāre (*to fly*) docuit, sed altius (*too high*) volāvit Īcarus. Itaque sōl (*the sun*) cēram solvit, et ālae dēcidērunt.
IŪLIA. Sed quid dē Īcarō?
MĀRCUS. Īcarus quoque dēcidit in ōceanum.
IŪLIA. Ēheu (*alas*), miserum Īcarum!

ROMANI PRO SOCIIS PUGNANT

170. Quod iniūriae multae fuērunt, sociī nostrī auxilium postulant. Itaque Rōmānī lēgātum cum virīs in terram Helvētiōrum mittent. Is lēgātus iam virōs convocāvit in oppidum. Cibum et carrōs ēmit et virōs gladiīs scūtīsque armāvit. Sociī interim frūmentum parāvērunt. Hodiē lēgātus animōs virōrum cōnfirmābit. Tum in agrōs fīnitimōs virōs dūcet et proelium exspectābit. Locus eius proelī propinquus Helvētiīs est. Nostrī virī magnō cum studiō prō sociīs pugnābunt et Helvētiōs superābunt. Multōs captīvōs in oppidum dūcent. Eī captīvī in vīcīs nostrīs hiemābunt.

ICARUS IN OCEANUM DECIDIT

LESSON XXIII

THE THIRD DECLENSION

171. The Third Declension. Nouns of the third declension end variously in the nominative singular. They are of masculine, feminine, or neuter gender. Their inflection is illustrated by the following words:

	rēx, m. *king*	mīles, m. *soldier*	virtūs, f. *valor*	caput, n. *head*	CASE ENDINGS M. AND F.	N.
			SINGULAR			
Nom.	rēx	mī′les	vir′tūs	ca′put	-s or ——	——
Gen.	rē′gis	mī′litis	virtū′tis	ca′pitis	-is	-is
Dat.	rē′gī	mī′litī	virtū′tī	ca′pitī	-ī	-ī
Acc.	rē′gem	mī′litem	virtū′tem	ca′put	-em	——
Abl.	rē′ge	mī′lite	virtū′te	ca′pite	-e	-e
			PLURAL			
Nom.	rē′gēs	mī′litēs	virtū′tēs	ca′pita	-ēs	-a
Gen.	rē′gum	mī′litum	virtū′tum	ca′pitum	-um	-um
Dat.	rē′gibus	mīli′tibus	virtū′tibus	capi′tibus	-ibus	-ibus
Acc.	rē′gēs	mī′litēs	virtū′tēs	ca′pita	-ēs	-a
Abl.	rē′gibus	mīli′tibus	virtū′tibus	capi′tibus	-ibus	-ibus

a. To decline a noun of the third declension it is necessary to know the gender, and the spelling of the nominative and the genitive singular. These things, therefore, must be learned about every noun of this declension. Often an English derivative will suggest the spelling of the genitive singular: as, *capital*, **capitis**; *military*, **mīlitis**.

b. No adequate rule for the gender of nouns of the third declension can be given. But

Nouns ending in -tor are masculine.

Nouns ending in -tās, -tūs, or -tūdō, and most nouns ending in -iō are feminine.

Nouns ending in -e, -al, or -ar are neuter.

THE THIRD DECLENSION

c. Learn the case endings. Then practice the declension of the nouns above and of those in the vocabulary. Observe that masculines and feminines are declined alike. The stem of nouns of this declension may end in a mute (**p, b, t, d, c, g**), as **rēx**, stem **rĕg-**; or in a liquid (**l, r**), as **soror**, stem **sorōr-**; or in a nasal (**m, n**), as **homō**, stem **homin-**.

172. VOCABULARY

caput, capitis, *n.*, head (*capital*)
dux, ducis, *m.*, leader, general (*conductor*)
eques, equitis, *m.*, horseman (*equestrian*)
et ... et, *conj.*, both ... and
fortiter, *adv.*, bravely

lapis, lapidis, *m.*, stone (*dilapidate*)
mīles, mīlitis, *m.*, soldier (*military*)
pedes, peditis, *m.*, foot soldier (*pedestrian*)
rēx, rēgis, *m.*, king (*regal*)
virtūs, virtūtis *f.*, valor courage (*virtue*)

EXERCISES

173. 1. Rēgem et ducem hodiē vīdī. 2. Capita multōrum peditum vīdimus. 3. Et rēgēs et ducēs mīlitēs nostrōs dūxērunt. 4. Etiam equitēs prō rēge et duce fortiter pugnābant. 5. Virtūte et studiō[1] sociōs superāvērunt. 6. Lapidibus et pīlīs multōs agricolās vulnerāvērunt. 7. Virtūs equitum atque studium peditum lēgātum certē dēlectābit.[2] 8. Quis iis equitibus scūta emet? 9. Nostrōs mīlitēs in silvās quoque mīsimus.

174. 1. The commands of the king have been many. 2. We shall approve of the commands of the kings. 3. By the valor of these soldiers we shall overcome the Helvetians. 4. I shall spend the winter with the general. 5. In a town I saw a king. 6. This king was a good general and ruled well. 7. He bought food for the wretched foot soldiers. 8. He sent both arms and grain into that town.

---

[1] Observe that the ablative of an abstract noun may express means.

[2] Observe that a singular verb may be used with two subjects, if the subjects are abstract nouns and considered as a single whole.

LESSON XXIV

THE THIRD CONJUGATION: VERBS IN -*IO* · THE ABLATIVE OF PLACE FROM WHICH · THE ACCUSATIVE OF PLACE TO WHICH

175. The Third Conjugation: Verbs in -*iō*. Certain verbs of the third conjugation differ in inflection from the regular verbs of that conjugation. Learn the present, imperfect, future, and perfect indicative active of **capiō**, *take* (661).

a. Wherein does the inflection of **capiō** differ from that of **regō** in the present? in the imperfect? in the future?

b. Verbs in -**iō**, with the infinitive in -**ĕre**, are conjugated like **capiō**. Like **capiō** inflect in the same tenses **fugiō** and **iaciō** (176).

176. VOCABULARY

ā (ab), *prep. with abl.*, away from, from, by (*avert*)
ad, *prep. with acc.*, to, toward (*adhere*)
conloquium, conlo'quiī, *n.*, conference, interview (*colloquial*)
ē (ex), *prep. with abl.*, out of, from (*exit*)
mūrus, -ī, *m.*, wall (*mural*)
pēs, pedis, *m.*, foot (*pedal*)
capiō, capere, cēpī, captus, take, capture, receive (*captive*)
dīmittō, dīmittere, dīmīsī, dīmissus, send away (*dismiss*)
fugiō, fugere, fūgī, fugitūrus, flee, run away (*fugitive*)
iaciō, iacere, iēcī, iactus, throw, hurl, cast, fling (*reject*)

a. **Ab** and **ex** are used instead of **ā** and **ē** before words beginning with a vowel or **h**; before consonants either **ā** or **ab**, **ē** or **ex** may be used.

177. The Ablative of Place from Which.

1. **Mīlitēs ab vīcō properant**, *the soldiers are hastening away from the village.*
2. **Mīlitēs ex vīcō properant**, *the soldiers are hastening out of the village.*
3. **Mīlitēs dē vīcō properant**, *the soldiers are hastening from (down from) the village.*

76

a. Observe that the phrases **ab vīcō, ex vīcō**, and **dē vīcō** denote the *place from which* the motion is directed. This usage is known as the *Ablative of Place from Which.* **Ab vīcō** (1) indicates that the soldiers started *from the vicinity of* the village; while **ex vīcō** (2) indicates that they started from some point or place *within* the village.

178. *Rule for the Ablative of Place from Which. Place from which is expressed by the ablative with* **ā** (ab), **dē, ē** (ex).

179. The Accusative of Place to Which.
1. **Lēgātōs in oppidum mīsērunt,** *they sent ambassadors into the town.*
2. **Lēgātōs ad oppidum mīsērunt,** *they sent ambassadors to the town.*

a. Observe that the phrases **in oppidum** and **ad oppidum** denote the *place to which* the motion is directed. This usage is known as the *Accusative of Place to Which.*

180. *Rule for the Accusative of Place to Which. Place to which is expressed by the accusative with* **ad** *or* **in**.

EXERCISES

181. 1. Capiet, capit, capiunt. 2. Iaciō, iaciam, iaciēbam. 3. Cēpērunt, iēcit, iēcimus. 4. Fūgimus, fugimus, dīmīsimus. 5. Ex conloquiō fugiunt. 6. Ab vīcō in agrōs fugient. 7. Dē oppidō ad ōceanum fūgit. 8. Quī litterās ad rēgem mīsērunt? 9. Dē mūrīs eius oppidī pīla iēcērunt. 10. Dēfessōs mīlitēs ex proeliō dīmīsit. 11. Cūr ab eō locō fugis? 12. Carrōs nostrōs capient.

182. 1. He will hurl, they will hurl, they hurl. 2. You throw, you will throw, you have thrown. 3. They wounded the feet of the horsemen. 4. I shall hasten from Italy into the province. 5. Both women and girls were fleeing from the fields. 6. They have hastened from Germany into Italy. 7. He led the tribune to the conference.

LESSON XXV

THE ABLATIVE OF CAUSE · PREPOSITIONAL PHRASES EXPRESSING CAUSE

183.   **VOCABULARY**

centuriō, centuriōnis, *m.*, centurion

corpus, corporis, *n.*, body (*corporal*)[1]

doleō, dolēre, doluī, dolitūrus, grieve (*doleful*)

explōrātor, explōrātōris, *m.*, scout (*explore*)

homō, hominis, *m.*, man (*homicide*)

inopia, -ae, *f.*, want, lack

ob, *prep. with acc.*, on account of

pater, patris, *m.*, father (*paternal*)

propter, *prep. with acc.*, on account of

soror, sorōris, *f.*, sister (*sorority*)

vulnus, vulneris, *n.*, wound (*vulnerable*)

a. Decline **centuriō miser, corpus magnum, homō dēfessus, id vulnus.**

184. The Ablative of Cause.

    1. **Lēgātus mīlitem virtūte laudāvit,** *the lieutenant praised the soldier for (because of, on account of) his valor.*

    2. **Peditēs viā longā sunt dēfessī,** *the foot soldiers are tired out with (from, because of) the long march.*

    a. Observe that the ablatives **virtūte** and **viā** denote *cause* or *reason*. Observe the various prepositions used in translating these ablatives: *for, with, from, because of, on account of.* This ablative answers the question *why?* and is known as the *Ablative of Cause.*

185. *Rule for the Ablative of Cause.* *The ablative without a preposition is used to express cause.*

186. Prepositional Phrases expressing Cause. Cause may also be expressed by a prepositional phrase consisting of **ob** or **propter** with the accusative, or of **dē** or **ex** with the ablative:

[1] See 171, *a.*

THE ABLATIVE OF CAUSE

1. **Lēgātus mīlitem ob (propter) virtūtem laudāvit,** *the lieutenant praised the soldier on account of his courage.*
2. **Multīs dē causīs in Italiam properābunt,** *for many reasons they will hurry into Italy.*

a. Observe the translation of **dē** in the phrase **dē causīs.**

EXERCISES

187. 1. Multīs dē causīs Rōmānī auxilium nōn mīsērunt. 2. Lapidibus pīlisque eōs hominēs vulnerāvērunt. 3. Multa vulnera in capitibus et in corporibus habent. 4. Hodiē patrēs vulneribus fīliōrum dolēbunt. 5. Dux noster magnā victōriā centuriōnēs laudābit. 6. Perīculum explōrātōrum mīlitēs terruit. 7. Tum in mūrōs oppidī ob iniūriās nōn fugiēbātis. 8. Propter inopiam cibī[1] magnō in perīculō fuimus. 9. Lēgātus equitēs et peditēs ad conloquium dūxit.

188. 1. We have often been tired because of wounds. 2. I shall praise our soldiers because of their courage and zeal. 3. Our fathers will fight for a long time and will capture much booty. 4. Which centurion was throwing javelins down from the wall? 5. On account of a lack of food and water Marcus and Galba, the centurions, did not fight with courage. 6. My sister is now grieving because the women of Britain are wretched. 7. In the meantime the scouts related the commands of the general.

CENTURIO

[1] This is a new usage of the genitive case. As used here, the genitive denotes that of which something consists or is made. It is called the *Genitive of Material.*

LESSON XXVI

THE THIRD DECLENSION: *I*-STEMS

189. The Third Declension: *i*-Stems. Certain nouns of the third declension have i-stems. These include:

1. Nouns which end in -is or -ēs in the nominative singular and have no more syllables in the genitive singular than in the nominative.
2. Neuters ending in -e, -al, or -ar.
3. Nouns ending in -ns or -rs.
4. Monosyllables ending in -s or -x, with a consonant preceding the -s or -x.

These nouns show the following peculiarities of declension:

1. The genitive plural ends in -ium.
2. The accusative plural of masculines and of feminines ends in -īs or -ēs.
3. The nominative and the accusative plural of neuters end in -ia.
4. The ablative singular of neuters and of a few other words ends in -ī.

The declension of nouns having i-stems is illustrated by the following paradigms:

	hostis, m., *enemy* STEM hosti-	mare, n., *sea* STEM mari-	cohors, f., *cohort* STEM cohorti-	mōns, m., *mountain* STEM monti-
		SINGULAR		
Nom.	hos'tis	ma're	co'hors	mōns
Gen.	hos'tis	ma'ris	cohor'tis	mon'tis
Dat.	hos'tī	ma'rī	cohor'tī	mon'tī
Acc.	hos'tem	ma're	cohor'tem	mon'tem
Abl.	hos'te	ma'rī	cohor'te	mon'te

80

I-STEMS

PLURAL

Nom.	hos'tēs	ma'ria	cohor'tēs	mon'tēs
Gen.	hos'tium	ma'rium	cohor'tium	mon'tium
Dat.	hos'tibus	ma'ribus	cohor'tibus	mon'tibus
Acc.	hos'tīs (-ēs)	ma'ria	cohor'tīs (-ēs)	mon'tīs (-ēs)
Abl.	hos'tibus	ma'ribus	cohor'tibus	mon'tibus

a. For the guidance of the learner, in the succeeding vocabularies nouns having i-stems will be followed by the stem.

b. Decline each noun in 190.

190. VOCABULARY

cīvis, cīvis (cīvi-), *m.*, citizen (*civil*)
cohors, cohortis (cohorti-), *f.*, cohort
collis, collis (colli-), *m.*, hill
fīnis, fīnis (fīni-), *m.*, end ; *plur.*, territories (*finish*)
hostis, hostis (hosti-), *m.*, enemy (*hostile*)
ignis, ignis (igni-), *m.*, fire (*ignite*)

mare, maris (mari-), *n.*, sea (*maritime*)
mōns, montis (monti-), *m.*, mountain (*mount*)
nāvis, nāvis (nāvi-), *f.*, ship (*navigate*)
urbs, urbis (urbi-), *f.*, city (*urban*)

EXERCISES

191. 1. Victōria hostium cīvīs urbis Rōmae terruit. 2. Collīs et montīs Italiae nōn vīdī. 3. Explōrātōrēs et centuriōnēs ex fīnibus Sabīnōrum fūgērunt. 4. Rōmānī multās nāvīs et nāvigia in marī habuērunt. 5. Magnō perīculō cīvēs cibum frūmentumque in urbem portant. 6. Cohortēs quoque mittēmus et hostīs superābimus. 7. Propinquum montī erat oppidum. 8. Virtūs cīvium grāta ducī fuit.

192. 1. Have we many ships to-day? 2. Formerly they lived on the hills and mountains. 3. The territories of the Romans were wide. 4. These citizens are not fit for war. 5. Our soldiers have captured many cities of Greece. 6. Who are throwing javelins down from the walls of the cities? 7. Boys see great fires in the city.

LESSON XXVII

THE ACCUSATIVE AND THE ABLATIVE WITH PREPOSITIONS ADJECTIVES USED AS NOUNS

193. Prepositions with the Accusative. The following prepositions are used with the accusative:

ad, to, toward, against (*adverse*)
ante, before, in front of (*antecedent*)
apud, near, with, among
contrā, against (*contradict*)
in, into, against (*inspire*)
inter, between (of two objects), among (of more than two objects) (*intervene*)
ob, on account of, because of
per, through (*perennial*)
post, after, behind (*postpone*)
propter, on account of, because of
trāns, across (*transatlantic*)

194. Prepositions with the Ablative. The following prepositions are used with the ablative:

ā, ab, away from, from, by (*ablative*)
cum, with (*compete*)
dē, down from, concerning (*depose*)
ē, ex, out of, from (*expose*)
in, in, at, on (*insist*)
prō, in front of, in behalf of (*protect*)
sine, without (*sinecure*)

a. Which preposition is used with both cases? With what difference in meaning?

b. Learn the meanings of all these prepositions.

195. Methods of saying "to," "on account of," "because of," and "with" in Latin:

a. To: If the phrase expresses the *indirect object*, use the dative.

If the phrase occurs with a verb of *motion* (as **mittō**), use **ad** or **in** with the accusative.

b. On account of, because of: Use either **ob** or **propter** with the accusative, or use the ablative.

Remember that the preposition **dē** or **ex** is used in certain phrases (as, **multīs dē causīs**, *for many reasons*).

c. With: If the phrase expresses *means*, use the ablative.

If the phrase expresses *manner*, use the ablative with **cum**; omit **cum**, if you wish, when there is an adjective in the phrase.

If the phrase expresses *accompaniment*, use the ablative with **cum**.

If the phrase expresses *cause*, use either **ob** or **propter** with the accusative, or use the ablative of cause.

196. Adjectives used as Nouns. Adjectives are often used as nouns (III, *f*); as, **amīcus, -ī**, m., *a friend*, from **amīcus, a, -um**, *friendly*; **multa, -ōrum**, n., *many things*, from **multī, -ae, -a**, *many*. So also **fīnitimī**, *neighbors*, and **nostrī**, *our men*.

EQUES ROMANUS

EXERCISES

197. 1. Nostrī centuriōnem inter captīvōs vīdērunt. 2. Fīnitimī propter eam victōriam Rōmānōrum dolent. 3. Cūr cohortēs per silvās ad oppidum fugiēbant? 4. Cum cūrā vestrās fīliās librīs docuistis. 5. Equitēs et peditēs ante portam sunt. 6. Sine perīculō in urbe manēbimus. 7. Atque multa ex eā urbe portāvērunt. 8. Trāns agrum lātum explōrātōrēs dūcit. 9. In prōvinciā cum multīs mīlitibus fuit.

198. 1. After this battle he will send our men into Germany. 2. They captured the town without help. 3. The neighbors were fighting bravely against the enemy. 4. In front of the town was a hill. 5. Near the lieutenant a messenger was waiting. 6. We shall hurry through Italy and shall spend the winter among those mountains.

LESSON XXVIII

READING LESSON

199.   VOCABULARY

exemplum, -ī, *n.,* example
factum, -ī, *n.,* act, deed (*fact*)
Horātius, Horātī, *m.,* Horatius, a Roman
nam, *conj.,* for
paucī, -ae, -a, *plur.,* few, only a few (*paucity*)
pōns, pontis (ponti-), *m.,* bridge (*pontoon*)
Porsena, -ae, *m.,* Porsena, a king of Etruria
Sublicius, -a, -um, Sublician (resting on piles)
tandem, *adv.,* at last, finally

tergum, -ī, *n.,* back; **ā tergō,** in the rear
terror, terrōris, *m.,* terror, fear
Tiberis, -is (*acc.* -im), *m.,* Tiber, a river
timidus, -a, -um, fearful (*timid*)
dēfendō, dēfendere, dēfendī, dēfēnsus, defend (*defense*)
obsideō, obsidēre, obsēdī, obsessus, besiege
servō, servāre, servāvī, servātus, save, protect (*preserve*)
sustineō, sustinēre, sustinuī, sustentus, hold up, sustain, hold in check

HORATIUS PONTEM DEFENDIT

200. Porsena, Rōmānōrum hostis, rēx fuit clārus. Ōlim urbem Rōmam obsidēbat. Magnus erat terror Rōmānōrum, quod Porsena multōs mīlitēs habēbat. Timidae fēminae in templīs deōs adōrābant. Sed virtūs validī virī Rōmam dēfendit. Nam paucīs cum sociīs prō ponte Subliciō Horātius hostīs sustinuit. Cīvēs interim ā tergō pontem solvunt et rescindunt (*break down*). Tum sociōs Horātius dīmittit et pontem contrā hostīs dēfendit. Tandem dēcidit pōns, et inter pīla hostium Horātius in Tiberim dēsilit (*jumps down*) et ad sociōs natat. Id exemplum virtūtis Rōmam servāvit. Hodiē facta Horātī laudāmus.

201. VOCABULARY

contendō, contendere, contendī, contentus, struggle (*contend*)
cotīdiānus, -a, -um, daily
ferē, *adv.*, almost
Gallia, -ae, *f.*, Gaul (*Gallic*)
Gallus, -ī, *m.*, a Gaul (inhabitant of Gaul)
Germānī, -ōrum, *m. plur.*, Germans
Hispānī, -ōrum, *m. plur.*, Spaniards
Hispānia, -ae, *f.*, Spain

incolō, incolere, incoluī, ——, dwell in, inhabit
magnopere, *adv.*, greatly
nātiō, nātiōnis, *f.*, race, people, tribe (*national*)
nōn sōlum . . . sed etiam, not only . . . but also
Rhēnus, -ī, *m.*, Rhine (*Rhenish*)
timeō, timēre, timuī, ——, fear, dread

DE NATIONIBUS EUROPAE

202. Hispānia et Gallia et Germānia erant nātiōnēs Eurōpae. Proxima ōceanō erat Hispānia. Gallī inter Hispāniam et Germāniam, Germānī trāns Rhēnum incolēbant. Germānī paucōs vīcōs etiam in Galliā habēbant. Quod eae nātiōnēs hostēs erant, Rōmānī cum Hispānīs et Gallīs et Germānīs saepe pugnāvērunt.

Inter Galliam et mare erat nova prōvincia Rōmae. Incolae eius prōvinciae iniūriās Gallōrum diū sustinuērunt. Tandem ab Rōmānīs auxilium postulāvērunt; nam Helvētiōs fīnitimōs magnopere timēbant. Helvētiī nōn sōlum prōvinciae sed etiam Germānīs inimīcī erant et cum Germānīs cotīdiānīs ferē proeliīs contendēbant.

HORATIUS PONTEM DEFENDIT

FIRST YEAR LATIN

FOURTH REVIEW LESSON

LESSONS XXII–XXVIII

203. Give the English meanings of the following words:

ā, ab	dēcidō	homō	nāvis	rēx
ad	dēfendō	hostis	nōn sōlum...	servō
ante	dīmittō	iaciō	sed etiam	sine
apud	doleō	iam	ob	solvō
capiō	dux	ignis	obsideō	soror
caput	ē, ex	incolō	pater	sustineō
centuriō	eques	inopia	paucī	tandem
cīvis	et... et	inter	pedes	tergum
cohors	exemplum	lapis	per	terror
collis	explōrātor	magnopere	pēs	timeō
cōnfirmō	factum	mare	pōns	timidus
conloquium	ferē	mīles	post	trāns
contendō	fingō	mōns	postulō	urbs
contrā	fīnis	mūrus	propter	virtūs
corpus	fortiter	nam	-que	volō
cotīdiānus	fugiō	nātiō	quoque	vulnus

204. Give the Latin meanings of the following words:

sister	back	after	on account of, because of
few, only a few	wall	and	near, with, among
fly	without	father	conference, interview
both... and	bridge	head	to, toward, against
across	enemy	daily	from, away from
hill	now	defend	not only... but also
foot soldier	horseman	stone	throw, hurl, cast
ship	at last	before	valor, courage
grieve	soldier	centurion	leader, general
fear, dread	bravely	for	fashion, devise
mountain	citizen	fall down	dwell in, inhabit
city	terror	loose	between, among

FOURTH REVIEW LESSON

take, capture	king	sea	race, people, tribe
fire	greatly	foot	end, territories
struggle	scout	flee	strengthen, encourage
man	against	body	hold up, sustain, hold in check
wound	lack, want	besiege	act, deed
send away	demand	cohort	example
out of, from	through	almost	save, protect
fearful			

205. Decline each noun in 203. Give the principal parts of each verb. Conjugate each verb of the third conjugation in the present, imperfect, future, and perfect indicative active. Use each preposition in a Latin phrase. Which nouns have i-stems?

206. Following the suggestions in 634, give English words derived from the Latin words in 203. Define these derivatives, and illustrate each by an English sentence.

207. Give the rule, if there is one, for each of the following constructions, and illustrate each by a sentence in Latin:

1. Ablative of place from which
2. Accusative of place to which
3. Ablative of cause
4. Prepositional phrases expressing cause
5. Prepositions with the accusative
6. Prepositions with the ablative
7. Adjectives used as nouns

NAVIS

LESSON XXIX

ADJECTIVES OF THE THIRD DECLENSION

208. Adjectives of the Third Declension. Besides the adjectives of the first and second declensions there are also adjectives of the third declension. They use the endings of the third declension of nouns.

a. Some of these adjectives have the same form for the nominative singular of all three genders: as, **audāx**, *bold*. Others have the same form for the masculine and feminine nominative singular, but a different form for the neuter nominative singular: as, **brevis, breve**, *short*. Still others have a different form in the nominative singular for each gender: as, **ācer, ācris, ācre**, *keen, eager*.

b. Learn the declension of **audāx, brevis,** and **ācer** (644).

c. Observe that the adjectives having two or three endings in the nominative singular have only -ī in the ablative singular. Adjectives of one ending more often have -ī than -e in the ablative. Compare the endings of these adjectives with the endings of nouns having i-stems (189). What differences are there?

d. Decline **proelium ācre,** *keen battle*; **corpus breve,** *short body*; **hostis audāx,** *bold enemy*; **vir ācer,** *bold man*.

209.   VOCABULARY

ācer, ācris, ācre, keen, eager, sharp (*acrid*)
audāx, audācis, bold (*audacious*)
brevis, -e, short, brief (*brevity*)
Caesar, Caesaris, *m.*, Caesar
commūnis, -e, common (*community*)
fortis, -e, brave, strong (*fortitude*)
gravis, -e, heavy, severe (*gravity*)
labor, labōris, *m.*, toil, hardship (*laborious*)
omnis, -e, all, every, the whole (*omnipresent*)
potestās, potestātis, *f.*, power

NOTE. In the vocabularies the genitive singular will be given of adjectives of one ending; but in the case of adjectives of two or of three endings all the forms of the nominative singular will be given.

88

ADJECTIVES OF THE THIRD DECLENSION

EXERCISES

210. 1. Caesar dux audāx Rōmānōrum erat. 2. Magna fuit potestās eius ducis. 3. Omnēs mīlitēs Caesarem magnopere amābant, quod hostīs saepe superāvit. 4. Labōrēs mīlitum in bellō saepe erant gravēs. 5. Hostēs multī et ācrēs erant et multa pīla contrā Rōmānōs iaciēbant. 6. Sed nostrae cohortēs propter commūne perīculum nōn fūgērunt. 7. Prō Rōmā fortiter pugnāvērunt. 8. Breve erat id bellum.

211. 1. The sword of the Romans was both short and heavy. 2. The foot soldier had a bold comrade. 3. Our men were carrying many heavy things. 4. To all my friends I shall give gifts. 5. The leader of the eager horsemen was grieving because of many hardships. 6. He dismissed all the tribunes from the conference.

CÆSAR

LESSON XXX

THE FOURTH CONJUGATION

212. The Fourth Conjugation. Learn the present, imperfect, future, and perfect indicative active of **audiō** (662).

a. Compare the inflection of **audiō** with that of **capiō**. Observe that three forms of **audiō** in the present differ in quantity from the corresponding forms of **capiō**: audīs, audīmus, audītis. In other respects the inflection is identical with that of **capiō**.

b. Inflect like **audiō** in the same tenses **reperiō**, *find*, and **veniō**, *come*.

213. VOCABULARY

flūmen, flūminis, *n.*, river (*fluent*)
nōbilis, -e, noble, of high birth (*nobility*)
audiō, audīre, audīvī, audītus, hear (*audible*)

oppugnō, oppugnāre, oppugnāvī, oppugnātus, attack (*impugn*)
reperiō, reperīre, repperī, repertus, find (*repertory*)
veniō, venīre, vēnī, ventūrus, come (*invent*)

EXERCISES

214. 1. Audiō, audiēbam, audiam. 2. Audītne? audiēbat, audiet. 3. Audiunt, audiēbant, audient. 4. Audīmus, audīvimus, audiētis. 5. Audīvī, audīs, audīvērunt. 6. Venīs, venit, vēnistī. 7. Vēnit, venīmus, vēnimus. 8. Reperīsne? repperistis, reperītis. 9. Repperī, reperit, repperit.

215. 1. He has found, they have found, they came. 2. You are hearing, you did come, he heard. 3. We have heard, we were finding, we came. 4. You are coming, they were finding, we shall come. 5. I shall hear, we hear, they heard. 6. He came, he has come, they hear. 7. They will defend, they have attacked, he has defended.

216. CONLOQUIUM

Mārcus. Hodiē fābulam dē Porsenā et Horātiō audīvī.

Iūlia. Quis fuit Porsena? Rōmānusne erat?

Mārcus. Porsena, rēx nōbilis, Rōmānōrum hostis ōlim fuit. Cum mīlitibus audācibus in fīnīs Rōmānōrum vēnit, et urbem Rōmam oppugnābat.

Iūlia. Fūgēruntne Rōmānī ob perīculum?

Mārcus. Magnum erat perīculum urbis et cīvium, quod hostēs erant fortēs et ācrēs, sed Rōmānī nōn fūgērunt.

Iūlia. Cēpitne Porsena Rōmam?

Mārcus. Urbem nōn cēpit, quod virtūs validī virī cīvīs dēfendēbat. Paucīs cum sociīs Horātius prō urbe fortiter pugnābat.

Iūlia. Diūne hostēs sustinuit Horātius?

Mārcus. Nōn diū, quod hostēs erant multī, et multa pīla iaciēbant. Tandem trāns flūmen ad sociōs natāvit. Rōmānī Horātium ob eam virtūtem laudāvērunt.

SOLDIERS MARCHING

LESSON XXXI

THE ABLATIVE OF TIME

217.   VOCABULARY

aestās, aestātis, *f.*, summer
annus, -ī, *m.*, year (*annual*)
decem, *adj., indecl.*, ten (*decimal*)
hiems, hiemis, *f.*, winter
hōra, -ae, *f.*, hour (*horoscope*)
lūx, lūcis, *f.*, light (*translucent*)
nox, noctis (nocti-), *f.*, night (*nocturnal*)
prīmus, -a, -um, first (*primary*)
secundus, -a, -um, second (*secondary*)
tempus, temporis, *n.*, time (*temporal*)
gerō, gerere, gessī, gestus, manage, carry on (*vicegerent*)
prīmā lūce, at dawn
bellum gerere, carry on war, wage war

218. The Ablative of Time.

1. **Hominēs aestāte et hieme labōrant,** *men toil in summer and in winter.*
2. **Decem annīs Caesar multa bella gessit,** *within ten years Cæsar carried on many wars.*

a. Observe that these ablatives are expressions of time. They answer the questions *when?* *in* or *within what time?* This usage of the ablative is known as the *Ablative of Time.* It may be translated by a phrase beginning with *in, at, within,* or *during.*

219. *Rule for the Ablative of Time. The time at which or within which a thing happens is expressed by the ablative without a preposition.*

EXERCISES

220. 1. Hieme ventī in marī sunt gravēs. 2. Aestāte agricolae in agrīs labōrābant. 3. Prīmā lūce ad Caesarem venient. 4. Caesar bellum fortibus cum hostibus gessit. 5. Omnēs prōvinciās paucīs annīs superāvit. 6. Quō tempore noctis in urbem vēnistī? 7. Secundā hōrā proelī decem explōrātōrēs capiunt. 8. Nūntius eō tempore lēgātō litterās dēmōnstrāvit.

221. 1. Welcome summer will come in a short time. 2. At the second hour of the night we heard these commands. 3. He found ten wounds on the body of the foot soldier. 4. At dawn Cæsar sent this cohort between the hill and the mountain. 5. They all fled from the province in the first year of the war. 6. Why did they not carry on war with the Romans in the winter?

LACONIC SPEECHES[1]

222. 1. Amīcus ōlim Spartānum rogāvit: "Cūr mūrōs nōn habet Sparta?" Spartānus respondit: "Nostra urbs mūrōs optimōs (*the very best*) habet, virtūtem incolārum fortium."

2. Rēx Spartānus ōlim dīxit: "Meī cīvēs numquam rogāvērunt, 'Quot sunt hostēs?' sed 'Ubi sunt?'"

3. Hostis ante pugnam Spartānō dīxit: "Sōlem propter pīlōrum multitūdinem et sagittārum nōn vidēbitis." "In umbrā igitur pugnābimus," respondit Spartānus.

[1] The meanings of words that are not given in the vocabularies of the lessons may be found in the general vocabulary.

AESTATE AGRICOLA IN AGRIS LABORAT

LESSON XXXII

THE PLUPERFECT AND FUTURE PERFECT INDICATIVE ACTIVE OF ALL CONJUGATIONS

223. The Formation of the Pluperfect and Future Perfect Tenses. The pluperfect (XXXIII, *b*) and the future perfect (XXXIII, *b*) indicative active of **amō** are inflected as follows:

PLUPERFECT

1. amā'veram, *I had loved*   amāverā'mus, *we had loved*
2. amā'verās, *you had loved*   amāverā'tis, *you had loved*
3. amā'verat, *he had loved*   amā'verant, *they had loved*

FUTURE PERFECT

1. amā'verō, *I shall have loved*   amāve'rimus, *we shall have loved*
2. amā'veris, *you will have loved*   amāve'ritis, *you will have loved*
3. amā'verit, *he will have loved*   amā'verint, *they will have loved*

a. Observe that the pluperfect is formed by adding the imperfect of **sum** (108) to the perfect stem; and the future perfect by adding the future of **sum** to the perfect stem. One form, however, is not spelled as it is in the inflection of **sum**. Which form?

b. The tense sign of the pluperfect is **-erā-**; of the future perfect, **-eri-**.

c. What are the perfect stems of **moneō, regō, capiō, audiō,** and **sum**? Inflect the pluperfect and future perfect tenses of these verbs, and of the verbs in 203.

d. What auxiliary verbs (IV, *f*) are to be used in translating these tenses? What English tense is the same as the pluperfect?

e. The perfect, pluperfect, and future perfect use the perfect stem, and so belong to the perfect system of the verb. Make synopses (671) in this system of the model verbs.

THE PLUPERFECT AND FUTURE PERFECT

224. VOCABULARY

cīvitās, cīvitātis, *f.*, state, clan
Labiēnus, -ī, *m.*, Labienus, a Roman officer
populus, -ī, *m.*, people (*population*)

prīnceps, prīncipis, *m.*, chief (*principal*)
Rōmānus, -a, -um, Roman
tēlum, -ī, *n.*, weapon

EXERCISES

225. 1. Ēmerint, gesseram, hiemāverātis. 2. Dēmōnstrāverant, audīveris, superāverāmus. 3. Tenuerō, complēveram, armāverās. 4. Habitāveris, vocāverat, mānserō. 5. Nārrāverātis, mīserās, fūgerimus. 6. Exspectāveram, doluerō, cōnfirmāverit. 7. Sustinuerat, rēxeram, properāveris.

8. Labiēnus prīncipem virtūte laudāverat. 9. Fortis homō amīcōs multōs et ācrīs habuerit. 10. Caesar bella nōn sōlum in Galliā sed etiam in Britanniā gesserat. 11. Quō tempore noctis arma cēperis? 12. Gallī oppida magnā cum virtūte dēfenderant. 13. Populus Rōmānus cīvēs eius cīvitātis līberāverat.

A GALLIC CHIEFTAIN

226. 1. We shall have frightened, you (*sing.*) had come, you (*plur.*) will have dismissed. 2. He will have fought, he had captured, they had defended. 3. We had led, they will have wounded, he will have thrown. 4. You (*sing.*) will have built, we had found, they will have carried.

5. The Roman people had long held the Gauls in check. 6. The chiefs had called together all the clans. 7. Labienus will have found many weapons in that place. 8. The Gauls had waited for aid. 9. At last we had attacked that hill.

LESSON XXXIII

THE DEMONSTRATIVES *HIC* AND *ILLE* · PLACE FROM WHICH AND TO WHICH, IN NAMES OF TOWNS

227. The Demonstratives *Hic* and *Ille*. Review the declension of is (654), and learn the declension of hic and ille (654).

a. Decline hic prīnceps, haec cīvitās, hoc tēlum, ille Gallus, illa nox, and illud tempus.

228. The Distinction between *Is*, *Hic*, and *Ille*. Is is used indifferently for *this* or *that* without emphasis (148). Hic means *this*, and ille *that*, with a certain emphasis. Hic is applied to what is *near* the speaker in place, time, or thought. Ille is applied to what is *not near* the speaker in place, time, or thought. Hic and ille, like is, are used both as demonstrative adjectives and as demonstrative pronouns: as, **hoc dōnum meum, illud tuum est,** *this gift is mine, that is yours.* Demonstratives, when used as adjectives, regularly precede their nouns.

229. Place from Which and to Which, in Names of Towns. You have already learned that *place from which* is expressed by the ablative with ā (ab), dē, ē (ex) (178); and that *place to which* is expressed by the accusative with ad or in (180). If, however, the *place from which* or *to which* is the name of a town, the prepositions are omitted: as, **Rōmā vēnit,** *he came from Rome*; **Rōmam vēnit,** *he came to Rome.* **Domus,** *home,* also omits the preposition: **domum vēnit,** *he came home (homeward).*

230. *Complete Rules for Place from Which and to Which.*
a. *Place from which is usually expressed by the ablative with ā (ab), dē, ē (ex); but with the names of towns, and with* **domus,** *the preposition is omitted.*

96

HIC AND ILLE

b. *Place to which is usually expressed by the accusative with* **ad** *or* **in**; *but with the names of towns, and with* **domus**, *the preposition is omitted.*

231.   **VOCABULARY**

Athēnae, -ārum, *f. plur.*, Athens
Capua, -ae, *f.*, Capua
Carthāgō, -inis, *f.*, Carthage
Corinthus, -ī, *f.*, Corinth [1]
Delphī, -ōrum, *m. plur.*, Delphi
domum, *acc.*, home, homeward
domō, *abl.*, from home

frāter, frātris, *m.*, brother (*fraternal*)
hic, haec, hoc, *dem. pron. or adj.*, this
ille, illa, illud, *dem. pron. or adj.*, that

EXERCISES

232. 1. Dux illōs equitēs peditēsque Capuam mīsit. 2. Tandem ex Italiā Carthāginem propter commūne perīculum properāvit. 3. Hī mīlitēs Athēnīs vēnerant et in Galliā pugnābant. 4. Secundā illīus noctis hōrā nūntium Corinthum mīsit. 5. Illī lēgātī praedam Rōmam portāverant. 6. Populus audāx in hāc īnsulā habitāverat. 7. Huic centuriōnī amīcus fueram. 8. Ex hīs fīnibus omnēs prīncipēs Delphōs fūgerant, quod illō tempore hostēs bellum parābant.

233. 1. From Delphi they had come to Athens. 2. From home my brother hastened to Corinth. 3. Cæsar had sent messengers through those states. 4. In these years the Gauls had been friendly to the Roman people. 5. These enemies will have fought with Cæsar with great courage. 6. This is a javelin, that is a sword.

[1] Most names of towns are feminine.

LESSON XXXIV

READING LESSON

VICTORIA CAESARIS

234. In Galliā multae et fortēs cīvitātēs erant. Prīncipēs hārum cīvitātum potestātem imperiaque Rōmānōrum timuērunt. Multōs mīlitēs igitur convocāverant et inter montīs et collīs Rōmānōs exspectābant.

Prīmō annō bellī populus Rōmānus Caesarem contrā Gallōs mīsit. Is dux, cum Labiēnō et peditibus et paucīs equitibus,

MILITES ROMANI

ex Italiā aestāte properāvit et sine perīculō in fīnīs Gallōrum vēnit. Hīs in locīs explōrātōrēs Caesaris hostēs repperērunt.

Prīmā lūce mīlitēs Rōmānī Gallōs oppugnāvērunt. Ācre erat proelium. Gallī lapidibus et tēlīs gravibus locum dēfendēbant. Nostrī pīla iaciēbant et gladiīs hostīs sustinēbant. Tandem Gallī dēfessī ob inopiam tēlōrum et vulnera trāns flūmen fūgērunt.

Decem annīs Caesar multa bella in Galliā gessit et multōs captīvōs Rōmam mīsit.

READING LESSON

235. VOCABULARY

Britannī, -ōrum, *m. plur.*, the Britons
Cassivellaunus, -ī, *m.*, Cassivellaunus
obses, obsidis, *m.*, hostage
tamen, *adv.*, yet, but, nevertheless

nāvigō, nāvigāre, nāvigāvī, nāvigātus, sail (*navigation*)
occupō, occupāre, occupāvī, occupātus, seize, take possession of (*occupy*)
vāstō, vāstāre, vāstāvī, vāstātus, lay waste (*devastate*)

DE CAESARE ET BRITANNIS

236. Quod Britannī ad Gallōs auxilium saepe mīserant, Caesar in īnsulam Britanniam nāvigāvit. Territī (*although frightened*) magnō numerō nāvium et virōrum, Britannī fortēs magnā cum virtūte prō patriā pugnāvērunt. Tandem tamen ab lītore fūgērunt. Post hoc proelium Rōmānī agrōs hostium vāstāvērunt et oppida occupāvērunt et multam praedam cēpērunt. Cassivellaunus, prīnceps Britannōrum, lēgātōs ad Caesarem mīsit. Caesar obsidēs postulāvit. Cum hīs obsidibus et captīvīs multīs ex Britanniā in Galliam vēnit. Propter hanc victōriam magna erat potestās Rōmānōrum in Britanniā.

IN BRITANNIAM CAESAR NAVIGAT

LESSON XXXV

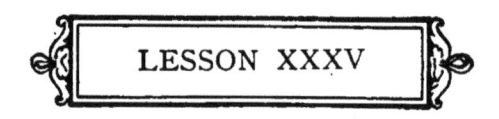

**THE PRESENT, IMPERFECT, AND FUTURE INDICATIVE PASSIVE OF THE FIRST AND SECOND CONJUGATIONS
THE ABLATIVE OF AGENT**

237. The Passive Voice. In the active voice the subject of the verb is *acting*; in the passive voice it is *acted on* (XXVIII): as,

The general praises the soldier (active).
The soldier is praised by the general (passive).

238. The Present Indicative Passive of the First Conjugation. The present indicative passive of **amō** is inflected as follows:

	Singular	Pers. Endings	Plural	Pers. Endings
1.	a'mor, *I am loved* (*I am being loved*)	-r	amā'mur, *we are loved*	-mur
2.	amā'ris, *you are loved*	-ris	amā'minī, *you are loved*	-minī
3.	amā'tur, *he, she, it is loved*	-tur	aman'tur, *they are loved*	-ntur

a. Observe that these passive forms differ from the active only in the personal endings. The endings are added to the present stem **amā-** exactly as they were in the active voice.

239. The Imperfect and Future Indicative Passive of the First Conjugation. Compare the imperfect and the future active and passive of **amō** (658). Observe that the passive endings are added to the tense stems **amābā-** and **amābi-**, exactly as in the active voice, except in the second person singular of the future, where -bi- is changed to -be-. Learn these tenses of **moneō** (659).

EXERCISES

240. 1. Amat, amātur. 2. Amābat, amābātur. 3. Amābit, amābitur. 4. Amant, amantur. 5. Amābant, amābantur. 6. Amābuntne? amābunturne? 7. Amāmus, amāmur. 8. Moneō,

THE PASSIVE VOICE

moneor. 9. Monēbam, monēbar. 10. Monēbō, monēbor. 11. Monēbitis, monēbiminī. 12. Monētis, monēminī.

241. 1. You praise, you are praised. 2. They were praising, they were being praised. 3. You will praise, you will be praised. 4. I teach, I am taught. 5. We teach, we are taught. 6. We shall teach, we shall be taught. 7. They teach, they are taught.

242. The Ablative of Agent.
  1. **Labiēnus mīlitem laudat,** *Labienus praises the soldier.*
  2. **Mīles ab Labiēnō laudātur,** *the soldier is being praised by Labienus.*

a. Observe the changes made in turning the active sentence into the passive: (1) the object in the active becomes the subject in the passive; (2) the subject of the active is expressed in the passive by the ablative with **ab**. This ablative is known as the *Ablative of Agent.*

b. The *agent* is the person doing something. The ablative of *agent* should not be confused with the ablative of *means* (122), which has no preposition: as, **mīles lapide vulnerātur,** *the soldier is wounded by a stone;* **mīles ā Gallō vulnerātur,** *the soldier is wounded by a Gaul.*

243. *Rule for the Ablative of Agent.* *The personal agent with a passive verb is expressed by the ablative with* **ā** *or* **ab.**

EXERCISES

244. 1. Hic puer ā frātre meō laudābātur. 2. Haec praeda Rōmam ā Caesare portābitur. 3. Ā quō nōn amātur potestās? 4. Fābulae multae dē Britanniā ab iīs nūntiīs nārrābuntur. 5. Oppidum ab mīlitibus oppugnātur. 6. In hāc pugnā decem hominēs ā Gallīs vulnerantur. 7. Nāvibus frūmentum portābitur.

245. 1. All these Gauls will be held in check by those horsemen. 2. My brothers were praised by that boy. 3. Aid is being awaited by the enemy. 4. A few cohorts were seen by the chief. 5. Rome was loved by all the Romans.

LESSON XXXVI

THE RELATIVE *QUI*

246. The Relative *Quī*. The relative **quī**, *who, which, that*, is declined as follows:

	Singular			Plural		
Nom.	quī	quae	quod	quī	quae	quae
Gen.	cuius	cuius	cuius	quōrum	quārum	quōrum
Dat.	cui	cui	cui	quibus	quibus	quibus
Acc.	quem	quam	quod	quōs	quās	quae
Abl.	quō	quā	quō	quibus	quibus	quibus

a. Compare the declension of the relative **quī** with that of the interrogative **quī** (154).

247. Agreement of the Relative with its Antecedent.

1. **Puellae quās laudāvimus bonae erant,** *the girls whom we praised were good.*
2. **Praemium quod ille homō portat laudātur,** *the reward which that man is bringing is praised.*
3. **Homō cuius gladium habeō est nauta,** *the man whose sword I have is a sailor.*

a. Observe that the relative (II, *d*) in each sentence refers to a certain word. This word is called its *antecedent* (II, *b*). Observe that the relative has the same gender and number as its antecedent, but that its case is different. Thus, in sentences 1 and 2 it is accusative because it is the object of **laudāvimus** or of **portat**; in sentence 3 it is genitive because it indicates the possessor of **gladium**.

b. A relative clause modifies its antecedent as an adjective modifies its noun.

248. *Rule for the Agreement of the Relative. A relative pronoun agrees with its antecedent in gender and number, but its case depends on the way it is used in its own clause.*

THE RELATIVE *QUI*

249.   VOCABULARY

cōnsilium, cōnsi'lī, *n.*, advice, plan (*counsel*)
frūstrā, *adv.*, in vain (*frustrate*)
legiō, legiōnis, *f.*, legion (*legionary*)
māter, mātris, *f.*, mother (*maternal*)

mercātor, mercātōris, *m.*, trader, merchant (*merchandise*)
quī, quae, quod, *rel. pron.*, who, which, that, as
turris, turris (turri-), *f.*, tower (*turret*)

EXERCISES

250. 1. Illa fēmina quam vidēs est māter Cornēliae. 2. Mercātōrēs multa in Germāniam portant. 3. Hostēs ācrēs, ā quibus nostra patria vāstātur, sunt Rōmānī. 4. Iī hominēs, quōrum virtūte et cōnsiliīs urbs tenēbātur, domum ē bellō venient. 5. Turrēs, quae cum cūrā aedificābantur, ab hostibus vāstābuntur. 6. Obsidēs quī ā Rōmānīs līberantur Athēnās properābunt. 7. Dux legiōnis quam Caesar trāns flūmen mīsit erat Labiēnus.

251. 1. The weapons which we have brought are not good. 2. This summer you will fight with Caesar, who is defending the province. 3. I shall praise the plan by which that town is being laid waste. 4. Caesar had

MATER CUM PUERIS

ten legions in the wars which he carried on with the Gauls. 5. The woman to whom I showed the way is the mother of this unhappy hostage.

FIFTH REVIEW LESSON

LESSONS XXIX–XXXVI

252. Give the English meanings of the following words:

ācer	decem	hōra	nox	quī
aestās	flūmen	ille	obses	reperiō
annus	fortis	labor	occupō	secundus
audāx	frāter	legiō	omnis	tamen
audiō	frūstrā	lūx	oppugnō	tēlum
brevis	gerō	māter	populus	tempus
cīvitās	gravis	mercātor	potestās	turris
commūnis	hic	nāvigō	prīmus	vāstō
cōnsilium	hiems	nōbilis	prīnceps	veniō

253. Give the Latin meanings of the following words:

legion	this	find
come	brother	toil, hardship
that	who, which, that, as	sail
ten	all	advice, plan
summer	mother	in vain
hostage	second	short, brief
time	brave, strong	trader
year	hour	power
river	night	chief
winter	bold	tower
first	manage, carry on, wage	yet, nevertheless
common	state, clan	heavy
light	noble, of high birth	people
weapon	attack	seize, take possession of
hear	keen, eager, sharp	lay waste

254. Decline each noun and each adjective in 252. Give the principal parts of each verb. Conjugate each verb of the fourth conjugation throughout the indicative mood. Make synopses (671) of each verb in the third person singular and plural. Decline **hic, ille,** and **qui.**

255. Following the suggestions in 634, give English words derived from the Latin words in 252. Define these derivatives, and illustrate each by an English sentence.

256. Give the rule for the following constructions, and illustrate each by a sentence in Latin:

       1. Ablative of time
       2. Place from which, in names of towns
       3. Place to which, in names of towns
       4. Ablative of agent
       5. Agreement of the relative

HOSTES CONTRA ROMANOS OPPIDUM DEFENDUNT

LESSON XXXVII

THE PRESENT, IMPERFECT, AND FUTURE INDICATIVE PASSIVE OF *REGO* AND *CAPIO*

257. The Present, Imperfect, and Future Indicative Passive of *Regō* and *Capiō*. Review the present, imperfect, and future indicative active of **regō** and **capiō**, and learn the passive of the same tenses (660, 661).

a. Observe that to form the passive you have only to substitute the passive personal endings for the active, except in one form. Which one is that, and what is the change?

b. Like **regō** inflect in both voices the same tenses of **dūcō, mittō,** and **gerō**; inflect **iaciō** and **recipiō** like **capiō**.

EXERCISES

258. 1. Regit, regitur. 2. Regēbat, regēbātur. 3. Reget, regētur. 4. Regunt, reguntur. 5. Regent, regentur. 6. Regis, regeris. 7. Regēbās, regēbāris. 8. Regēs, regēris. 9. Regimus, regimur. 10. Regitis, regiminī. 11. Regam, regar. 12. Capiunt, capiuntur. 13. Capiēbat, capiēbātur. 14. Capiet, capiētur. 15. Capient, capientur. 16. Capiēs, capiēris. 17. Capis, caperis. 18. Capiēbās, capiēbāris.

259. 1. He leads, he is led. 2. They will lead, they will be led. 3. They lead, they are led. 4. You lead, you are led. 5. We shall lead, we shall be led. 6. We send, we are sent. 7. Is he sent? are they sent? 8. He will send, he will be sent. 9. You are sent, you will be sent. 10. They were waging, I was waging. 11. We wage, we shall wage. 12. We throw, we are thrown. 13. We threw, we were being thrown. 14. Who receives? who was being received?

260.   VOCABULARY

castra, -ōrum, *n. plur.*, camp (*Lancaster*)
cōnsul, cōnsulis, *m.*, consul (*consular*)
nōn iam, *adv.*, no longer

pāx, pācis, *f.*, peace (*pacify*)
recipiō, recipere, recēpī, receptus, receive, welcome (*recipient*)
vincō, vincere, vīcī, victus, defeat, conquer (*invincible*)

EXERCISES

261. 1. Lēgātī dē pāce in castra cōnsulis vēnērunt. 2. Iam ad cōnsulem dūcuntur hī lēgātī. 3. Bene ā cōnsule recipientur. 4. Nōn iam urbs hostium dēfenditur. 5. Tēla quae dē mūrīs iaciēbantur multōs vulnerābant. 6. Mīlitēs cōnsulis nōn saepe ā Gallīs vincuntur. 7. Pāx populō Rōmānō grāta erit.

262. 1. Labienus with only a few cohorts will be sent from Rome into Gaul. 2. Those towns of Gaul will be defended bravely. 3. The legion is being led out of the camp. 4. Many states of Gaul are being conquered to-day. 5. The new plans of our allies were being announced to the neighbors. 6. They will be received by Cæsar, who has conquered the Helvetians.

CASTRA ROMANA

LESSON XXXVIII

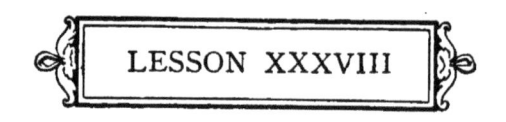

THE PERSONAL AND REFLEXIVE PRONOUNS

263. The Personal Pronouns. The personal pronouns (II, c) are **ego**, *I*; **tū**, *you*; **is**, *he*; **ea**, *she*; **id**, *it*.

In reality there is no pronoun of the third person in Latin. The demonstrative **is** (148, 228) is so often used as a personal pronoun that it may be classed as the pronoun of the third person. Sometimes the demonstratives **hic** and **ille** are similarly used. Learn the declension of the personal pronouns (652).

264. The Personal Pronouns as Subjects of Verbs. The personal pronouns are expressed as subjects only for emphasis, especially the emphasis of contrast: as, **ego tē laudō, tū mē nōn laudās**, *I praise you, you do not praise me.*

265. The Reflexive Pronouns. A reflexive pronoun refers to the subject of its clause (II, h). Learn the declension of the reflexive pronouns (653).

266. The Use of the Reflexive Pronouns. The use of the reflexive pronouns is illustrated by the following sentences:

    1. **Tū tē amās**, *you love yourself.*
    2. **Omnēs hominēs sē amant**, *all men love themselves.*

a. Observe that **tē** and **sē** refer to the subjects of their sentences.

b. Remember that **is**, *he*; **ea**, *she*; and **id**, *it*, are used as personal pronouns, but not as reflexive pronouns; and that **suī** is always a reflexive pronoun, and not a personal pronoun.

267. Relative Clauses referring to Personal Pronouns.

Tū, quī venīs, es amīcus meus, *you, who are coming, are my friend.*

a. Observe that the verb of the relative clause is in the same person as the antecedent.

PERSONAL AND REFLEXIVE PRONOUNS

268. **VOCABULARY**

cotīdiē, *adv.*, daily
ego, *pers. pron.*, I (*egotistic*)
interficiō, interficere, interfēcī, interfectus, kill
is, ea, id, *pers. pron.*, he, she, it
reliquus, -a, -um, rest of, remaining (*relic*)
reliquī, -ōrum, *m. plur.*, the rest
suī, *reflex. pron.*, of himself, herself, itself, themselves
tempestās, tempestātis, *f.*, weather, storm (*tempest*)
tū, *pers. pron.*, you

EXERCISES

269. 1. Scūtum eius erat grave. 2. Amīcī eōrum fuerant mīlitēs. 3. Studium eārum laudātur. 4. Vōbīscum[1] propter tempestātem manēbō. 5. Contrā eōs bellum geritur. 6. Estne Mārcus tēcum? 7. Cum eā ambulābat. 8. Sine vōbīs Athēnās properābunt. 9. Nōs sumus miserī, vōs aegrī et dēfessī estis. 10. Omnia vestra cōnsilia nōbīs sunt grāta. 11. Pater et māter eius ab vōbīs bene recipiēbantur. 12. Reliquī prīncipēs, quī sē armābant, ad conloquium nōn vēnērunt. 13. Itaque ad sē centuriōnem vocat et eī cōnsilium nārrat. 14. Cotīdiē Caesar peditēs ē castrīs dūcēbat.

270. 1. His mother and my father saw you. 2. They are now with me. 3. To him, to her, to them I shall give rewards. 4. Their camp is being attacked. 5. *I* shall hurry into town with you. 6. We shall free ourselves with severe hardship. 7. *She* has wounded herself with her father's sword. 8. The rest will kill themselves. 9. Their towns are being laid waste by the Gauls this summer.

[1] The preposition **cum** is appended to the ablative of personal and reflexive pronouns in the manner of an enclitic (22); so usually to relative and interrogative pronouns.

LESSON XXXIX

THE PRESENT, IMPERFECT, AND FUTURE INDICATIVE PASSIVE OF THE FOURTH CONJUGATION

271. The Present, Imperfect, and Future Indicative Passive of Audiō. Review the active voice of **audiō** in the present, imperfect, and future indicative, and learn the passive of the same tenses (662)

a. Like **audiō** inflect **impediō**, *hinder*, and **reperiō**, *find*, in the present, imperfect, and future tenses.

EXERCISES

272. 1. Audit, audītur. 2. Audiēbat, audiēbātur. 3. Audiet, audiētur. 4. Audīmus, audīmur. 5. Audiēmus, audiēmur. 6. Audiam, audiar. 7. Audītis, audīminī. 8. Audiētis, audiēminī. 9. Audīs, audīris. 10. Audiēbam, audiēbar. 11. Audiunt, audiuntur. 12. Audiēbant, audiēbantur.

273. 1. I hinder, I am hindered. 2. I was hindering, I was being hindered. 3. I shall hinder, I shall be hindered. 4. They hinder, they are hindered. 5. They will hinder, they will be hindered. 6. He finds, he is found. 7. He found, he was found. 8. He will find, he will be found.

274.   VOCABULARY

aedificium, aedifi′cī, *n.*, building (*edifice*)
Coriolānus, -ī, *m.*, Coriolanus
maximē, *adv.*, greatly, very much (*maximum*)
statim, *adv.*, at once
Veturia, -ae, *f.*, Veturia
Volscī, -ōrum, *m.*, Volscians

dīcō, dīcere, dīxī, dictus, say (*diction*)
impediō, impedīre, impedīvī, impedītus, hinder (*impede*)
incitō, incitāre, incitāvī, incitātus, arouse, impel (*incite*)
praebeō, praebēre, praebuī, praebitus, cause, furnish, show

PASSIVE OF THE FOURTH CONJUGATION

EXERCISES

VETURIA, MATER CORIOLANI

275. Urbī Rōmae ōlim magnum perīculum ā Volscīs, quī erant populī Rōmānī hostēs audācēs, praebēbātur. Volscī ā Coriolānō, Rōmānō, incitābantur et dūcēbantur. Iam aedificia multa in agrīs ab hostibus vāstābantur. Cīvēs sē armābant. Urbs cibō complēbātur ā cōnsule. Frūstrā hostēs impediēbantur. Tum perīculō magnō Rōmānī mātrem Coriolānī dē pāce ad eum misērunt, quod ea ab fīliō maximē amābātur. Veturia, māter Coriolānī, in castra ad fīlium vēnit. In castrīs eum repperit. Coriolānus eam vīdit et dīxit, "Mea patria mē et sociōs meōs vīcit." Statim ab urbe fūgit cum hostibus.

276.   **VOCABULARY**

autem, *postpositive*[1] *conj.*, but, however, besides

enim, *postpositive conj.*, for

perturbō, perturbāre, perturbāvī,

perturbātus, disturb, throw into confusion (*perturbation*)

pōnō, pōnere, posuī, positus, put, place (*postpone*)

DE PERSEO

277. Dē Perseō multae fābulae nārrantur ā poētīs. Perseus fīlius fuit Iovis (642), rēgis deōrum. Avus eius Ācrisius fuit. Ille Perseum interficere volēbat[2]; nam propter imperia deōrum puerum timēbat. Cēpit igitur eum adhūc īnfantem, et cum mātre in arcā posuit. Tum in mare arcam iēcit. Danaē, Perseī māter, maximē timēbat, tempestās enim magna mare perturbābat. Perseus autem in sinū (*in the arms*) mātris dormiēbat.

---

[1] Never the first word in the sentence or clause.

[2] **interficere volēbat**, *wished to kill*. The infinitive used in this way is called a complementary infinitive (394).

LESSON XL

THE POSSESSIVE ADJECTIVES · THE ABLATIVE OF SEPARATION

278. The Possessive Adjectives. The possessive adjectives are as follows:

    meus, -a, -um, *my*   tuus, -a, -um, *your* (sing.)
    noster, -tra, -trum, *our*   vester, -tra, -trum, *your* (plur.)
       suus, -a, -um, *his, her, its, their* (*own*), used reflexively

a. To show possession the possessive adjectives are used instead of the genitives **meī, tuī, nostrum, vestrum,** and **suī.** They may also be used as possessive pronouns: as, **mea,** *mine*; **nostrī,** *our men.*

279. The Distinction between *Suus* and the Possessive Genitive of *Is*.

    1. **Mīles scūtum eius habet,** *the soldier has his shield* (i. e. somebody else's shield).
    2. **Mīles suum scūtum habet,** *the soldier has his own shield.*

a. **Eius** (sentence 1) does not refer to the subject; **suum** (sentence 2) does refer to the subject. **Suus** is always reflexive, but the genitives of **is, ea, id** are never reflexive.

280. When Possessive Adjectives are used in Latin. When the meaning is clear, a possessive adjective is omitted unless emphatic: as,

    1. **Caesar mīlitēs in castra redūxit,** *Cæsar led his soldiers back into camp.*
    2. **Caesar suōs mīlitēs in castra redūxit,** *Cæsar led his* (*own*) *soldiers back into camp* (but the others he left outside).

281. The Ablative of Separation.

    1. **Hic homō cibō caret,** *this man lacks* (is separated from) *food.*
    2. **Germānī Rōmānōs ā fīnibus suīs prohibēbant,** *the Germans were keeping the Romans away from their lands.*

THE POSSESSIVE ADJECTIVES

a. Observe that the ablative is here used to denote that from which there is freedom, removal, or separation, or that which is lacking. The ablative so used answers the questions *from what? of what?* and is called the *Ablative of Separation.* It is of the same nature as the ablative of *place whence.*

282. Rule for the Ablative of Separation. *Words signifying* **privation, removal,** *or* **separation** *are followed by the ablative without a preposition, or with the prepositions* ā (ab), dē, ē (ex).

283. VOCABULARY

posteā, *adv.*, afterwards
suus, -a, -um, his (own), her (own), its (own), their (own)
careō, carēre, caruī, caritūrus, lack, want (*caret*)
dēsistō, dēsistere, dēstitī, dēstitūrus, leave off, cease (*desist*)
interclūdō, interclūdere, interclūsī, interclūsus, cut off, shut off (*conclude*)
prīvō, prīvāre, prīvāvī, prīvātus, keep from, deprive of (*privation*)
prohibeō, prohibēre, prohibuī, prohibitus, keep away (from), restrain (*prohibit*)

EXERCISES

284. 1. Caesar autem suōs mīlitēs trāns flūmen mīsit. 2. Caesar eius frātrem in castrīs reperiet. 3. Ille vir aeger aquā prīvābātur. 4. Posteā ea cīvitās cibō et frūmentō carēbat. 5. Ab aedificiīs et pecūniā huius populī mīlitēs diū prohibuit. 6. Ob inopiam armōrum proeliō Germānī dēstitērunt. 7. Nostrī, quī in castra Germānōrum properāverant, eōs tēlīs prīvāvērunt. 8. Flūmen nostrōs viā interclūdēbat. 9. Apud flūmen nāvigia ab hostibus eō tempore aedificābantur.

285. 1. Our friends lacked money. 2. The enemy will defend their own buildings. 3. You will free us from care. 4. Cæsar announced to his (men) his plans concerning peace. 5. They will afterwards deprive the Germans of all power. 6. The rest of the chiefs were being shut off from their towns.

LESSON XLI

THE PERFECT, PLUPERFECT, AND FUTURE PERFECT INDICATIVE PASSIVE OF ALL CONJUGATIONS

286. The Perfect, Pluperfect, and Future Perfect of All Conjugations.

a. Review the principal parts of **amō**, and notice especially the perfect passive participle. Examine the formation of the perfect indicative passive (658). Observe that it is formed by using the present tense of **sum** with the perfect passive participle **amātus**. Those tenses which are formed with the help of the perfect passive participle belong to the participial system of the verb (671).

b. Examine the pluperfect and the future perfect indicative passive. Observe that they are formed by using the imperfect and the future of **sum** with the perfect passive participle.

c. The perfect, pluperfect, and future perfect indicative passive of all verbs are formed in the same way.

d. The participle **amātus** is declined like **bonus**; and so in the nominative singular and plural it is changed to agree with the subject of the verb in number and gender. These changes are made because a participle is an adjective in its nature. Observe these changes as illustrated in 287.

e. Recall the principal parts of **moneō, regō, capiō,** and **audiō**, and inflect the perfect, pluperfect, and future perfect passive of these verbs and of those in 252.

EXERCISES

287. 1. Vir amātus est, fēmina amāta est, bellum amātum est. 2. Virī amātī sunt, fēminae amātae sunt, bella amāta sunt. 3. Mīlitēs monitī erant, puer monitus erit, oppidum monitum erat. 4. Agricola captus est, urbs rēcta est, prōvincia rēcta erat. 5. Captus sum, captus eram, captus erō. 6. Audītus es, audītus erās, audītus eris. 7. Audītī sumus, audītī erāmus, audītī erimus.

THE PERFECT INDICATIVE PASSIVE

288. 1. The Gaul was warned, had been warned, will have been warned. 2. The buildings have been taken, had been taken, will have been taken. 3. The territories had been ruled by the Germans. 4. The cities will have been defended. 5. And so we (*fem.*) shall have been heard.

289.   VOCABULARY

concilium, conci'lī, *n.*, meeting (*council*)
ibi, *adv.*, there
impedīmentum, -ī, *n.*, hindrance; *plur.*, baggage (*impediment*)

imperātor, imperātōris, *m.*, general, commander (*emperor*)
mora, -ae, *f.*, delay (*moratorium*)
verbum, -ī, *n.*, word (*verbal*)

EXERCISES

290. 1. Multa in Italiā oppida ā Rōmānīs aedificāta sunt. 2. Paucī Germānī ibi tēlīs nostrōrum interfectī sunt. 3. Tua verba ā mē audīta erunt. 4. Eō tempore imperātor ab impedīmentīs carrīsque interclūsus erat. 5. Bellum, quod ā Caesare gestum est, longum fuit. 6. Mīlitēs, quī ab eō in Galliam missī sunt, frūmentō caruērunt. 7. Praeda, quae ab imperātōre nostrō capta erat, sine morā Rōmam portāta est. 8. In conciliō suīs Caesar dīxit, "Cōnsilia mea ab hostibus nōn impedīta sunt."

IUPPITER PERSEUM SERVAT (CONTINUED FROM 277)

291. Iuppiter tamen haec omnia vīdit, et fīlium suum servāre cōnstituit (*determined to save*). Tranquillum igitur fēcit mare, et arcam ad īnsulam Serīphum dūxit. Huius īnsulae Polydectēs tum rēx erat. Postquam[1] arca ad lītus ducta est, Danaē in harēnā dormiēbat. Post breve tempus ā virō reperta est, et ad rēgem adducta est. Ille mātrem et puerum bene recēpit, et eīs sēdem tūtam in fīnibus suīs praebuit.

[1] **Postquam** introduces a subordinate clause of time (xx, *e*).

LESSON XLII

THE FOURTH DECLENSION

292. The Fourth Declension. Nouns of the fourth declension end in the nominative singular in **-us** or **-ū**. Those ending in **-us** are masculine, with a few exceptions; those ending in **-ū** are neuter. These nouns are inflected as follows:

	exercitus, m. *army*	cornū, n. *horn, wing*	CASE ENDINGS Masc.	Neut.
	SINGULAR			
Nom.	exer'cit**us**	cor'n**ū**	-us	-ū
Gen.	exer'cit**ūs**	cor'n**ūs**	-ūs	-ūs
Dat.	exerci'tu**ī** (-ū)	cor'n**ū**	-uī (-ū)	-ū
Acc.	exer'cit**um**	cor'n**ū**	-um	-ū
Abl.	exer'cit**ū**	cor'n**ū**	-ū	-ū
	PLURAL			
Nom.	exer'cit**ūs**	cor'n**ua**	-ūs	-ua
Gen.	exerci't**uum**	cor'n**uum**	-uum	-uum
Dat.	exerci't**ibus**	cor'n**ibus**	-ibus (-ubus)	-ibus
Acc.	exer'cit**ūs**	cor'n**ua**	-ūs	-ua
Abl.	exerci't**ibus**	cor'n**ibus**	-ibus (-ubus)	-ibus

a. A few nouns of this declension may have the dative and the ablative plural in **-ubus**; such nouns in this book are **lacus**, *lake*, and **portus**, *harbor*.

b. **Domus**, *house*, and **manus**, *hand*, are the only feminine nouns of this declension used in this book; and **cornū** is the only neuter so used. Learn the declension of **domus**, which has forms of the second declension as well as those of the fourth (642).

c. Decline **exercitus magnus, mea manus,** and **cornū longum.**

THE FOURTH DECLENSION

293.   **VOCABULARY**

adventus, -ūs, *m.*, coming (*advent*)
commeātus, -ūs, *m.*, supplies
cornū, -ūs, *n.*, horn, wing (of an army) (*cornucopia*)
domus, -ūs, *f.*, house, home (*domicile*)
exercitus, -ūs, *m.*, army (*exercise*)

lacus, -ūs, *m.*, lake (*lake*)
manus, -ūs, *f.*, hand, handful, band (of men) (*manufacture*)
palūs, palūdis, *f.*, marsh, swamp
portus, -ūs, *m.*, harbor (*port*)
mūniō, mūnīre, mūnīvī, mūnītus, fortify (*munitions*)

EXERCISES

294. 1. Adventus legiōnum nōs dēlectat. 2. Noster exercitus tamen Germānōs commeātibus interclūsit. 3. Inter nostrōs et hostīs erat lacus. 4. Cōnsulēs erant exercituum Rōmānōrum imperātōrēs. 5. In cornibus diū et fortiter pugnāverant. 6. Castra Labiēnī palūde et lacū mūniēbantur. 7. Graeciae in portubus nāvēs multās hieme vīdimus. 8. Manūs hostium spectāvimus.

295. 1. They fight both with feet and with horns. 2. Many lakes are seen by them among the mountains. 3. We had been delighted by the coming of the traders. 4. This house is mine, that is yours. 5. However, at daybreak they carried the supplies from the camp to the harbor. 6. Rome was at once fortified by the hands of the citizens. 7. Why are you hurrying home?

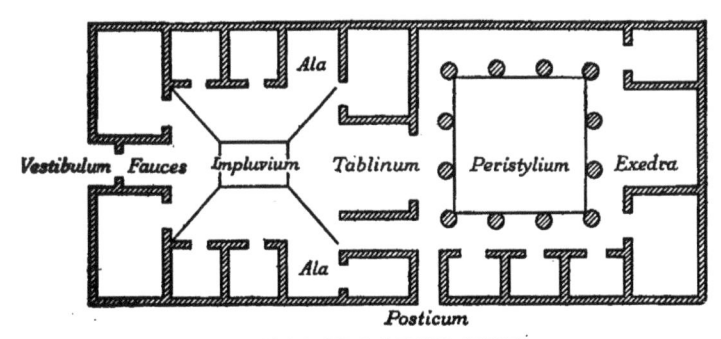

PLAN OF A ROMAN HOUSE

LESSON XLIII

THE COMPARISON OF ADJECTIVES

296. Degrees of Comparison. Latin adjectives have three degrees of comparison, the positive, the comparative, and the superlative. But in Latin, as in English, there are certain adjectives which are not compared.

Positive	Comparative
lātus, -a, -um, *wide* (BASE lāt-)	lātior, lātius, *wider*
brevis, -e, *short* (BASE brev-)	brevior, brevius, *shorter*
audāx, *bold* (BASE audāc-)	audācior, audācius, *bolder*

Superlative
lātissimus, -a, -um, *widest*
brevissimus, -a, -um, *shortest*
audācissimus, -a, -um, *boldest*

a. Observe that the comparative is formed by adding to the base of the positive the endings **-ior** for the masculine and the feminine, and **-ius** for the neuter; the superlative by adding to the base of the positive **-issimus, -issima, -issimum.**

b. Compare **clārus, grātus, longus, fortis,** and **gravis.**

c. The comparative may be translated *wider, more wide, rather wide, too wide*; the superlative *widest, most wide, very wide*.

297. The Declension of the Comparative. The comparative is declined as follows:

	SINGULAR		PLURAL	
	M. AND F.	N.	M. AND F.	N.
Nom.	lā'tior	lā'tius	lātiō'rēs	lātiō'ra
Gen.	lātiō'ris	lātiō'ris	lātiō'rum	lātiō'rum
Dat.	lātiō'rī	lātiō'rī	lātiō'ribus	lātiō'ribus
Acc.	lātiō'rem	lā'tius	lātiō'rēs (-īs)	lātiō'ra
Abl.	lātiō're	lātiō're	lātiō'ribus	lātiō'ribus

THE COMPARISON OF ADJECTIVES

a. The superlative is declined like **bonus** (643).

b. Decline the positive, the comparative, and the superlative of the adjectives in 296, *b.*

298.   VOCABULARY

amīcitia, -ae, *f.*, friendship
equitātus, -ūs, *m.*, cavalry
impetus, -ūs, *m.*, attack (*impetuous*)
iter, itineris, *n.*, way, march, journey (642) (*itinerary*)

senātus, -ūs, *m.*, senate (*senator*)
faciō, facere, fēcī, factus, make; impetum facere, to make an attack; iter facere, to march, travel
peto, petere, petīvī (petiī), petītus, seek, ask (*petition*)

EXERCISES

299. 1. Quod iter brevius est? 2. Quod iter brevissimum est? 3. Equitātus autem iter per vīcōs propinquōs fēcerat. 4. Germānī dē senātū Rōmānō pācem petīvērunt. 5. Amīcitia sociōrum populō Rōmānō grātissima erit. 6. Noster exercitus impetum in (*against, upon*) hostēs faciet. 7. Hoc flūmen est lātum, sed mare lātius est. 8. Gallī in bellō certē fortissimī erant. 9. Ubi cīvis fortiōrēs vīdistī?

300. 1. Your house is very new. 2. The general sent the cavalry by a longer way. 3. The summer in Britain is not very short. 4. This javelin is too heavy. 5. Peace, however, will be sought by all the clans of Gaul. 6. They are making an attack against the turret with little zeal. 7. The army was marching through the woods and swamps.

ROMAN SHOES

SIXTH REVIEW LESSON

LESSONS XXXVII–XLIII

301. Give the English meanings of the following words:

adventus	ego	iter	praebeō
aedificium	enim	lacus	prīvō
amīcitia	equitātus	manus	prohibeō
autem	exercitus	maximē	recipiō
careō	faciō	mora	reliquī
castra	ibi	mūniō	reliquus
commeātus	impedīmentum	nōn iam	senātus
concilium	impediō	palūs	statim
cōnsul	imperātor	pāx	suī
cornū	impetus	perturbō	suus
cotīdiē	incitō	petō	tempestās
dēsistō	interclūdō	pōnō	tū
dīcō	interficiō	portus	verbum
domus	is	posteā	vincō

302. Give the Latin meanings of the following words:

daily	horn, wing	but, however, besides
senate	put, place	cause, furnish, show
say	I	seek, ask
army	camp	greatly, very much
lack, want	lake	keep from, deprive of
no longer	kill	he, she, it, they
for	hinder	disturb, throw into confusion
peace	make	leave off, cease
hand, band	meeting	harbor
cut off, shut off	delay	his (own), her (own), its (own)
you	the rest	rest of, remaining
at once	fortify	arouse, impel
house, home	afterwards	keep away, restrain

SIXTH REVIEW LESSON

marsh, swamp	word	cavalry
weather, storm	consul	hindrance, baggage
receive, welcome	coming	general, commander
supplies	building	way, march, journey
there	attack	of himself, of herself, etc.
defeat, conquer	friendship	

303. Decline each noun in 301. Give the principal parts of each verb. Inflect those tenses of **dīcō, impediō, pōnō,** and **prīvō** which are formed from the present stem. Make synopses of each verb in 301 in the third person singular and plural. Decline **ego, is,** and **tū.**

304. Following the suggestions in 634, give English words derived from the Latin words in 301. Define these derivatives, and illustrate each by an English sentence.

305. Give the rule, if there is one, for each of the following constructions, and illustrate each by a sentence in Latin:

1. A personal pronoun of each person as the object of a verb
2. A personal pronoun of each person as the subject of a verb
3. A reflexive pronoun of the third person as the object of a verb
4. Ablative of separation

MILITES CASTRA MUNIUNT

LESSON XLIV

THE COMPARISON OF ADJECTIVES ENDING IN -ER OR -LIS
THE PARTITIVE GENITIVE

306. The Comparison of Adjectives in -er. Adjectives ending in -er are compared as follows:

miser, misera, miserum, *wretched*	miserior, miserius	miserrimus, -a, -um
ācer, ācris, ācre, *keen*	ācrior, ācrius	ācerrimus, -a, -um

a. Observe that the comparative of these adjectives is regular; but the superlative is formed by adding **-rimus, -rima, -rimum** to the nominative masculine of the positive. Compare similarly **aeger**.

307. The Comparison of Adjectives in -lis. The comparative of the following adjectives ending in -lis is regular; but the superlative is formed by adding **-limus, -lima, -limum** to the base of the positive. Learn their meaning and comparison.

facilis, -e, *easy*	facilior, -ius	facillimus, -a, -um
difficilis, -e, *hard*	difficilior, -ius	difficillimus, -a, -um
similis, -e, *like*	similior, -ius	simillimus, -a, -um
dissimilis, -e, *unlike*	dissimilior, -ius	dissimillimus, -a, -um

Most other adjectives in -lis are compared regularly: as, **nōbilis, nōbilior, nōbilissimus**.

308. The Partitive Genitive.

1. **Ille amīcus cōpiam pecūniae habet,** *that friend has plenty of money.*
2. **Multī mīlitum vulnerātī sunt,** *many of the soldiers were wounded.*

a. Observe that each genitive denotes a whole, and the word on which it depends denotes a part of that whole. Such a genitive, of which a part is taken, is called a *Partitive Genitive*.

THE COMPARISON OF ADJECTIVES

309. *Rule for the Partitive Genitive.* Words denoting a part may have with them a genitive of the whole from which the part is taken.

a. Numerals and a few other words have the ablative with **ē (ex)** or **dē** instead of the partitive genitive: as, **decem ex mīlitibus**, *ten of the soldiers.*

310. VOCABULARY

angustus, -a, -um, narrow (*anguish*)
celer, -eris, -ere, swift, quick (*celerity*)
cōpia, -ae, *f.*, plenty, supply; *plur.*, troops (*copious*)
lītus, lītoris, *n.*, shore (*littoral*)
pars, partis (parti-), *f.*, part (*partition*)
quīnque, *adj., indecl.*, five (*quinquennial*)

EXERCISES

311. 1. Magna pars itineris est angusta sed facillima. 2. Prīmā lūce partem hostium in monte vīdimus. 3. Illa omnium urbis viārum brevissima fuit. 4. Hominēs Britanniae hominibus Italiae dissimillimī sunt. 5. Statim decem ex mīlitibus proeliō dēsistunt. 6. In lītore fēminae dolēbant quod iter erat difficile. 7. Omnium Gallōrum ācerrimī atque celerrimī erant hostēs. 8. Difficillima saepe facillima sunt. 9. Cum cīvitātibus proximīs amīcitiam cōnfirmābunt.

312. 1. Have we plenty of arms? 2. The march through the mountains will not be easy. 3. Five of my friends will be sent by me by an easier way to the shore. 4. Part of the soldiers were cut off from the rest of the army. 5. Your hand is like mine. 6. This is the easiest of all the ways through the territories of the Gauls.

LESSON XLV

READING LESSON

313.   VOCABULARY

adulēscēns, adulēscentis, *m.*, young man (*adolescent*)
vīta, -ae, *f.*, life (*vital*)
appellō, appellāre, appellāvī, appellātus, call, name (*appeal*)

expugnō, expugnāre, expugnāvī, expugnātus, take by storm, capture
iūrō, iūrāre, iūrāvī, iūrātūrus, swear, take oath (*abjure*)

SCIPIO ET HANNIBAL

314. Scīpiō et Hannibal erant clārissimī imperātōrēs. Ille (*the former*) erat Rōmānus, quī victōriās magnās reportāvit; hic (*the latter*) Poenus, quī Rōmānōs multīs pugnīs vīcit. Hannibal puer [1] ad ārās ā patre adductus est. Ibi odium iūrāvit in [2] Rōmānōs. Adulēscēns oppida multa in Hispāniā expugnāvit, tum Alpīs montīs superāvit [3] Rōmānōsque saepe vīcit in Italiā. Scīpiō ad [4] Tīcīnum flūmen vītam patris virtūte servāvit posteāque ad [4] Cannās contrā Hannibalem sē fortem praebuit. Bellum in Āfricam trānsportātum est ibique Scīpiō Hannibalem ad [4] Zamam superāvit. Ā Rōmānīs appellātus est Āfricānus.

315.   VOCABULARY

nātūra, -ae, *f.*, nature, character (*natural*)
omnīnō, *adv.*, wholly, altogether, entirely
prīmum, *adv.*, first, at first
accipiō, accipere, accēpī, acceptus, receive (*accept*)

discēdō, discēdere, discessī, discessūrus, withdraw
perveniō, pervenīre, pervēnī, perventūrus, come through, reach, arrive
quaerō, quaerere, quaesīvī, quaesītus, seek, ask (*inquire*)

[1] puer, *when a boy.*   [2] in, *against.*   [3] superāvit, *passed over.*   [4] ad, *near.*

READING LESSON

PERSEUS MEDUSAM QUAERIT (CONTINUED FROM 291)

316. Perseus adulēscēns ex īnsulā Serīphō discessit, et, postquam ad continentem vēnit, Medūsam quaesīvit. Diū frūstrā eam quaerēbat, nam nātūram locī ignōrābat. Tandem Mercurius et Minerva eī viam dēmōnstrāvērunt. Prīmum ad Graeās, sorōrēs Medūsae, pervēnit. Hārum auxiliō tālāria et galeam magicam accēpit. Mercurius et Minerva eī falcem et speculum dedērunt. Tum, postquam tālāria pedibus induit,[1] in āera[2] ascendit. Diū per āera volābat; tandem tamen ad eum locum vēnit ubi Medūsa cum reliquīs Gorgonibus incolēbat. Gorgonēs mōnstra erant quārum capita anguibus omnīnō contēcta[3] erant. Manūs autem ex aere[4] erant factae.

[1] **pedibus induit,** *put on his feet.*   [2] **āera,** acc. of āer.   [3] **contēcta,** from contegō.   [4] **aere,** from aes.

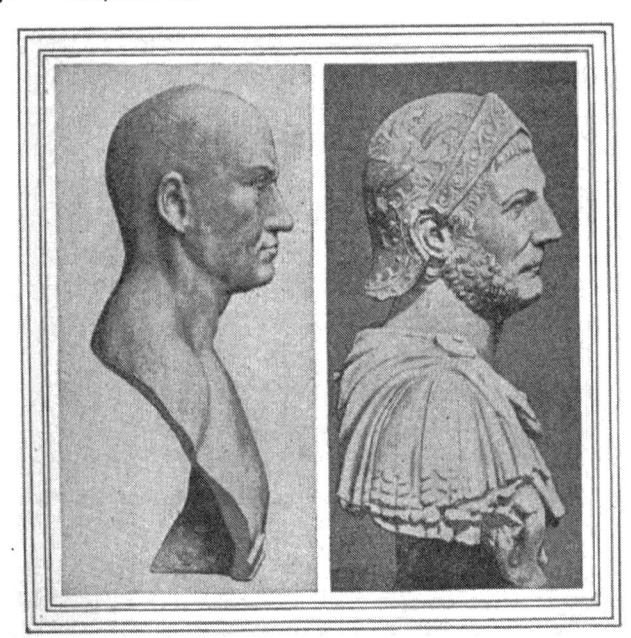

SCIPIO AND HANNIBAL

LESSON XLVI

IRREGULAR COMPARISON OF ADJECTIVES · THE ABLATIVE OF DEGREE OF DIFFERENCE

317. Adjectives Compared Irregularly. Both the comparative and the superlative of several common adjectives are irregular. Commit to memory the following:

bonus, -a, -um, *good*	melior, melius, *better*	optimus, -a, -um, *best*
magnus, -a, -um, *large*	maior, maius, *larger*	maximus, -a, -um, *largest*
malus, -a, -um, *bad*	peior, peius, *worse*	pessimus, -a, -um, *worst*
multus, -a, -um, *much*	——, plūs, *more*	plūrimus, -a, -um, *most*
multī, -ae, -a, *many*	plūrēs, plūra, *more*	plūrimī, -ae, -a, *most*
parvus, -a, -um, *little, small*	minor, minus, *less, smaller*	minimus, -a, -um, *least, smallest*

318. The Declension of *Plūs*. In the singular **plūs**, *more*, is used only as a neuter noun. Learn the declension of **plūs** (648).

319. Other Adjectives Compared Irregularly. There are other adjectives that are compared irregularly, some of which have no positive, but form their comparative and superlative from prepositions or adverbs, and others of which have two forms in the superlative. See 649. These should be learned as they occur in the vocabularies.

320. The Ablative of Degree of Difference.

1. **Pater pede altior est quam fīlius,** *the father is a foot taller than his son.*
2. **Pāx multō grātior erit quam bellum,** *peace will be much more welcome than war.*

a. Observe that the ablatives **pede** and **multō** answer the question (*by*) *how much?* They denote the *degree of difference* between the objects compared. This usage is called the *Ablative of Degree of Difference.*

IRREGULAR COMPARISON

321. Rule for the Ablative of Degree of Difference. *The degree of difference is expressed by the ablative.*

322.   VOCABULARY

centum, *adj., indecl.*, a hundred (*century*)
inferus, -a, -um, low, below (649) (*inferior*)
interdum, *adv.*, sometimes
malus, -a, -um, bad (*malice*)
opera, -ae, *f.*, work, activity (*opera*)
quam, *conj.*, than
sex, *adj., indecl.*, six (*sextant*)
superus, -a, -um, high, above (649) (*superior*)

EXERCISES

323. 1. In inferiōrem partem prōvinciae sex legiōnēs ā Caesare dūcuntur. 2. Viae urbis nostrae pedibus multīs angustiōrēs sunt. 3. Maximae manūs hostium convocātae erant et Rōmānōs itinere prohibēbant. 4. Dē locīs superiōribus plūrima tēla iēcērunt. 5. Illa turris decem pedibus altior quam mūrus est. 6. Minōra castra ā centum mīlitibus dēfendēbantur. 7. Tua operae pars est maior quam mea. 8. Interdum amīcī nōbīs cōnsilium malum dant. 9. Summum montem[1] videō. 10. Italiae pars inferior propter multās Graecōrum urbēs Magna Graecia appellābātur; superior pars Italiae, quod ibi Gallī incolēbant, Gallia Cisalpīna vel (*or*) Gallia Citerior appellābātur.

324. 1. The best men sometimes do not have the most friends. 2. On the journey a great many men were killed; the rest fled into a very large forest. 3. Cornelia was a foot taller than Julia. 4. The Gauls had more horsemen than the Romans. 5. Part of the army was waiting in higher places. 6. A better plan was shown to the senate. 7. The largest towns sent a hundred hostages to Caesar.

---

[1] **summum montem**, *top of the mountain.*

LESSON XLVII

THE FORMATION AND THE COMPARISON OF ADVERBS

325. The Formation of Adverbs. Many adverbs are formed from adjectives. From adjectives of the first and second declensions adverbs are formed by the addition of **-ē** to the base of the positive; from adjectives of the third declension they may be formed by the addition of -iter to the base: as, **cārē**, *dearly*, from **cārus**, *dear*; **miserē**, *wretchedly*, from **miser**, *wretched*; **ācriter**, *eagerly*, from **ācer**, *eager*; but most adjectives of one ending add -ter to the base: as, **audācter**, from **audāx**.

a. Form adverbs from **grātus, lātus, longus, līber, aeger, brevis, fortis, gravis**.

326. The Irregular Formation of Adverbs. Some adverbs are the accusative or ablative singular neuter of the adjective: as, **multum**, *much*, from **multus**; **multō**, *much*, from **multus**; **facile**, *easily*, from **facilis**.

327. The Comparison of Adverbs.

Positive	Comparative	Superlative
cārē	cārius	cārissimē
miserē	miserius	miserrimē
ācriter	ācrius	ācerrimē
facile	facilius	facillimē
bene	melius	optimē
male	peius	pessimē
multum	plūs	plūrimum

a. Observe that the comparative of the adverb is the same as the neuter singular comparative of the adjective; and that the superlative, with one exception, is formed from the superlative of the adjective by changing final **-us** to **-ē**.

FORMATION AND COMPARISON OF ADVERBS

328.   **VOCABULARY**

amplus, -a, -um, large, spacious (*ample*)
arbor, arboris, *f.*, tree (*arboreal*)
dīligenter, *adv.*, diligently (*diligent*)
diū (diūtius, diūtissimē), *adv.*, long
hinc, *adv.*, hence, from here, from this place
līberī, -ōrum, *m. plur.*, children (*liberty*)

multitūdō, -inis, *f.*, great number (*multitude*)
subitō, *adv.*, suddenly
praemittō, praemittere, praemīsī, praemissus, send ahead (*premise*)
relinquō, relinquere, relīquī, relictus, leave behind, leave (*relinquish*)

EXERCISES

329. 1. Patrēs et mātrēs suōs līberōs maximē amant. 2. Eīs cōnsilia optima dant et prō eīs dīligentissimē labōrant. 3. Tum in illam silvam amplam, quam hinc vidēmus, multitūdinem peditum praemittēmus. 4. Ex hōc summō monte facile videō sex urbēs centumque viās. 5. In īmīs terrae partibus sunt flūmina minima. 6. Diūtius lacū quam montibus impedītae sunt cōpiae nostrae. 7. Plūrimī mīlitēs apud portum relictī erant; reliquī impetum in hostīs subitō fēcērunt. 8. Arboribus et lapidibus mūrōs facient. 9. Hoc flūmen centum pedibus lātius est quam illud.

330. 1. Sometimes Cæsar's enemies fought much more bravely than the Roman soldiers. 2. But his soldiers fought very eagerly and boldly. 3. He carried on wars with the Gauls for a very long time. 4. Often he gave ample rewards to his centurions because they had captured much booty. 5. He was killed in the city of Rome by his personal enemies (**inimīcus**).

GALLIC SWORD

LESSON XLVIII

THE FIFTH DECLENSION · THE ACCUSATIVE OF EXTENT

331. The Fifth Declension. Nouns of the fifth declension end in **-ēs**. They are feminine, with the exception of **diēs**, *day*, which is usually masculine. They are inflected as follows:

	SING.	PLUR.	SING.	PLUR.	CASE ENDINGS	
Nom.	di'ēs	di'ēs	rēs	rēs	-ēs	-ēs
Gen.	diē'ī	diē'rum	re'ī	rē'rum	-ĕī	-ērum
Dat.	diē'ī	diē'bus	re'ī	rē'bus	-ĕī	-ēbus
Acc.	di'em	di'ēs	rem	rēs	-em	-ēs
Abl.	di'ē	diē'bus	rē	rē'bus	-ē	-ēbus

a. The vowel **e** of the case endings is regularly long. It is shortened, however, in the ending **-eī** after a consonant, and in the ending **-em**: as, **rĕī** and **rem**.

b. Only **diēs** and **rēs** are complete in the plural. A few other nouns have the nominative and the accusative plural. Decline **aciēs**, **fidēs**, and **spēs**.

332. The Accusative of Extent.

1. **Decem annōs urbs oppugnābātur**, *the city was besieged for ten years.*
2. **Turris est centum pedēs alta**, *the tower is a hundred feet high.*

a. The accusative **decem annōs** denotes *extent* of *time*; the accusative **centum pedēs** denotes *extent* of *space*. Such accusatives answer the questions *how long? how far?* in time or in space. This usage is called the *Accusative of Extent*.

333. *Rule for the Accusative of Extent.* *Extent of time or of space is expressed by the accusative.*

334. VOCABULARY

aciēs, -ēī, *f.*, line of battle
altus, -a, -um, high, deep (*alto*)
diēs, -ēī, *m.*, day (*diary*)
fidēs, -ēī, *f.*, trust, confidence (*fidelity*)
plānitiēs, -ēī, *f.*, plain (*plane*)
posterus, -a, -um, next (649)

rēs, -ēī, *f.*, thing, event, fact (*reality*)
spēs, -ēī, *f.*, hope
īnstruō, īnstruere, īnstrūxī, īnstrūctus, draw up, marshal (*instruct*)
castra pōnere, to pitch camp

EXERCISES

335. 1. Caesar castra summō in monte prīmum posuit. 2. Castra summō in monte ā Caesare posita sunt. 3. Hinc hostēs magnā in plānitiē vīsī sunt. 4. Inter hunc montem et illam plānitiem erat flūmen, quod centum pedēs lātum et quīnque pedēs altum erat. 5. Caesar autem aciem īnstrūxit et impetum hostium exspectābat. 6. Eius equitēs maiōrem partem diēī in cornibus manēbant. 7. Sed hostēs impetum nōn fēcērunt, quod parvam victōriae spem habuērunt. 8. Tum adulēscentēs frūmentō plūris diēs caruērunt. 9. Collēs post castra nostra multīs pedibus altiōrēs sunt.

336. 1. Cæsar heard about this fact from very many messengers. 2. The confidence of the Gauls was very slight on that day. 3. The river was ten feet deep at this place; and so they left all the baggage on the shore. 4. This fact deprived our soldiers of all hope. 5. We shall remain six days in Italy.

AN OFFERING TO THE GODS

LESSON XLIX

READING LESSON

A LETTER FROM POMPEII

337. Sī tū valēs, bene est; ego quoque valeō. Hās litterās ad tē laetus[1] scrībō. Medicī cōnsiliō cum parentibus in Italiā hiemāvī. Apud[2] vōs nivēs (*snow*) omnia complent, sed nōs hīc nivēs rārō vidēmus. Āēr est lēnissimus; caelum rīdet. Interdum in lītore ambulō vel in hortīs amplīs errō, nam grāmen arborēsque iam virent. Hinc videō Vesuvium montem, hinc tōtam ferē urbem, hinc pulchrās īnsulās in marī sitās.[3] Linguae Latīnae cotīdiē multum operae dō. Eam linguam multō facilius quam Graecam discō. Sed iam fīnem faciam epistulae; mox cōram omnia tibi nārrābō. Valē,[4] mī amīce.[5]

[1] **laetus**, *gladly*. [2] **apud**, *with*. [3] **sitās**, *situated*. [4] **valē**, *farewell*. This form is the imperative singular of **valeō**. See XXXI, *a*. [5] **mī amīce**, *my friend*. These words are in the vocative case (XXIV, *b*). When a person is addressed in Latin, a special case, called the vocative, is used. Generally it is the same in spelling as the nominative.

A VIEW IN POMPEII

338.   VOCABULARY

cōnspectus, -ūs, *m.*, look, view, sight (*conspectus*)
modus, -ī, *m.*, way, manner (*mood*)
saxum, -ī, *n.*, stone, rock
excēdō, excēdere, excessī, excessūrus, go out, withdraw

prōcēdō, prōcēdere, prōcessī, prōcessūrus, go forward, advance (*proceed*)
vertō, vertere, vertī, versus, turn, change (*convert*)

PERSEUS MEDUSAM INTERFICIT (CONTINUED FROM 316)

339. Rēs difficillima erat caput Gorgonis abscīdere,[1] eius enim cōnspectū hominēs in saxum vertēbantur. Propter hanc causam Minerva speculum Perseō dederat. Ille igitur tergum vertit, et in speculum īnspiciēbat; hōc modō ad locum prōcessit ubi Medūsa dormiēbat. Tum falce suā caput eius ūnō ictū abscīdit. Reliquae Gorgones statim ē somnō excitātae sunt, et, ubi[2] rem vīdērunt, perturbātae sunt. Arma rapuērunt, et Perseum interficere volēbant.[3] Ille autem dum fugit,[4] galeam magicam induit; et, ubi hoc fēcit, statim ē cōnspectū eārum excessit.

[1] **abscīdere**, *to cut off.* The infinitive is here used as the subject of **erat** (393). [2] What two meanings has ubi in this paragraph? What kind of clause does it introduce here? [3] **interficere volēbant**, *wished to kill.* [4] **dum fugit**, *while he was fleeing.* The present tense with dum is translated as if it were the imperfect tense.

HEAD OF MEDUSA

LESSON L

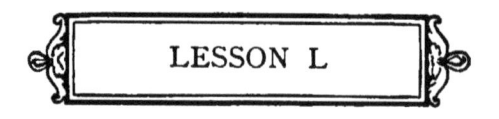

THE SUBJUNCTIVE MOOD · THE PRESENT SUBJUNCTIVE
PURPOSE CLAUSES WITH *UT* AND *NE*

340. The Subjunctive Mood. The Latin subjunctive is used in both independent and dependent clauses, but the kinds of dependent clauses in which the subjunctive is used are far more numerous than the independent. In this book only some uses in dependent clauses will be studied.

341. The Tenses of the Subjunctive. There are four tenses of the subjunctive: present, imperfect, perfect, and pluperfect. No meanings are given for the tenses of the subjunctive, because the translation varies with the use of the mood (cf. 343, 357, 372).

342. The Present Subjunctive. The present subjunctive of the several conjugations and of **sum** is inflected as follows:

	Active		Passive	
1.	a′mem	amē′mus	a′mer	amē′mur
2.	a′mēs	amē′tis	amē′ris	amē′minī
3.	a′met	a′ment	amē′tur	amen′tur

mone, reg, capi, audi { -am, -ās, -at ; -āmus, -ātis, -ant
{ -ar, -āris, -ātur ; -āmur, -āminī, -antur

sim, sīs, sit   sīmus, sītis, sint

a. Observe that the mood sign of the present subjunctive of the regular verbs is -ē- in the first conjugation, and -ā- in the others.

b. Learn the present subjunctive of the verbs above. Then inflect the present subjunctive active and passive of **dūcō, mittō, recipiō, reperiō,** and **videō**. The present subjunctive belongs in the present system (671).

SUBJUNCTIVE MOOD · PURPOSE CLAUSES

343. Purpose Clauses.
1. **Cīvēs sē armant ut pugnent,** *the citizens arm themselves that they may fight* (or, *in order that they may fight, in order to fight, for the purpose of fighting, to fight*).
2. **Cīvēs sē armant nē superentur,** *the citizens arm themselves that they may not be overcome* (or, *in order not to be overcome, so that they may not be overcome, lest they be overcome*).

a. Observe that the dependent clauses express the *purpose* of the action of the principal clause, **ut,** *that,* introducing the affirmative clause, and **nē,** *that not,* the negative clause.

b. Observe the various ways of translating **ut** and **nē** and the subjunctive in these clauses. In English, purpose is most often expressed by the infinitive. In the best Latin prose, however, the purpose of an action is not expressed by the infinitive.

344. *Rule for Purpose Clauses.* *The subjunctive is used with* ut *or* nē *in a dependent clause to express the purpose of the action stated in the independent clause.*

EXERCISES

345. 1. Nūntium mittit ut cīvēs moneat. 2. Adulēscēns mittitur ut cīvēs moneantur. 3. Legiō mittitur nē oppidum ab hostibus capiātur. 4. Legiōnēs fortiter pugnant ut oppidum capiant. 5. Puer venit ut fābulam audiat. 6. Puerī veniunt ut verba tua audiant. 7. Eōs mittimus ut prōvinciam regant. 8. Eōs mittimus ut prōvincia ab eīs regātur. 9. In Galliam properātis ut bellum gerātis. 10. Centum mīlitēs praemittimus ut castra mūniant.

346. 1. He is sent to fight. 2. We send them to find the way. 3. You are sent that the enemy may not make an attack on the city. 4. The soldiers are led out of the camp that a line of battle may be drawn up. 5. I am coming to see you and your mother. 6. He fights to defend himself.

LESSON LI

THE IMPERFECT SUBJUNCTIVE · SEQUENCE OF TENSES

347. The Imperfect Subjunctive. The imperfect subjunctive may be formed by adding the personal endings to the present infinitive active; but the final -e of the infinitive is lengthened in certain forms.

a. Learn the imperfect subjunctive of the model verbs and of **sum** (658–663). The imperfect subjunctive belongs in the present system (671).

348. Sequence of Tenses. Examine the following English sentences:

1. He *comes* (*is coming*) that he *may* fight.
2. He *will come* that he *may* fight.
3. He *came* that he *might* fight.

a. Observe that in sentences 1 and 2 the verbs in the independent clauses are present and future, and that in sentence 3 the verb in the independent clause is past. Observe the change from *may* (present) to *might* (past) when a past tense takes the place of a present or a future in the verb of the independent clause. This following of one tense by another of the same kind is called *Sequence of Tenses.*

349. Primary and Secondary Tenses. Those tenses of the indicative which refer to present or to future time (present, future, and future perfect) are called *Primary Tenses.* Those tenses of the indicative which refer to past time (imperfect, perfect, and pluperfect) are called *Secondary Tenses.*

350. *Rule for Primary Sequence.* *When the verb of the independent clause of a sentence is in a primary tense, a verb in the dependent clause is in the present tense if its action is incomplete, but in the perfect tense if its action is completed.*

A GLIMPSE INTO A ROMAN THEATER

SEQUENCE OF TENSES

351. Rule for Secondary Sequence. *When the verb of the independent clause of a sentence is in a secondary tense, a verb in the dependent clause is in the imperfect tense if its action is incomplete, but in the pluperfect if its action is completed.*

a. Observe that all the verbs in the independent clauses in 345 are in the present tense, and that all the verbs in the dependent clauses are in the present subjunctive. If the verbs in the independent clauses should be changed to the future or the future perfect tense, what would be the tense of the subjunctive in the dependent clauses?

352. Rule for the Tense of the Subjunctive in Purpose Clauses. *Since a purpose clause expresses an incomplete action, its verb will be in the present subjunctive if the verb in the independent clause is in a primary tense, and in the imperfect subjunctive if the verb of the independent clause is in a secondary tense.*

EXERCISES

353. 1. Veniunt ut pācem petant. 2. Veniēbant ut pācem peterent. 3. Venient ut pācem petant. 4. Vēnerant ut pācem peterent. 5. Fortiter pugnābant nē ā Gallīs vincerentur. 6. Trāns flūmen properāverant ut oppidum oppugnārent. 7. Legiōnēs mittentur ut hostēs commeātibus interclūdantur. 8. Ut portum dēfenderent nostrī praemissī sunt. 9. Cōnsul audācissimē dīcet ut populum Rōmānum incitet.

354. 1. They labor that they may be praised. 2. They were laboring that they might be praised. 3. They will labor that they may be praised. 4. They had labored that they might be praised. 5. They threw weapons from the higher places in order to hinder the Romans. 6. He had called together the chiefs to hear the new plan. 7. They will desist from battle that they may not be killed.

LESSON LII

SUBSTANTIVE CLAUSES OF PURPOSE · RESULT CLAUSES

355. Substantive Clauses of Purpose. A substantive clause is a clause used like a noun (xx, *d*); it may be the subject or the object of a verb. Purpose clauses with **ut** and **nē** are often used in Latin as the objects of certain verbs: as,

> **Petit ut obsidēs dent,** *he asks them to give hostages (that they give hostages).*

a. Observe that the clause **ut obsidēs dent** is the object of **petit.** This is, therefore, a noun clause. The purpose clauses in the preceding lessons were adverbial in nature (xx, *c*).

356. *Rule for Substantive Clauses of Purpose. Verbs meaning* **ask, command, persuade,** *and* **urge** *may have for their object a clause of purpose with its verb in the subjunctive.*

a. In English an infinitive is generally used in the object clause.

357. Result Clauses.
1. **Iter tam longum est ut puer sit dēfessus,** *the journey is so long that the boy is tired out.*
2. **Puer tam malus fuit ut ā patre nōn laudārētur,** *the boy was so bad that he was not praised by his father.*

a. Observe that the dependent clauses beginning with **ut** express the result of the statements in the independent clauses, and that the subjunctive is translated by an English indicative.

b. Observe that the sequence is the same as in purpose clauses, but that the negative clause contains **ut nōn** (not **nē**).

358. *Rule for Result Clauses. The subjunctive is used with* **ut** *or* **ut nōn** *in a dependent clause to express the result of the action stated in the independent clause. The sequence of tenses is generally the same as in purpose clauses.*

359. VOCABULARY

ita, *adv.*, so, in such a way
tam, *adv.*, so
tantus, -a, -um, so great
agō, agere, ēgī, āctus, act, do (*agent*)

circumveniō, circumvenīre, circumvēnī, circumventus, surround (*circumvent*)
imperō, imperāre, imperāvī, imperātus, command, order (*imperative*)

EXERCISES

360. 1. Puer ita ēgit ut ab omnibus amārētur. 2. Urbs vāstāta est nē ab hostibus caperētur. 3. Eum monēmus nē mīles sit. 4. Imperāvit nē per nostram prōvinciam iter facerent. 5. Tanta est inopia cibī ut plūrimī aegrī sint. 6. Urbs tam fortiter dēfēnsa est ut decem diēbus nōn caperētur. 7. Hostēs in silvās fūgērunt nē ā nostrīs circumvenīrentur. 8. Caesar prīmum postulāvit ut nostrīs auxilium darētur.

361. 1. They were so few that they fled. 2. They were so brave that they did not flee. 3. I advise him to be more bold. 4. The lieutenant led the soldiers out of the camp in order to draw up a line of battle. 5. He demands that they pitch camp in this place. 6. The marsh is so great that our men are hindered.

A ROMAN CUP

SEVENTH REVIEW LESSON

LESSONS XLIV-LII

362. Give the English meanings of the following words:

accipiō	cōpia	īnstruō	opera	rēs
aciēs	diēs	interdum	pars	saxum
adulēscēns	difficilis	ita	perveniō	sex
agō	dīligenter	iūrō	plānitiēs	similis
altus	discēdō	līberī	posterus	spēs
amplus	dissimilis	lītus	praemittō	subitō
angustus	excēdō	malus	prīmum	superus
appellō	expugnō	modus	prōcēdō	tam
arbor	facilis	multitūdō	quaerō	tantus
celer	fidēs	nātūra	quam	ut
centum	hinc	nē	quīnque	vertō
circumveniō	imperō	omnīnō	relinquō	vīta
cōnspectus	īnferus			

363. Give the Latin meanings of the following words:

children	hundred	high, deep	swear, take oath
bad	so	turn, change	so, in such a way
hope	next	young man	nature, character
five	plain	that not, lest	thing, event, fact
suddenly	narrow	way, manner	leave behind, leave
so great	day	send ahead	look, view, sight
part	withdraw	command, order	plenty, supply; troops
easy	hard	stone, rock	trust, confidence
than	six	wholly, entirely	draw up, marshal
unlike	seek, ask	great number	take by storm, capture
tree	act, do	so that, to	go forward, advance
sometimes	high, above	large, spacious	hence, from here
diligently	call, name	first, at first	come through, reach, arrive
shore	like	work, activity	
receive	low, below	line of battle	go out, withdraw
life	surround	swift, quick	

364. Decline each noun and each adjective in 362. Conjugate each verb in the present and the imperfect subjunctive, active and passive. Make synopses in the third person singular and plural.

365. Following the suggestions in 634, give English words derived from the Latin words in 362. Define these derivatives, and illustrate each by an English sentence.

366. Give the rule for the following constructions, and illustrate each by a sentence in Latin:

1. Partitive genitive
2. Ablative of degree of difference
3. Accusative of extent
4. Adverbial clause of purpose
5. Substantive clause of purpose
6. Adverbial clause of result
7. Sequence of tenses

THE ATRIUM OF A ROMAN HOUSE

LESSON LIII

READING LESSON

367. VOCABULARY

cēdō, cēdere, cessī, cessūrus, give way, retire (*secede*)

conlocō, conlocāre, conlocāvī, conlocātus, place, station (*collocation*)

ēdūcō, ēdūcere, ēdūxī, ēductus, lead out, lead forth

iuvō, iuvāre, iūvī, iūtus, help, aid (*adjutant*)

CAESAR HOSTIS VINCIT

368. Posterō diē Caesar ex castrīs exercitum ēdūxit et iter ad flūmen fēcit. Quae (*this*) rēs hostibus nūntiāta est, quōrum peditēs ā nostrīs summō in colle vīsī sunt. Tum Caesar equitēs in cornibus conlocāvit ut peditēs iuvārent, et mīlitum animōs ad pugnam ita incitāvit: "Omnis reī pūblicae spēs in nostrā virtūte posita est. Audācēs fortūna iuvat. Fortēs vincent." Hostēs tam ācriter in nostram aciem impetum fēcērunt ut hī cēderent. Brevī autem tempore hostēs ita superātī sunt ut ex omnibus pugnae partibus trāns flūmen fugerent. Eōrum dux captus est et Rōmam missus est.

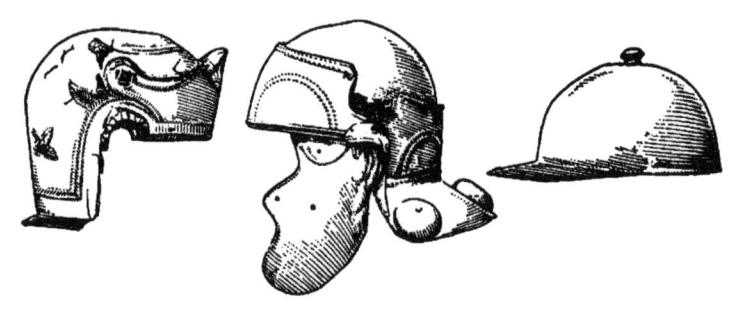

ROMAN HELMETS

369. VOCABULARY

cōnstituō, cōnstituere, cōnstituī, cōnstitūtus, establish, determine (*constitution*)

cōnsulō, cōnsulere, cōnsuluī, cōnsultus, plan, deliberate, consult (*consultation*)

trādō, trādere, trādidī, trāditus, give over, surrender (*tradition*)

ANDROMEDA FILIA CEPHEI (CONTINUED FROM 339)

370. Post haec Perseus in fīnēs Aethiopum vēnit. Ibi Cēpheus illō tempore regēbat. Hīc Neptūnum, maris deum, ōlim offenderat; itaque Neptūnus mōnstrum saevissimum mīserat. Hoc mōnstrum cotīdiē ē marī veniēbat et hominēs dēvorābat. Quam (*this*) ob causam terror animōs omnium occupāverat. Cēpheus igitur ōrāculum deī Hammōnis cōnsuluit, et ā deō iussus est[1] fīliam Andromedam mōnstrō trādere.[2] Illa autem virgō pulcherrima erat. Cēpheus, ubi haec audīvit, maximē doluit. Volēbat tamen cīvīs suōs ē tantō perīculō servāre,[3] et ob eam causam imperāta Hammōnis facere[4] cōnstituit.

[1] **iussus est**, from **iubeō**. [2] **trādere**, translate with **iussus est**. [3] **servāre**, translate with **volēbat** (394). [4] **facere**, translate with **cōnstituit** (394).

AN ETRUSCAN CHARIOT

LESSON LIV

THE PERFECT AND THE PLUPERFECT SUBJUNCTIVE
INDIRECT QUESTIONS

371. The Perfect and the Pluperfect Subjunctive. The perfect and the pluperfect subjunctive active are formed on the perfect stem (671):

amāv	-erim, -erīs, -erit,	-erīmus, -erītis, -erint
amāv	-issem, -issēs, -isset,	-issēmus, -issētis, -issent

The perfect and the pluperfect subjunctive passive belong to the participial system (671).

a. Learn these tenses of the model verbs and of **sum** (658-663). Inflect the entire subjunctive of **agō**, **pōnō**, **dō**, and **videō**.

372. Indirect Questions. An indirect question is a subordinate clause which contains the substance of a direct question: as,

1. **Ubi sunt?** *where are they?*
2. **Audit ubi sint,** *he hears where they are.*

a. Observe that the dependent clause in 2 begins with an interrogative word (**ubi**) and contains the substance of the direct question in 1. Observe that the subjunctive mood is used, and that the clause is substantive in nature. Every subordinate clause introduced by an interrogative word is an indirect question.

b. An indirect question, with its verb in the subjunctive, may be used as the subject or the object of another verb. Indirect questions usually follow the general rule for the sequence of tenses: as,

1. **Audit,** *he hears*
2. **Audiet,** *he will hear*
3. **Audīverit,** *he will have heard*

   ubi sint, *where they are*
   ubi fuerint, *where they were* or *where they have been*

1. **Audiēbat,** *he was hearing*
2. **Audīvit,** *he heard*
3. **Audīverat,** *he had heard*

ubi essent, *where they were*
ubi fuissent, *where they had been*

373. Rule for Indirect Questions. *The verb of an indirect question is in the subjunctive. If the verb of the independent clause is in a primary tense, the verb of the indirect question is put in the present subjunctive for an incomplete action, but in the perfect for a completed action. If the verb of the independent clause is in a secondary tense, the verb of the indirect question is put in the imperfect subjunctive for an incomplete action, but in the pluperfect for a completed action.*

374. VOCABULARY

num, *adv.,* whether
quot, *adj.,* how many (*quotient*)
unde, *adv.,* whence

rogō, rogāre, rogāvī, rogātus, ask (*arrogant*)
sciō, scīre, scīvī, scītus, know (*science*)

EXERCISES

375. 1. Rogat quid agant, quid ēgerint. 2. Sciēbat quid agerent, quid ēgissent. 3. Tibi dīcam cūr labōrent, cūr labōrāverint. 4. Audīverant unde mīlitēs venīrent, unde vēnissent. 5. Rogāvērunt cūr laudārētur, cūr laudātī essent. 6. Scit cūr maneant, cūr mānserint. 7. Nōbīs dīxit quid illī puerī fēcissent. 8. Rogāvī num saepe in Italiā fuisset. 9. Scīsne quot annōs Rōmānī Britanniam tenuerint?

376. 1. I shall tell you where they were and what they did. 2. These come to see, those to be seen. 3. They are so tired that they are not working to-day. 4. He asked me why I had come. 5. I had heard where he had been. 6. The general asked whether they had all come. 7. Do you know how many soldiers are coming?

LESSON LV

NUMERAL ADJECTIVES · THE OBJECTIVE GENITIVE

377. Numeral Adjectives. For the definition of numeral adjectives see III, *c*. A list of Latin cardinal and ordinal numerals is given in 651.

378. The Declension of Numeral Adjectives. The cardinals **ūnus**, *one*, **duo**, *two*, **trēs**, *three*, are declined; so, too, are the words for the *hundreds*, as, **ducentī**, *two hundred*, **trecentī**, *three hundred*, and (in the plural) **mīlle**, *thousand*. The other cardinals are not declined. The ordinals are declined as adjectives of the first and second declensions.

a. Learn the declension of **ūnus**, **duo**, **trēs**, and **mīlle** (646).

379. The Use of *Mīlle*. The singular of **mīlle** is indeclinable, and is used either as an adjective or as a neuter noun: **mīlle** (adj.) **hominēs**, *a thousand men*, or **mīlle** (noun) **hominum**. The plural is used only as a noun. When used as a noun it takes the partitive genitive: **mīlle hominum**, *a thousand (of) men*; **quattuor mīlia hominum**, *four thousand(s of) men*.

380. The Objective Genitive.

Spēs praedae hominēs incitat, *hope of booty impels the men.*

a. Observe that the genitive **praedae** expresses the thing hoped for, the object of the hope. This usage of the genitive case is called the *Objective Genitive*. The difference between the possessive and the objective genitive is illustrated by **timor canis**, *fear of the dog*, which may mean the dog's fear (possessive) or fear felt for the dog (objective).

381. *Rule for the Objective Genitive. Some nouns of action and feeling may have with them a genitive to express the object of the action or feeling implied in the nouns.*

NUMERAL ADJECTIVES

382. **VOCABULARY**

dexter, dextra, dextrum, right (*dexterous*)
duo, duae, duo, *adj.*, two (*dual*)
memoria, -ae, *f.*, memory (*memorable*)
mille, *adj. or noun*, thousand (*million*)
mille passuum, mile (a thousand of paces)
octō, *adj., indecl.*, eight (*October*)

passus, -ūs, *m.*, pace (*pace*)
quārtus, -a, -um, *adj.*, fourth (*quarto*)
quattuor, *adj., indecl.*, four
sinister, sinistra, sinistrum, left (*sinister*)
tertius, -a, -um, *adj.*, third (*tertiary*)
timor, timōris, *m.*, fear (*timorous*)
trēs, tria, *adj.*, three (*trio*)
ūnus, -a, -um, *adj.*, one (*unify*)

EXERCISES

383. 1. In itinere duo flūmina reperientur decem pedēs alta. 2. Memoria hārum rērum exercitum incitāverat. 3. Tria mīlia passuum iter fēcerant et prīma aciēs instruēbātur. 4. Caesar imperāvit ut in dextrō cornū tertia, in sinistrō quārta legiō conlocārētur. 5. Trium frātrum Mārcus erat fortissimus. 6. Propter studium victōriae haec ūna legiō Gallōs sustinuit. 7. Pīlum Rōmānum fuit sex pedēs longum. 8. Posterō diē octō mīlia passuum ex illō locō discessērunt. 9. Quattuor explōrātōrēs, quī praemissī erant, propter timōrem hostium fūgērunt.

384. 1. Hope of a reward impelled the children of Marcus. 2. On that hill were drawn up ten thousand foot soldiers and two thousand horsemen. 3. The baggage of the army had been left a mile from the shore. 4. The general will station the second legion in front of the camp. 5. At the arrival of two legions the enemy departed from the left flank. 6. Fear of Cæsar and of the Romans will hinder one clan. 7. One of the men was unfriendly to me.

LESSON LVI

ADJECTIVES HAVING THE GENITIVE IN -ĪUS

385. Adjectives having the Genitive in -īus. The adjectives of the following vocabulary end in -īus in the genitive singular and in -ī in the dative singular of all genders (except that the genitive of **alter** ends in -īus).

386. VOCABULARY

alius, alia, aliud, other, another (*alias*)
alter, altera, alterum, the other (of two) (*alternate*)
neuter, neutra, neutrum, neither (of two) (*neutrality*)
nūllus, -a, -um, no, no one, none (*nullify*)
sōlus, -a, -um, alone, sole, only (*solitude*)
tōtus, -a, -um, whole, all (*total*)
ūllus, -a, -um, any (at all)
ūnus, -a, -um, one (*unite*)
uter, utra, utrum, which (of two)
uterque, utraque, utrumque, each (of two), both

a. Learn the declension of **alius** (646). Decline the other words.

b. These adjectives are usually emphatic, and so stand before their nouns. They are often used as pronouns.

387. The Idiomatic Uses of *Alius* and of *Alter*. Alius and alter, when repeated in the same sentence, have the following meanings:

alter . . . alter, *one . . . the other* (of two only)
alius . . . alius, *one . . . another* (of any number)
aliī . . . aliī, *some . . . others*

1. Alterum oppidum in Italiā, alterum in Galliā est, *one town is in Italy, the other in Gaul* (only two towns are thought of).
2. Aliud oppidum magnum, aliud parvum est, *one town is large, another small* (here the thought is not limited to two towns).
3. Aliī gladiīs, aliī pīlīs pugnant, *some are fighting with swords, others with javelins.*

ADJECTIVES HAVING THE GENITIVE IN -ĪUS

EXERCISES

388. 1. In alterō flūminis lītore urbs, in alterō fuit mōns. 2. Duōrum hominum alter imperātor, alter tribūnus erat. 3. Tertiae legiōnis sōlīus virtūte tōtus exercitus dēfendēbātur. 4. Altera legiō in dextrō, altera in sinistrō cornū ā Caesare conlocāta est. 5. Neutrī obsidī cibum dabō. 6. Uter puer est tuus fīlius? 7. Eā aestāte erant in marī nūllae nāvēs. 8. Cūr utrumque incitās?

389. 1. Cæsar had praised the valor of the whole legion. 2. Which of the two young men showed the greater courage? 3. Cæsar will march without any delay with the second legion alone. 4. Some were pitching camp, others were drawing up a line of battle. 5. In no place did we find very many trees.

390.   **VOCABULARY**

celeritās, celeritātis, *f.*, speed (*celerity*)
dolor, dolōris, *m.*, grief, pain (*dolorous*)
fremitus, -ūs, *m.*, noise
lacrima, -ae, *f.*, tear (*lachrymose*)
nec, neque, *conj.*, and not, nor
simul, *adv.*, at the same time (*simultaneous*)

MONSTRUM APPROPINQUAT (CONTINUED FROM 370)

391. Tum rēx diem dīxit et omnia parāvit. Ubi is diēs vēnit, Andromeda ad lītus ducta est, et in cōnspectū omnium ad rūpem adligāta est. Omnēs propter fātum eius dolēbant, nec lacrimās tenēbant. Subitō autem, dum mōnstrum exspectant, Perseus ad lītus pervenit; et, ubi lacrimās vīdit, causam dolōris quaerit. Illī rem tōtam expōnunt et puellam dēmōnstrant. Dum haec geruntur, fremitus terribilis audītur; simul mōnstrum saevissimum procul vidētur. Eius cōnspectus timōrem maximum praebuit. Magnā celeritāte ad lītus mōnstrum properāvit, iamque ad locum appropinquābat ubi puella stābat.

LESSON LVII

THE INFINITIVE AS SUBJECT AND AS COMPLEMENT

392. The Infinitive. The infinitives of **amō** are as follows:

	ACTIVE	PASSIVE
Pres.	amāre, *to love*	amārī, *to be loved*
Perf.	amāvisse, *to have loved*	amātus esse, *to have been loved*
Fut.	amātūrus esse, *to be about to love, to be going to love*	(amātum īrī, *to be about to be loved*)

a. Observe that the present infinitive passive is formed from the active by changing final -e to -ī. But in the third conjugation final -ere is changed to -ī.

b. The perfect infinitive active is formed by adding **-isse** to the perfect stem.

c. The perfect infinitive passive is formed by using the perfect participle with **esse**, the present infinitive of **sum**.

d. The future infinitive active is formed by using the future active participle, **amātūrus**, with **esse**. The future active participle is made by changing final -tus or -sus of the perfect passive participle to -tūrus or -sūrus. Form the future active participles of **pōnō**, **īnstruō**, **videō**, **mittō**, and **gerō**.

e. Learn the infinitives and meanings of the model verbs and of **sum** (658–663). The future infinitive passive may be omitted. It is rare.

393. The Infinitive as Subject. Since the infinitive is a noun, it may be used as the subject or the object of a verb. Since it is a *verbal* noun, it may have a subject or an object of its own, and be modified by adverbs, adverb phrases, or adverb clauses.

1. **Laudārī est grātum**, *to be praised is pleasing.*
2. **Iter per fīnēs hostium facere erit difficile**, *to march through the territory of the enemy will be difficult.*

INFINITIVE AS SUBJECT AND AS COMPLEMENT

a. Observe that **laudārī** is the subject of **est**, and **iter per fīnēs hostium facere** of **erit**, while **iter** is the object of **facere**. Of what gender are **grātum** and **difficile**? What, then, is the gender of the infinitive?

394. The Complementary Infinitive.

1. **Vincere potest,** *he is able to conquer.*
2. **Bonī esse dēbēmus,** *we ought to be good.*

a. Observe that **vincere** and **esse** complete the meaning of **potest** and **dēbēmus**. An infinitive so used is called a *Complementary Infinitive*, and it is common in Latin, as in English, with verbs meaning *be able, decide, ought, wish, begin,* etc. You have already met this usage of the infinitive in several of the selections for reading.

b. The predicate adjective used with a complementary infinitive agrees in gender, number, and case with the subject of the main verb.

395.   **VOCABULARY**

coepī, coepisse (*lacks the present system*), began
dēbeō, dēbēre, dēbuī, dēbitus, ought, be obliged to (*debit*)
decimus, -a, -um, tenth (*decimate*)
potest, is able, can
possunt, are able, can (*possible*)

EXERCISES

396. 1. Venīre, dare, discēdere potest. 2. Impedīrī, pōnī, conlocārī possunt. 3. Praemia recipere saepe est grātum. 4. Caesar reliquōs agrōs et oppida illīus cīvitātis vāstāre coepit. 5. Tua verba audīre est difficillimum. 6. Germānī Rōmānōs commeātibus interclūdere nōn possunt. 7. Statim multitūdō pācem petere coepit. 8. Sē dēfendere dēbent. 9. Quis tōtīus exercitūs tam fortis fuit ut impetum hostium sustinēret? 10. Hieme diēs quīnque hōrīs breviōrēs quam aestāte sunt.

397. 1. It will be easy to fortify the camp with a high wall. 2. You ought to offer help. 3. He is not able to arouse the soldiers of the tenth legion. 4. To carry on a war is not often best. 5. We ought to be brave and good. 6. Some have begun to fight, others to flee.

LESSON LVIII

THE INFINITIVE AS OBJECT · THE ACCUSATIVE AS SUBJECT OF THE INFINITIVE · INDIRECT STATEMENTS

398. The Infinitive as Object.

Mē venīre iussit, *he ordered me to come.*

a. Observe that in the English sentence the object of *ordered* is *me to come*; and that *me* is in the objective case and subject of the infinitive *to come*. The Latin sentence is like the English; **mē** is in the accusative case. Verbs meaning *order* and *wish* are the commonest verbs having an infinitive as their object; but **imperō**, *order*, takes a substantive clause of purpose (356). The objective infinitive is also used in indirect statements (400-402).

399. *Rule for the Accusative as Subject of the Infinitive.* *The subject of the infinitive is in the accusative.*

400. Indirect Statements. A direct statement gives the exact words used by a speaker or writer: as, *He says* (or *said*), "*Soldiers are coming.*" In an indirect statement the words of a speaker or writer are made to depend on a verb of *saying*, *thinking*, etc., and in English may or may not be the same as they were in the original statement or thought: as, *He says that soldiers are coming, he said that soldiers were coming.* Observe the same sentences in Latin:

1. **Mīlitēs veniunt,** *soldiers are coming.*
2. **Dīcit mīlitēs venīre,** *he says that soldiers are coming.*
3. **Dīxit mīlitēs venīre,** *he said that soldiers were coming.*

a. Observe that in turning a direct statement into an indirect statement in Latin the nominative is changed to the accusative (399) and the indicative to the infinitive.

INFINITIVE AS OBJECT · INDIRECT STATEMENTS

401. Rule for Indirect Statements. *Indirect statements, with verb in the infinitive and subject in the accusative, are found in dependence on verbs of* saying, thinking, knowing, perceiving, *and the like.*

402. The Use of the Tenses of the Infinitive in Indirect Statements. The *present* infinitive is used when the action of the indirect statement is going on at the *same* time as the action indicated by the verb of *saying, thinking,* etc.: as,

1. Dīcit mīlitēs venīre, *he says that soldiers are coming.*
2. Dīxit mīlitēs venīre, *he said that soldiers were coming.*
3. Dīcet mīlitēs venīre, *he will say that soldiers are coming.*

The *perfect* infinitive is used when the action of the indirect statement occurred *before* that of the verb of *saying, thinking,* etc.: as,

1. Dīcit mīlitēs vēnisse, *he says that soldiers came* (or *have come*).
2. Dīxit mīlitēs vēnisse, *he said that soldiers came* (or *had come*).
3. Dīcet mīlitēs vēnisse, *he will say that soldiers came* (or *have come*).

The *future* infinitive is used when the action of the indirect statement occurs *after* that of the verb of *saying, thinking,* etc.: as,

1. Dīcit mīlitēs ventūrōs esse, *he says that soldiers will come.*
2. Dīxit mīlitēs ventūrōs esse, *he said that soldiers would come.*
3. Dīcet mīlitēs ventūrōs esse, *he will say that soldiers will come.*

403.   **VOCABULARY**

cognōscō, cognōscere, cognōvī, cognitus, learn, know, understand (*recognize*)

cupiō, cupere, cupīvī (cupiī), cupītus, desire, wish (*cupidity*)

iubeō, iubēre, iussī, iussus, bid, order, command (*jussive*)

respondeō, respondēre, respondī, respōnsus, answer, reply (*respond*)

EXERCISES

404. 1. Caesar per duōs explōrātōrēs cognōvit hostēs sex mīlia passuum iter fēcisse. 2. Sociī respondent sē sine morā auxilium ad Caesarem missūrōs esse. 3. Imperātor dīxit sē suīs praemia ampla datūrum esse. 4. Omnēs cupiunt esse līberī. 5. Omnēs cupiunt Italiam esse līberam. 6. Omnēs vident oppidum fortiter dēfendī. 7. Statim tertiam aciem īnstruī Caesar iussit. 8. Sciēbat Gallōs venīre ut impetum facerent.

405. 1. That lieutenant will order his men to build towers. 2. I know that two legions have been sent ahead. 3. From the captives he learned that the enemy lacked food. 4. He ordered (**iubeō**) them to spend the winter in that state. 5. The traders replied that there was no grain in the territory of the Germans.

A ROMAN AND HIS WIFE

THE ROMAN FORUM TO-DAY

LESSON LIX

READING LESSON

CAESAR IN CONCILIO DICIT

406. Post hoc proelium Caesar mīlitibus in conciliō ita dīxit: Eōs fortiter pugnāvisse; itaque hostīs omnibus in partibus victōs esse et in montīs et palūdēs fugere; praedam eīs sē datūrum esse; sē scīre eōs longō bellō esse dēfessōs et statim eōs in Italiam missūrum esse; sē velle [1] in Galliā manēre per hiemem, sed proximā aestāte suōs in Germānōs ductūrum esse; multōs captīvōs Rōmam missōs esse, et populum Rōmānum victōriā eōrum dēlectārī.

407.   **VOCABULARY**

paene, *adv.,* nearly, almost (*peninsula*)

regiō, regiōnis, *f.,* place (*region*)

undique, *adv.,* from all sides, everywhere

dēpōnō, dēpōnere, dēposuī, dēpositus, put down, lay aside (*deposit*)

ostendō, ostendere, ostendī, ostentus, show, display (*ostensible*)

reddō, reddere, reddidī, redditus, give back, return (*render*)

sentiō, sentīre, sēnsī, sēnsus, feel, know, perceive (*sentiment*)

PERSEUS CEPHEO ANDROMEDAM REDDIT
(CONTINUED FROM 391)

408. At Perseus ubi haec vīdit, gladium suum ēdūxit, et postquam tālāria induit, per āera volāvit. Tum dēsuper in mōnstrum impetum subitō fēcit, et gladiō suō collum eius graviter vulnerāvit. Mōnstrum ubi sēnsit vulnus, fremitum horribilem ēdidit et sine morā tōtum corpus in aquam mersit. Perseus dum circum lītus volat, reditum eius exspectābat. Mare

[1] **velle,** infin. of **volō,** *wish.*

autem interim undique sanguine inficitur. Post breve tempus bēlua rūrsus caput ostendit; mox tamen ā Perseō ictū graviōre vulnerāta est. Tum iterum sē in undās mersit, neque posteā vīsa est.

Perseus postquam ad lītus dēscendit, prīmum tālāria exuit; tum ad rūpem vēnit ubi Andromeda vīncta erat. Ea autem omnem spem salūtis dēposuerat, et ubi Perseus pervēnit, terrōre paene exanimāta erat. Ille vincula statim solvit, et puellam patrī reddidit. Cēpheus ob hanc rem maximō gaudiō adfectus est. Itaque Andromedam Perseō in mātrimōnium dedit. Paucōs annōs Perseus cum uxōre in eā regiōne habitābat, et in magnō honōre erat apud omnīs Aethiopēs.

IMPERATOR ET CAPTIVI

LESSON LX

THE DEMONSTRATIVES *IDEM, IPSE, ISTE* · THE IRREGULAR VERB *POSSUM*

409. The Demonstratives *Īdem, Ipse,* and *Iste*. Review the declension of **is, hic,** and **ille** (654), and learn the declension of **īdem,** *same,* **ipse,** *-self,* and **iste,** *this of yours, that of yours* (654).

a. Observe that **īdem** is declined like **is** with **-dem** added, except that in the accusative singular and the genitive plural **m** is changed to **n**, and in the nominative and accusative singular **is** is changed to **ī, id** to **i.**

b. Decline together **īdem diēs, rēs ipsa,** and **istud cōnsilium.**

410. The Distinction between *Īdem, Ipse,* and *Iste*.

a. **Īdem** and **iste** may be used both as demonstrative adjectives and as demonstrative pronouns.

b. **Iste** is used of that which has some relation to the second person, and is translated *this of yours, that of yours, your*: as, **istam dīligentiam laudō,** *I praise that diligence of yours (your diligence).*

c. **Ipse** means *-self (himself, herself, itself, themselves).* It is an intensive word, used to emphasize a noun or pronoun, expressed or understood, with which it agrees as an adjective: as, **amīcus ipse ad mē vēnit,** *my friend himself came to me.* It must be distinguished from **sē,** *-self,* which is reflexive, not emphatic (266). Sometimes **ipse** may be translated *even* or *very*: as, **in flūmine ipsō pugnant,** *they are fighting in the very river.*

411. The Irregular Verb *Possum*. The irregular verb **possum,** *I can,* is a compound of **potis,** *able,* and **sum,** *I am*; **pot-sum** changed to **possum.** Wherever, in the inflection of this verb, **t** comes before **s**, it is changed to **s**, and wherever it comes before **f**, **f** is dropped. Learn the principal parts and the complete inflection (664).

IDEM, IPSE, ISTE

412. VOCABULARY

difficultās, difficultātis, *f.*, difficulty
īdem, eadem, idem, same (*identity*)
īdem ... quī, same ... as
ipse, ipsa, ipsum, *intensive*, -self
iste, ista, istud, this of yours, that of yours
nihil, *n., indecl.*, nothing (*annihilate*)
ōrātiō, ōrātiōnis, *f.*, speech, plea (*oration*)

rūrsus, *adv.*, again
nūntiō, nūntiāre, nūntiāvī, nūntiātus, report, announce (*annunciator*)
possum, posse, potuī, ———, be able, can (*potent*)
putō, putāre, putāvī, putātus, think, believe, reckon (*compute*)
spērō, spērāre, spērāvī, spērātus, hope (*prosperous*)

EXERCISES

413. 1. Potest, poterat, poterit. 2. Potuimus, potuerant, poterant. 3. Scīsne cūr ista verba audīrī nōn possint? 4. Eaedem erant difficultātēs bellī quās vōbīs nūntiāre potuī. 5. Labiēnus ipse scīvit causās bellī plūrimās esse. 6. Putō mē hodiē nihil ēmptūrum esse. 7. Nōn iam postulant ut populus Rōmānus nāvēs praebeat. 8. Centuriō, quī cum octō explōrātōribus missus erat ut viam cognōsceret, nūntiāvit sē viam cognōscere nōn potuisse. 9. Omnēs spērābant Caesarem eā aestāte Gallōs victūrum esse. 10. Virī ipsī dīcunt tēla iacī nōn posse.

414. 1. They have been able, he will be able, I could. 2. He had been able, they will have been able, we could. 3. The very children no longer desired peace. 4. They say that our allies are in the same danger to-day. 5. I think that I can stay two days with that friend of yours. 6. The traders reported that many bands of horsemen had been sent into the mountains. 7. I think that you can fight. 8. You thought that I could not come.

EIGHTH REVIEW LESSON
LESSONS LIII-LX

415. Give the English meanings of the following words:

alius	difficultās	nec	putō	sōlus
alter	dolor	neque	quārtus	spērō
cēdō	duo	neuter	quattuor	tertius
celeritās	ēdūcō	nihil	quot	timor
coepī	fremitus	nūllus	reddō	tōtus
cognōscō	īdem	num	regiō	trādō
conlocō	ipse	nūntiō	respondeō	trēs
cōnstituō	iste	octō	rogō	ūllus
cōnsulō	iubeō	ōrātiō	rūrsus	unde
cupiō	iuvō	ostendō	sciō	undique
dēbeō	lacrima	paene	sentiō	ūnus
decimus	memoria	passus	simul	uter
dēpōnō	mīlle	possum	sinister	uterque
dexter	mīlle passuum			

416. Give the Latin meanings of the following words:

two	answer, reply	memory	give way, retire
one	nearly, almost	the other	think, believe, reckon
left	and not, nor	know	put down, lay aside
tear	give back, return	began	from all sides, everywhere
speed	other, another	three	no, no one, none
eight	how many	whence	lead out, lead forth
again	be able, can	help, aid	at the same time
four	show, display	hope	bid, order, command
mile	which (of two)	difficulty	this of yours, that of yours
ask	speech, plea	place	establish, determine
third	place, station	noise	alone, sole, only
neither	desire, wish	thousand	learn, know, understand
pace	report, announce	right	ought, be obliged to
nothing	whole, all	-self	give over, surrender

same	each, both	whether	feel, know, perceive
fourth	any (at all)	fear	plan, deliberate, consult
tenth	grief, pain		

417. Decline each noun, adjective, and pronoun in 415. Conjugate each verb in all tenses of the subjunctive mood. Make synopses. Give the infinitives of each verb.

418. Following the suggestions of 634, give English words derived from the Latin words in 415. Define these derivatives, and illustrate each by an English sentence.

419. Give the rule for the following constructions, and illustrate each by a sentence in Latin:

1. Indirect questions
2. Objective genitive
3. Infinitive as subject
4. Infinitive as complement
5. Infinitive as object
6. Indirect statements
7. Accusative as subject of the infinitive

INTERIOR OF A ROMAN HOUSE

LESSON LXI

THE INDEFINITE PRONOUNS

420. The Indefinite Pronouns. The indefinite pronouns (II, *g*) are compounds of **quis** and of **quī**. The following indefinite pronouns will be used in this book:

aliquis, aliqua, aliquid, aliquod, *some, some one, any, any one*
quīdam, quaedam, quiddam, quoddam, *a certain one, a certain*
quisquam, ——, quidquam (no plural), *any one (at all)*
quisque, quaeque, quidque, quodque, *each, each one, every, every one*

a. Learn the meanings and the declension of these pronouns (657).

b. The meanings of the neuters (*something, anything*, etc.) are easily inferred.

c. Observe how **aliqua**, which is both the feminine nominative singular and the neuter nominative and accusative plural of **aliquis**, differs from the corresponding forms of **quis**.

d. Observe that **quīdam** (**quī + dam**) is declined like **quī**, except that in the accusative singular and genitive plural **m** is changed to **n**; also that the neuter has **quiddam** and **quoddam** in the nominative and accusative singular.

e. In the neuter of all indefinites the **quid** forms are used as pronouns, and the **quod** forms as adjectives.

EXERCISES

421. 1. Duo nova flūmina ā quibusdam virīs audācibus reperta sunt. 2. Nōn iam quemquam ante domum vidēre possum. 3. Ut cīvēs timōre līberāret, arma statim trādī iussit. 4. Quīdam captīvus idem rūrsus nūntiāvit. 5. Quisque aliquid respondēre potuerit. 6. Aliquae fēminae nōn sōlum perturbātae erant, sed etiam fūgerant. 7. Lēgātus quemque ex fīnibus frūmentum portāre iubēbit. 8. Quaedam legiō spē victōriae Delphōs properābat. 9. Īnsulae similis est ista terra.

422. 1. Each says that the Gauls are approaching. 2. He does not demand anything at all. 3. That girl has something in her right hand. 4. A part of each summer we live among the mountains and hills. 5. To-day a story was told to us by somebody. 6. At the same time certain (men) came to Cæsar to demand help. 7. I know what each is able to do.

THE NATIONS OF GAUL

423. Gallia est omnis dīvīsa (*divided*) in partīs trēs, quārum ūnam incolunt Belgae, aliam Aquītānī, tertiam eī quī Gallī appellantur. Hōrum omnium fortissimī sunt Belgae, quod prōvinciae Rōmānae propinquī nōn sunt neque mercātōrēs ad eōs saepe perveniunt; proximīque sunt Germānīs quī trāns Rhēnum incolunt, quibuscum bellum gerunt. Quā dē causā (*for this reason*, 186) Helvētiī quoque fortiōrēs quam reliquī Gallī sunt. Cotīdiānīs ferē proeliīs cum Germānīs contendunt, cum (*when*) aut (*either*) suīs fīnibus eōs prohibent aut (*or*) ipsī in eōrum fīnibus bellum gerunt. Ea pars quam Gallī obtinent initium capit ā flūmine Rhodanō; continētur Garumnā (*Garonne*) flūmine, ōceanō, fīnibus Belgārum.

TABLE, VASE, AND LAMP STANDS

LESSON LXII

THE DATIVE WITH COMPOUNDS · THE DATIVES OF PURPOSE AND REFERENCE

424. The Dative with Compounds.

1. Quis equitibus praefuit? *who commanded the horsemen?*
2. Huic legiōnī lēgātum praefēcit, *he put a lieutenant in charge of this legion.*

a. Observe that **praefuit**, which is a compound of **sum**, is intransitive. It does not admit a direct object, but does admit the indirect object **equitibus**. There are a number of Latin verbs which in their simple form take neither a direct nor an indirect object; when these verbs are compounded with a preposition, they have a meaning which may take an indirect object. Some compound verbs take both a direct and an indirect object: as, **praefēcit** in sentence 2.

425. Rule for the Dative with Compounds. *Some verbs compounded with* **ad, ante, con, dē, in, inter, ob, post, prae, prō, sub,** *and* **super,** *take a dative of the indirect object. Transitive compounds may take both an accusative and a dative.*

426. The Datives of Purpose and Reference.

1. Mīlitēs ibi erant praesidiō, *soldiers were there as (for) a defense.*
2. Mīlitēs auxiliō eīs mittuntur, *soldiers are sent as (for) a help to them.*

a. Observe that the datives **praesidiō** and **auxiliō** are used to express the purpose for which something serves. This usage is called the *Dative of Purpose*. Often the dative of purpose is accompanied by another dative, called the *Dative of Reference*, denoting the person or thing served: as, **eīs** in sentence 2. This combination is known as the *Double Dative*.

427. Rule for the Dative of Purpose. *The dative is used to denote the purpose for which a thing serves.*

THE DATIVE WITH COMPOUNDS

428. Rule for the Dative of Reference. *The dative is used to denote the person (or, rarely, the thing) affected by the action or situation expressed by the verb.*

429. VOCABULARY

mūnītiō, mūnītiōnis, *f.*, fortification, defense (*ammunition*)

praesidium, praesi'dī, *n.*, defense, protection, guard

subsidium, subsi'dī, *n.*, help, aid

ūsus, -ūs, *m.*, use, benefit, advantage (*useful*)

dēsum, deesse, dēfuī, dēfutūrus, be lacking, be wanting, fail

occurrō, occurrere, occurrī, occursūrus, run toward, meet (*occur*)

praeficiō, praeficere, praefēcī, praefectus, place in command of (*prefect*)

praestō, praestāre, praestitī, praestitus, surpass, be superior to

praesum, praeesse, praefuī, praefutūrus, be at the head of, command

supersum, superesse, superfuī, superfutūrus, be left over, survive

EXERCISES

430. 1. Ūnum oppidum sociōrum ab hostibus diū oppugnātum erat, et mūnītiōnēs cotīdiē vāstābantur. 2. Quod cibus et arma cīvibus deesse coepērunt, sociī rogāvērunt ut Caesar cōpiās auxiliō mitteret. 3. Itaque Caesar Labiēnum ūnī legiōnī praefēcit et eum subsidiō cīvibus mīsit. 4. In itinere Labiēnus hostibus occurrit, quī omnibus ex partibus vēnerant ut oppidum caperent. 5. Pīla impedīmentō nostrīs, sed magnō ūsuī gladiī erant. 6. Nostrī hostibus praestitērunt et · eōs superāvērunt. 7. Labiēnus dīxit sē cīvibus praesidiō futūrum esse. 8. Scīsne quis eī oppidō praefuerit?

431. 1. Courage did not often fail Cæsar. 2. He commanded brave men. 3. He was a protection to his country. 4. He did not survive his last (**proximus**) wars many years. 5. He was superior to the chiefs of the Gauls and the Germans. 6. He placed lieutenants in charge over the nations which had been conquered. 7. The sea is many feet deeper than this lake.

LESSON LXIII

THE DATIVE WITH SPECIAL INTRANSITIVE VERBS · THE IRREGULAR VERBS *VOLO, NOLO, MALO*

432. The Dative with Special Intransitive Verbs.

1. Legiōnī imperat, *he commands a legion.*
2. Amīcō meō persuādet, *he persuades my friend.*

a. Observe that **legiōnī** and **amīcō** are in the dative case, while the English equivalents are in the objective case. It is obvious, therefore, that the Latin verbs **imperō** and **persuādeō** are intransitive, and that they admit an indirect object.

433. *Rule for the Dative with Special Intransitive Verbs. Most verbs meaning* believe, favor, help, please, trust, *and their opposites, also* command, obey, pardon, persuade, resist, serve, spare, *and the like, take a dative of the indirect object.*

a. Such verbs used in this book are **crēdō**, *believe*; **faveō**, *favor*; **imperō**, *command*; **noceō**, *harm*; **persuādeō**, *persuade*; **placeō**, *please*; **resistō**, *resist*; and **studeō**, *desire, be eager for.*

b. Observe that **imperō** has an indirect object, while **iubeō** takes a direct object.

434. The Irregular Verbs *Volō, Nōlō,* and *Mālō*. Learn the principal parts and the conjugation of **volō**, *wish*, **nōlō** (nē + volō), *be unwilling*, and **mālō** (magis volō), *be more willing, prefer*, in the indicative, subjunctive, and infinitive (665).

435. VOCABULARY

mulier, mulieris, *f.*, woman
neque . . . neque, neither . . . nor
occāsus, -ūs, *m.*, setting (*occasion*)
sōl, sōlis, *m.*, sun (*solstice*)

crēdō, crēdere, crēdidī, crēditus, believe, trust (*creditor*)
faveō, favēre, fāvī, fautūrus, favor (*favor*)

THE DATIVE WITH SPECIAL VERBS

mālō, mālle, māluī, ———, be more willing, prefer
noceō, nocēre, nocuī, nocitūrus, harm, injure (*obnoxious*)
nōlō, nōlle, nōluī, ———, be unwilling
persuādeō, persuādēre, persuāsī, persuāsus, persuade (*persuasive*)

placeō, placēre, placuī, placitūrus, please, be pleasing to (*placidly*)
resistō, resistere, restitī, ———, resist, oppose (*resistance*)
studeō, studēre, studuī, ———, be eager for, desire (*student*)
volō, velle, voluī, ———, be willing, wish (*volition*)

EXERCISES

436. 1. Vultis, nōlumus, māvīs. 2. Mercātōribus nōn crēdidit. 3. Nōlle, māluisse. 4. Vōbīs persuādēre volunt. 5. Vult mihi favēre. 6. Neque nōlunt tibi nocēre. 7. Tibi auxiliō esse mālumus. 8. Cūr nōn vīs mātrī tuae esse praesidiō? 9. Putāmus eum voluisse equitātuī praeesse. 10. Sōlis occāsū mīlitēs castra hostium capient. 11. Paucae enim ex hīs nātiōnibus bellō student. 12. Mīlitibus imperāvit ut fortiter Gallīs resisterent. 13. Neque mulierēs neque līberī timēbant.

437. 1. They were wishing, I shall be unwilling, she will prefer. 2. They were not willing to help our men. 3. They were not able to please your friends. 4. And they did not persuade the general. 5. He will command them not to harm the women. 6. Neither the Gauls nor the Germans desired war at that time.

WALL DECORATION OF A POMPEIAN HOUSE

LESSON LXIV

READING LESSON

BELLING THE CAT

438. Quīdam mūrēs aliquandō concilium habēbant, nam fēlem maximē timēbant. Cōnsilia quae prōposita sunt omnibus nōn placēbant. Tandem ūnus ex mūribus ita dīxit: "Tintinnābulum caudae fēlis adnectere dēbēmus. Sīc enim sonitū eius monēbimur et fugere poterimus. Quis vestrum hoc facere vult?" Sed nūllī ex sociīs persuādēre potuit ut tintinnābulum fēlī adnecteret, et ipse nōluit. Ea fābula docet plūrimōs in suādendō[1] esse audācēs sed in ipsō perīculō timidōs.

NASICA AND ENNIUS

439. Nāsīca aliquandō ad poētam[2] Ennium vēnit et dē eō quaesīvit. Ancilla respondit Ennium domī[3] nōn esse. Nāsīca autem sēnsit illam dominī iussū hoc dīxisse et Ennium domī[3] esse. Paucīs post diēbus[4] Ennius ad Nāsīcam vēnit. Eī exclāmat Nāsīca sē domī nōn esse. Tum Ennius dīxit, "Quid? Ego nōn cognōscō vōcem tuam?" Hīc[5] Nāsīca: "Homō es impudēns. Ego ancillae tuae crēdidī; tū mihi ipsī nōn crēdis?"

ORGETORIX AND THE HELVETIANS

440. Apud Helvētiōs longē nōbilissimus erat Orgetorīx. Is rēgnī cupiditāte inductus est et coniūrātiōnem nōbilitātis fēcit. Tum cīvitātī persuāsit ut dē fīnibus suīs cum omnibus cōpiīs properārent. Facilius eīs persuāsit quod undique locī nātūrā

---

[1] **suādendō**, *offering advice.* [2] **ad poētam**, *to the house of the poet.* [3] **domī**, *at home.* [4] **paucīs post diēbus**, *a few days later.* [5] **hīc**, adv., *hereupon.*

Helvētiī continentur: ūnā ex parte (*on one side*) flūmine Rhēnō, lātissimō atque altissimō, quī agrum Helvētiōrum ā Germānīs dīvidit; alterā ex parte monte Iūrā altissimō, quī est inter Sēquanōs et Helvētiōs; tertiā (ex parte) lacū Lemannō et flūmine Rhodanō, quī prōvinciam nostram ab Helvētiīs dīvidit. Propter multitūdinem hominum et glōriam bellī angustōs sē fīnēs habēre putābant, quī in longitūdinem mīlia passuum CCXL (ducenta quadrāgintā), in lātitūdinem CLXXX (centum octōgintā) patēbant.

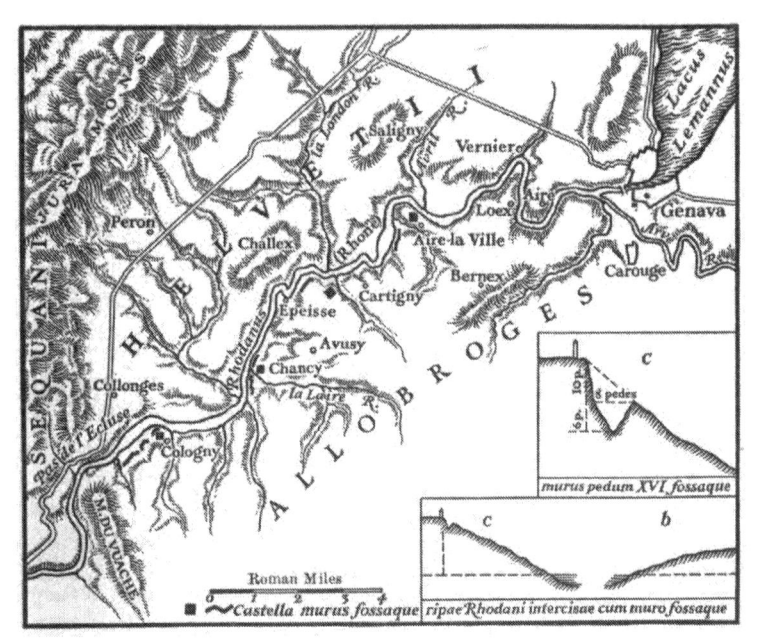

MAP OF HELVETIA

LESSON LXV

PARTICIPLES

441. Participles. Learn the participles of the model verbs (658–662), and their meanings.

a. Observe that the present active and the future passive participles are formed from the present stem by the addition of -ns and -ndus, with certain changes in quantity; and the future active and the perfect passive from the participial stem by the addition of -ūrus and -us. But observe that in verbs of the fourth conjugation and of the third conjugation ending in -iō the present active participle has -iēns and the future passive participle has -iendus. Form the participles of **gerō, videō, iaciō, vāstō,** and **mūniō**.

442. The Declension of Participles. Participles in -ns are declined like **amāns** (645). The ablative singular ending is -e; but the ending is -ī when the word is used as an adjective. The other participles are declined like **bonus** (643). Decline the participles of **gerō**.

443. The Agreement of Participles. Since participles are verbal adjectives (XXXIV), they agree with nouns or pronouns in gender, number, and case.

444. The Tenses of Participles. The present active participle is used of an action going on at the same time as the action of the main verb: as, **tē labōrantem videō,** *I see you working;* **tē labōrantem vīdī,** *I saw you working.*

The perfect passive participle is used of an action that is completed at the time of the action of the main verb: as, **mīles vulnerātus domum vēnit,** *the soldier, having been wounded, came home.*

The future active and passive participles are used of actions which are to occur after the time of the action of the main

PARTICIPLES

verb. In this book the future active participle is used only in the formation of the future active infinitive (392, *d*). The uses of the future passive participle will be explained later (471–473).

445. The Translation of Participles.

1. Tē in urbe manentem vīdī, *I saw you when you were staying in the city.*
2. Urbs diū oppugnāta nōn capta est, *the city, though besieged for a long time, was not taken.*
3. Caesar eā rē commōtus in Galliam properāvit, *Cæsar, because he was alarmed by this circumstance, hastened into Gaul.*
4. Dux victus sē recipiet, *the general, if defeated, will retreat.*
5. Dōna missa recēpit, *he received the gifts which had been sent.*
6. Caesar prīncipem captum Rōmam mīsit, *Cæsar captured a chieftain and sent him to Rome.*

a. Observe that in the first five sentences the participle is translated by clauses of *time, concession, cause,* and *condition,* and by a *relative clause.* In 6 the participle is translated by a coördinate verb. Note the words which introduce the different clauses. When you meet a participle, consider which of these six ways best brings out the thought of the sentence and translate accordingly. Do not translate a participle literally.

446.   **VOCABULARY**

hīberna, -ōrum, *n. plur.*, winter quarters (*hibernate*)
commoveō, commovēre, commōvī, commōtus, disturb, move, arouse (*commotion*)
moveō, movēre, mōvī, mōtus, move (*motion*)
redūcō, redūcere, redūxī, reductus, lead back (*reduce*)

EXERCISES

447. 1. Aliī mīlitēs fugientēs captī sunt. 2. Hīs rēbus impedītī eō diē impetum nōn fēcērunt. 3. Alter centuriō prīmā in aciē pugnāns vulnerātus est. 4. Ad nostrōs mīlitēs castra oppugnantīs auxilium missum erat. 5. Quaedam mulierēs in oppidō relictae sē dēfendere cōnstituērunt. 6. Pars hostium adventū Caesaris commōta sōlis occāsū discessit. 7. In hībernīs reductōs mīlitēs relinquēbat. 8. Multitūdō servōrum territa ex urbe fugiēbat. 9. Posterō diē castra mōvērunt.

448. 1. A certain man, while resisting, was wounded by an enemy. 2. Although wounded, they fought so bravely that they could not be captured. 3. Since he was disturbed by the difficulties of the march, he decided to lead back his legions. 4. Those horsemen who were sent ahead resisted the Gauls long and bravely. 5. If asked concerning your plans, I shall say nothing. 6. The leaders will be captured and sent to Italy.

GALLI CAPTI IN CASTRA REDUCUNTUR

LESSON LXVI

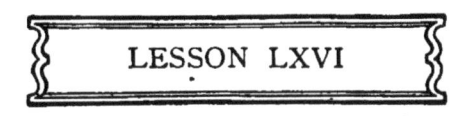

READING LESSON

DICTA ANTIQUORUM

449. 1. Lacaena filiō in proelium properantī dīxit, "Aut in scūtō aut cum scūtō."

2. Leōnidās mīlitī nūntiantī, "Hostēs nōbīs propinquī sunt," respondit, "Etiam nōs hostibus propinquī sumus."

3. Thalēs interrogātus, "Quid hominibus commūne est?" respondit, "Spēs; hanc enim etiam illī habent quī nihil aliud habent."

4. Āgis mūrōs firmōs altōsque Corinthī spectāns rogāvit, "Quārum mulierum haec urbs est?"

5. Aristotelem quīdam rogāvit, "Quid est amīcitia?" Ille respondit, "Ūnus animus in duōbus corporibus."

6. Cicerō dīxit, "Nōn potest exercitum is continēre imperātor quī sē ipse nōn continet."

450.   **VOCABULARY**

rēgnum, -ī, *n.*, kingdom (*interregnum*)
addūcō, addūcere, addūxī, adductus, lead to, influence (*adduce*)
obtineō, obtinēre, obtinuī, obtentus, possess, occupy, hold (*obtain*)
suscipiō, suscipere, suscēpī, susceptus, take up, undertake (*susceptible*)

ORGETORIX AND THE HELVETIANS (CONTINUED FROM 440)

451. Hīs rēbus adductī et auctōritāte Orgetorīgis permōtī Helvētiī cōnstituērunt carrōrum maximum numerum emere, cōpiam frūmentī parāre, pācem et amīcitiam cum proximīs cīvitātibus cōnfirmāre. Orgetorīx interim lēgātiōnem ad cīvitātēs suscēpit. In eō itinere persuāsit Casticō, Sēquanō, cuius pater rēgnum in Sēquanīs multōs annōs obtinuerat et ā senātū populī Rōmānī amīcus appellātus erat, ut rēgnum in cīvitāte suā occupāret. Cuidam aliī prīncipī persuāsit ut idem faceret. Ōrātiōne Orgetorīgis adductī hī prīncipēs inter sē obsidēs dant, et tōtam Galliam sēsē occupāre posse spērant. Helvētiī autem hoc cōnsilium nōn probāvērunt. Itaque multitūdinem hominum ex agrīs coēgērunt ut cōnsilia Orgetorīgis prohibērent. Sed eō tempore Orgetorīx subitō mortuus est (*died*).

ROMAN STYLES OF HAIRDRESSING

LESSON LXVII

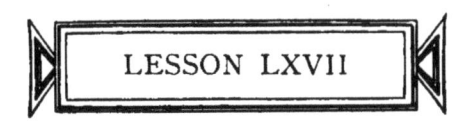

THE ABLATIVE ABSOLUTE

452. The Ablative Absolute.

1. Cōnsul, castrīs mūnītīs, Rōmam vēnit, *with the camp fortified, the consul came to Rome.*
2. Caesare dūcente, semper vincimus, *with Cæsar leading, we always conquer.*
3. Caesare duce, vincēmus, *with Cæsar as leader, we shall conquer.*

a. Observe that the ablatives in these sentences are so loosely connected with the rest of the sentence that they are grammatically independent. Because of its loose connection with the sentence this usage of the ablative is known as the *Ablative Absolute* (ab + solvō).

453. How to translate the Ablative Absolute. The ablative absolute is usually translated, not as above, but by a clause: thus,

1. *When (because, although, if) the camp had been fortified, the consul came to Rome.*
2. *When (because, although, if) Cæsar is leading, we always conquer.*
3. *When (because, although, if) Cæsar is leader, we shall conquer.*

The method of translation in any particular sentence must be determined by asking which kind of clause best expresses the thought of the sentence as a whole.

454. The Formation of the Ablative Absolute. The ablative absolute may be formed by a noun or pronoun with a participle (as in 452, 1 and 2); or by a noun or pronoun with another noun or an adjective (as in 452, 3). The present active and perfect passive participles are used in this construction. Since the verb **sum** has no present participle, a participle is not expressed when the ablative absolute is formed as it is in 452, 3 : **Caesare duce,** *Cæsar (being) leader.*

a. An ablative absolute containing a perfect passive participle expresses an action that occurred before the action expressed by the main verb of the sentence; one containing a present participle expresses an action occurring at the same time as that of the main verb.

b. The Latin perfect participle is not found in the active voice. Accordingly such a sentence as *Cæsar, having defeated the Gauls, returned to Rome* has to be recast into the form *Cæsar, the Gauls having been defeated, returned to Rome*, **Caesar, Gallīs victīs, Rōmam rediit.**

c. The noun of the ablative absolute is always a different person or thing from the subject or object of the sentence.

455. Rule for the Ablative Absolute. *The ablative of a noun or pronoun, with a participle, a noun, or an adjective in agreement, is used to express time, cause, concession, condition, or other relations.*

456.   VOCABULARY

dēditiō, dēditiōnis, *f.*, surrender   **medius, -a, -um,** middle of
ēruptiō, ēruptiōnis, *f.*, sally, sortie   (*medium*)
     (*eruption*)   **rīpa, -ae,** *f.*, bank (*riparian*)

EXERCISES

457. 1. Hostibus victīs, per mediam prōvinciam iter facere cōnstituit. 2. Caesare cōnsule, cum Gallīs longum erat bellum. 3. Oppidō quōdam expugnātō, castra in rīpīs ipsīs huius flūminis posuērunt. 4. Helvētiī omnium rērum inopiā adductī lēgātōs dē dēditiōne ad Caesarem mīsērunt. 5. Hīs rēbus repertīs, omnēs bellō studēbant. 6. Hoc oppidum, paucīs dēfendentibus, Rōmānī capere nōn potuērunt. 7. Captīvīs in dēditiōnem acceptīs, dux subsidiō castrīs trēs cohortēs relīquit. 8. Hī captīvī eīdem fortissimē pugnantēs captī erant. 9. Quis praefuit equitibus quī imperātōrī auxiliō missī sunt? 10. Urbe mūnītā, cīvēs nōn iam terrēbantur.

THE ABLATIVE ABSOLUTE

458. 1. When he had heard these words, he was much disturbed. 2. When the city had been taken, the soldiers set the prisoners free. 3. The enemy resisted our men all day. 4. If Labienus is leader, our army will be able to injure the enemy. 5. Labienus, having captured the mountain, was waiting for our men. 6. Although a sortie was made, they were not able to approach our first line.

A COUNTRY VILLA

LESSON LXVIII

THE GERUND · THE IRREGULAR VERB *EO*

459. The Gerund. The gerund (XXXII, *c*) is a verbal noun used in the genitive, dative, accusative, and ablative singular. It is formed by adding **-ndī, -ndō, -ndum, -ndō** to the present stem, with certain changes in quantity and spelling. Learn the gerunds of the model verbs (658–662).

460. What the Gerund is. The gerund is like the English verbal noun in *-ing*, as, *loving*; but it lacks a nominative case. For the nominative the infinitive is used.

Nom. amāre, *to love, loving*
Gen. amandī, *of loving*
Dat. amandō, *for loving*
Acc. amandum, *loving*
Abl. amandō, *by loving*

461. The Uses of the Gerund. The gerund is used in the various constructions of nouns. Since it is a *verbal* noun, it may have a direct or an indirect object: as, **vincendō hostēs**, *by overcoming the enemy*; **resistendō hostibus**, *by resisting the enemy*. Also observe the following:

1. **Ad pugnandum vēnērunt**, *they came for fighting, for the purpose of fighting, to fight.*
2. **Pugnandī causā vēnērunt**, *they came for the sake of fighting, to fight.*

a. Observe that the accusative of the gerund with **ad**, or the genitive of the gerund with **causā**, is used to express purpose. **Causā** when so used follows its genitive. This method of expressing purpose is used in brief statements.

THE GERUND

462. The Irregular Verb *Eō*. Learn the principal parts and conjugation of the irregular verb **eō** (667).

a. Observe where **i** (the root of **eō**) is changed to **e** in the present indicative and subjunctive, in the present participle, and in the gerund. In the perfect system **-v-** is regularly dropped. For the declension of the present participle see 645.

463.   VOCABULARY

causā, *abl. of* **causa**, for the sake of, to
nōmen, nōminis, *n.*, name (*nominate*)
spatium, spati, *n.*, room, space, time, opportunity (*spacious*)
vāllum, -ī, *n.*, rampart, earthworks (*interval*)

accēdō, accēdere, accessī, accessūrus, come near, approach (*accession*)
coniciō, conicere, coniēcī, coniectus, throw, hurl (*conjecture*)
eō, īre, iī (īvī), itūrus, go (*initial*)
ōrō, ōrāre, ōrāvī, ōrātus, speak, plead, beg (*orator*)

EXERCISES

464. 1. It, īmus, ībant. 2. Īre, īsse, ībunt. 3. Eunt, ierant, iit. 4. Difficultātem nāvigandī nūntiāvit. 5. Haec est causa mittendī. 6. Litterās mittendī causā vēnit. 7. Dīligentia in agendō ducī placet. 8. Spatium pugnandī nōn datum est. 9. Caesar fīnem ōrandī fēcit. 10. Spatium pīla in hostīs coniciendī breve fuit. 11. Accessērunt ad dīcendum. 12. Vōbīscum ībit ut nōmina eōrum roget. 13. Voluit cognōscere quō īssent. 14. Labiēnus imperāvit ut castra vāllō mūnīrentur.

465. 1. You are going, they were going, he had gone. 2. We shall go, you will have gone. 3. Whither have they gone? 4. He persuades them to go. 5. He ordered them to go. 6. They came near for the sake of seeking peace. 7. Time was not given for pleading. 8. They went toward the sea for the purpose of sailing. 9. That day they went three miles, and at sunset pitched camp.

NINTH REVIEW LESSON

LESSONS LXI-LXVIII

466. Give the English meanings of the following words:

accēdō	ēruptiō	noceō	praesidium	sōl
addūcō	faveō	nōlō	praestō	spatium
aliquis	hīberna	nōmen	praesum	studeō
causā	mālō	obtineō	quīdam	subsidium
commoveō	medius	occāsus	quisquam	supersum
coniciō	moveō	occurrō	quisque	suscipiō
crēdō	mulier	ōrō	redūcō	ūsus
dēditiō	mūnītiō	persuādeō	rēgnum	vāllum
dēsum	neque...	placeō	resistō	volō
eō	neque	praeficiō	rīpa	

467. Give the Latin meanings of the following words:

neither ... nor	kingdom	use, benefit, advantage
be unwilling	bank	each, each one, every, every one
be left over, survive	throw, hurl	possess, occupy, hold
be willing, wish	favor	disturb, move, arouse
resist, oppose	sun	surpass, be superior to
believe, trust	surrender	rampart, earthworks
place in command	move	be at the head of, command
for the sake of, to	harm, injure	some, some one, any, any one
be eager for, desire	help, aid	be more willing, prefer
speak, plead, beg	middle of	defense, protection, guard
sally, sortie	name	be lacking, be wanting, fail
lead to, influence	woman	come near, approach
winter quarters	persuade	please, be pleasing to
take up, undertake	lead back	room, space, time, opportunity
run towards, meet	setting	a certain one, a certain
any one (at all)	go	fortification, defense

468. Decline the nouns in 466. Decline the indefinite pronouns. Give the principal parts of each verb. Give the participles of each verb. Make synopses in the third person singular and plural. Conjugate **volō, nōlō**, and **eō** throughout.

469. Following the suggestions in 634, give English words derived from the Latin words in 466. Define these derivatives, and illustrate each by an English sentence.

470. Give the rule, if there is one, for the following constructions, and illustrate each by a sentence in Latin:

1. Dative with compounds
2. Dative of purpose
3. Dative of reference
4. Dative with special intransitive verbs
5. Participles as the equivalent of certain clauses
6. Ablative absolute
7. Gerund

WALL DECORATION OF A POMPEIAN HOUSE

LESSON LXIX

THE GERUNDIVE · THE IRREGULAR VERB *FERO*

471. The Gerundive. The future passive participle (441, 444) is more commonly called the *Gerundive*. It is a verbal adjective, and must be distinguished from the gerund, which is a verbal noun. The gerund, being a noun, may be used alone or with an object; but the gerundive, being an adjective, must agree with a noun.

472. The Gerundive used in Place of the Gerund.
1. Pācem petendī causā vēnērunt, *they came for the purpose of seeking peace.*
2. Pācis petendae causā vēnērunt, *they came for the purpose of seeking peace.*

a. Observe that the Latin sentences have the same meaning, and that 1 contains a gerund, **petendī**, with an object, **pācem**; while 2 contains a gerundive, **petendae**, in agreement with **pācis**. Instead of a gerund with an object, the Romans much preferred the gerundive construction, except occasionally in the genitive and in the ablative without a preposition.

473. The Gerundive used in the Passive Periphrastic Conjugation. The gerundive is also used with forms of **sum** as a predicate adjective. This is known as the *Passive Periphrastic Conjugation*. For a synopsis see 670.

1. Mīles laudandus est, *the soldier is to be praised, must be praised, ought to be praised.*
2. Cornēlia laudanda erat, *Cornelia was to be praised, ought to have been praised, needed to be praised.*

a. Observe that these sentences express necessity. Observe, too, the methods of translation.

THE GERUNDIVE

474. The Irregular Verb *Ferō*. Learn the principal parts and the conjugation of the irregular verb ferō (666).

475.   VOCABULARY

lībertās, lībertātis, *f.*, freedom (*liberty*)

signum, -ī, *n.*, sign, signal (*signify*)

vīs, vīs, *f.*, force, strength, power, might (642) (*violence*)

augeō, augēre, auxī, auctus, increase, enlarge (*auction*)

conveniō, convenīre, convēnī, conventūrus, come together, assemble (*convene*)

ferō, ferre, tulī, lātus, bear, bring; report, say (*transfer*)

EXERCISES

476. 1. Fert, ferimus, ferent. 2. Ferre, feret, tulisse. 3. Rūrsus veniunt ut auxilium ferant. 4. Tulerant, lātus esse. 5. In petendā pāce. 6. Lībertātis petendae causā. 7. Vīribus augendīs. 8. Pontis faciendī. 9. Legiō ad bellum gerendum sē parat. 10. Multī convēnērunt urbis novae videndae causā. 11. Signum dandum erat. 12. Signō datō, mīlitēs impetum summā celeritāte fēcērunt. 13. Omnia ūnō tempore agenda erant. 14. Putāmus bellum parandum esse. 15. Ad pīla conicienda tempus dēfuit. 16. Arma in hīberna ferenda sunt.

477. 1. You are bearing, they bear, he had borne. 2. You have borne, they were bearing, by bearing. 3. Help was being brought. 4. They said that they should bring the shields. 5. Of seeing the town. 6. For the sake of drawing up a line of battle. 7. By carrying on war. 8. In laying waste the fields. 9. The strength of the allies is being increased daily. 10. The force of the enemy must be borne. 11. The cohort must be led back with speed. 12. A lieutenant ought to have been put in command of these troops.

LESSON LXX

READING LESSON

478.   VOCABULARY

mors, mortis, *f.*, death (*mortality*)
prīvātus, -a, -um, private, personal (*private*)
vadum, -ī, *n.*, ford, shoal
vel . . . vel, *conj.*, either . . . or
exeō, exīre, exiī, exitūrus, go out, go forth (*exit*)
incendō, incendere, incendī, incēnsus, burn, kindle, excite (*incendiary*)

incipiō, incipere, incēpī, inceptus, begin (*incipient*)
pācō, pācāre, pācāvī, pācātus, subdue, pacify
permittō, permittere, permīsī, permissus, allow, suffer, give up (*permission*)
pertineō, pertinēre, pertinuī, ——, extend, pertain to (*pertinent*)
trānseō, trānsīre, trānsiī, trānsitus, go across, cross (*transit*)

THE HELVETIANS LEAVE THEIR TERRITORY

479. Post Orgetorīgis mortem tamen Helvētiī id quod cōnstituerant facere incēpērunt, ut ē fīnibus suīs exīrent. Ubi iam sē ad eam rem parātōs esse putāvērunt, oppida sua omnia et vīcōs et prīvāta aedificia incendērunt. Frūmentum et cibum sibi quemque domō ferre iussērunt. Persuāsērunt quibusdam cīvitātibus fīnitimīs ut oppidīs suīs vīcīsque incēnsīs cum eīs exīrent.

Erant omnīnō itinera duo quibus itineribus domō exīre poterant: ūnum per Sēquanōs, angustum et difficile, inter montem Iūram et flūmen Rhodanum; mōns autem altissimus impendēbat, ut facile paucī prohibēre possent; alterum per prōvinciam Rōmānam, multō facilius, quod inter fīnēs Helvētiōrum et Allobrogum, quī nūper pācātī erant, Rhodanus fluit, isque nōn nūllīs locīs vadō trānsitur.

READING LESSON

Extrēmum oppidum Allobrogum est proximumque Helvētiōrum fīnibus Genāva. Ex eō oppidō pōns ad Helvētiōs pertinet. Allobrogibus sēsē vel persuāsūrōs esse vel vī coāctūrōs esse spērābant ut per suōs fīnēs eōs īre permitterent. Omnibus rēbus parātīs diem conveniendī dīcunt.

Caesar per nūntiōs audīvit Helvētiōs per prōvinciam nostram iter facere coepisse. Statim properāvit Rōmā et quam maximīs potuit itineribus[1] in Galliam ulteriōrem contendit et ad Genāvam pervēnit. Prōvinciae tōtī quam maximum potuit mīlitum numerum imperāvit (erat omnīnō in Galliā ulteriōre legiō ūna), pontem quī erat ad Genāvam iussit rescindī. Ubi dē eius adventū Helvētiī cognōvērunt, lēgātōs ad eum mīsērunt.

[1] **quam maximīs potuit itineribus,** *by as long journeys as possible.* Sometimes Cæsar traveled a hundred miles a day.

DINING COUCHES

LESSON LXXI

THE ABLATIVE OF SPECIFICATION · DEPONENT VERBS

480. The Ablative of Specification.

Gallōs virtūte superant, *they surpass the Gauls in courage.*

a. Observe that the ablative **virtūte** tells in what respect the Gauls are surpassed. This usage is known as the *Ablative of Specification*.

481. Rule for the Ablative of Specification. *The ablative without a preposition is used to denote in what respect something is true.*

482. Deponent Verbs. Deponent verbs are verbs which have passive forms with active meanings. They occur in each of the regular conjugations, and are distinguished by the ending of the present infinitive: first conjugation, -ārī; second, -ērī; third, -ī; fourth, -īrī. Learn the principal parts, the meanings, and the conjugation of the deponent verbs in 669.

483. The Active Forms and the Participles of Deponent Verbs. A deponent verb has the following active forms:

Fut. Infin. hortātūrus esse *Gerund* hortandī, etc.

It has the participles of both voices:

Pres.	hortāns, *urging*	*Perfect*	hortātus, *having urged*
Fut.	hortātūrus, *about to urge, going to urge*	*Gerundive*	hortandus, *to be urged*

a. Observe that the perfect participle of deponent verbs is active in meaning; the gerundive is passive. As the perfect participle is active in meaning, an ablative absolute (454, *b*) is seldom necessary with this participle; instead, the construction is the same as in English: as,

Hortātus mīlitēs signum dedit, *having encouraged the soldiers he gave the signal*, or, *when he had encouraged*, etc.

THE ABLATIVE OF SPECIFICATION

484.   VOCABULARY

cōnor, cōnārī, cōnātus sum, try, attempt (*conative*)

experior, experīrī, expertus sum, test, make trial of (*experience*)

hortor, hortārī, hortātus sum, urge, entreat (*exhortation*)

polliceor, pollicērī, pollicitus sum, promise, offer

proficīscor, proficīscī, profectus sum, set out, march

prōgredior, prōgredī, prōgressus sum, go forward, advance (*progress*)

sequor, sequī, secūtus sum, follow (*sequence*)

vereor, verērī, veritus sum, fear, respect (*reverence*)

EXERCISES

485. 1. Experiēbāminī, cōnāmur, hortāberis. 2. Pollicēbantur, experiuntur, veritī erāmus. 3. Ut sequātur, verēns, sequendō. 4. Proficīscētur, sequendī causā, secūtūrus esse. 5. Veritī sunt, secūtūrus, prōgredientur. 6. Cōnātur, expertus esse, ad prōgrediendum. 7. Verēminī mortem. 8. Caesar hortātus est mīlitēs ut ducēs sequerentur. 9. Illō diē exercitus proficīscēbātur. 10. Ipse cum celeritāte eōs sequētur. 11. His persuāserant ut eandem fortūnam bellī experīrentur. 12. Nātiōnēs Germāniae subsidium pollicitae erant. 13. Per fīnēs nostrōs īre cōnantur. 14. Puer patrī virtūte similis erat.

486. 1. He was urging, they urge, they will follow. 2. She has followed, he fears, to attempt. 3. They had followed many miles. 4. You will set out, they will advance, going to follow. 5. Having followed, to have advanced. 6. Caesar ordered the same two legions to set out. 7. They do not follow the tribune. 8. They will set out at daybreak in order to follow the enemy. 9. Although they promised grain, they were unable to bring it because of a lack of carts. 10. The poor soldiers are tired in body, but they surpass the enemy in speed.

LESSON LXXII

TEMPORAL CLAUSES WITH *CUM* · THE IRREGULAR VERB *FIO*

487. Temporal Clauses with *Cum*. The Latin conjunction cum, *when, while,* introduces temporal clauses (xx, *e*).

1. Cum Caesar in Italiā erat, bellum in Galliā ortum est, *when (while) Cæsar was in Italy, a war began in Gaul.*
2. Caesar, cum id nūntiātum esset, in Galliam contendit, *Cæsar, when this had been reported, hastened into Gaul.*
3. Cum nūntius pervēnerit, Caesar prōgrediētur, *when the messenger arrives, Cæsar will advance.*

a. Observe that the temporal clause in sentence 1 *fixes the time* at which the war began, and that its verb is in the indicative. Observe that the clause in sentence 2 *describes the circumstances* under which Cæsar was impelled to hasten into Gaul, and that its verb is in the subjunctive. Observe that the temporal clause in sentence 3 *refers to future time,* and that its verb is in the indicative.

488. *Rule for Temporal Clauses with* **Cum.** *Temporal clauses referring to past time, when introduced by* **cum,** *have their verb in the indicative if they fix the time of an action, but in the subjunctive if they describe the circumstances of an action. The indicative is used in temporal clauses introduced by* **cum** *referring to present or to future time.*

489. The Irregular Verb *Fīō*. The verb **faciō,** which you have frequently used in the active voice, forms its present system in the passive from the irregular verb **fīō.** Learn the principal parts of **fīō** and its conjugation (668). Review the complete inflection of **faciō.** The passive voice of the compounds of **faciō** is inflected regularly.

TEMPORAL CLAUSES WITH *CUM*

490.   **VOCABULARY**

certus, -a, -um, certain, sure
cum, *conj.*, when, while
frūmentārius, -a, -um, of grain; **rēs frūmentāria**, grain supply, provisions
nē ... quidem, not even (*the word or words between* **nē** *and* **quidem** *are emphasized*)

paulō, *adv.*, a little
fīō, fierī, factus sum, be made, be done, happen
certiōrem facere (to make more sure), to inform
certior fierī (to be made more sure), to be informed

EXERCISES

491. 1. Fit, fiunt. 2. Fierī, factus esse. 3. Fīet, fīēbant, fīō. 4. Fīētis, fīēmus. 5. Eum certiōrem fēcimus. 6. Certior fit dē hīs rēbus. 7. Gallī, cum oppidum cēpissent, omnēs captīvōs interfēcērunt. 8. Cum dē inopiā reī frūmentāriae certior factus esset, in ulteriōrem partem prōvinciae paulō ante mediam noctem profectus est. 9. Nē amīcī quidem dē adventū tuō certiōrēs fient. 10. Cum proelī fīnem nox fēcisset, quīdam ad Caesarem vēnit. 11. Cum equitātum hostium vīdērunt, nostrī in eōs impetum fēcērunt.

A ROMAN STOVE

492. 1. You are becoming, they become. 2. It happens, to be made, it will be made. 3. When you come, you will learn this. 4. They have been informed. 5. I shall inform them. 6. When he was not able to persuade them, he went to the general. 7. Not even the general had been informed about this. 8. When the lieutenant had exhorted the soldiers, he gave the signal for battle.

LESSON LXXIII

READING LESSON

493.   VOCABULARY

altitūdō, altitūdinis, *f.*, height (*altitude*)
castellum, -ī, *n.*, fort, redoubt (*castle*)
cōnsuētūdō, cōnsuētūdinis, *f.*, custom
facultās, facultātis, *f.*, power, opportunity (*faculty*)
fossa, -ae, *f.*, ditch, trench (*fosse*)

exīstimō, exīstimāre, exīstimāvī, exīstimātus, think, judge, consider (*estimate*)
pellō, pellere, pepulī, pulsus, beat, drive, defeat (*repel*)
perficiō, perficere, perfēcī, perfectus, accomplish, finish (*perfect*)
temperō, temperāre, temperāvī, temperātus, control, refrain, abstain from (*temperance*)

CÆSAR REFUSES THE HELVETIANS PERMISSION TO GO THROUGH THE ROMAN PROVINCE

494. Cum lēgātī Helvētiōrum rogāvissent ut per prōvinciam īre permitterentur, Caesar, quod memoriā tenēbat cōnsulem Rōmānum interfectum (esse)[1] ab Helvētiīs et exercitum eius pulsum (esse) et sub iugum missum (esse), concēdendum (esse) nōn putābat; neque Helvētiōs, datā facultāte per prōvinciam itineris faciendī, temperātūrōs ab iniūriā exīstimābat. Tamen, ut spatium mīlitum cōgendōrum, quōs imperāverat, esset, lēgātīs respondit diem sē ad conloquium dictūrum.

Intereā eā legiōne quam sēcum habēbat mīlitibusque quī ex prōvinciā convēnerant ā lacū Lemannō, quī in flūmen Rhodanum fluit, ad montem Iūram, quī fīnis Sēquanōrum ab

[1] Frequently **esse** is omitted in Latin infinitive forms. From which infinitives in this lesson is it omitted?

READING LESSON

Helvētiīs dīvidit, mīlia passuum xviiii mūrum in altitūdinem pedum xvi fossamque perdūxit. Eō opere perfectō praesidia conlocāvit, castella mūnīvit, ut facilius eōs prohibēre posset.

Ubi ea diēs quam cōnstituerat cum lēgātīs vēnit, et lēgātī ad eum vēnērunt, dīxit sē propter cōnsuētūdinem populī Rōmānī iter nūllī per prōvinciam dare posse; et eōs prohibitūrum ostendit.

ROMAN ARMY CROSSING A BRIDGE OF BOATS

LESSON LXXIV

**SUBSTANTIVE CLAUSES OF FACT INTRODUCED BY *QUOD*
THE INDICATIVE IN ADVERBIAL CLAUSES**

495. Substantive Clauses of Fact with *Quod*.

Quod eum laudās, mihi grātum est, *the fact that you praise him is pleasing to me.*

a. Observe that the clause **quod eum laudās** is the subject of **est**. Such clauses, which should be translated by *that* or *the fact that*, are called *Quod Clauses of Fact*, and have their verb in the indicative. They are found as the subject of a verb or in apposition with some word.

496. *Rule for Substantive Clauses of Fact. The indicative is used with* **quod** *in a substantive clause to state something which is regarded as a fact.*

497. Adverbial Clauses with the Verb in the Indicative.

1. Ībunt quā iter facillimum est, *they will go where the way is easiest.*
2. Quaedam nātiōnēs Galliae, ut dīximus, fortissimae erant, *certain nations of Gaul, as we said, were very brave.*

a. Observe that the clauses introduced by **quā** and **ut** are adverbial in nature, and that their verbs are in the indicative. **Quā** and **ut**, so used, are adverbs.

498.   **VOCABULARY**

condiciō, condiciōnis, *f.*, terms, condition (*condition*)

lātitūdō, lātitūdinis, *f.*, breadth, width (*latitude*)

lēgātiō, lēgātiōnis, *f.*, mission, embassy (*legation*)

numerus, -ī, *m.*, number (*numerical*)

cōgō, cōgere, coēgī, coāctus, gather together, force, compel (*with acc. and infin., or a substantive clause of purpose*) (*cogent*)

ēgredior, ēgredī, ēgressus sum, go out, go forth (*egress*)

pateō, patēre, patuī, ——, lie open, extend, spread (*patent*)

EXERCISES

499. 1. Inopia commeātūs hostēs ēgredī coēgit. 2. Quā proximum iter in ulteriōrem Galliam per montēs erat, cum legiōnibus īre contendit. 3. Quod maiōrēs manūs hostium coāctae sunt, ducem nōn perturbāvit. 4. Ūna rēs Caesarem impedīvit, quod lātitūdinem flūminis nōn cognōverat. 5. Eōrum agrī in lātitūdinem centum et sex mīlia passuum patēbant. 6. Quod Gallī vīcōs nostrōs vāstābant, Caesarī persuāsit ut prīncipēs eōrum in conloquium convocāret. 7. In Italiam contendit ut magnum numerum equitum et peditum cōgeret. 8. Quod condiciōnēs pācis petunt, nūntiandum est. 9. Omnia paranda sunt ad ēgrediendum. 10. Ad cognōscendās condiciōnēs dēditiōnis, ut dēmōnstrāvimus, lēgātiōnēs ab proximīs nātiōnibus missae erant.

500. 1. Bands of horsemen must be gathered together. 2. The fact that a great number of men are now going forth from the villages to make war disturbs us. 3. In the conference he said that the terms of surrender would be pleasing to him. 4. A great number of scouts went forth from the camp where the width of the river was least. 5. Do you know how many miles the lake extends? 6. The fact that the enemy were greatly confused was of help to us in attacking the town.

ROMAN LAMPS

LESSON LXXV

SUBORDINATE CLAUSES IN INDIRECT STATEMENTS

501. Subordinate Clauses in Indirect Statements.

1. Dīcunt Germānōs, quī trāns Rhēnum incolant, ex fīnibus ēgredī, *they say that the Germans, who live across the Rhine, are going forth from their territories.*
2. Dīxērunt Germānōs, quī trāns Rhēnum incolerent, ex fīnibus ēgredī, *they said that the Germans, who lived across the Rhine, were going forth from their territories.*

a. Observe that in each sentence there is an indirect statement containing a subordinate clause. The direct statement of both sentences is the same, **Germānī, quī trāns Rhēnum incolunt, ex fīnibus ēgrediuntur.** Observe that the subordinate verbs are in the subjunctive in an indirect statement, and that the tense is changed according to the rule for the sequence of tenses (348–351).

502. *Rule for Subordinate Clauses in Indirect Statements. The verbs of the subordinate clauses of an indirect statement are in the subjunctive. The tense of the subjunctive is decided by the rule for the sequence of tenses after the verb of* **saying, knowing,** *etc.*

a. Subordinate verbs that were in the subjunctive before they were indirectly quoted of course remain in the subjunctive.

503. VOCABULARY

barbarus, -ī, *m.*, barbarian (*barbarous*)
celeriter, *adv.*, swiftly (*celerity*)
initium, ini'tī, *n.*, beginning (*initial*)
satis, *adv. and n. noun*, enough, sufficiently (*satisfy*)

cōnsuēscō, cōnsuēscere, cōnsuēvī, cōnsuētus, become accustomed
moror, morārī, morātus sum, hinder, delay (*moratorium*)
revertō, revertere, revertī, reversus (*or, in the present system,* revertor, *deponent*), turn back, return (*revert*)

SUBORDINATE CLAUSES

EXERCISES

504. 1. Caesar pollicētur sē celeriter reversūrum esse quod barbarī initium bellī faciant. 2. Caesar pollicitus est sē celeriter reversūrum esse quod barbarī initium bellī facerent. 3. Explōrātōrēs nūntiāvērunt hostēs vīcōs quōs oppugnāvissent nōn cēpisse. 4. Per captīvōs cognōscit hostēs, quod agrī et vīcī omnēs vāstātī sint, nūllum frūmentum habēre. 5. Putō cōnsilia quae mihi dare cōnsuēveris bona fuisse. 6. Aliquis dīcit dolōrem hostium tantum esse ut in castrīs Rōmānīs audiātur. 7. Barbarī putāvērunt Caesarem, quī in Galliam citeriōrem quōque annō revertī cōnsuēvisset, diūtius nōn morātūrum esse. 8. Habēsne satis nāvium ad nāvigandum?

505. 1. They say that the legions which are spending the winter across the river will return. 2. A scout announced that Labienus, who had captured the town, was awaiting the coming of Cæsar. 3. I think that the enemy will go forth from our territories because they have not enough food. 4. We know that many nations which contended with the Romans have been conquered. 5. The barbarians, when they had delayed three days in front of the camp, sent an embassy to our general.

ROMAN PITCHERS

TENTH REVIEW LESSON
LESSONS LXIX-LXXV

506. Give the English meanings of the following words:

altitūdō	conveniō	hortor	pācō	rēs frūmentāria
augeō	cum	incendō	pateō	revertō
barbarus	ēgredior	incipiō	paulō	satis
castellum	exeō	initium	pellō	sequor
celeriter	exīstimō	lātitūdō	perficiō	signum
certus	experior	lēgātiō	permittō	temperō
cōgō	facultās	lībertās	pertineō	trānseō
condiciō	ferō	moror	polliceor	vadum
cōnor	fīō	mors	prīvātus	vel ... vel
cōnsuēscō	fossa	nē ... quidem	proficīscor	vereor
cōnsuētūdō	frūmentārius	numerus	prōgredior	vīs

507. Give the Latin meanings of the following words:

test, make trial of	promise, offer	barbarian
allow, suffer, give up	terms, condition	not even
come together, assemble	urge, entreat	try, attempt
enough, sufficiently	either ... or	death
accomplish, finish	ditch, trench	sign, signal
bear, bring; report, say	go across, cross	a little
mission, embassy	certain, sure	height
become accustomed	fort, redoubt	begin
turn back, return	breadth, width	follow
extend, pertain to	private, personal	swiftly
lie open, extend, spread	set out, march	number
control, refrain, abstain from	increase, enlarge	hinder, delay
power, opportunity	fear, respect	beginning
be made, be done, happen	burn, kindle, excite	ford, shoal
force, strength, power, might	go forward, advance	go out, go forth
gather together, force, compel	think, judge, consider	of grain
beat, drive, defeat	subdue, pacify	freedom
grain supply, provisions	when, while	custom

TENTH REVIEW LESSON

508. Decline each noun in 506. Conjugate each deponent verb throughout. Make synopses in the third person singular and plural. Give the infinitives and the participles of each verb. Conjugate **ferō** and **fīō** throughout.

509. Following the suggestions in 634, give English words derived from the Latin words in 506. Define these derivatives, and illustrate each by an English sentence.

510. Give the rule, if there is one, for the following constructions, and illustrate each by a sentence in Latin:

1. Gerundive with **ad** and with **causā**
2. Passive periphrastic conjugation
3. Ablative of specification
4. Temporal clauses with **cum**
5. Substantive clauses of fact with **quod**
6. Adverbial clauses with the verb in the indicative
7. Subordinate clauses in indirect discourse

511. Give Latin words suggested by the following English words:

popular	magnanimous	petition	prefect	total
temporal	audible	posterity	depredation	fidelity
real	local	intellect	malefactor	itinerary
neutral	habitable	novelty	humility	science
vulnerable	lucid	extremity	longitude	premium
ultimate	subterranean	solitude	identity	fortitude
post mortem	numerous	exhortation	altitude	egress
versatile	cognizant	tenant	deity	ignite
subsidiary	innocent	instruction	factory	satisfy
nocturnal	permanent	magnitude	postulate	assimilate
impetuous	alternate	gladiator	contention	minimize
final	urban	avocation	mission	nullify
insular	cogent	multitude	position	intervene
military	marine	pedestrian	audacity	contradict
hostile	naval	constitution	vicinity	expatriate

SUMMARY

THE USES OF NOUNS AND VERBS

512. From your study of the book to this point you are supposed to be familiar with the uses of nouns and verbs summarized below.

USES OF NOUNS

Nominative
  Subject, 27, 28
  Predicate noun, 86, 87
Genitive
  Possessive, 43, 44
  Material, p. 79, note 1
  Partitive, 308, 309
  Objective, 380, 381
Dative
  Indirect object, 56, 57
  With adjectives, 110, 111
  With compound verbs, 424, 425
  Purpose, 426, 427
  Reference, 426, 428
  With special verbs, 432, 433
Accusative
  Direct object, 32, 33
  Place to which, 179, 180, 230
  With prepositions, 193
  Extent of time and space, 332, 333
  Subject of infinitive, 399
Ablative
  Place where, 58, 59
  Means, 121, 122
  Manner, 128, 129
  Accompaniment, 142, 143
  Place from which, 177, 178, 230
  Cause, 184, 185
  With prepositions, 194
  Time, 218, 219
  Agent, 242, 243
  Separation, 281, 282
  Degree of difference, 320, 321
  Absolute, 452–455
  Specification, 480, 481

513. USES OF VERBS

Indicative
  Main verb: Declaratory sentence
  Main verb: Question
  Subordinate verb: Causal clause with **quod**, 50, 51
  Subordinate verb: Temporal clause with **cum**, 487, 488
  Subordinate verb: Relative clause
  Subordinate verb: Substantive clause of fact with **quod**, 495, 496
  Subordinate verb: Adverbial clause with **quā** and **ut**, 497

Subjunctive
  Purpose clause: Adverbial, 343, 344
  Purpose clause: Substantive, 355, 356
  Result clause: Adverbial, 357, 358
  Indirect Question: Substantive, 372, 373
  Temporal clause: with **cum**, 487, 488
  Subordinate clause in indirect statements, 501, 502

Infinitive
  Subject of another verb, 393
  Complement of another verb, 394
  Object of another verb, 398
  Verb of an indirect statement, 401

Participle
  As an adjective, 443
  Ablative absolute, 452–455
  Equivalent to a clause of time, concession, cause, condition, etc., 444, 445

Gerund
  As a noun, 460
  With **ad** or **causā** to show purpose, 461

Gerundive
  With **ad** or **causā** to show purpose, 472
  With forms of **sum** in the passive periphrastic conjugation, 473

Whenever in your translation of the subsequent Selections for Reading you meet a noun or a verb, at once ask yourself which of these uses the particular noun or verb has. Then translate accordingly.

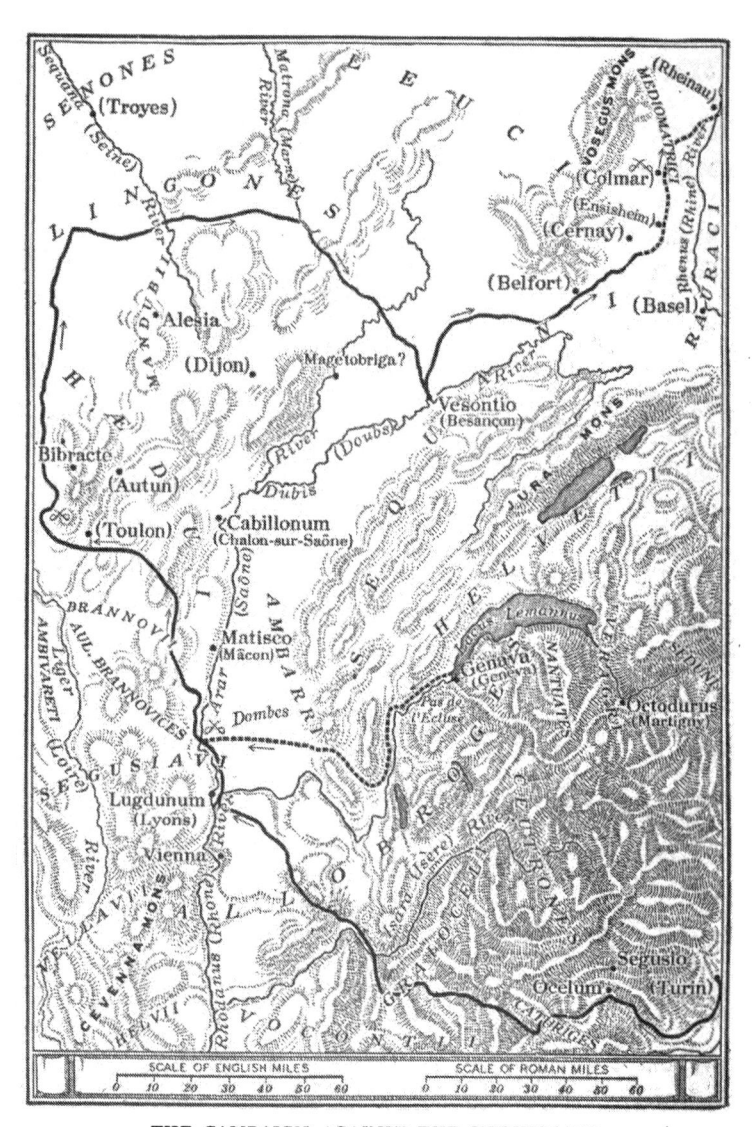

THE CAMPAIGN AGAINST THE HELVETIANS

SELECTIONS FOR READING

CÆSAR: THE CAMPAIGN AGAINST THE HELVETIANS
(CONTINUED FROM 494)

The Helvetians are allowed to proceed through the land of the Sequani

514. Helvētiī, eā spē dēiectī, vadīs Rhodanī, quā minima altitūdō flūminis erat, trānsīre cōnātī sunt, sed mūnītiōne et tēlīs repulsī hōc cōnātū dēstitērunt. Relinquēbātur ūna per Sēquanōs via. Hīs cum persuādēre nōn possent, lēgātōs ad Dumnorīgem Haeduum mīsērunt. Dumnorīx apud Sēquanōs plūrimum poterat[1] et Helvētiīs erat amīcus, quod ex eā cīvitāte Orgetorīgis fīliam in mātrimōnium dūxerat. Etiam cupiditāte rēgnī adductus est. Itaque Sēquanīs persuāsit ut per fīnēs suōs Helvētiōs īre permitterent et obsidēs inter sēsē darent: Sēquanī, nē itinere Helvētiōs prohibērent; Helvētiī, ut sine iniūriā trānsīrent.

Cæsar opposes this plan of the Helvetians and crosses the Rhone

515. Caesar certior factus est Helvētiōs cōnstituisse per agrum Sēquanōrum et Haeduōrum iter in Santonum fīnēs facere, quī nōn longē ā Tolōsātium fīnibus aberant, quae cīvitās erat in prōvinciā. Inimīcōs populī Rōmānī eam regiōnem incolere nōlēbat. Ob eam causam eī mūnītiōnī quam fēcerat Labiēnum lēgātum praefēcit; ipse in Italiam magnīs itineribus[2] contendit duāsque ibi legiōnēs cōnscrīpsit, et trēs quae circum Aquilēiam hiemābant ex hībernīs ēdūxit, et, quā proximum iter in ulteriōrem Galliam per Alpēs erat, cum hīs quīnque legiōnibus īre contendit. Ibi quaedam cīvitātēs, locīs

---

[1] **plūrimum poterat**, *had a great deal of influence.* [2] **magnīs itineribus,** *by long journeys.* See p. 185, note 1.

superiōribus occupātīs, itinere exercitum prohibēre cōnātae sunt. Complūribus hīs proeliīs victīs,[1] ab Ocelō, quod est oppidum citeriōris prōvinciae[2] extrēmum, in fīnēs Vocontiōrum ulteriōris prōvinciae diē septimō pervēnit; inde in Allobrogum fīnēs, ab Allobrogibus in Segusiāvōs exercitum dūxit. Hī sunt extrā prōvinciam trāns Rhodanum prīmī.

The Hædui and other tribes ask for Cæsar's help against the Helvetians

516. Helvētiī interim per fīnēs Sēquanōrum suās cōpiās dūxerant, et in Haeduōrum fīnēs pervēnerant eōrumque agrōs vāstābant. Haeduī sē suaque[3] ab eīs dēfendere nōn poterant. Itaque lēgātōs ad Caesarem mīsērunt ut auxilium rogārent. Eī dīxērunt paene in cōnspectū exercitūs nostrī agrōs vāstārī, līberōs in servitūtem abdūcī, oppida expugnārī nōn dēbuisse.[4] Eōdem tempore Ambarrī Caesarem certiōrem fēcērunt sēsē, vāstātīs agrīs, nōn facile ab oppidīs vim hostium prohibēre. Item Allobrogēs, quī trāns Rhodanum vīcōs habēbant, fugā sē ad Caesarem recēpērunt. Quibus rēbus adductus Caesar diūtius nōn exspectandum esse[5] cōnstituit.

Cæsar destroys one division of the Helvetians

517. Flūmen est Arar, quod per fīnēs Haeduōrum et Sēquanōrum in Rhodanum fluit. Id Helvētiī trānsībant. Ubi per explōrātōrēs Caesar certior factus est trēs iam partēs cōpiārum Helvētiōs id flūmen trādūxisse, quārtam fere partem citrā flūmen Ararim relictam esse, dē tertiā vigiliā cum legiōnibus tribus ē castrīs profectus ad eam partem pervēnit quae nōndum flūmen trānsierat. Eōs impedītōs adgressus magnam partem interfēcit; reliquī sēsē fugae mandāvērunt atque in proximās silvās abdidērunt.

---

[1] Translate **complūribus** with **proeliīs** and **hīs** with **victīs**. [2] The Roman province on the Italian side of the Alps. [3] **suaque**, *and their possessions.* [4] **vāstārī . . . nōn dēbuisse,** *ought not to have been* etc. [5] **nōn exspectandum esse,** *that he must not wait.* The verb, however, is used impersonally.

CAMPAIGN AGAINST THE HELVETIANS

The Helvetians send an embassy to Cæsar

518. Hōc proeliō factō, reliquās cōpiās Helvētiōrum ut cōnsequī posset, pontem in Ararī[1] fēcit atque ita exercitum trādūxit. Helvētiī repentīnō eius adventū commōtī, cum illum ūnō diē flūmen trānsīsse intellegerent, lēgātōs ad eum mīsērunt; cuius lēgātiōnis Dīvicō prīnceps fuit. In conloquiō Caesar imperāvit ut obsidēs populō Rōmānō darentur. Dīvicō respondit Helvētiōs obsidēs accipere, nōn dare cōnsuēvisse. Hōc respōnsō datō discessit.

Cæsar follows the Helvetians

519. Posterō diē castra ex eō locō mōvērunt. Idem fēcit Caesar, equitātumque omnem, ad numerum quattuor mīlium, quem ex omnī prōvinciā et Haeduīs atque eōrum sociīs coēgerat, praemīsit, ut vidērent quās in partēs hostēs iter facerent. Quī cupidius novissimum agmen[2] secūtī aliēnō locō cum equitātū Helvētiōrum proelium commīsērunt; et paucī dē nostrīs interfectī sunt. Quō proeliō dēlectātī Helvētiī, quod paucīs equitibus tantam multitūdinem equitum vīcerant, audācius in nostrōs impetum facere coepērunt. Caesar suōs ā proeliō continēbat, et ita diēs circiter XV iter fēcērunt ut inter novissimum hostium agmen et nostrum prīmum[3] quīnque mīlia passuum interessent.

Cæsar prepares to attack the Helvetians

520. Tandem ab explōrātōribus certior factus est hostēs mīlia passuum ab ipsīus castrīs octō abesse. Dē tertiā vigiliā Labiēnum lēgātum cum duābus legiōnibus et eīs ducibus quī iter cognōverant, summum iugum montis ascendere iussit. Ipse dē quārtā vigiliā eōdem itinere quō hostēs ierant ad eōs contendit, equitātumque omnem ante sē mīsit. Cōnsidius cum explōrātōribus praemissus est.

---

[1] **in Ararī,** *over the Arar.* [2] **novissimum agmen,** *the rear.* [3] **prīmum (agmen),** *vanguard.*

Considius becomes panic-stricken

521. Prīmā lūce, cum summus mōns ā Labiēnō tenērētur, ipse ab hostium castrīs mīlle passuum abesset, neque (ut posteā ex captīvīs intellēxit) aut ipsīus adventus aut Labiēnī cognitus esset, Cōnsidius equō admissō[1] ad eum properāvit. Dīxit mon-
5 tem quem Caesar ā Labiēnō occupārī voluisset ab hostibus tenērī; id sē ā Gallicīs armīs cognōvisse. Caesar suās cōpiās ad proximum collem dūxit et aciem īnstrūxit. Labiēnus interim, monte occupātō, nostrōs exspectābat. Multō diē[2] per explōrātōrēs Caesar cognōvit et montem ā suīs tenērī et Hel-
10 vētiōs castra mōvisse et Cōnsidium timōre perterritum quod nōn vīdisset prō vīsō sibi nūntiāvisse. Eō diē, quō cōnsuēverat intervāllō, hostēs secūtus est et mīlia passuum tria ab eōrum castrīs castra posuit.

The battle between Cæsar and the Helvetians

522. Posterō diē cōpiās suās Caesar in proximum collem
15 dūxit equitātumque, ut sustinēret hostium impetum, mīsit. Ipse interim in colle mediō aciem legiōnum quattuor īnstrūxit. In summō iugō duās legiōnēs, quās in Galliā citeriōre proximā aestāte cōnscrīpserat, et omnia auxilia[3] conlocāvit. Helvētiī cum omnibus suīs carrīs secūtī impedīmenta in ūnum locum
20 contulērunt; ipsī sub prīmam nostram aciem successērunt. Caesar hortātus suōs proelium commīsit. Mīlitēs ē locō superiōre pīlīs missīs in hostēs impetum fēcērunt. Tandem vulneribus dēfessī hostēs ad montem, quī circiter mīlle passuum aberat, sē recipere coepērunt. Diū atque ācriter pugnāvērunt. Diūtius
25 cum sustinēre nostrōrum impetūs nōn possent, alterī sē, ut coeperant, in montem recēpērunt, alterī[4] ad impedīmenta et

---

[1] **equō admissō**, *at full gallop.* [2] **multō diē**, *late in the day.* [3] **auxilia**, *auxiliaries.* [4] **alterī ... alterī**, *one body ... the other.*

CAMPAIGN AGAINST THE HELVETIANS

.carrōs suōs iērunt. Ad multam noctem[1] etiam ad impedīmenta contendērunt, quod Helvētiī prō vāllō carrōs conlocāverant et ē locō superiōre in nostrōs venientēs tēla coniciēbant. Tandem nostrī impedīmenta et castra cēpērunt. Ibi Orgetorīgis fīlia atque ūnus ē fīliīs captus est.

The Helvetians retreat and offer to surrender

523. Ex eō proeliō circiter hominum mīlia cxxx superfuērunt, eāque tōtā nocte continenter iērunt. In fīnēs Lingonum diē quārtō pervēnērunt. Nostrī autem propter vulnera mīlitum eōs sequī nōn potuērunt. Caesar litterās nūntiōsque ad Lingonēs mīsit et imperāvit nē eōs frūmentō nēve aliā rē iuvārent. Ipse trīduō intermissō cum omnibus cōpiīs eōs sequī coepit.

Helvētiī omnium rērum inopiā adductī lēgātōs dē dēditiōne ad eum mīsērunt. Quī cum eum in itinere convēnissent sēque ad pedēs[2] prōiēcissent pācemque petīssent atque eōs in eō locō quō tum erant suum adventum exspectāre iussisset, pāruērunt. Eō cum Caesar pervēnisset, obsidēs et arma postulāvit. Obsidibus armīsque trāditīs, eōs in dēditiōnem accēpit. Helvētiōs in fīnēs suōs, unde erant profectī, revertī iussit. Id eā maximē ratiōne fēcit, quod nōluit eum locum unde Helvētiī discesserant vacāre, nē propter bonitātem agrōrum Germānī, quī trāns Rhēnum incolunt, ex suīs fīnibus in Helvētiōrum fīnēs trānsīrent et fīnitimī Galliae prōvinciae Allobrogibusque essent.

[1] **ad multam noctem,** *until late at night.* [2] **ad pedēs,** *at his feet.*

CARRI

CÆSAR: THE STORY OF THE ADUATUCI

The Aduatuci prepare to make a desperate resistance to Cæsar

524. Aduatucī[1] cum omnibus cōpiīs auxiliō[2] Nerviīs veniēbant. Hāc pugnā[3] nūntiātā, ex itinere domum revertērunt; omnibus oppidīs castellīsque dēsertīs sua omnia in ūnum oppidum ēgregiē nātūrā mūnītum contulērunt. Quod[4] ex omnibus in circuitū partibus[5] altissimās rūpēs habēbat, sed ūnā ex parte aditus relinquēbātur. Quem locum duplicī altissimō mūrō mūnierant et magna saxa in mūrō conlocābant.

From their walls they taunt the Romans

525. Prīmō adventū exercitūs nostrī[6] crēbrās ēruptiōnēs faciēbant parvīsque proeliīs cum nostrīs contendēbant. Posteā, vāllō crēbrīsque castellīs ā Rōmānīs circummūnītī, oppidō[7] sē continēbant. Ubi, vīneīs āctīs[8] aggere exstrūctō, turrim[9] procul cōnstituī vīdērunt, prīmum inrīdēre ex mūrō atque increpitāre vōcibus[10] coepērunt, quod tanta māchinātiō ab tantō spatiō[11] īnstruēbātur. Rogāvērunt quibus manibus aut quibus vīribus tantulī[12] hominēs tantam turrim in mūrō[13] conlocāre possent.

---

[1] The Aduatuci lived about the river Mosa (Meuse), in what is now Belgium. [2] *for an aid = to aid.* What use of the case? [3] The reference is to a battle in which the Nervii had been almost annihilated. [4] *this town.* [5] **ex ... partibus,** *from all parts in a circuit = all around.* [6] **prīmō ... nostrī,** *as soon as our army got there.* What literally? [7] **oppidō** = in oppidō. [8] **vīneīs āctīs,** *the vineæ had been brought up.* These vineæ were wooden sheds, open in front and rear, used to protect men who were building an agger, undermining a wall, or filling up a ditch in front of fortifications. They were about eight feet high, of like width, and double that length, covered with raw hides to protect them from being set on fire, and moved on wheels or rollers. [9] **turrim** = turrem. [10] **increpitāre vōcibus,** *taunt.* What literally? [11] **ab tantō spatiō,** *so far away.* [12] To the taller Belgians the Romans looked like "little chaps." [13] The Aduatuci, unacquainted with Roman siege operations, supposed the Romans intended to hoist the tower upon their wall.

THE STORY OF THE ADUATUCI

But they lose confidence and offer to surrender

526. Ubi turrim movērī[1] et appropinquāre mūrīs vīdērunt, novā speciē commōtī, lēgātōs ad Caesarem dē pāce mīsērunt, quī ad hunc modum locūtī[2] sunt: Aduatucōs nōn exīstimāre Rōmānōs sine auxiliō deōrum bellum gerere, quod tantās māchinātiōnēs tantā celeritāte movēre possent; itaque sē suaque omnia eōrum potestātī permissūrōs esse. Ūnum[3] petēbant, nē Caesar sē armīs prīvāret. Omnēs ferē fīnitimī erant inimīcī, ā quibus sē dēfendere armīs trāditīs nōn poterant. Mālēbant quamvīs fortūnam[4] ā populō Rōmānō patī quam ab inimīcīs interficī.

Cæsar says they must disarm, but promises them protection

527. Ad haec Caesar respondit: Magis cōnsuētūdine suā[5] quam meritō eōrum cīvitātem sē cōnservātūrum esse; sed dēditiōnis nūllam esse condiciōnem nisi[6] armīs trāditīs; id quod in[7] Nerviīs fēcisset factūrum esse, et fīnitimīs imperātūrum esse nē iniūriam eīs īnferrent. Rē nūntiātā ad suōs, quae imperārentur sē factūrōs esse dīxērunt. Armōrum tanta multitūdō dē mūrō in fossam quae erat ante oppidum iacta est ut prope summam mūrī aggerisque altitūdinem[8] acervī eōrum adaequārent, et tamen circiter pars tertia, ut posteā cognōvit Caesar, cēlāta[9] atque in oppidō retenta est.

A brave dash for freedom, with a tragic ending

528. Sub vesperum Caesar portās claudī mīlitēsque ex oppidō exīre iussit. Oppidānī, quod dēditiōne factā nostrōs[10] praesidia dēductūrōs crēdiderant, tertiā vigiliā, quā facilis ad nostrās

---

[1] *was moving.* [2] From *loquor.* [3] *one thing,* namely, **nē ... prīvāret.**
[4] **quamvīs fortūnam,** *any fate whatsoever.* [5] *according to his custom.* [6] **nisi** is to be translated with the ablative absolute **armīs trāditīs,** *unless their arms were given up.* [7] *in the case of.* [8] **summam ... altitūdinem,** *top.* [9] Supply **est.** [10] **nostrōs,** *our commanders.*

mūnītiōnēs ascēnsus vidēbātur, omnibus cōpiīs subitō ex oppidō
ēruptiōnem fēcērunt. Celeriter, ut Caesar ante imperāverat,
ignibus[1] signō factō, ex proximīs castellīs eō nostrī properā-
vērunt. Ācriter hostēs pugnābant in extrēmā spē salūtis[2]
5 inīquō locō contrā nostrōs, quī ex vāllō turribusque tēla iacie-
bant. Interfectīs ad[3] hominum mīlibus quattuor, reliquōs in
oppidum nostrī reiēcērunt. Posterō diē, intrōmissīs mīlitibus
nostrīs, sectiōnem eius oppidī ūniversam Caesar vēndidit.[4] Ab
eīs quī ēmerant capitum[5] numerus ad eum relātus est mīlium
10 quīnquāgintā trium.[6]

STORIES OF HERCULES

The infant Hercules

529. Herculēs, Alcmēnae fīlius, ōlim in Graeciā habitābat.
Hīc dīcitur omnium hominum validissimus fuisse. Sed Iūnō,
rēgīna deōrum, Alcmēnam nōn amāvit et Herculem, quī adhūc
īnfāns erat, interficere voluit. Mīsit igitur duo serpentīs sae-
15 vissimōs, quī mediā nocte in cubiculum Alcmēnae vēnērunt,
ubi Herculēs cum frātre dormiēbat. Nōn tamen in cūnīs sed
in scūtō magnō dormiēbant. Serpentēs iam appropinquāverant
et scūtum movēbant. Itaque puerī ē somnō excitātī sunt.

Īphiclēs, frāter Herculis, magnā vōce auxilium petiit; at
20 Herculēs ipse parvīs manibus serpentēs statim prehendit et
colla eōrum magnā vī compressit. Hōc modō serpentēs ā puerō
interfectī sunt. Alcmēna autem, māter puerōrum, clāmōre audītō, marītum ē somnō excitāverat. Ille lūmen accendit et

---

[1] *by fires.* [2] **in . . . salūtis,** *as their last chance of saving themselves.* What literally? [3] *about,* an adverb. [4] **sectiōnem . . . vēndidit,** *Caesar sold the whole town* (the people and their property) *as booty.* [5] *souls.* We say so many "head" of cattle. [6] **relātus . . . trium,** *was reported to be 53,000.* These 53,000 captives were probably driven to the Province or to Italy and sold in lots to suit purchasers, there to wear out their lives in bondage.

WITH THE ROMANS AT THE FRONT

gladium rapuit ad auxilium ferendum; tum ad pueros properāvit, sed, ubi ad locum vēnit, rem mīram vīdit, Herculēs enim rīdēbat et serpentēs interfectōs dēmōnstrābat.

Hercules studies music

530. Herculēs ā puerō (*from boyhood*) corpus dīligenter exercēbat; magnam partem diēī in palaestrā cōnsūmēbat; didicit etiam arcum intendere et tēla conicere. Hīs exercitātiōnibus vīrēs eius cōnfirmātae sunt. In mūsicā ā Linō centaurō ērudiēbātur. Hī centaurī equī erant, sed caput hominis habēbant. Huic artī nōn dīligenter Herculēs studēbat. Hāc rē cognitā, Linus puerum reprehendēbat, quod nōn studiōsus erat. Tum Herculēs, īrā commōtus, citharam subitō rapuit, et omnibus vīribus caput magistrī īnfēlīcis percussit.[1] Ille ictū prōstrātus[2] est, et paulō post ē vītā excessit, neque quisquam posteā id officium suscipere voluit.

Hercules consults the oracle

531. Herculēs post paucōs annōs cōnstituit ad ōrāculum Delphicum īre, hoc enim ōrāculum erat omnium celeberrimum. Ibi templum erat Apollinis plūrimīs dōnīs ōrnātum. Hōc in templō sedēbat fēmina quaedam, Pȳthia, et cōnsilium dabat iīs quī ad ōrāculum veniēbant. Haec autem fēmina ab ipsō Apolline docēbātur et voluntātem deī hominibus ēnūntiābat. Herculēs igitur, quī Apollinem maximē colēbat, hūc vēnit. Pȳthia iussit eum ad urbem Tīryntha īre et Eurysthei rēgis omnia imperāta facere. Hīs audītīs, Herculēs ad illam urbem contendit, et Eurystheō rēgī sē in servitūtem trādidit. Duodecim annōs in servitūte Eurysthei tenēbātur, et duodecim labōrēs quōs ille imperāverat cōnfēcit, hōc enim ūnō modō tantum scelus[3] expiārī potuit. Dē hīs labōribus plūrima ā poētīs scrīpta sunt. Multa tamen quae poētae nārrant vix crēdibilia sunt.

[1] From **percutiō**.   [2] From **prōsternō**.   [3] The murdering of his own children.

The golden apples of the Hesperides

532. Eurystheus labōrem ūndecimum Herculī imposuit graviōrem quam eōs quōs anteā imperāverat. Imperāvit enim eī ut aurea pōma ex hortō Hesperidum ferret. Hesperidēs autem nymphae erant quaedam pulcherrimae, quae in terrā longinquā habitābant et quibus aurea quaedam pōma ā Iūnōne commissa erant. Multī hominēs, aurī cupiditāte inductī, haec pōma auferre iam anteā cōnātī erant. Rēs tamen difficillima erat, nam hortus in quō pōma erant mūrō ingentī undique circumdatus est; praetereā dracō quīdam, quī centum capita habuit, portam hortī dīligenter custōdiēbat. Opus igitur quod Eurystheus Herculī imperāverat erat difficillimum, nōn sōlum ob causās quās memorāvimus, sed etiam quod Herculēs omnīnō ignōrābat quō in locō hortus situs esset.

Atlas, who upheld the heavens

533. Herculēs quiētem vehementer cupiēbat, sed cōnstituit Eurystheō pārēre; et, cum iussa eius accēpisset, proficīscī mātūrāvit. Ā multīs mercātōribus quaesīvit quō in locō Hesperidēs habitārent; nihil tamen certum reperīre potuit. Frūstrā per multās terrās iter fēcit et multa perīcula subiit. Tandem, cum in hīs itineribus tōtum annum cōnsūmpsisset, ad extrēmam partem orbis, quae proxima erat Ōceanō, pervēnit. Hīc stābat vir quīdam, nōmine Atlās, quī caelum umerīs sustinēbat, nē in terram dēcideret. Herculēs, tantum labōrem magnopere mīrātus, paulō post in conloquium cum Atlante vēnit, et, cum causam itineris docuisset, auxilium ab eō petiit.

Hercules takes the place of Atlas

534. Atlās autem potuit Herculem maximē iuvāre, ille enim erat pater Hesperidum et bene scīvit quō in locō esset hortus. Cum igitur audīvisset quam ob causam Herculēs vēnisset, dīxit:

"Ipse ad hortum ībō, et fīliābus[1] meīs persuādēbō ut pōma suā sponte[2] trādant." Herculēs, cum haec audīvisset, magnopere gāvīsus est,[3] nōluit enim vim adhibēre; cōnstituit igitur oblātum[4] auxilium accipere. Atlās tamen postulāvit ut, dum ipse abesset (*while he was himself away*), Herculēs caelum umerīs sustinē- ret. Hoc negōtium Herculēs libenter suscēpit et, quamquam rēs difficillima erat, tōtum pondus caelī continuōs complūrīs diēs sōlus sustinuit.

The return of Atlas

535. Atlās intereā abierat[5] et ad hortum Hesperidum, quī pauca mīlia passuum aberat, sē quam celerrimē[6] contulerat. Eō cum vēnisset, causam veniendī exposuit et fīliās vehementer hortātus est ut pōma trāderent. Illae diū haerēbant, nōlēbant enim hoc facere, quod ab ipsā Iūnōne, ut ante dictum est, hoc mūnus accēperant. Atlās tamen post multa verba eīs persuāsit ut sibi[7] pārērent, et pōma ad Herculem rettulit. Herculēs intereā, cum plūrīs diēs exspectāvisset, neque ūllam fāmam dē reditū Atlantis accēpisset, hāc morā graviter commōtus est. Tandem quīntō diē Atlantem redeuntem[8] vīdit et mox magnō cum gaudiō pōma accēpit; tum, postquam grātiās prō tantō beneficiō ēgit, in Graeciam proficīscī mātūrāvit.

Nessus, the Centaur

536. Post haec Herculēs multa alia praeclāra perfēcit, quae nunc perscrībere[9] longum est.[10] Tandem aetāte prōvectus[11]

---

[1] The ending -ābus is regularly used for the dative and ablative plural of dea and of fīlia.   [2] **suā sponte**, *of their own accord*.   [3] **gāvīsus est**, from gaudeō, which is deponent in the perfect system.   [4] From offerō.   [5] From abeō. From what verb does aberat come?   [6] **quam celerrimē**, *as quickly as possible*. Quam with a superlative usually has the force *as ... as possible* (see p. 185, note 1).   [7] **sibi** is an indirect reflexive here, and refers to the subject of persuāsit rather than to that of pārērent.   [8] Present participle of redeō.   [9] See 393.   [10] **longum est**, *it would be tedious*. What is the subject of est?   [11] From prōvehō. How translated?

Dēianīram, Oeneī fīliam, in mātrimōnium dūxit[1]; post tamen trēs annōs puerum quendam, nōmine[2] Eunomum, cāsū interfēcit. Itaque cum uxōre ē fīnibus eius cīvitātis exīre mātūrāvit. Dum tamen iter faciunt, ad flūmen quoddam pervēnērunt,
5 quod nūllō ponte iūnctum erat, et, dum quaerunt quō modō flūmen trāicerent, accurrit centaurus quīdam, nōmine Nessus, quī auxilium viātōribus obtulit. Herculēs igitur uxōrem in tergum Nessī imposuit; tum ipse flūmen nandō[3] trānsiit, quā flūmen angustissimum erat. At Nessus, paulum in aquam
10 prōgressus, ad rīpam subitō revertit et Dēianīram auferre cōnābātur. Quod cum animadvertisset[4] Herculēs, īrā graviter commōtus, arcum intendit et pectus Nessī sagittā trānsfīxit.

The poisoned robe

537. Nessus igitur sagittā Herculis trānsfīxus humī (*on the ground*) iacēbat; at, nē occāsiōnem suī ulcīscendī dīmitteret,
15 ita locūtus est: "Sī vīs amōrem marītī tuī cōnservāre, aliquid huius sanguinis, quī ē pectore meō effunditur, sūmēs et repōnēs. Tum sī quandō suspīciō in mentem tuam vēnerit,[5] vestem marītī hōc sanguine īnficiēs." Haec locūtus, Nessus animam efflāvit; Dēianīra autem, nihil malī[6] suspicāta, imperāta fēcit.
20 Post breve tempus Herculēs bellum contrā Eurytum, rēgem propinquum, suscēpit et, cum rēgem ipsum cum fīliīs interfēcisset, Iolēn, fīliam Eurytī, captīvam redūxit. Antequam tamen domum vēnit, nāvem ad Cēnaeum prōmunturium appulit et, in terram ēgressus, āram cōnstituit, ut Iovī sacrificāret. Dum
25 tamen sacrificium parat, Licham, comitem suum, domum mīsit

---

[1] **in mātrimōnium dūxit,** *married.* How literally? [2] See 481. [3] From nō; *by swimming*; see 460. [4] **quod cum animadvertisset,** *when he had noticed this*; refers to the whole preceding sentence. Quod referring to a preceding sentence is commonly translated by a personal or a demonstrative pronoun. [5] **vēnerit,** *shall have come;* but it is better translated *comes.* [6] Partitive genitive with **nihil;** *nothing of evil* = *no evil.*

ut vestem albam referret; mōs enim erat apud antīquōs vestem albam gerere[1] cum sacrificia facerent. At Dēïanīra, verita[2] Iolēn, vestem, priusquam Lichae dedit, sanguine Nessī īnfēcit.

The death of Hercules

538. Herculēs, nihil malī suspicātus, vestem quam Lichās attulit statim induit; post tamen breve tempus dolōrem per 5 omnia membra sēnsit, et quae causa eius reī esset magnopere mīrābātur. Dolōre paene exanimātus vestem dētrahere cōnātus est; illa tamen in corpore haesit neque ūllō modō dīvellī potuit. Tum dēmum Herculēs, quasi furōre impulsus, in montem Oetam sē contulit et in rogum, quem summā celeritāte ex- 10 strūxerat, sē imposuit. Quod cum fēcisset, eōs quī circumstābant ōrāvit ut rogum quam celerrimē accenderent. Omnēs diū recūsābant; tandem tamen pāstor quīdam, ad misericordiam inductus, ignem subdidit. Tum, dum omnia fūmō obscūrantur, Herculēs dēnsā nūbe vēlātus ā Iove in Olympum abreptus est. 15

STORIES OF ULYSSES

Polyphemus, the one-eyed giant

539. Ulixēs comitēsque, postquam tōtam noctem rēmīs contenderant, ad terram ignōtam nāvem appulērunt; tum, quod nātūram eius regiōnis ignōrābat, ipse Ulixēs, cum duodecim ē sociīs in terram ēgressus, locum explōrāre cōnstituit. Paulum ā lītore prōgressī, ad antrum ingēns pervēnērunt, quod habitārī 20 sēnsērunt, eius enim introitum arte et manibus[3] mūnītum esse animadvertērunt. Mox, etsī intellegēbant sē nōn sine perīculō id factūrōs esse, antrum intrāvērunt. Quod cum fēcissent,

---

[1] **gerere**, *to wear*; subject of **erat**. [2] **verita**, *fearing*; the perfect participle of some deponent verbs is often translated like a present participle. [3] **arte et manibus**, *by skill and hands* = *by skillful hands*.

magnam cōpiam lactis invēnērunt in vāsīs ingentibus conditam. Dum tamen mīrantur quis eam sēdem incoleret, sonitum terribilem audīvērunt, et oculīs ad portam versīs, mōnstrum horribile vīdērunt, quod hūmānam speciem et figūram sed corpus
5 ingēns habuit. Cum autem animadvertissent gigantem ūnum tantum[1] oculum habēre in mediā fronte positum, intellēxērunt hunc esse ūnum ē Cyclōpibus, dē quibus fāmam iam accēperant.

The giant's supper

540. Cyclōpēs autem pāstōrēs erant quīdam, quī īnsulam Siciliam et praecipuē montem Aetnam incolēbant; ibi enim
10 Vulcānus, praeses fabrōrum et ignis repertor, cuius servī Cyclōpēs erant, officīnam habēbat. Graecī igitur, simul ac mōnstrum vīdērunt, terrōre paene exanimātī, in interiōrem partem spēluncae refūgērunt et sē ibi cēlāre cōnābantur. Polyphēmus autem (ita enim gigās appellātus est) pecora sua in spēluncam
15 ēgit; tum, cum saxō ingentī portam obstrūxisset, ignem mediō in antrō accendit. Hōc factō, omnia oculō perlūstrābat, et cum sēnsisset hominēs in interiōre parte antrī cēlārī, magnā vōce exclāmāvit: " Quī estis hominēs? Mercātōrēs an latrōnēs?" Tum Ulixēs respondit sē neque mercātōrēs esse neque
20 praedandī causā vēnisse, sed ā Trōiā redeuntēs,[2] vī tempestātum ā rēctō cursū dēpulsōs esse; ōrāvit etiam ut sē sine iniūriā dīmitteret. Tum Polyphēmus quaesīvit ubi nāvis eōrum esset. Ulixēs autem respondit nāvem in rūpēs coniectam et omnīnō perfrāctam[3] esse. Polyphēmus, nūllō respōnsō datō, duo ē
25 sociīs manū corripuit et membrīs eōrum dīvulsīs[4] carnem[5] dēvorāre coepit.

[1] **tantum,** *only.* [2] Modifies **sē** understood from the preceding clause; *that they, while returning.* [3] From **perfringō.** [4] From **dīvellō.** [5] From **carō.**

No way of escape

541. Dum haec geruntur, Graecōrum animōs tantus terror occupāvit ut nē vōcem quidem ēdere possent, sed, omnī spē salūtis dēpositā, mortem praesentem exspectārent. At Polyphēmus, postquam famēs hāc tam horribilī cēnā dēpulsa est, humī (*on the ground*) prōstrātus somnō sē dedit. Quod cum vīdisset Ulixēs, arbitrātus est mōnstrum interficiendum esse. Prīmum cōnstituit explōrāre quā ratiōne ex antrō ēvādere possent. At, cum saxum animadvertisset quō introitus obstrūctus erat, intellēxit mortem Polyphēmī auxiliō sibi nōn futūram esse. Tanta enim erat eius saxī magnitūdō ut nē ā decem quidem hominibus āmovērī posset. Ulixēs igitur hōc cōnātū dēstitit et ad sociōs rediit; quī, cum intellēxissent quō in locō[1] rēs esset, nūllā spē salūtis oblātā, dē fortūnīs suīs dēspērāre coepērunt. Ille tamen vehementer hortātus est nē animōs dēmitterent,[2] et dēmōnstrāvit sē ipsōs iam anteā ē multīs et magnīs perīculīs ēvāsisse.

A plan for vengeance

542. Ortā lūce[3] Polyphēmus, iam ē somnō excitātus, idem quod[4] hesternō diē fēcit, correptīs enim duōbus ē reliquīs virīs carnem eōrum sine morā dēvorāvit. Tum, cum saxum āmōvisset, ipse cum pecore ex antrō prōgressus est. Quod cum vidērent Graecī, magnam in spem vēnērunt[5] sē post paulum ēvāsūrōs. Mox tamen ab hāc spē repulsī sunt, nam Polyphēmus, postquam omnēs ovēs exiērunt, saxum in locum restituit. Graecī, omnī spē salūtis dēpositā, lāmentīs lacrimīsque sē dēdidērunt. Ulixēs vērō, quī, ut suprā dēmōnstrāvimus, vir

---

[1] locō, *state, condition*, not *place*. [2] nē ... dēmitterent, *not to lose heart.* [3] ortā lūce = prīmā lūce, *at daybreak*; ortā is from orior. [4] idem quod, *the same as.* [5] magnam ... vēnērunt, *had great hopes.*

fortis fuit, etsī bene intellegēbat rem in discrīmine esse, nōndum omnīnō dēspērābat. Tandem, postquam diū tōtō animō cōgitāvit, hoc cēpit cōnsilium. Ē lignīs quae in antrō reposita sunt pālum magnum dēlēgit; hunc summā cum dīligentiā
5 praeacūtum fēcit; tum, postquam sociīs quid[1] fierī vellet ostendit, reditum Polyphēmī exspectābat.

Polyphemus thrice drains a wine bowl

543. Sub vesperum Polyphēmus ad antrum rediit et eōdem modō quō anteā cēnāvit. Tum Ulixēs ūtrem vīnī prōmpsit,[2] quem forte, ut in tālibus rēbus saepe accidit, sēcum attu-
10 lerat, et postquam magnam crātēram vīnō replēvit, gigantem ad bibendum prōvocāvit. Polyphēmus, quī numquam anteā vīnum gustāverat, tōtam crātēram statim hausit.[3] Quod cum fēcisset, tantam voluptātem percēpit ut iterum et tertium crātēram replērī iubēret. Tum, cum quaesīvisset quō nōmine
15 Ulixēs appellārētur, ille respondit sē Nēminem[4] appellārī. Quod cum audīvisset Polyphēmus, ita locūtus est: "Ut tibi grātiam prō tantō beneficiō referam, tē ultimum omnium dēvorābō." Hīs dictīs, cibō vīnōque gravātus recubuit[5] et post breve tempus somnō oppressus est. Tum Ulixēs, sociīs convocā-
20 tīs, dīxit: "Habēmus quam petiimus facultātem.[6] Tanta occāsiō nōn omittenda est."

Noman

544. Hāc ōrātiōne habitā, postquam extrēmum pālum[7] ignī calefēcit, oculum Polyphēmī, dum dormit, flagrante lignō trānsfōdit. Quō factō, omnēs in dīversās spēluncae partīs sē abdi-
25 dērunt. At ille subitō illō dolōre, quod necesse fuit,[8] ē somnō

---

[1] In what case is quid? [2] From prōmō. [3] From hauriō. [4] *Noman.*
[5] From recumbō. [6] quam . . . facultātem = facultātem quam petiimus.
[7] extrēmum pālum = extrēmam partem pālī. [8] quod necesse fuit, *which was necessary = necessarily*; the reference is to what follows.

STORIES OF ULYSSES

excitātus, clāmōrem terribilem sustulit,[1] et dum per spēluncam errat, Ulixī manum inicere cōnābātur. Hoc tamen, quod iam omnīnō caecus erat, nūllō modō efficere potuit. Intereā reliquī Cyclōpēs, clāmōre audītō, undique ad spēluncam convēnērunt, et apud introitum adstantēs, quid Polyphēmus ageret[2] quaesīvērunt et quam ob causam tantum clāmōrem sustulisset. Ille respondit sē graviter vulnerātum esse et magnō dolōre adficī. Cum tamen cēterī quaesīvissent quis eī[3] vim intulisset, respondit ille Nēminem id fēcisse. Hōc audītō, Cyclōpēs, eum in īnsāniam incidisse arbitrātī,[4] abiērunt.

The escape

545. Sed Polyphēmus, cum sociōs suōs abiisse sēnsisset, furōre atque āmentiā impulsus, Ulixem iterum quaerere coepit. Tandem cum portam invēnisset, saxum quō obstrūcta[5] erat āmōvit, ut pecus ad agrōs exīret. Tum ipse in introitū sēdit, et cum quaeque ovis ad locum vēnerat, tergum eius manibus tractābat, nē virī inter ovēs exīre possent. Quod cum animadvertisset Ulixēs, hoc cōnsilium iniit, bene enim intellēxit omnem spem salūtis iam in dolō magis quam in virtūte pōnī. Prīmum trēs quās vīdit pinguissimās ex ovibus dēlēgit.. Quibus inter sē[6] vīminibus cōnexīs,[7] ūnum ex sociīs ventribus eōrum ita subiēcit ut omnīnō latēret; deinde ovīs hominem sēcum ferentēs ad portam ēgit. Id accidit quod fore[8] suspicātus erat. Polyphēmus enim, postquam manūs tergīs eōrum imposuit, ovīs praeterīre passus[9] est. Ulixēs, postquam rem fēlīciter ēvēnisse vīdit, omnēs sociōs suōs ex ōrdine eōdem modō ēmīsit; quō factō, ipse ultimus ēvāsit.

---

[1] From **tollō**. [2] **quid ... ageret**, *what Polyphemus was doing = what ailed Polyphemus*. [3] Which usage of the dative? [4] Translate as if it were a present participle. See p. 213, note 2. [5] The subject is **porta**. [6] **inter sē**, *together*. [7] From **cōnectō**. [8] **fore** = **futūrum esse**, *would be, would happen*. [9] From **patior**.

Out of danger

546. His rēbus ita cōnfectīs, Ulixēs cum sociīs quam celerrimē ad lītus contendit. Quō[1] cum vēnissent, ab eīs quī praesidiō nāvī relictī erant magnā cum laetitiā acceptī sunt. Hī enim, cum iam anxiīs animīs trēs diēs reditum eōrum in
5 hōrās[2] exspectāvissent, eōs in perīculum grave incidisse suspicātī, ipsī auxiliandī causā ēgredī parābant. Tum Ulixēs, nōn satis tūtum esse arbitrātus in eō locō manēre, quam celerrimē proficīscī cōnstituit. Iussit igitur omnēs nāvem cōnscendere, et, ancorīs sublātīs, paulum ā lītore in altum prōvectus est. Tum
10 magnā vōce exclāmāvit: "Tū, Polyphēme,[3] quī iūra hospitī spernis, iūstam et dēbitam poenam immānitātis tuae solvistī." Hāc vōce audītā, Polyphēmus, īrā vehementer commōtus, ad mare sē contulit, et ubi intellēxit nāvem paulum ā lītore remōtam esse, saxum ingēns correptum in eam partem coniēcit unde
15 vōcem venīre sēnsit. Graecī autem, nūllō damnō acceptō, cursum tenuērunt.

EUTROPIUS: HISTORY OF ROME[4]

The founding of Rome by Romulus

547. Rōmānum imperium[5] ā Rōmulō initium habet, quī Rhēae Silviae fīlius et Mārtis erat. Is decem et octō annōs nātus urbem parvam in Palātīnō monte[6] cōnstituit. Conditā
20 cīvitāte, quam ex nōmine suō Rōmam vocāvit, haec ferē ēgit.[7] Multitūdinem fīnitimōrum in cīvitātem recēpit, centum ex seniōribus[8] lēgit, quōrum cōnsiliō omnia agēbat, quōs senātōrēs

---

[1] **quō**, *thither*; begin to translate with **cum**. [2] **in hōrās**, *hourly*. [3] Vocative case, denoting the person addressed. [4] Eutropius, a Roman historian of the fourth century of our era, wrote a brief history of Rome from its founding to the year 364. [5] **imperium**, *power, state*. [6] **Palātīnō monte**, *the Palatine Hill*, one of the seven hills on which Rome was built. [7] **haec ferē ēgit**, *he did about as follows.* [8] **seniōribus**, *older men*; comparative of **senex**, *old*.

nōmināvit propter senectūtem. Tum, cum uxōrēs ipse et populus suus nōn habērent,[1] invītāvit ad spectāculum lūdōrum vīcīnās urbī Rōmae nātiōnēs atque eārum virginēs rapuit. Commōtīs bellīs propter raptārum[2] iniūriam Caenīnēnsēs vīcit, Antemnātēs, Crustumīnōs, Sabīnōs,[3] Fīdēnātēs, Vēientēs. Haec omnia oppida urbem cingunt. Et cum, ortā subitō tempestāte, nōn compāruisset,[4] annō rēgnī trīcēsimō septimō ad deōs trānsīsse crēditus est et cōnsecrātus.[5]

The kings who succeeded Romulus

548. Posteā Numa Pompilius rēx creātus est, quī bellum quidem nūllum gessit, sed nōn minus cīvitātī[6] quam Rōmulus prōfuit. Nam et lēgēs Rōmānīs mōrēsque cōnstituit et annum dēscrīpsit in decem mēnsēs, et īnfīnīta sacra ac templa cōnstituit.

Huic successit Tullus Hostīlius. Hic bella reparāvit, Albānōs vīcit; Vēientēs et Fīdēnātēs bellō superāvit; urbem ampliāvit adiectō Caeliō monte.[7]

Post hunc Ancus Mārcius suscēpit imperium. Contrā Latīnōs dīmicāvit, Aventīnum montem cīvitātī adiēcit et Iāniculum; apud ōstium Tiberis cīvitātem condidit.

Deinde rēgnum Prīscus Tarquinius accēpit. Hic numerum senātōrum duplicāvit, circum[8] Rōmae[9] aedificāvit, lūdōs Rōmānōs[10] īnstituit, quī ad nostram memoriam permanent. Vīcit īdem etiam Sabīnōs et nōn parum[11] agrōrum urbis Rōmae territōriō iūnxit, prīmusque triumphāns urbem intrāvit. Mūrōs fēcit et cloācās, Capitōlium incohāvit.

[1] **cum ... habērent**, *because ... had.* A causal clause introduced by **cum**, *because, as, since*, has its verb in the subjunctive mood. [2] Understand **virginum**. [3] In apposition with **Caenīnēnsēs**, **Antemnātēs**, and **Crustumīnōs**. Fidenæ and Veii were Etruscan towns. [4] **nōn compāruisset**, *had disappeared.* [5] **cōnsecrātus (est)**, *was deified.* [6] Which use of the dative? [7] **adiectō Caeliō monte**, *by the addition of the Cælian Hill.* [8] **circum**, the Circus Maximus, where races and other sports were held. [9] **Rōmae**, *at Rome.* [10] The **lūdī Rōmānī** consisted of a variety of games and contests held each year in September in the Circus Maximus. [11] **nōn parum**, *not a little*; **parum** is here used as a noun.

Post hunc Servius Tullius suscēpit imperium. Hic quoque Sabīnōs subēgit, montēs trēs, Quirīnālem, Vīminālem, Ēsquilīnum, urbī adiūnxit, fossās circum mūrum dūxit. Prīmus omnium cēnsum ōrdināvit, quī adhūc per orbem terrārum incognitus erat. Sub eō Rōma, omnibus in cēnsum dēlātis,[1] habuit capita[2] LXXXIII mīlia cīvium Rōmānōrum cum hīs quī in agrīs erant.

Tarquinius Superbus, septimus atque ultimus rēgum, Volscōs, quae gēns ad Campāniam euntibus[3] nōn longē ab urbe est, vīcit, Gabiōs cīvitātem[4] et Suessam Pōmētiam subēgit, cum Tuscīs pācem fēcit et templum Iovī in Capitōliō[5] aedificāvit. Posteā Ardeam oppugnāns imperium perdidit[6]; cumque imperāvisset annōs quattuor et vīgintī, cum uxōre et līberīs suīs fūgit.

The first consuls

549. Hinc cōnsulēs coepērunt, prō ūnō rēge duo, hāc causā creātī, ut, sī ūnus malus esse voluisset,[7] alter eum habēns potestātem similem coercēret. Et placuit[8] nē imperium longius quam annum habērent, nē per diūturnitātem potestātis insolentiōrēs redderentur. Fuērunt igitur annō prīmō ab expulsīs rēgibus cōnsulēs Iūnius Brūtus et Tarquinius Collātīnus. Sed Tarquiniō Collātīnō statim sublāta est dignitās. Placuerat[9] enim nē quisquam in urbe manēret quī Tarquinius vocārētur. Ergō, acceptō omnī patrimōniō suō, ex urbe migrāvit, et locō ipsīus[10] factus est L. Valerius Pūblicola cōnsul.

[1] **omnibus...dēlātīs,** *when all had been enumerated.* [2] See p. 208, note 5.
[3] **ad Campāniam euntibus,** *to those going toward Campania, in the direction of Campania;* **euntibus** is a dative of reference. [4] **Gabiōs cīvitātem,** *the city* (or *community*) *of Gabii.* [5] **in Capitōliō,** *on the Capitoline Hill.* [6] A crime committed by a son of Tarquinius aroused such indignation that Tarquinius and his family were obliged to leave Rome. [7] **sī...voluisset,** *if one of the consuls were inclined to be troublesome;* **voluisset** is attracted into the subjunctive mood, because it depends on a clause the verb of which is in the subjunctive. [8] **placuit,** *it was decided.* The subject is the clause **nē...habērent.**
[9] **placuerat,** *it had been decided.* [10] **locō ipsīus,** *in his place.*

Wars against the Tarquins

550. Commōvit tamen bellum urbī Rōmae rēx Tarquinius, quī fuerat expulsus, et, collēctīs multīs gentibus, ut in rēgnum posset restituī, dīmicāvit. In prīmā pugnā Brūtus cōnsul et Arrūns, Tarquinī fīlius, invicem sē occīdērunt,[1] Rōmānī tamen ex eā pugnā victōrēs recessērunt. Brūtum mātrōnae Rōmānae quasi commūnem patrem per annum lūxērunt.[2]

Secundō quoque annō iterum Tarquinius, ut reciperētur in rēgnum, bellum Rōmānīs[3] intulit, auxilium[4] eī ferente Porsenā,[5] Tusciae rēge, et Rōmam paene cēpit. Vērum tum quoque victus est.

Tertiō annō post rēgēs exāctōs Tarquinius, cum suscipī nōn posset in rēgnum neque eī Porsena, quī pācem cum Rōmānīs fēcerat, praestāret auxilium, Tusculum sē contulit, quae cīvitās nōn longē ab urbe est, atque ibi per quattuordecim annōs prīvātus incoluit.

Pyrrhus and the Romans

551. Eōdem tempore Tarentīnīs, quī iam in ultimā Italiā sunt, bellum indictum est, quod lēgātīs Rōmānōrum iniūriam fēcerant. Hī Pyrrhum, Ēpīrī rēgem, contrā Rōmānōs in auxilium poposcērunt.[6] Is mox ad Italiam vēnit, tumque prīmum Rōmānī cum trānsmarīnō hoste dīmicāvērunt. Missus est contrā eum cōnsul P. Valerius Laevīnus, quī cum explōrātōrēs Pyrrhī cēpisset, iussit eōs per castra dūcī, ostendī omnem exercitum, tumque dīmittī, ut renūntiārent Pyrrhō quae ā Rōmānīs agerentur. Commissā mox pugnā, cum iam Pyrrhus fugeret, elephantōrum auxiliō vīcit, quōs incognitōs[7] Rōmānī timuērunt. Sed nox proeliō fīnem dedit; Laevīnus tamen per noctem fūgit, Pyrrhus Rōmānōs mīlle octingentōs cēpit et eōs

---

[1] **invicem sē occīdērunt,** *killed each other.* [2] From **lūgeō.** [3] Which usage of the dative? [4] **auxilium**, object of **ferente.** [5] **ferente Porsenā**, ablative absolute. [6] From **poscō.** [7] Translate so as to show cause.

summō honōre trāctāvit, occīsōs sepelīvit. Quōs cum adversō vulnere[1] et trucī vultū[1] etiam mortuōs iacēre vīdisset, tulisse ad caelum manūs dīcitur cum hāc vōce: Sē tōtīus orbis dominum esse potuisse, sī tālēs sibi mīlitēs contigissent.[2]

Posteā Pyrrhus, coniūnctīs sibi Samnītibus, Lūcānīs, Bruttiīs, Rōmam perrēxit,[3] omnia ferrō ignīque vāstāvit, Campāniam populātus est, et ad Praeneste vēnit. Mox terrōre exercitūs, quī eum cum cōnsule sequēbātur, in Campāniam sē recēpit. Lēgātī ad Pyrrhum dē redimendīs captīvīs missī ab eō bene receptī sunt. Captīvōs sine pretiō Rōmam mīsit. Ūnum ex lēgātīs Rōmānōrum, Fabricium, sīc admīrātus, cum eum pauperem esse cognōvisset, ut quārtā parte rēgnī prōmissā[4] sollicitāre voluerit[5] ut ad sē trānsīret, contemptusque[6] est ā Fabriciō. Quārē cum Pyrrhus Rōmānōrum ingentī admīrātiōne tenērētur,[7] lēgātum mīsit, ut pācem aequīs condiciōnibus peteret, praecipuum virum, Cīneam nōmine, ita ut Pyrrhus partem Italiae quam iam armīs occupāverat obtinēret.

Pāx displicuit remandātumque Pyrrhō est[8] ā senātū eum cum Rōmānīs, nisi ex Italiā recessisset, pācem habēre nōn posse. Ita lēgātus Pyrrhī reversus est. Ā quō cum quaereret Pyrrhus quālem Rōmam[9] comperisset, Cīneās dīxit rēgum sē patriam vīdisse: tālēs illīc ferē omnēs esse, quālis ūnus Pyrrhus apud Ēpīrum[10] et reliquam Graeciam putārētur.

Missī sunt contrā Pyrrhum ducēs P. Sulpicius et Decius Mūs cōnsulēs. Certāmine commissō Pyrrhus vulnerātus est,

---

[1] **adversō vulnere** and **trucī vultū** are descriptive ablatives. Translate, *when he saw these men lying with wounds on the front of their bodies and with stern expressions on their faces even in death.* [2] *if it had been his lot to have such soldiers.* [3] From **pergō**. [4] **quārtā ... prōmissā**, *by the offer of a fourth of his kingdom.* [5] The perfect subjunctive is often used in result clauses in secondary sequence. [6] From **contemnō**. [7] **cum ... tenērētur**, *since Pyrrhus felt great admiration for the Romans.* How literally? The clause is causal. [8] **remandātum ... est**, *word was sent back to Pyrrhus that*, etc. [9] **quālem Rōmam**, *what sort of city he had found Rome to be.* [10] **apud Ēpīrum**, *in Epirus.*

elephantī interfectī, vīgintī mīlia caesa[1] hostium, et ex Rōmānīs tantum quīnque mīlia; Pyrrhus Tarentum fugātus.[2]

Interiectō annō contrā Pyrrhum Fabricius est missus, quī prius inter lēgātōs sollicitārī nōn poterat, quārtā rēgnī parte prōmissā. Tum, cum vīcīna castra ipse et rēx habērent, medi- 5 cus Pyrrhī nocte ad eum vēnit, prōmittēns venēnō sē Pyrrhum occīsūrum, sī sibi aliquid pollicērētur.[3] Quem Fabricius vīnctum redūcī iussit ad dominum Pyrrhōque dīcī quae contrā caput eius medicus spopondisset.[4] Tum rēx admīrātus eum dīxisse fertur[5]: "Ille est Fabricius quī difficilius ab honestāte quam 10 sōl ā cursū suō āvertī potest." Tum rēx in Siciliam profectus est.

Cōnsulēs deinde M. Curius Dentātus et Cornēlius Lentulus adversus Pyrrhum missī sunt. Curius contrā eum pugnāvit, exercitum eius cecīdit,[6] ipsum Tarentum fugāvit, castra cēpit. 15 Eō diē caesa hostium vīgintī tria mīlia. Curius in cōnsulātū triumphāvit. Prīmus Rōmam elephantōs quattuor dūxit. Pyrrhus etiam ā Tarentō mox recessit et apud Argōs, Graeciae cīvitātem, occīsus est.

STORIES FROM ROMAN HISTORY

The brave deed of Horatius Cocles

552. Porsena, rēx Etrūscōrum, ad restituendōs Tarquiniōs 20 cum īnfestō exercitū vēnit. Prīmō impetū Iāniculum cēpit. Nōn umquam aliās ante tantus terror Rōmānōs invāserat; ex agrīs in urbem dēmigrant; urbem ipsam saepiunt praesidiīs. Alia pars urbis mūrīs,[7] alia Tiberī obiectō[8] tūta vidēbātur.[9] Pōns Sublicius iter paene hostibus dedit. Ūnus vir autem erat, 25

---

[1] From **caedō**. [2] Supply **est**. [3] **sī ... pollicērētur**, *if some reward were promised to him*. [4] From **spondeō**. [5] **fertur**, *is reported*. [6] From **caedō**.
[7] **mūrīs**, *by reason of its walls*. [8] **Tiberī obiectō**, *by the interposed Tiber = by the Tiber's being between*. [9] **vidēbātur**, *seemed*.

Horātius Cocles, illō cognōmine appellātus quod in aliō proeliō oculum āmīserat. Is, extrēmā pontis parte occupātā, aciem hostium solus sustinuit. Intereā pōns ā tergō interrumpēbātur. Ipsa audācia obstupefēcit hostis; ponte rescissō,[1] armātus in
5 Tiberim dēsiluit et, multīs superincidentibus tēlīs, incolumis ad suōs trānāvit. Ob virtūtem Horātiō cīvitās grātiam solvit[2]: eī tantum agrī pūblicē datum est quantum[3] ūnō diē circumarāre potuit. Statua quoque eī in Comitiō posita est.

The fortitude of Mucius

553. Cum Porsena Rōmam obsidēret, Mūcius senātum adiit
10 et veniam trānsfugiendī[4] petiit, necem rēgis reprōmittēns. Acceptā potestāte, in castra Porsenae vēnit. Ibi in cōnfertissimā turbā prope rēgium tribūnal cōnstitit. Stīpendium tunc forte mīlitibus dabātur, et proximus rēgī erat scrība, quī similem vestem gerēbat. Mūcius, ignōrāns uter rēx esset, scrībam prō
15 rēge occīdit. Apprehēnsus et ad rēgem pertrāctus,[5] dextram accēnsō[6] ad sacrificium foculō iniēcit, velut manum pūniēns. Attonitus mīrāculō, rēx iuvenem āmovērī ab altāribus iussit. Tum Mūcius, quasi beneficium remūnerāns, dīxit trecentōs[7] sibi similīs adversus eum coniūrāvisse. Quā rē ille territus,
20 bellum acceptīs obsidibus dēposuit.

Clœlia, the hostage, escapes

554. Porsena Cloeliam, virginem nōbilem, inter obsidēs accēperat. Castra Porsenae haud procul ab rīpā Tiberis locāta erant. Cloelia, dēceptīs custōdibus, nocte castrīs ēgressa, equō quem fors dederat arreptō,[8] Tiberim trāiēcit. Quod ubi rēgī
25 nūntiātum est, prīmō incēnsus īrā, Rōmam lēgātōs mīsit ad

---

[1] From **rescindō**. [2] **grātiam solvit**, *showed its gratitude*. [3] **tantum ... quantum**, *as much ... as*. [4] **veniam trānsfugiendī**, *favor of deserting* = *permission to desert*. [5] From **pertrahō**. [6] From **accendō**; order: **foculō accēnsō ad sacrificium**. [7] **trecentōs**, *three hundred*; subject of **coniūrāvisse**. [8] **equō ... arreptō**, *seizing a horse*; **arreptō** is from **arripiō**.

STORIES FROM ROMAN HISTORY

Cloeliam obsidem reposcendam. Rōmānī eam* ex foedere restituērunt. Tum rēx virginis virtūtem admīrātus[1] eam laudāvit ac partem obsidum eī datūrum esse sē dīxit, permīsitque ut ipsa obsidēs legeret. Prōductīs obsidibus, Cloelia virginēs puerōsque ēlēgit, quōrum aetātem iniūriae obnoxiam[2] sciēbat, et cum eīs in patriam rediit. Rōmānī novam in fēminā virtūtem novō genere honōris, statuā equestrī, dōnāvērunt. In summā[3] Viā Sacrā[4] est posita virgō īnsidēns equō.

Caius Marcius Coriolanus

555. C. Mārcius captīs Coriolīs,[5] urbe Volscōrum, Coriolānus dictus est. Puer patre[6] orbātus sub mātris tūtēlā adolēvit. Cum prīma stīpendia facere coepisset[7] adulēscēns, ē multīs proeliīs quibus interfuit numquam rediit nisi corōnā aliōve mīlitārī praemiō dōnātus. In omnī vītae ratiōne nihil aliud sibi prōpōnēbat quam ut mātrī placēret; cumque illa audīret fīlium[8] laudārī aut corōnā dōnārī vidēret, tum dēmum fēlīcem sē ipsa putābat. Cōnsul factus gravī annōnā[9] advectum[10] ē Siciliā frūmentum magnō pretiō dandum populō cūrāvit, ut plēbs agrōs, nōn sēditiōnēs, coleret. Quā dē causā damnātus ad Volscōs īnfestōs tunc Rōmānīs cōnfūgit eōsque adversus Rōmānōs concitāvit. Imperātor ā Volscīs factus, castrīs ad quārtum ab urbe lapidem[11] positīs, agrum Rōmānum est populātus.

Missī sunt Rōmā ad Coriolānum lēgātī dē pāce, sed atrōx* respōnsum rettulērunt. Iterum deinde iīdem missī nē in castra

---

[1] Translate as if it were a present participle. [2] **obnoxiam**, *liable to*. [3] **summā**, *highest part of*. [4] **Viā Sacrā**, a street running through the Roman Forum up to the Capitol. [5] **captīs Coriolīs**, *because of the capture of Corioli*. [6] Which usage of the ablative? [7] **prīma ... coepisset**, *had begun to earn first wages (as a soldier)* = *had begun his first military service*. [8] Subject accusative of **laudārī** and **dōnārī**. [9] **gravī annōnā**, *in a time of extreme scarcity*. [10] Agrees with **frūmentum**, which is the subject accusative of **dandum** (**esse**). Translate, *had* (**cūrāvit**) *corn, which had been brought from Sicily, distributed to the people at a high price*. [11] **lapidem**, *milestone*.

quidem receptī sunt. Stupēbat senātus, trepidābat populus, virī pariter ac mulierēs exitium imminēns lāmentābantur. Tum Veturia, Coriolānī māter, et Volumnia uxor, duōs parvōs fīliōs sēcum trahēns, castra hostium petiērunt. Ubi mātrem adspexit
5 Coriolānus, exclāmāvit : " Ō patria, vīcistī īram meam admōtīs mātris meae precibus,[1] cui[2] tuam in mē iniūriam condōnō." Complexus inde suōs castra mōvit et exercitum ex agrō Rōmānō abdūxit.

[1] **admōtīs ... precibus,** *by employing the prayers.* [2] **cui,** *for whose sake.*

REVIEW QUESTIONS

LESSON I

556. What use of the nominative do you know? What are the case endings of a noun, and what is their use? What are the personal endings of the third person singular and plural? Translate **puella ambulat** to show three kinds of action. What is the case ending in the nominative plural for words ending in **-a** in the nominative singular? What is an enclitic? To which word in a sentence is **-ne** generally attached? Accent **ambulant** and **ambulantne**. Divide **agricola** and **ambulant** into syllables, and give a reason for the accent of each word.

LESSON II

557. What are the case endings for the nominative and the accusative singular? for the same cases in the plural? What usage has the accusative? Give the accusative singular and plural of **agricola**. What is the difference in meaning between **agricola puellās convocat** and **puellās agricola convocat**? What Latin words are suggested by the English words *laudatory, aquarium, convocation, cantata, aëronaut*? Tell why each noun in 36 stands in the case in which it is found.

LESSON III

558. What is the use of the personal endings in the inflection of a verb? Give the personal endings of the present tense. What does each mean? Inflect **convocō** in the present indicative active. If a verb ends in **-mus**, what is its subject? If it ends in **-s**? Say in Latin *it swims* and *she walks*. Spell the present stem of each verb in 39, *c*. How many conjugations of Latin verbs are there? How are they distinguished from each other? Give the present infinitive active of each verb in 39, *c*.

LESSON IV

559. What three Latin cases have you learned? To which English case does each correspond? What is the usage of each case you have met? Inflect **fugō** in the present indicative active. Give the nominative, genitive, and accusative singular and plural of the Latin word for *daughter*. Express in Latin *whose land? whom does he see? what has he?* Give English words that appear to be derived from **līberō** and **portō**. Give the genitive and the accusative forms of the nouns in 45. Tell the reason for the case of each noun in 46.

LESSON V

560. Spell the present stem of the Latin verb meaning *see*. What endings do you add in the inflection of the present indicative active? Where is the vowel **e** of the present stem of the second conjugation short in the inflection of the present tense? Inflect **doceō, habeō, videō**, and **portō** in the present indicative active. What Latin words are suggested by the English words *fortune, expectation, piratical, export, monitor*? Why is the infinitive given with each verb in the vocabularies? What kind of clause is introduced by **quod**?

LESSON VI

561. How many cases of Latin nouns have you learned? Name them. Give a usage of each case, and give the rule for the usage. With which Latin case have you used a preposition? What is the general character of the dative and of the ablative case? Give the dative and the ablative singular and plural of each noun in 55. What do you observe about the endings of the dative and the ablative plural? Explain the normal order of words in a Latin sentence. What is the effect of a change from the normal order of words? Give English words that appear to be derived from **fābula, dō**, and **nārrō**. Conjugate each verb in 49 in the present indicative active. Tell the reason for the case of each noun in 61.

REVIEW QUESTIONS

LESSON VII

562. How many declensions of Latin nouns are there? What nouns belong to the first declension? What is the base of a noun? Give in their order the case endings of the first declension. How do you recognize a noun of this declension? Decline **rēgīna, pīrāta,** and **domina.** What is the gender of most nouns of the first declension? Give five masculine nouns of this declension. What three case endings in this declension are the same? Say in Latin *in the fight, in the forests.* Give English words that appear to be derived from the words in 65.

LESSON VIII

563. What is the case of the direct object in Latin? of the indirect object? for the *to* or *for* relation? for the *of* relation? How is the *in* or *on* relation expressed? What two genders are there in nouns of the second declension? What are the case endings of the second declension? Decline **dominus** and **oppidum.** Express in Latin *of the horses, in the garden, to the friends.* What cases are alike in the second declension? What four pairs of cases of neuter nouns in this declension are alike? What English words are suggested by **dominus?** Tell the reason for the case of each noun in 75.

LESSON IX

564. Decline **bonus.** Decline **pīlum magnum.** What is the rule for the agreement of adjectives? What is the normal position of an adjective? of an indirect object? How many declensions of adjectives are there? What adjectives precede their nouns? Decline **nauta validus.** Give the ablative singular and plural of each noun in 82. Give the case endings of an adjective of the first and second declensions, reciting first the nominative endings for the three genders, then the genitive endings, and so on. What English words are suggested by **magnus?** Conjugate in the present indicative active each verb in 83.

LESSON X

565. State the rule for the gender of nouns of the first declension. Is the ending of the adjective always the same as that of the noun with which it agrees? Why is **nauta bona** not correct? Express in Latin *you are a poet, your fortune is large, in Europe, to the kind goddess*. Decline **longus** and **puella parva**. Inflect **sum** and **dēmōnstrō** in the present indicative active. What kind of verb is **sum**? What are predicate nouns and adjectives? Give two uses of the nominative.

LESSON XII

566. What cases of the second declension end in **-ō**? What cases end in **-īs**? What two cases in the neuter plural end in **-a**? Decline **puer, ager, vir, praemium**, and **socius**. How do the English derivatives of these words help you to decline them? Point out the predicate nouns and adjectives in 101. How is the present stem of a verb found? Give English words that appear to be derived from the nouns of 100. What is the rule for the gender of nouns of the second declension? Tell the reason for the case of each noun in 101.

LESSON XIII

567. Decline **miser** and **vester**. Inflect **superō** in the present indicative active. How does the meaning of **tuus** differ from that of **vester**? What is an appositive? Find examples of an appositive in 96 and in 101. What is the rule for the case of an appositive? What is the rule for the agreement of an adjective? Say in Latin *for my friend Galba*. What English words appear to be derived from **miser, multus,** and **vocō**? What kind of clause begins with **quod** in sentence 7 of 105?

LESSON XIV

568. Give two uses of the nominative and two of the dative, and one usage of each of the other cases. Give seven Latin adjectives that are accompanied by the dative. How do you say in

Latin *there is? there are?* Inflect **sum** in the present, imperfect, and future tenses. Decline **servus, vir, filius**. What adjectives have you learned that keep **e** in their inflection? In what two ways have you used **amicus**? What is the rule for the dative with adjectives? Give English derivatives of **propinquus** and **proximus**.

LESSON XV

569. Decline **lēgātus** and **scūtum**. Inflect **pugnō** and **compleō** in the imperfect indicative active. Give two uses of the ablative. Which use requires a preposition? By what sort of prepositional phrases is the ablative of means to be translated? What is the tense sign of the imperfect indicative active? Divide **exspectābāmus** in such a way as to show the stem, the tense sign, and the personal ending. Which personal ending of the imperfect is unlike that of the present? Express in Latin *by an oar, with water, by means of money*. What kind of action is expressed by the imperfect?

LESSON XVI

570. Inflect **labōrō** and **teneō** in the future indicative active. Give three uses of the ablative, two of the dative, and one of the genitive. Which two cases are used with prepositions in Latin? Give two uses of the accusative. What preposition in Latin is used with two cases? What is the tense sign of the future indicative active? Translate **cum cūrā** in two ways. When may **cum** be omitted in phrases of manner? Say in Latin *with a sword* and *with zeal*. Give English derivatives of **labōrō**. Decline **aeger**.

LESSON XVII

571. What forms are given as the principal parts of a verb? Give the principal parts of **laudō**. What are the present and the perfect stem of **laudō**? What tenses use the present stem in their inflection (as far as you have studied the verb)? What are the personal endings of the perfect indicative active? What tenses use the perfect stem in their inflection? Inflect **laudō** in the perfect indicative active. What is the difference between the perfect definite and the perfect indefinite? Translate the perfect of **laudō** in both ways. Tell the reason for the case of each noun and adjective in 138.

LESSON XVIII

572. Give four uses of the ablative. Which uses of the ablative take **cum**? Inflect **videō** in the perfect indicative active and **maneō** in the imperfect indicative active. Express in Latin *with the Romans, with danger, with a shield, in Italy, into Germany.* Decline **perīculum** and **locus**. What are the perfect stems of the verbs in 139? Give English derivatives of **captīvus, causa,** and **locus**.

LESSON XIX

573. What is a demonstrative? Give an example in English. In what ways is the demonstrative **is** used? Inflect **sum, hiemō,** and **maneō** in the tenses of the indicative active through the perfect. Express in Latin *she has been kind, they have been friends.* Decline **is** and **proximus**. What is the normal position of a modifying adjective? What is the normal position of **is** when it is an adjective? Tell the reason for the case of each noun and adjective in 150.

LESSON XX

574. What is the difference in the action expressed by the imperfect and the perfect tense? What is the perfect stem of **sum**? Decline the interrogative pronoun **quis**. Decline the interrogative adjective **quī**. Express in Latin *whose horse? of those men, with that girl, with which spears?* Make a synopsis (671) of **sum** in each person for the tenses you have studied. Decline **animus** and **imperium**.

LESSON XXI

575. Give the infinitives of **amō, moneō,** and **regō**. What letter of the infinitive needs to be especially noticed? Why? What are the perfect stems of **amō, moneō,** and **mittō**? Translate the third person

REVIEW QUESTIONS

singular of the perfect indicative active of **dūcō** in two ways. What is the tense sign of the future in the first and second conjugations? in the third? Inflect **mittō** in the indicative active through the perfect. Inflect **dūcō** and **emō** in the present and future indicative active. Give English derivatives of **dūcō** and **mittō**. Make a synopsis of **amō** in each person through the perfect indicative.

LESSON XXIII

576. What three things must you know about each noun of the third declension to be able to decline it? What are the case endings of this declension? What case endings are the same? Decline **eques, dux, lapis**, and **caput**. Decline **rēx noster**. Make a synopsis of **mittō** in each person for the tenses you have studied. Give English derivatives of the words in 172.

LESSON XXIV

577. What uses of the accusative and ablative cases have you now studied? What is the difference between phrases of place from which introduced by **ab, ex**, and **dē**? Give the rules for place from which and place to which. In what forms is the inflection of **capiō** unlike that of **regō**? Inflect **fugiō** in the present, imperfect, future, and perfect indicative active. Decline **mūrus** and **pēs**. Express in Latin *he fled toward the gate, he fled out of the gate, he fled away from the gate*. Give the genitive endings for the first three declensions; then the dative endings, and so on. From what Latin words are *pedal, mural*, and *dismiss* derived? Tell the reason for the case of each noun in 181.

LESSON XXV

578. Give five uses of the ablative case, and illustrate each with a Latin phrase. Decline **homō bonus, quod vulnus**, and **corpus**. What English words are used to translate the ablative of cause? What uses of the ablative require a preposition? In what two uses of the ablative is **cum** employed? Inflect **doleō** in the present, imperfect, future, and perfect indicative active. In what two ways may the dative case be used? What two ways are there of expressing a phrase introduced by *to*? Make a synopsis of **capiō** in each person through the perfect indicative active.

LESSON XXVI

579. What are the regular case endings for nouns of the third declension of each gender? What nouns have i-stems? How do nouns with i-stems differ in declension from other nouns of the third declension? What is an enclitic? Give two examples. Decline **lapis**, **cīvis**, and **urbs**. Express in Latin *because of our courage, sons of these citizens*. From what Latin words are *civilize, finite, ignition, marine,* and *interurban* derived?

LESSON XXVII

580. What preposition is used with both the accusative and the ablative case? Decline **fīnis** and **mare**. Decline **aeger**. What two meanings has **inter**? How do you say *with* and *because of* in Latin? What forms of adjectives are used as nouns? Say in Latin *among the allies, after the war, across the sea, against the soldiers, toward the province, through the cities, without a friend.*

LESSON XXIX

581. Decline **audāx**, **brevis**, and **ācer**. Decline **omnēs Rōmānī**, **perīculum commūne**, and **dux fortis**. What English words are derived from **gravis, omnis,** and **fortis**? What is the more common ending for the ablative singular of adjectives of the third declension? How can you tell from the vocabularies whether an adjective of the third declension has one, two, or three terminations? Express in Latin *for an eager man, with all the citizens, among the brave centurions.* Tell the reason for the case of each noun in 202.

LESSON XXX

582. How can you tell a verb of the fourth conjugation from a verb in -iō of the third conjugation? How do verbs of the fourth conjugation differ in inflection from verbs in -iō of the third conjugation?

REVIEW QUESTIONS

Inflect **dēfendō** and **veniō** in the present, imperfect, future, and perfect indicative active, and make synopses of each. What are the present and perfect stems of the verbs in 213? Decline **flūmen** and **dux nōbilis**. What English words are derived from **paucī, nōbilis, audiō**, and **dēfendō**? What are the principal parts of **dūcō, mittō, capiō, fugiō**, and **iaciō**?

LESSON XXXI

583. Give eight uses of the ablative case, two of the dative, and two of the accusative. Inflect **gerō** in all the tenses you have studied. Decline **ea aestās, secundus annus, nox**, and **tempus breve**. Express in Latin *within ten hours, at that time, during the second summer*. What is the rule for the expression of time when in Latin? From what Latin words are *perennial, decimate, primitive, extemporaneous*, and *belligerent* derived?

LESSON XXXII

584. What auxiliary word must be used in translating the pluperfect? How are the pluperfect and future perfect tenses formed? Inflect **veniō, sum**, and **gerō** in these tenses. What is the Latin way of saying *the Roman people*? What is the perfect system of a verb? What is the difference in the meaning of **Gallus** and **Gallia**? What is the meaning of **fuerat**? of **habuerat**? Write a Latin sentence containing an ablative of cause, an ablative of accompaniment, and a pluperfect indicative active.

LESSON XXXIII

585. In what two ways may a demonstrative be used? Distinguish between **is, hic**, and **ille**. Decline these words. Give the complete rules for place from which and place to which. Express in Latin *from Italy, from Rome, to Gaul, to Athens*. Make a synopsis of **gerō** in the third person singular and plural of the indicative active. From the derivation of the words what is the difference between a *society* and a *fraternity*?

LESSON XXXV

586. What is the passive voice? What are the personal endings of the passive voice? In passive sentences how is the person doing the act expressed in Latin? How is the thing doing the act expressed? Inflect **superō** and **videō** in the present, imperfect, and future indicative passive, and make synopses of each. In how many ways have you used the ablative case? How many of these uses employ **ā** or **ab**? How many employ **cum**? Express in Latin *they are overcome by weapons, they are overcome by the Gauls.* Where does the tense sign in the passive differ from the tense sign in the active?

LESSON XXXVI

587. What is the antecedent of a relative pronoun? In what respects does a relative agree with its antecedent? In what case is a relative? Decline **quī.** Inflect **vāstō** in the active indicative, and make a synopsis of the third person singular and plural in the passive. Decline **vestrum cōnsilium, legiō prīma,** and **turris.** Express in Latin *the traders to whom I gave, the traders toward whom, among the mountains which I see, against those men whose sons are.* Give English derivatives from the words in 249.

LESSON XXXVII

588. Decline **castra** and **cōnsul Rōmānus.** Inflect **vincō** and **recipiō** in the present system active and passive. Make synopses in the third person singular and plural of **vincō.** What is the second person singular of the present passive of **gerō**? the second person singular of the future passive of **vincō**? What are the third persons plural of the present and future active and passive of **dūcō** and **iaciō**? From what Latin words are *pacific, consulate, reception,* and *victor* derived?

LESSON XXXVIII

589. Decline the personal pronouns of the first, second, and third persons. Decline the reflexive pronouns of the first, second, and third persons. Why is the nominative of reflexive pronouns not needed? Express in Latin *his, her, their, to him, to himself, him, himself, to me, with us.* Inflect **interficiō** in the active and passive indicative through the perfect tense, and make synopses in the third person singular and plural. What is the position of cum when it is used with personal pronouns?

LESSON XXXIX

590. Inflect **dicō** in the perfect system, and **impediō** in the present system. Make a synopsis of **incitō** in the third person singular and of **praebeō** in the third person plural. Give English words derived from **dicō, impediō**, and **incitō**. What is the difference in meaning of the perfect indefinite and the imperfect? Decline **aedificium**. Tell the reason for the case of each noun, adjective, and relative pronoun in 275.

LESSON XL

591. What kind of word is **suus**? When should it be used? When may it be omitted? How do you say *his, her, its, their*, when they are not reflexive? What kind of words are followed by an ablative of separation? Give six verbs that may be followed by this ablative. What prepositions are used with the ablative of separation? What other ablative is of the same nature as the ablative of separation? Inflect **dēsistō** in the indicative active, and **interclūdō** in the indicative passive. Give English derivatives from **prīvō, prohibeō**, and **dēsistō**.

LESSON XLI

592. What tenses of the verb belong to the present system? to the perfect system? to the participial system? Point out six uses of the ablative in 290. Inflect **gerō** throughout the indicative passive. Decline **impedīmentum, imperātor**, and **mora brevis**. How do concilium and cōnsilium differ in meaning? Why does a participle change its endings?

LESSON XLII

593. What are the case endings of the fourth declension? What is the rule for the gender of nouns of the fourth declension? What exceptions are there to this rule? Decline **lacus, adventus, domus**, and cornū. Inflect **mūniō** in the participial system, and make a synopsis in the third person plural active and passive. How are place from which and place to which expressed with the word **domus**? Give English words derived from **adventus, manus,** and **mūniō**.

LESSON XLIII

594. What are the three degrees of comparison of adjectives? Compare **fortis** and **longus**. Decline the positive, comparative, and superlative of **gravis**. Inflect **petō** in the indicative active and passive. Make a synopsis of **faciō** in the first person plural of the active voice. Decline **senātus Rōmānus** and **iter longum**. How do you say in Latin *rather long, too new, very brave, I shall march, we were attacking*?

LESSON XLIV

595. Compare **similis, dissimilis,** and **nōbilis**. Give two uses of the genitive and two of the dative case. What is a partitive genitive? Give an exception to the rule for the partitive genitive. Decline **pars** and **lītus angustum**. What adjectives are compared like **similis**? Compare **ācer**, and decline its comparative.

LESSON XLVI

596. Compare **bonus, summus, peior, plūrimus, minus,** and **maiōrem**, and decline each in the comparative degree. How is the comparative of **multus** used? What does **summus mōns** mean? Give English words that are derived from the words in 316. Give all the ways in which you have used each case.

LESSON XLVII

597. What do adverbs modify? What is the regular way of forming adverbs from adjectives? What cases of adjectives are used as adverbs? Give examples. Form and compare an adverb from an adjective of the first and second declensions; from an adjective of the third declension of one ending. Form and compare adverbs from **ācer, miser,** and **bonus**. Decline **multitūdō**. Inflect **dō** throughout the indicative. Inflect **praemittō** in the participial system. Make a synopsis of **relinquō** in the third person plural. Tell the reason for the case of the nouns in 329.

LESSON XLVIII

598. What are the case endings for each declension in the nominative singular? in the genitive singular? in the other cases? What is the gender of nouns of the fourth declension? of the fifth? Give the case endings of the fifth declension. Decline **diēs**, **rēs**, and **aciēs**. Inflect **pōnō** in the present and the future indicative active, and **instruō** in the present system. Make a synopsis of **pōnō** in the third person singular. Give three uses of the accusative case. How is time during which expressed? How is duration of time expressed?

LESSON L

599. What tenses has the subjunctive? What vowels characterize the present subjunctive of the several conjugations? Inflect the present subjunctive active and passive of **laudō, videō, gerō, recipiō, audiō**, and **sum**. To which system of the verb does the present subjunctive belong? How is purpose expressed in English? How in Latin? When is **ut** used in purpose clauses? When is **nē** used? Translate **venit ut videat** in five ways. Are purpose clauses independent or dependent? Are they adjectives, adverbs, or nouns in nature?

LESSON LI

600. How is the imperfect subjunctive formed? Inflect the present and the imperfect subjunctive active and passive of **portō, terreō, mittō, iaciō**, and **mūniō**. To which system does the imperfect subjunctive belong? What do you understand by sequence of tenses? What are the primary tenses? What are the secondary tenses? Give the rules for the sequence of tenses, and for the tense of the subjunctive in purpose clauses. Translate **vēnit ut vidēret** in as many ways as you can. Tell the reason for the tense of each subjunctive in 353.

LESSON LII

601. Explain the difference between a substantive clause of purpose and an adverbial clause of purpose. Give an example of each. With what verbs are substantive clauses of purpose found? What is the rule for result clauses? What words in the independent clause indicate that a result clause will follow? Inflect **agō** in the present system. What English words are derived from **agō** and **imperō**?

LESSON LIV

602. What is an indirect question? In what mood is its verb? State when each tense may be used. How is the perfect subjunctive formed in the active voice? in the passive? Inflect **rogō** in all the tenses of the subjunctive active. To which system do the perfect and the pluperfect passive subjunctive belong? Inflect **audiō** in all tenses of that system. Make a synopsis of **rogō** in the third person singular. Express in Latin *I know who is fighting, I knew who had fought.* Tell the reason for the mood and tense of each subjunctive in 375.

LESSON LV

603. Count in Latin to ten. What are cardinals? What are ordinals? Decline **ūnus, duo, trēs,** and **mīlle**. How is **mīlle** used? What is the difference between the possessive and the objective genitive? Give examples of each. Inflect the subjunctive active of **discēdō**. Decline **passus** and **dexter**. What Latin words are suggested by *timorous, million, unicorn, dual, dexterity, memory*? Give all the English words you can think of that are derived from **ūnus**.

LESSON LVI

604. Decline **aeger** and **neuter**. Decline **magnus** and **nūllus**. What are the ten irregular adjectives of the first and second declensions? Give English derivatives from the words in 386. Say in Latin *which of the two do you see? one is a farmer, another is a slave, a third is a poet.*

LESSON LVII

605. How many tenses has the infinitive mood? What are they? How is each formed? To which system of the verb does the perfect infinitive active belong? the perfect infinitive passive? the future infinitive active? How is the future active participle of a verb formed? What are the infinitives of **gerō**? What do they mean? What part of speech is an infinitive? Name two uses of the infinitive, and illustrate each by a Latin sentence. What is a complementary infinitive? What is the case of a predicate adjective after a complementary infinitive? What English words are suggested by **dēbeō**? Tell how each infinitive in 396 is used.

LESSON LVIII

606. Mention three uses of the infinitive mood. Say in Latin *I desire to learn the way* and *I desire you to learn the way*. What uses of the infinitive do these sentences illustrate? What kind of clause is used with **imperō**? with **iubeō**? What is an indirect statement? In what mood is its verb? When are the different tenses of this mood used in indirect statements? What is an indirect question? In what mood is the verb of an indirect question? When are the different tenses of this mood used in indirect questions? When **sē** and **suus** occur in indirect statements, to what do they frequently refer? Express in Latin *Cæsar was a general*; then express it indirectly after *I know*, *I knew*, and *I shall know*. Give English derivatives from the words in 403. Make a synopsis of **iubeō** in the third person singular. Give the infinitives of **iubeō** and of **cognōscō**. Explain the reason for the tense of each infinitive in 404.

LESSON LX

607. Give the meanings of **is, īdem, hic, ille, iste, ipse**. Of what is **īdem** compounded? What part of **īdem** remains unchanged in declension? How is the accusative singular masculine written? Pronounce the neuter nominative singular. What does **ipse** do in a sentence? Inflect **possum** throughout and make synopses. What usage of the infinitive generally accompanies **possum**? What English words are derived from **nihil, putō, respondeō,** and **nūntiō**?

LESSON LXI

608. Name four indefinite pronouns. Decline **quīdam** and **aliquis**. Name seven kinds of pronouns, giving an example of each. Review the declension of the various pronouns. Give the usages that you have learned for the several cases of nouns. Illustrate each by a brief Latin sentence.

LESSON LXII

609. Recite the rule for the dative with compounds. Give some compound verbs with which the dative is used. What is the double dative? Inflect **dēsum** in all moods. Name a compound verb which takes both an accusative and a dative. What Latin words are suggested by the English words *munitions, prefect, subsidize, occurrence*? Illustrate the dative of purpose by a Latin sentence. Tell the reason for the case of the nouns and for the mood and tense of the subjunctives in 430.

LESSON LXIII

610. Inflect **volō** and **nōlō**. Make a synopsis of each in the third person singular and plural. Give the rule for the dative with special intransitive verbs, and name verbs followed by such a dative. Say in Latin in two ways *Cæsar ordered the men to come into the camp*. Decline **mulier, sōl,** and **occāsus**. Inflect **resistō** in the present subjunctive and the future indicative active. Explain sequence of tenses. What tenses are used in purpose clauses, and when?

LESSON LXV

611. How is the present participle formed? the future active participle? the future passive participle? Give the participles of **gerō** and their meanings. Decline **fugiēns**. What part of speech is a participle? What is the rule for the agreement of participles? Explain the tenses of participles. Translate **Gallī territī ex agrīs**

fugiēbant in six ways. Give English words derived from **commoveō** and **redūcō**. Inflect **commoveō** in the present system. Give the infinitives and the participles of **redūcō**.

LESSON LXVII

612. What is an ablative absolute? In what three ways is it formed? Give examples. Which participles are used in making the ablative absolute, and what time do they express? Translate **bellō factō** in five ways. Express in Latin *having captured the town they freed the captives*. Decline **dēditiō** and **rīpa**. What does **media urbs** mean? Give the rule for the ablative absolute.

LESSON LXVIII

613. Name two parts of the verb which are verbal nouns. Decline the gerunds of **iaciō** and of **mittō**. What is used in place of the nominative of the gerund? Translate **ad petendum**. What other ways of expressing the same idea are there in Latin? Inflect **eō** throughout. Make synopses in each person. Decline **nōmen** and **spatium**. Give English words suggested by the Latin words of 463. Give the infinitives and the participles of **ōrō**, with their meanings.

LESSON LXIX

614. What other name has the gerundive? What part of speech is a gerund? What part of speech is a gerundive? Decline the gerund and the gerundive of **videō**. Name two uses of the gerundive. Express in Latin *for the purpose of capturing the city* and *the signal had to be given*. Decline **vīs**. Inflect **augeō** in the indicative active, **conveniō** in the subjunctive active, and **ferō** throughout, and give synopses of each. State what you know about the uses of participles.

LESSON LXXI

615. What is a deponent verb? What active forms has a deponent verb? Inflect **cōnor** throughout. Give a Latin sentence containing an ablative of specification. What uses of the ablative case do you know? What English words are suggested by **sequor, hortor,** and **experior**? Make a synopsis of **sequor** in the third person singular.

LESSON LXXII

616. Inflect **faciō** in the active and the passive voice. Make a synopsis of **vereor** in the third person plural. What is a clause? What clauses thus far studied have had a verb in the subjunctive? in the infinitive? Recite the rule for temporal clauses introduced by **cum**. Say in Latin *I was informed by you, you informed me.*

LESSON LXXIV

617. What substantive clauses have you studied? In which mood are their verbs? Give the rule for **quod** clauses of fact. Say in Latin *that road, as we have shown, was more difficult.* Decline **lēgātiō**. Inflect **ēgredior** throughout. Make synopses of **cōgō**. Give English words suggested by the words in 498.

LESSON LXXV

618. What is the rule for the main verb of a statement that is given indirectly? for the subordinate verb of such a statement? What determines the sequence of tenses in indirect statements? Compare **celeriter** and decline **initium**. Inflect **moror** and **revertor** throughout. What uses do you know for each case of nouns (512)? How have you used the subjunctive mood (513)? the infinitive (513)? the participle (513)?

APPENDIX I

RULES OF SYNTAX

NOTE. These rules are here numbered consecutively for the convenience of teachers and pupils. The number in parentheses following a rule is its section number.

619. Agreement.

1. A verb agrees with its subject in person and number (29).

2. A predicate noun agrees in case with the subject of the verb (87).

3. A predicate adjective agrees in gender, number, and case with the subject of the verb (88).

4. An appositive agrees in case with the noun which it explains (94).

5. Adjectives agree with their nouns in gender, number, and case (79).

6. A predicate adjective used with a complementary infinitive agrees in gender, number, and case with the subject of the main verb (394, *b*).

7. A relative pronoun agrees with its antecedent in gender and number, but its case depends on the way it is used in its own clause (248).

620. Nominative Case.

8. The subject of a verb is in the nominative case (28).

621. Genitive Case.

9. The word denoting the owner or possessor is in the genitive case (44).

10. Words denoting a part may have with them a genitive of the whole from which the part is taken (309).

11. Some nouns of action and feeling may have with them a genitive to express the object of the action or feeling implied in the nouns (381).

12. The genitive denotes that of which something consists or is made (p. 79, note 1)

622. Dative Case.

13. The indirect object of a verb is in the dative case (57).

14. Certain adjectives meaning *near, fit, friendly, pleasing, like,* and their opposites, may be accompanied by a dative to show the person or the thing toward which the quality of the adjective is directed (111).

15. Some verbs compounded with **ad, ante, con, dē, in, inter, ob, post, prae, prō, sub,** and **super,** take a dative of the indirect object. Transitive compounds may take both an accusative and a dative (425).

16. The dative is used to denote the purpose for which a thing serves (427).

17. The dative is used to denote the person (or, rarely, the thing) affected by the action or situation expressed by the verb (428).

18. Most verbs meaning *believe, favor, help, please, trust,* and their opposites, also *command, obey, pardon, persuade, resist, serve, spare,* and the like, take a dative of the indirect object (433).

623. Accusative Case.

19. The object of a verb is in the accusative case (33).

20. Place *to which* is usually expressed by the accusative with **ad** or **in**; but with the names of towns, and with **domus,** the preposition is omitted (230, *b*).

21. The accusative is used with certain prepositions (193).

22. Extent of time or of space is expressed by the accusative (333).

23. The subject of the infinitive is in the accusative (399).

624. Ablative Case.

24. Place *where* is commonly expressed by a phrase consisting of a preposition, usually **in,** with the ablative case (59).

APPENDIX I

25. The means by which an action is accomplished is expressed by the ablative without a preposition (122).

26. The ablative with **cum** is used with abstract nouns to denote the manner of an action; but **cum** may be omitted if an adjective modifies the noun of the phrase (129).

27. The ablative with **cum** is used to show accompaniment (143).

28. Place *from which* is usually expressed by the ablative with ā (ab), dē, ē (ex); but with the names of towns, and with **domus**, the preposition is omitted (230, *a*).

29. The ablative without a preposition is used to express cause (185).

30. The ablative is used with certain prepositions (194).

31. The time at which or within which a thing happens is expressed by the ablative without a preposition (219).

32. The personal agent with a passive verb is expressed by the ablative with ā or ab (243).

33. Words signifying *privation*, *removal*, or *separation* are followed by the ablative without a preposition, or with the prepositions ā (ab), dē, ē (ex) (282).

34. The degree of difference is expressed by the ablative (321).

35. The ablative of a noun or pronoun, with a participle, a noun, or an adjective in agreement, is used to express *time, cause, concession, condition*, or other relations (455).

36. The ablative without a preposition is used to denote in what respect something is true (481).

625. Adverbial Clauses.

37. The cause of an action may be expressed by a dependent clause introduced by **quod** (51).

38. The subjunctive is used with **ut** or **nē** in a dependent clause to express the purpose of the action stated in the independent clause (344).

39. The subjunctive is used with **ut** or **ut nōn** in a dependent clause to express the result of the action stated in the independent clause (358).

40. Temporal clauses referring to past time, when introduced by **cum**, have their verb in the indicative if they fix the time of an action, but in the subjunctive if they describe the circumstances of an action (488).

41. Adverbial clauses introduced by **quā** and **ut** (= *as*) have their verbs in the indicative (497).

626. Adjective Clauses.

42. A relative clause modifies its antecedent as an adjective modifies its noun (247, *b*).

627. Substantive Clauses.

43. Verbs meaning *ask, command, persuade,* and *urge* may have for their object a clause of purpose with its verb in the subjunctive (356).

44. An indirect question, with its verb in the subjunctive, may be used as the subject or the object of another verb (372, *b*).

45. An infinitive with subject accusative may be used as the subject of another verb (393).

46. An infinitive with subject accusative may be used as the object of another verb (393).

47. An infinitive with subject accusative may be used with verbs meaning *say, think, know, perceive,* and the like, to express an indirect statement (401).

48. The indicative is used with **quod** in a substantive clause to state something which is regarded as a fact (496).

628. Participles, the Gerund, and the Gerundive.

49. A participle may be used as an adjective to modify a noun; or it may express the idea that might otherwise be expressed by a clause of *time, concession, cause,* or *condition,* or by a *relative* clause (443-445).

APPENDIX I

50. The gerund is a verbal noun used in the genitive, dative, accusative, and ablative singular, with the constructions of regular nouns (461).

51. When a gerund with an object might be used, the gerundive is the more usual construction. The gerundive is a verbal adjective in agreement with a noun (471, 472).

52. The gerund or the gerundive with **ad** or **causā** may be used to express the purpose of an action (461, 472).

53. The gerundive is used with the forms of the verb **sum** to express necessary action (473).

629. Subordinate Clauses in Indirect Statements.

54. The verbs of the subordinate clauses of an indirect statement are in the subjunctive (502).

FORMATION OF LATIN WORDS

During the first year of the study of Latin the pupil should learn the force of the prefixes and suffixes given below.

630. Prefixes.

ā- (ab-, abs-), *away from, from*	ab + dūcō = abdūcō, *lead away*
ad-, *to, toward, against*	ad + dūcō = addūcō, *lead to*
con-, *together; completely*	con + dūcō = condūcō, *lead together*
dē-, *down from; from*	dē + dūcō = dēdūcō, *lead down*
ex- (ē-), *out from, out of; completely*	ē + dūcō = ēdūcō, *lead out*
in-, *in, into, on, toward*	in + dūcō = indūcō, *lead in, lead on*
in-, *not;* like English *un-, in-*	in + amīcus = inimīcus, *unfriendly*
inter-, *between*	inter + cēdō = intercēdō, *go between*
per-, *through; thoroughly*	per + dūcō = perdūcō, *lead through*
prae-, *in front of, in advance*	prae + mittō = praemittō, *send ahead*
prō-, *forward, forth, for*	prō + dūcō = prōdūcō, *lead forth*
re- (red-), *back, again*	re + dūcō = redūcō, *lead back*
sub- (subs-), *under, from under, up*	su(b)s + teneō = sustineō, *hold up, sustain*
trāns- (trā-), *across, through*	trā + dūcō = trādūcō, *lead across*

631. Explain the formation of the following verbs, and give the meaning of each:

appropinquō	cognōscō	incolō	īnstruō	persuādeō
convocō	dēpōnō	sustineō	conlocō	addūcō
exspectō	reddō	reperiō	cōnstituō	redūcō
dēmōnstrō	dēsum	respondeō	ēdūcō	suscipiō
compleō	coniciō	recipiō	trādō	accēdō
perturbō	permittō	impediō	commoveō	perficiō
praebeō	trānseō	incitō	praeficiō	ēgredior
prohibeō	prōgredior	expugnō	praestō	cōgō
dēsistō	exīstimō	perveniō	praesum	cōnsuēscō
accipiō	cōnfirmō	praemittō	resistō	revertor
dēbeō	dēfendō	conveniō	excēdō	prōcēdō

632. Suffixes.

a. The suffixes **-tās, -tūs,** and **-ia,** when added to the stems of nouns, make other nouns denoting *condition* or *characteristic*:

cīvi (stem of **cīvis,** *citizen*) + **tās** = **cīvitās,** *citizenship* (the condition or characteristic of a citizen); *state, tribe.*

vir (weakened stem of **vir,** *man*) + **tūs** = **virtūs,** *manliness, valor* (the characteristic of a man).

b. The suffixes **-ia, -tia, -tās,** and **-tūdō,** when added to the stems of adjectives, make abstract nouns denoting *quality* or *condition*:

alti (weakened stem of **altus,** *high*) + **tūdō** = **altitūdō,** *height* (the quality or condition of being high).

c. The suffixes **-iō, -tiō, -tus,** and **-ium,** when added to the stems of verbs, make verbal nouns denoting an *act* or the *result of an act*:

mūnī (stem of **mūniō,** *fortify*) + **tiō** = **mūnītiō,** *a fortifying, a fortification* (the act of fortifying, or the result of the act of fortifying).

633. Explain the formation of the following nouns:

victōria	nātiō	aedificium	celeritās	dēditiō
praemium	cōnsilium	adventus	difficultās	ēruptiō
studium	legiō	exercitus	mūnītiō	altitūdō
imperium	multitūdō	equitātus	praesidium	facultās
virtūs	cīvitās	cōnspectus	subsidium	lēgātiō
conloquium	tempestās	memoria	occāsus	condiciō

APPENDIX I

ENGLISH DERIVATIVES

634. Suggestions for a Notebook. In making a collection of the English words that are derived from the Latin words of the vocabularies, the pupil should keep the results of his work in a notebook. Such a book should contain, in addition to the list of derivatives, the definition of each derivative, and a brief sentence illustrating its use. A suggested form of arrangement for the notebook follows:

Derivatives of Vocō, *call*

vocō, vocāre, vocāvī, vocātus	vocation, vocational, vocal, evoke, convoke, convocation, vocative, revoke, invoke, vociferous, invocation
	vocation: a *calling*, occupation vocational: pertaining to a vocation or *calling* vocal: pertaining to the voice evoke: *call* out convoke: *call* together convocation: a *calling* together, an assembly vocative: case of *calling*, case of address revoke: *call* back invoke: *call* upon, ask for vociferous: of large *calling* power, with a loud voice invocation: a *calling* upon, a prayer
	vocation: The choice of a vocation is not always easy vocational: Vocational guidance is often necessary vocal: He is receiving vocal instruction evoke: His remarks evoked applause convoke: He will convoke the council convocation: Convocation day is at hand vocative: The vocative is not common in Cæsar revoke: Their punishment will be revoked invoke: The ancients invoked many gods vociferous: The audience became vociferous invocation: The invocation was then made

635. The following verbs are especially worthy of study in the manner suggested above because of the large number of English words derived from them:

amō	dūcō	audiō	locō (conlocō)	nāvigō
videō	mittō	dīcō	cēdō	pōnō
habeō	capiō	vincō	parō	cognōscō
doceō	iaciō	faciō	pugnō	putō
moneō	sedeō (obsideō)	dō	teneō	moveō
terreō	timeō	agō	veniō	sūmō

The prefixes listed in 630, and also **ante**, *before*, **circum**, *around*, **ob**, *toward*, and **super**, *above*, usually are evident in the English derivatives of Latin words. But sometimes the prefix appears in a different spelling: thus,

> **ab-** appears as a-, abs-, as- (*abstain*)
> **ad-** appears as ac-, ag-, al-, ap-, ar-, as-, at- (*apparatus*)
> **con-** appears as com-, co-, col-, cor- (*composition*)
> **in-** appears as im-, ir-, il- (*impose*)
> **ob-** appears as oc-, of-, obs-, o- (*occur*)
> **sub-** appears as suc-, suf-, sug-, sup-, sur- (*suppose*)

APPENDIX II

DECLENSION, CONJUGATION, ETC.

NOUNS

636. FIRST DECLENSION

	SINGULAR	Case Endings	PLURAL	Case Endings
Nom.	hasta	-a	hastae	-ae
Gen.	hastae	-ae	hastārum	-ārum
Dat.	hastae	-ae	hastīs	-īs
Acc.	hastam	-am	hastās	-ās
Abl.	hastā	-ā	hastīs	-īs

637. SECOND DECLENSION

	SINGULAR	Case Endings MASC.	PLURAL	Case Endings MASC.
Nom.	hortus	-us	hortī	-ī
Gen.	hortī	-ī	hortōrum	-ōrum
Dat.	hortō	-ō	hortīs	-īs
Acc.	hortum	-um	hortōs	-ōs
Abl.	hortō	-ō	hortīs	-īs

	SINGULAR	Case Endings NEUT.	PLURAL	Case Endings NEUT.
Nom.	dōnum	-um	dōna	-a
Gen.	dōnī	-ī	dōnōrum	-ōrum
Dat.	dōnō	-ō	dōnīs	-īs
Acc.	dōnum	-um	dōna	-a
Abl.	dōnō	-ō	dōnīs	-īs

SINGULAR

Nom.	puer	ager	vir	fīlius
Gen.	puerī	agrī	virī	fīlī
Dat.	puerō	agrō	virō	fīliō
Acc.	puerum	agrum	virum	fīlium
Abl.	puerō	agrō	virō	fīliō

PLURAL

Nom.	puerī	agrī	virī	fīliī
Gen.	puerōrum	agrōrum	virōrum	fīliōrum
Dat.	puerīs	agrīs	virīs	fīliīs
Acc.	puerōs	agrōs	virōs	fīliōs
Abl.	puerīs	agrīs	virīs	fīliīs

	SINGULAR	PLURAL
Nom.	proelium	proelia
Gen.	proelī	proeliōrum
Dat.	proeliō	proeliīs
Acc.	proelium	proelia
Abl.	proeliō	proeliīs

638. THIRD DECLENSION

SINGULAR

					CASE ENDINGS	
					M. AND F.	N.
Nom.	rēx	mīles	virtūs	caput	-s or —	—
Gen.	rēgis	mīlitis	virtūtis	capitis	-is	-is
Dat.	rēgī	mīlitī	virtūtī	capitī	-ī	-ī
Acc.	rēgem	mīlitem	virtūtem	caput	-em	—
Abl.	rēge	mīlite	virtūte	capite	-e	-e

PLURAL

Nom.	rēgēs	mīlitēs	virtūtēs	capita	-ēs	-a
Gen.	rēgum	mīlitum	virtūtum	capitum	-um	-um
Dat.	rēgibus	mīlitibus	virtūtibus	capitibus	-ibus	-ibus
Acc.	rēgēs	mīlitēs	virtūtēs	capita	-ēs	-a
Abl.	rēgibus	mīlitibus	virtūtibus	capitibus	-ibus	-ibus

APPENDIX II

639. *I*-STEMS

SINGULAR

CASE ENDINGS

					M. AND F.	N.
Nom.	hostis	cohors	mōns	mare	-s (-is, -ēs)	—
Gen.	hostis	cohortis	montis	maris	-is	-is
Dat.	hostī	cohortī	montī	marī	-ī	-ī
Acc.	hostem	cohortem	montem	mare	-em (-im)	—
Abl.	hoste	cohorte	monte	marī	-e (-ī)	-ī

PLURAL

Nom.	hostēs	cohortēs	montēs	maria	-ēs	-ia
Gen.	hostium	cohortium	montium	marium	-ium	-ium
Dat.	hostibus	cohortibus	montibus	maribus	-ibus	-ibus
Acc.	hostīs (-ēs)	cohortīs (-ēs)	montīs (-ēs)	maria	-īs (-ēs)	-ia
Abl.	hostibus	cohortibus	montibus	maribus	-ibus	-ibus

	SING.	PLUR.		SING.	PLUR.
Nom.	ignis	ignēs		turris	turrēs
Gen.	ignis	ignium		turris	turrium
Dat.	ignī	ignibus		turrī	turribus
Acc.	ignem	ignīs (-ēs)		turrim (-em)	turrīs (-ēs)
Abl.	ignī (-e)	ignibus		turrī (-e)	turribus

640. FOURTH DECLENSION

SINGULAR

		CASE ENDINGS MASC.		CASE ENDINGS NEUT.
Nom.	exercitus	-us	cornū	-ū
Gen.	exercitūs	-ūs	cornūs	-ūs
Dat.	exercituī (-ū)	-uī (-ū)	cornū	-ū
Acc.	exercitum	-um	cornū	-ū
Abl.	exercitū	-ū	cornū	-ū

PLURAL

	CASE ENDINGS MASC.			CASE ENDINGS NEUT.
Nom.	exercitūs	-ūs	cornua	-ua
Gen.	exercituum	-uum	cornuum	-uum
Dat.	exercitibus	-ibus (-ubus)	cornibus	-ibus
Acc.	exercitūs	-ūs	cornua	-ua
Abl.	exercitibus	-ibus (-ubus)	cornibus	-ibus

641.   FIFTH DECLENSION

					CASE ENDINGS	
	SING.	PLUR.	SING.	PLUR.	SING.	PLUR.
Nom.	diēs	diēs	rēs	rēs	-ēs	-ēs
Gen.	diēī	diērum	reī	rērum	-ēī	-ērum
Dat.	diēī	diēbus	reī	rēbus	-ēī	-ēbus
Acc.	diem	diēs	rem	rēs	-em	-ēs
Abl.	diē	diēbus	rē	rēbus	-ē	-ēbus

642.   SPECIAL PARADIGMS

SINGULAR

Nom.	deus	domus	iter	vīs
Gen.	deī	domūs (-ī)	itineris	vīs
Dat.	deō	domuī (-ō)	itinerī	vī
Acc.	deum	domum	iter	vim
Abl.	deō	domō (-ū)	itinere	vī

PLURAL

Nom.	deī (diī, dī)	domūs	itinera	vīrēs
Gen.	deōrum (deum)	domuum (-ōrum)	itinerum	vīrium
Dat.	deīs (diīs, dīs)	domibus	itineribus	vīribus
Acc.	deōs	domōs (-ūs)	itinera	vīrīs (-ēs)
Abl.	deīs (diīs, dīs)	domibus	itineribus	vīribus

SINGULAR

Nom.	Iuppiter
Gen.	Iovis
Dat.	Iovī
Acc.	Iovem
Abl.	Iove

APPENDIX II

ADJECTIVES

643. FIRST AND SECOND DECLENSIONS

SINGULAR

	Masc.	Fem.	Neut.
Nom.	bonus	bona	bonum
Gen.	bonī	bonae	bonī
Dat.	bonŏ	bonae	bonŏ
Acc.	bonum	bonam	bonum
Abl.	bonŏ	bonā	bonŏ

PLURAL

	Masc.	Fem.	Neut.
Nom.	bonī	bonae	bona
Gen.	bonŏrum	bonārum	bonŏrum
Dat.	bonīs	bonīs	bonīs
Acc.	bonŏs	bonās	bona
Abl.	bonīs	bonīs	bonīs

SINGULAR

	Masc.	Fem.	Neut.
Nom.	līber	lībera	līberum
Gen.	līberī	līberae	līberī
Dat.	līberŏ	līberae	līberŏ
Acc.	līberum	līberam	līberum
Abl.	līberŏ	līberā	līberŏ

PLURAL

	Masc.	Fem.	Neut.
Nom.	līberī	līberae	lībera
Gen.	līberŏrum	līberārum	līberŏrum
Dat.	līberīs	līberīs	līberīs
Acc.	līberŏs	līberās	lībera
Abl.	līberīs	līberīs	līberīs

SINGULAR

	Masc.	Fem.	Neut.
Nom.	noster	nostra	nostrum
Gen.	nostrī	nostrae	nostrī
Dat.	nostrŏ	nostrae	nostrŏ
Acc.	nostrum	nostram	nostrum
Abl.	nostrŏ	nostrā	nostrŏ

FIRST YEAR LATIN

PLURAL

	MASC.	FEM.	NEUT.
Nom.	nostrī	nostrae	nostra
Gen.	nostrōrum	nostrārum	nostrōrum
Dat.	nostrīs	nostrīs	nostrīs
Acc.	nostrōs	nostrās	nostra
Abl.	nostrīs	nostrīs	nostrīs

644. THIRD DECLENSION

	SINGULAR		SINGULAR	
	M. AND F.	N.	M. AND F.	N.
Nom.	audāx	audāx	brevis	breve
Gen.	audācis	audācis	brevis	brevis
Dat.	audācī	audācī	brevī	brevī
Acc.	audācem	audāx	brevem	breve
Abl.	audācī (-e)	audācī (-e)	brevī	brevī

	PLURAL		PLURAL	
Nom.	audācēs	audācia	brevēs	brevia
Gen.	audācium	audācium	brevium	brevium
Dat.	audācibus	audācibus	brevibus	brevibus
Acc.	audācīs (-ēs)	audācia	brevīs (-ēs)	brevia
Abl.	audācibus	audācibus	brevibus	brevibus

	SINGULAR			PLURAL		
	MASC.	FEM.	NEUT.	MASC.	FEM.	NEUT.
Nom.	ācer	ācris	ācre	ācrēs	ācrēs	ācria
Gen.	ācris	ācris	ācris	ācrium	ācrium	ācrium
Dat.	ācrī	ācrī	ācrī	ācribus	ācribus	ācribus
Acc.	ācrem	ācrem	ācre	ācrīs (-ēs)	ācrīs (-ēs)	ācria
Abl.	ācrī	ācrī	ācrī	ācribus	ācribus	ācribus

645. PRESENT ACTIVE PARTICIPLES

	SINGULAR		PLURAL	
	M. AND F.	N.	M. AND F.	N.
Nom.	amāns	amāns	amantēs	amantia
Gen.	amantis	amantis	amantium	amantium
Dat.	amantī	amantī	amantibus	amantibus
Acc.	amantem	amāns	amantīs (-ēs)	amantia
Abl.	amante (-ī)	amante (-ī)	amantibus	amantibus

APPENDIX II

	SINGULAR		PLURAL	
	M. AND F.	N.	M. AND F.	N.
Nom.	iēns	iēns	euntēs	euntia
Gen.	euntis	euntis	euntium	euntium
Dat.	euntī	euntī	euntibus	euntibus
Acc.	euntem	iēns	euntīs (-ēs)	euntia
Abl.	eunte (-ī)	eunte (-ī)	euntibus	euntibus

646. IRREGULAR ADJECTIVES

	SINGULAR			PLURAL		
	Masc.	Fem.	Neut.	Masc.	Fem.	Neut.
Nom.	alius	alia	aliud	aliī	aliae	alia
Gen.	alīus	alīus	alīus	aliōrum	aliārum	aliōrum
Dat.	aliī	aliī	aliī	aliīs	aliīs	aliīs
Acc.	alium	aliam	aliud	aliōs	aliās	alia
Abl.	aliō	aliā	aliō	aliīs	aliīs	aliīs

	Masc.	Fem.	Neut.	M. AND F.	N.
Nom.	ūnus	ūna	ūnum	trēs	tria
Gen.	ūnīus	ūnīus	ūnīus	trium	trium
Dat.	ūnī	ūnī	ūnī	tribus	tribus
Acc.	ūnum	ūnam	ūnum	trīs (trēs)	tria
Abl.	ūnō	ūnā	ūnō	tribus	tribus

	Masc.	Fem.	Neut.	Sing.	Plur.
Nom.	duo	duae	duo	mīlle	mīlia
Gen.	duōrum	duārum	duōrum	mīlle	mīlium
Dat.	duōbus	duābus	duōbus	mīlle	mīlibus
Acc.	duōs (duo)	duās	duo	mīlle	mīlia
Abl.	duōbus	duābus	duōbus	mīlle	mīlibus

647. COMPARISON OF ADJECTIVES

POSITIVE	COMPARATIVE	SUPERLATIVE
lātus	lātior, lātius	lātissimus, -a, -um
brevis	brevior, brevius	brevissimus, -a, -um
audāx	audācior, audācius	audācissimus, -a, -um
miser	miserior, miserius	miserrimus, -a, -um
ācer	ācrior, ācrius	ācerrimus, -a, -um

648. DECLENSION OF COMPARATIVES

	SINGULAR		PLURAL	
	M. AND F.	N.	M. AND F.	N.
Nom.	lātior	lātius	lātiōrēs	lātiōra
Gen.	lātiōris	lātiōris	lātiōrum	lātiōrum
Dat.	lātiōrī	lātiōrī	lātiōribus	lātiōribus
Acc.	lātiōrem	lātius	lātiōrēs (-īs)	lātiōra
Abl.	lātiōre (-ī)	lātiōre (-ī)	lātiōribus	lātiōribus

	M. AND F.	N.	M. AND F.	N.
Nom.	——	plūs	plūrēs	plūra
Gen.	——	plūris	plūrium	plūrium
Dat.	——	——	plūribus	plūribus
Acc.	——	plūs	plūrīs (-ēs)	plūra
Abl.	——	plūre	plūribus	plūribus

649. IRREGULAR COMPARISON

POSITIVE	COMPARATIVE	SUPERLATIVE
bonus, -a, -um	melior, melius	optimus, -a, -um
malus, -a, -um	peior, peius	pessimus, -a, -um
magnus, -a, -um	maior, maius	maximus, -a, -um
multus, -a, -um	——, plūs	plūrimus, -a, -um
multī, -ae, -a	plūrēs, plūra	plūrimī, -ae, -a
parvus, -a, -um	minor, minus	minimus, -a, -um
facilis, -e	facilior, -ius	facillimus, -a, -um
difficilis, -e	difficilior, -ius	difficillimus, -a, -um
similis, -e	similior, -ius	simillimus, -a, -um
dissimilis, -e	dissimilior, -ius	dissimillimus, -a, -um
exterus, *outward*	exterior, *outer, exterior*	extrēmus ⎱ *outermost,* extimus ⎰ *last*
īnferus, *below*	īnferior, *lower*	īnfimus ⎱ *lowest* īmus ⎰
posterus, *following*	posterior, *later*	postrēmus ⎱ *last* postumus ⎰
superus, *above*	superior, *higher*	suprēmus ⎱ *highest* summus ⎰

APPENDIX II

POSITIVE	COMPARATIVE	SUPERLATIVE
[cis, citrā, *on this side*]	citerior, *hither*	citimus, *hithermost*
[in, intrā, *in, within*]	interior, *inner*	intimus, *inmost*
[prae, prō, *before*]	prior, *former*	prīmus, *first*
[prope, *near*]	propior, *nearer*	proximus, *next*
[ultrā, *beyond*]	ulterior, *farther*	ultimus, *farthest*

650. COMPARISON OF ADVERBS

POSITIVE	COMPARATIVE	SUPERLATIVE
cārē (cārus)	cārius	cārissimē
miserē (miser)	miserius	miserrimē
ācriter (ācer)	ācrius	ācerrimē
facile (facilis)	facilius	facillimē
bene (bonus)	melius	optimē
male (malus)	peius	pessimē
multum (multus)	plūs	plūrimum
parum, *little*	minus	minimē
diū, *long, a long time*	diūtius	diūtissimē
saepe, *often*	saepius	saepissimē

651. NUMERALS

CARDINALS	ORDINALS
1. ūnus, -a, -um	prīmus, -a, -um
2. duo, duae, duo	secundus (*or* alter)
3. trēs, tria	tertius
4. quattuor	quārtus
5. quīnque	quīntus
6. sex	sextus
7. septem	septimus
8. octō	octāvus
9. novem	nōnus
10. decem	decimus
11. ūndecim	ūndecimus
12. duodecim	duodecimus
13. tredecim	tertius decimus
14. quattuordecim	quārtus decimus

CARDINALS		ORDINALS
15.	quīndecim	quīntus decimus
16.	sēdecim	sextus decimus
17.	septendecim	septimus decimus
18.	duodēvīgintī	duodēvīcēnsimus
19.	ūndēvīgintī	ūndēvīcēnsimus
20.	vīgintī	vīcēnsimus
21.	{ vīgintī ūnus *or* ūnus et vīgintī	{ vīcēnsimus prīmus *or* ūnus et vīcēnsimus
22.	{ vīgintī duo *or* duo et vīgintī	{ vīcēnsimus secundus *or* alter et vīcēnsimus
28.	duodētrīgintā	duodētrīcēnsimus
29.	ūndētrīgintā	ūndētrīcēnsimus
30.	trīgintā	trīcēnsimus
40.	quadrāgintā	quadrāgēnsimus
50.	quīnquāgintā	quīnquāgēnsimus
60.	sexāgintā	sexāgēnsimus
70.	septuāgintā	septuāgēnsimus
80.	octōgintā	octōgēnsimus
90.	nōnāgintā	nōnāgēnsimus
100.	centum	centēnsimus
101.	{ centum ūnus *or* centum et ūnus	{ centēnsimus prīmus *or* centēnsimus et prīmus
200.	ducentī, -ae, -a	ducentēnsimus
300.	trecentī	trecentēnsimus
400.	quadringentī	quadringentēnsimus
500.	quīngentī	quīngentēnsimus
600.	sescentī	sescentēnsimus
700.	septingentī	septingentēnsimus
800.	octingentī	octingentēnsimus
900.	nōngentī	nōngentēnsimus
1000.	mīlle	mīllēnsimus
2000.	duo mīlia	bis mīllēnsimus
100,000.	centum mīlia	centiēns mīllēnsimus

APPENDIX II

PRONOUNS

652. PERSONAL

	SING.	PLUR.	SING.	PLUR.
Nom.	ego, *I*	nōs, *we*	tū, *you*	vōs, *you*
Gen.	meī	nostrum (-trī)	tuī	vestrum (-trī)
Dat.	mihi	nōbīs	tibi	vōbīs
Acc.	mē	nōs	tē	vōs
Abl.	mē	nōbīs	tē	vōbīs

	SING.	PLUR.	SING.	PLUR.	SING.	PLUR.
Nom.	is, *he*	iī (eī), *they*	ea, *she*	eae, *they*	id, *it*	ea, *they*
Gen.	eius, *his*	eōrum, *their*	eius, *her*	eārum, *their*	eius, *its*	eōrum, *their*
Dat.	eī	iīs (eīs)	eī	iīs (eīs)	eī	iīs (eīs)
Acc.	eum	eōs	eam	eās	id	ea
Abl.	eō	iīs (eīs)	eā	iīs (eīs)	eō	iīs (eīs)

a. **Hic** (654) and **ille** (654) are also used as pronouns of the third person.

653. REFLEXIVE

	SING.	PLUR.	SING.	PLUR.	SING.	PLUR.
Nom.	—	—	—	—	—	—
Gen.	meī, *of myself*	nostrī, *of ourselves*	tuī, *of yourself*	vestrī, *of yourselves*	suī, *of himself, herself, itself*	suī, *of themselves*
Dat.	mihi	nōbīs	tibi	vōbīs	sibi	sibi
Acc.	mē	nōs	tē	vōs	sē (sēsē)	sē (sēsē)
Abl.	mē	nōbīs	tē	vōbīs	sē (sēsē)	sē (sēsē)

654. DEMONSTRATIVE

	SINGULAR			PLURAL		
	MASC.	FEM.	NEUT.	MASC.	FEM.	NEUT.
Nom.	hic	haec	hoc	hī	hae	haec
Gen.	huius	huius	huius	hōrum	hārum	hōrum
Dat.	huic	huic	huic	hīs	hīs	hīs
Acc.	hunc	hanc	hoc	hōs	hās	haec
Abl.	hōc	hāc	hōc	hīs	hīs	hīs

	SINGULAR			PLURAL		
	Masc.	Fem.	Neut.	Masc.	Fem.	Neut.
Nom.	ille	illa	illud	illī	illae	illa
Gen.	illīus	illīus	illīus	illōrum	illārum	illōrum
Dat.	illī	illī	illī	illīs	illīs	illīs
Acc.	illum	illam	illud	illōs	illās	illa
Abl.	illō	illā	illō	illīs	illīs	illīs

	Masc.	Fem.	Neut.	Masc.	Fem.	Neut.
Nom.	is	ea	id	iī (eī)	eae	ea
Gen.	eius	eius	eius	eōrum	eārum	eōrum
Dat.	eī	eī	eī	iīs (eīs)	iīs (eīs)	iīs (eīs)
Acc.	eum	eam	id	eōs	eās	ea
Abl.	eō	eā	eō	iīs (eīs)	iīs (eīs)	iīs (eīs)

	Masc.	Fem.	Neut.	Masc.	Fem.	Neut.
Nom.	iste	ista	istud	istī	istae	ista
Gen.	istīus	istīus	istīus	istōrum	istārum	istōrum
Dat.	istī	istī	istī	istīs	istīs	istīs
Acc.	istum	istam	istud	istōs	istās	ista
Abl.	istō	istā	istō	istīs	istīs	istīs

	Masc.	Fem.	Neut.	Masc.	Fem.	Neut.
Nom.	īdem	e'adem	idem	iīdem / eīdem	eaedem	e'adem
Gen.	eiusdem	eiusdem	eiusdem	eōrundem	eārundem	eōrundem
Dat.	eīdem	eīdem	eīdem	iīsdem / eīsdem	iīsdem / eīsdem	iīsdem / eīsdem
Acc.	eundem	eandem	idem	eōsdem	eāsdem	e'adem
Abl.	eōdem	eādem	eōdem	iīsdem / eīsdem	iīsdem / eīsdem	iīsdem / eīsdem

	Masc.	Fem.	Neut.	Masc.	Fem.	Neut.
Nom.	ipse	ipsa	ipsum	ipsī	ipsae	ipsa
Gen.	ipsīus	ipsīus	ipsīus	ipsōrum	ipsārum	ipsōrum
Dat.	ipsī	ipsī	ipsī	ipsīs	ipsīs	ipsīs
Acc.	ipsum	ipsam	ipsum	ipsōs	ipsās	ipsa
Abl.	ipsō	ipsā	ipsō	ipsīs	ipsīs	ipsīs

APPENDIX II

655. RELATIVE

	SINGULAR			PLURAL		
	Masc.	Fem.	Neut.	Masc.	Fem.	Neut.
Nom.	quī	quae	quod	quī	quae	quae
Gen.	cuius	cuius	cuius	quōrum	quārum	quōrum
Dat.	cui	cui	cui	quibus	quibus	quibus
Acc.	quem	quam	quod	quōs	quās	quae
Abl.	quō	quā	quō	quibus	quibus	quibus

656. INTERROGATIVE

	SINGULAR			PLURAL		
	Masc.	Fem.	Neut.	Masc.	Fem.	Neut.
Nom.	quis (quī)	quae	quid (quod)	quī	quae	quae
Gen.	cuius	cuius	cuius	quōrum	quārum	quōrum
Dat.	cui	cui	cui	quibus	quibus	quibus
Acc.	quem	quam	quid (quod)	quōs	quās	quae
Abl.	quō	quā	quō	quibus	quibus	quibus

657. INDEFINITE

	SINGULAR		
	Masc.	Fem.	Neut.
Nom.	aliquis (aliquī)	aliqua	aliquid (aliquod)
Gen.	alicuius	alicuius	alicuius
Dat.	alicui	alicui	alicui
Acc.	aliquem	aliquam	aliquid (aliquod)
Abl.	aliquō	aliquā	aliquō

	PLURAL		
Nom.	aliquī	aliquae	aliqua
Gen.	aliquōrum	aliquārum	aliquōrum
Dat.	aliquibus	aliquibus	aliquibus
Acc.	aliquōs	aliquās	aliqua
Abl.	aliquibus	aliquibus	aliquibus

	SINGULAR		
Nom.	quīdam	quaedam	quiddam (quoddam)
Gen.	cuiusdam	cuiusdam	cuiusdam
Dat.	cuidam	cuidam	cuidam
Acc.	quendam	quandam	quiddam (quoddam)
Abl.	quōdam	quādam	quōdam

PLURAL

	MASC.	FEM.	NEUT.
Nom.	quīdam	quaedam	quaedam
Gen.	quōrundam	quārundam	quōrundam
Dat.	quibusdam	quibusdam	quibusdam
Acc.	quōsdam	quāsdam	quaedam
Abl.	quibusdam	quibusdam	quibusdam

SINGULAR

	MASC.	FEM.	NEUT.	MASC. AND FEM.	NEUT.
Nom.	quisque	quaeque	quidque (quodque)	quisquam	quicquam (quidquam)
Gen.	cuiusque	cuiusque	cuiusque	cuiusquam	cuiusquam
Dat.	cuique	cuique	cuique	cuiquam	cuiquam
Acc.	quemque	quamque	quidque (quodque)	quemquam	quicquam (quidquam)
Abl.	quōque	quāque	quōque	quōquam	quōquam

Plural rare   *Plural missing*

REGULAR VERBS

658.   FIRST CONJUGATION — Ā-Verbs

amō, *love*

PRINCIPAL PARTS: **a′mō, amā′re, amā′vī, amā′tus**

Pres. Stem **amā-**   *Perf. Stem* **amāv-**   *Part. Stem* **amāt-**

INDICATIVE

ACTIVE VOICE   PASSIVE VOICE

PRESENT

I love, am loving, do love, etc.   *I am loved,* etc.

a′mō	amā′mus	a′mor	amā′mur
a′mās	amā′tis	amā′ris	amā′minī
a′mat	a′mant	amā′tur	aman′tur

IMPERFECT (PAST)

I loved, was loving, did love, etc.   *I was loved,* etc.

amā′bam	amābā′mus	amā′bar	amābā′mur
amā′bās	amābā′tis	amābā′ris	amābā′minī
amā′bat	amā′bant	amābā′tur	amāban′tur

APPENDIX II

FUTURE

I shall love, etc.   *I shall be loved*, etc.

amā´bō	amā´bimus	amā´bor	amā´bimur
amā´bis	amā´bitis	amā´beris	amābi´minī
amā´bit	amā´bunt	amā´bitur	amābun´tur

PERFECT

I have loved, loved, did love, etc.   *I have been (was) loved*, etc.

amā´vī	amā´vimus	amā´tus { sum / es / est	amā´tī { sumus / estis / sunt
amāvis´tī	amāvis´tis
amā´vit	amāvē´runt

PLUPERFECT (PAST PERFECT)

I had loved, etc.   *I had been loved*, etc.

amā´veram	amāverā´mus	amā´tus { eram / erās / erat	amā´tī { erāmus / erātis / erant
amā´verās	amāverā´tis
amā´verat	amā´verant

FUTURE PERFECT

I shall have loved, etc.   *I shall have been loved*, etc.

amā´verō	amāve´rimus	amā´tus { erō / eris / erit	amā´tī { erimus / eritis / erunt
amā´veris	amāve´ritis
amā´verit	amā´verint

SUBJUNCTIVE

PRESENT

a´mem	amē´mus	a´mer	amē´mur
a´mēs	amē´tis	amē´ris	amē´minī
a´met	a´ment	amē´tur	amen´tur

IMPERFECT (PAST)

amā´rem	amārē´mus	amā´rer	amārē´mur
amā´rēs	amārē´tis	amārē´ris	amārē´minī
amā´ret	amā´rent	amārē´tur	amāren´tur

PERFECT

amā´verim	amāverī´mus	amā´tus { sim / sīs / sit	amā´tī { sīmus / sītis / sint
amā´verīs	amāverī´tis
amā´verit	amā´verint

PLUPERFECT (PAST PERFECT)

amāvis'sem	amāvissē'mus	amā'tus	essem / essēs / esset	amā'tī	essēmus / essētis / essent
amāvis'sēs	amāvissē'tis				
amāvis'set	amāvis'sent				

IMPERATIVE
PRESENT

a'mā, *love thou*   amā're, *be thou loved*
amā'te, *love ye*   amā'minī, *be ye loved*

FUTURE

amātō, *thou shalt love*   amātor, *thou shalt be loved*
amātō, *he shall love*   amātor, *he shall be loved*
amātōte, *you shall love*
amantō, *they shall love*   amantor, *they shall be loved*

INFINITIVE

PRES. amā're, *to love*   amā'rī, *to be loved*
PERF. amāvis'se, *to have loved*   amā'tus esse, *to have been loved*
FUT. amātū'rus esse, *to be about to love*   [amā'tum īrī, *to be about to be loved*]

PARTICIPLES

PRES. a'māns, -antis, *loving*   PRES. ———
FUT. amātū'rus, -a, -um, *about to love*   GER.[1] aman'dus, -a, -um, *to be loved*
PERF. ———   PERF. amā'tus, -a, -um, *having been loved, loved*

GERUND

Nom. ———
Gen. aman'dī, *of loving*
Dat. aman'dō, *for loving*
Acc. aman'dum, *loving*
Abl. aman'dō, *by loving*

SUPINE

Acc. [amātum, *to love*]
Abl. [amātū, *to love, in the loving*]

---

[1] Gerundive, sometimes called *future passive participle.*

APPENDIX II

659. SECOND CONJUGATION — Ē-Verbs

moneō, *advise*

PRINCIPAL PARTS: **mo′neō, monē′re, mo′nuī, mo′nitus**

Pres. Stem **monē-**   *Perf. Stem* **monu-**   *Part. Stem* **monit-**

INDICATIVE

ACTIVE VOICE   PASSIVE VOICE

PRESENT

I advise, etc.   *I am advised*, etc.

mo′neō	monē′mus	mo′neor	monē′mur
monē′s	monē′tis	monē′ris	monē′minī
mo′net	mo′nent	monē′tur	monen′tur

IMPERFECT (PAST)

I was advising, etc.   *I was advised*, etc.

monē′bam	monēbā′mus	monē′bar	monēbā′mur
monē′bās	monēbā′tis	monēbā′ris	monēbā′minī
monē′bat	monē′bant	monēbā′tur	monēban′tur

FUTURE

I shall advise, etc.   *I shall be advised*, etc.

monē′bō	monē′bimus	monē′bor	monē′bimur
monē′bis	monē′bitis	monē′beris	monēbi′minī
monē′bit	monē′bunt	monē′bitur	monēbun′tur

PERFECT

I have advised, I advised, etc.   *I have been (was) advised*, etc.

mo′nuī	monu′imus		sum		sumus
monuis′tī	monuis′tis	mo′nitus { es	mo′nitī { estis
mo′nuit	monuē′runt		est		sunt

PLUPERFECT (PAST PERFECT)

I had advised, etc.   *I had been advised*, etc.

monu′eram	monuerā′mus		eram		erāmus
monu′erās	monuerā′tis	mo′nitus { erās	mo′nitī { erātis
monu′erat	monu′erant		erat		erant

Future Perfect

I shall have advised, etc.   *I shall have been advised*, etc.

monu′erō	monue′rimus		(erō		(erimus
monu′eris	monue′ritis	mo′nitus{ eris	mo′nitī{ eritis
monu′erit	monu′erint		(erit		(erunt

SUBJUNCTIVE

Present

mo′neam	moneā′mus	mo′near	moneā′mur
mo′neās	moneā′tis	moneā′ris	moneā′minī
mo′neat	mo′neant	moneā′tur	monean′tur

Imperfect (Past)

monē′rem	monērē′mus	monē′rer	monērē′mur
monē′rēs	monērē′tis	monērē′ris	monērē′minī
monē′ret	monē′rent	monērē′tur	monēren′tur

Perfect

monu′erim	monuerī′mus		(sim		(sīmus
monu′erīs	monuerī′tis	mo′nitus{ sīs	mo′nitī{ sītis
monu′erit	monu′erint		(sit		(sint

Pluperfect (Past Perfect)

monuis′sem	monuissē′mus		(essem		(essēmus
monuis′sēs	monuissē′tis	mo′nitus{ essēs	mo′nitī{ essētis
monuis′set	monuis′sent		(esset		(essent

IMPERATIVE

Present

mo′nē, *advise thou*   monē′re, *be thou advised*
monē′te, *advise ye*   monē′minī, *be ye advised*

Future

monētō, *thou shalt advise*   monētor, *thou shalt be advised*
monētō, *he shall advise*   monētor, *he shall be advised*
monētōte, *you shall advise*   ———
monentō, *they shall advise*   monentor, *they shall be advised*

APPENDIX II

INFINITIVE

Pres.	monē´re, *to advise*	monē´rī, *to be advised*
Perf.	monuis´se, *to have advised*	mo´nitus esse, *to have been advised*
Fut.	monitū´rus esse, *to be about to advise*	[mo´nitum īrī, *to be about to be advised*]

PARTICIPLES

Pres.	mo´nēns, -entis, *advising*	Pres.	————
Fut.	monitū´rus, -a, -um, *about to advise*	Ger.	monen´dus, -a, -um, *to be advised*
Perf.	————	Perf.	mo´nitus, -a, -um, *having been advised, advised*

GERUND

Nom. ————
Gen. monen´dī, *of advising*
Dat. monen´dō, *for advising*
Acc. monen´dum, *advising*
Abl. monen´dō, *by advising*

SUPINE

Acc. [monitum, *to advise*]
Abl. [monitū, *to advise, in the advising*]

660.   THIRD CONJUGATION — Ĕ-Verbs

regō, *rule*

Principal Parts: re´gō, re´gere, rē´xī, rēc´tus

Pres. Stem rege-   *Perf. Stem* rēx-   *Part. Stem* rēct-

INDICATIVE

Active Voice   Passive Voice

Present

I rule, etc.   *I am ruled*, etc.

re´gō	re´gimus	re´gor	re´gimur
re´gis	re´gitis	re´geris	regi´minī
re´git	re´gunt	re´gitur	regun´tur

Imperfect (Past)

I was ruling, etc.   *I was ruled*, etc.

regē'bam	regēbā'mus	regē'bar	regēbā'mur
regē'bās	regēbā'tis	regēbā'ris	regēbā'minī
regē'bat	regē'bant	regēbā'tur	regēban'tur

Future

I shall rule, etc.   *I shall be ruled*, etc.

re'gam	regē'mus	re'gar	regē'mur
re'gēs	regē'tis	regē'ris	regē'minī
re'get	re'gent	regē'tur	regen'tur

Perfect

I have ruled, etc.   *I have been ruled*, etc.

rē'xī	rē'ximus	rēc'tus {	sum	rēc'tī {	sumus
rēxis'tī	rēxis'tis		es		estis
rē'xit	rēxē'runt		est		sunt

Pluperfect (Past Perfect)

I had ruled, etc.   *I had been ruled*, etc.

rē'xeram	rēxerā'mus	rēc'tus {	eram	rēc'tī {	erāmus
rē'xerās	rēxerā'tis		erās		erātis
rē'xerat	rē'xerant		erat		erant

Future Perfect

I shall have ruled, etc.   *I shall have been ruled*, etc.

rē'xerō	rēxe'rimus	rēc'tus {	erō	rēc'tī {	erimus
rē'xeris	rēxe'ritis		eris		eritis
rē'xerit	rē'xerint		erit		erunt

SUBJUNCTIVE

Present

re'gam	regā'mus	re'gar	regā'mur
re'gās	regā'tis	regā'ris	regā'minī
re'gat	re'gant	regā'tur	regan'tur

Imperfect (Past)

re'gerem	regerē'mus	re'gerer	regerē'mur
re'gerēs	regerē'tis	regerē'ris	regerē'minī
re'geret	re'gerent	regerē'tur	regeren'tur

APPENDIX II

Perfect

rē′xerim	rēxerī′mus	rēc′tus { sim / sīs / sit	rēc′tī { sīmus / sītis / sint
rē′xerīs	rēxerī′tis
rē′xerit	rē′xerint

Pluperfect (Past Perfect)

rēxis′sem	rēxissē′mus	rēc′tus { essem / essēs / esset	rēc′tī { essēmus / essētis / essent
rēxis′sēs	rēxissē′tis
rēxis′set	rēxis′sent

Imperative

Present

re′ge, *rule thou* re′gere, *be thou ruled*
re′gite, *rule ye* regi′minī, *be ye ruled*

Future

regitō, *thou shalt rule* regitor, *thou shalt be ruled*
regitō, *he shall rule* regitor, *he shall be ruled*
regitōte, *ye shall rule*
reguntō, *they shall rule* reguntor, *they shall be ruled*

Infinitive

Pres. re′gere, *to rule* re′gī, *to be ruled*
Perf. rēxis′se, *to have ruled* rēc′tus esse, *to have been ruled*
Fut. rēctū′rus esse, *to be about to rule* [rēc′tum īrī, *to be about to be ruled*]

Participles

Pres. re′gēns, -entis, *ruling* Pres. ———
Fut. rēctū′rus, -a, -um, *about to rule* Ger. regen′dus, -a, -um, *to be ruled*
Perf. ——— Perf. rēc′tus, -a, -um, *having been ruled, ruled*

Gerund

Nom. ———
Gen. regen′dī, *of ruling*
Dat. regen′dō, *for ruling*
Acc. regen′dum, *ruling*
Abl. regen′dō, *by ruling*

Supine

Acc. [rēctum, *to rule*]
Abl. [rēctū, *to rule, in the ruling*]

661. THIRD CONJUGATION — Verbs in -iō

capiō, *take*

PRINCIPAL PARTS: **ca′piō, ca′pere, cē′pī, cap′tus**

Pres. Stem **cape-**   *Perf. Stem* **cēp-**   *Part. Stem* **capt-**

INDICATIVE

ACTIVE VOICE   **PASSIVE VOICE**

PRESENT

I take, etc.   *I am taken*, etc.

ca′piō	ca′pimus	ca′pior	ca′pimur
ca′pis	ca′pitis	ca′peris	capi′minī
ca′pit	ca′piunt	ca′pitur	capiun′tur

IMPERFECT (PAST)

I was taking, etc.   *I was taken*, etc.

capiē′bam	capiēbā′mus	capiē′bar	capiēbā′mur
capiē′bās	capiēbā′tis	capiēbā′ris	capiēbā′minī
capiē′bat	capiē′bant	capiēbā′tur	capiēban′tur

FUTURE

I shall take, etc.   *I shall be taken*, etc.

ca′piam	capiē′mus	ca′piar	capiē′mur
ca′piēs	capiē′tis	capiē′ris	capiē′minī
ca′piet	ca′pient	capiē′tur	capien′tur

PERFECT

cē′pī, cēpis′tī, cē′pit, etc.   cap′tus sum, es, est, etc.

PLUPERFECT (PAST PERFECT)

cē′peram, cē′perās, cē′perat, etc.   cap′tus eram, erās, erat, etc.

FUTURE PERFECT

cē′perō, cē′peris, cē′perit, etc.   cap′tus erō, eris, erit, etc.

SUBJUNCTIVE

PRESENT

ca′piam, ca′piās, ca′piat, etc.   ca′piar, -iā′ris, -iā′tur, etc.

IMPERFECT (PAST)

ca′perem, ca′perēs, ca′peret, etc.   ca′perer, -erē′ris, -erē′tur, etc.

PERFECT

cē′perim, cē′perīs, cē′perit, etc.   cap′tus sim, sīs, sit, etc.

PLUPERFECT (PAST PERFECT)

cēpis′sem, cēpis′sēs, cēpis′set, etc.   cap′tus essem, essēs, esset, etc.

IMPERATIVE

PRES. ca′pe, *take thou*   ca′pere, *be thou taken*
     ca′pite, *take ye*   capi′minī, *be ye taken*
FUT. capitō, *thou shalt take*, etc.   capitor, *thou shalt be taken*, etc.

INFINITIVE

PRES. ca′pere, *to take*   ca′pī, *to be taken*
PERF. cēpis′se, *to have taken*   cap′tus esse, *to have been taken*
FUT. captū′rus esse, *to be about to take*   [cap′tum īrī, *to be about to be taken*]

PARTICIPLES

PRES. ca′piēns, -ientis, *taking*   PRES. ———
FUT. captū′rus, -a, -um, *about to take*   GER. capien′dus, -a, -um, *to be taken*
PERF. ———   PERF. cap′tus, -a, -um, *having been taken, taken*

GERUND

Gen. capien′dī, *of taking*, etc.

SUPINE

Acc. [captum, *to take*]
Abl. [captū, *to take, in the taking*]

662. FOURTH CONJUGATION — Ī-Verbs

audiō, *hear*

PRINCIPAL PARTS: au′diō, audī′re, audī′vī, audī′tus

Pres. Stem audī-   *Perf. Stem* audīv-   *Part. Stem* audīt-

INDICATIVE

ACTIVE VOICE   PRESENT   PASSIVE VOICE
I hear, etc.   *I am heard*, etc.

au′diō	audī′mus	au′dior	audī′mur
au′dīs	audī′tis	audī′ris	audī′minī
au′dit	au′diunt	audī′tur	audiun′tur

Imperfect (Past)

I was hearing, etc.   *I was heard*, etc.

audiē′bam	audiēbā′mus	audiē′bar	audiēbā′mur
audiē′bās	audiēbā′tis	audiēbā′ris	audiēbā′minī
audiē′bat	audiē′bant	audiēbā′tur	audiēban′tur

Future

I shall hear, etc.   *I shall be heard*, etc.

au′diam	audiē′mus	au′diar	audiē′mur
au′diēs	audiē′tis	audiē′ris	audiē′minī
au′diet	au′dient	audiē′tur	audien′tur

Perfect

I have heard, etc.   *I have been heard*, etc.

audī′vī	audī′vimus				
audīvis′tī	audīvis′tis	audī′tus {	sum / es / est	audī′tī {	sumus / estis / sunt
audī′vit	audīvē′runt				

Pluperfect (Past Perfect)

I had heard, etc.   *I had been heard*, etc.

audī′veram	audīverā′mus				
audī′verās	audīverā′tis	audī′tus {	eram / erās / erat	audī′tī {	erāmus / erātis / erant
audī′verat	audī′verant				

Future Perfect

I shall have heard, etc.   *I shall have been heard*, etc.

audī′verō	audīve′rimus				
audī′veris	audīve′ritis	audī′tus {	erō / eris / erit	audī′tī {	erimus / eritis / erunt
audī′verit	audī′verint				

SUBJUNCTIVE

Present

au′diam	audiā′mus	au′diar	audiā′mur
au′diās	audiā′tis	audiā′ris	audiā′minī
au′diat	au′diant	audiā′tur	audian′tur

Imperfect (Past)

audī′rem	audīrē′mus	audī′rer	audīrē′mur
audī′rēs	audīrē′tis	audīrē′ris	audīrē′minī
audī′ret	audī′rent	audīrē′tur	audīren′tur

APPENDIX II

PERFECT

audī′verim	audīverī′mus	audī′tus {	sim / sīs / sit	audī′tī {	sīmus / sītis / sint
audī′veris	audīverī′tis				
audī′verit	audī′verint				

PLUPERFECT (PAST PERFECT)

audīvis′sem	audīvissē′mus	audī′tus {	essem / essēs / esset	audī′tī {	essēmus / essētis / essent
audīvis′sēs	audīvissē′tis				
audīvis′set	audīvis′sent				

IMPERATIVE

PRESENT

au′dī, *hear thou* audī′re, *be thou heard*
audī′te, *hear ye* audī′minī, *be ye heard*

FUTURE

audītō, *thou shalt hear* audītor, *thou shalt be heard*
audītō, *he shall hear* audītor, *he shall be heard*
audītōte, *ye shall hear* ———
audiuntō, *they shall hear* audiuntor, *they shall be heard*

INFINITIVE

Pres. audī′re, *to hear* audī′rī, *to be heard*
Perf. audīvis′se, *to have heard* audī′tus esse, *to have been heard*
Fut. audītū′rus esse, *to be about to hear* [audī′tum īrī, *to be about to be heard*]

PARTICIPLES

Pres. au′diēns, -ientis, *hearing* Pres. ———
Fut. audītū′rus, -a, -um, *about to hear* Ger. audien′dus, -a, -um, *to be heard*
Perf. ——— Perf. audī′tus, -a, -um, *having been heard, heard*

GERUND

Nom. ———
Gen. audien′dī, *of hearing*
Dat. audien′dō, *for hearing*
Acc. audien′dum, *hearing*
Abl. audien′dō, *by hearing*

SUPINE

Acc. [audītum, *to hear*]
Abl. [audītū, *to hear, in the hearing*]

IRREGULAR VERBS

663. **sum,** *be*

PRINCIPAL PARTS: **sum, esse, fuī, futūrus**

Pres. Stem **es-**   *Perf. Stem* **fu-**   *Part. Stem* **fut-**

INDICATIVE

PRESENT

SINGULAR	PLURAL
sum, *I am*	su′mus, *we are*
es, *you are*	es′tis, *you are*
est, *he (she, it) is*	sunt, *they are*

IMPERFECT (PAST)

e′ram, *I was*	erā′mus, *we were*
e′rās, *you were*	erā′tis, *you were*
e′rat, *he was*	e′rant, *they were*

FUTURE

e′rō, *I shall be*	e′rimus, *we shall be*
e′ris, *you will be*	e′ritis, *you will be*
e′rit, *he will be*	e′runt, *they will be*

PERFECT

fuī, *I have been, was*	fu′imus, *we have been, were*
fuis′tī, *you have been, were*	fuis′tis, *you have been, were*
fu′it, *he has been, was*	fuē′runt, *they have been, were*

PLUPERFECT (PAST PERFECT)

fu′eram, *I had been*	fuerā′mus, *we had been*
fu′erās, *you had been*	fuerā′tis, *you had been*
fu′erat, *he had been*	fu′erant, *they had been*

FUTURE PERFECT

fu′erō, *I shall have been*	fue′rimus, *we shall have been*
fu′eris, *you will have been*	fue′ritis, *you will have been*
fu′erit, *he will have been*	fu′erint, *they will have been*

SUBJUNCTIVE

Present
SING.	PLUR.
sim	sī′mus
sīs	sī′tis
sit	sint

Imperfect (Past)
SING.	PLUR.
es′sem	essē′mus
es′sēs	essē′tis
es′set	es′sent

Perfect
SING.	PLUR.
fu′erim	fuerī′mus
fu′erīs	fuerī′tis
fu′erit	fu′erint

Pluperfect (Past Perfect)
SING.	PLUR.
fuis′sem	fuissē′mus
fuis′sēs	fuissē′tis
fuis′set	fuis′sent

IMPERATIVE

Present
es, *be thou*
es′te, *be ye*

Future
estō, *thou shalt be*
estō, *he shall be*
estōte, *ye shall be*
suntō, *they shall be*

INFINITIVE
- PRES. es′se, *to be*
- PERF. fuis′se, *to have been*
- FUT. futū′rus esse, or fo′re, *to be about to be*

PARTICIPLE
futū′rus, -a, -um, *about to be*

664.   possum, *be able, can*

PRINCIPAL PARTS: **possum, posse, potuī, ———**

INDICATIVE / SUBJUNCTIVE

	SING.	PLUR.	SING.	PLUR.
PRES.	possum	possumus	possim	possīmus
	potes	potestis	possīs	possītis
	potest	possunt	possit	possint
IMPF.	poteram	poterāmus	possem	possēmus
FUT.	poterō	poterimus	———	———
PERF.	potuī	potuimus	potuerim	potuerīmus
PLUP.	potueram	potuerāmus	potuissem	potuissēmus
F. P.	potuerō	potuerimus	———	———

INFINITIVE
PRES. posse   PERF. potuisse

665. volō, nōlō, mālō

PRINCIPAL PARTS:
- volō, velle, voluī, ———, *be willing, will, wish*
- nōlō, nōlle, nōluī, ———, *be unwilling, will not*
- mālō, mālle, māluī, ———, *be more willing, prefer*

INDICATIVE

SINGULAR

PRES. volō	nōlō	mālō
vīs	nōn vīs	māvīs
vult	nōn vult	māvult

PLURAL

volumus	nōlumus	mālumus
vultis	nōn vultis	māvultis
volunt	nōlunt	mālunt
IMPF. volēbam	nōlēbam	mālēbam
FUT. volam, volēs, etc.	nōlam, nōlēs, etc.	mālam, mālēs, etc.
PERF. voluī	nōluī	māluī
PLUP. volueram	nōlueram	mālueram
F. P. voluerō	nōluerō	māluerō

SUBJUNCTIVE

SINGULAR

PRES. velim	nōlim	mālim
velīs	nōlīs	mālīs
velit	nōlit	mālit

PLURAL

velīmus	nōlīmus	mālīmus
velītis	nōlītis	mālītis
velint	nōlint	mālint
IMPF. vellem	nōllem	māllem
PERF. voluerim	nōluerim	māluerim
PLUP. voluissem	nōluissem	māluissem

IMPERATIVE

PRES. ———	nōlī	———
	nōlīte	
FUT. ———	nōlītō, etc.	———

APPENDIX II

	INFINITIVE	
Pres. velle	nōlle	mālle
Perf. voluisse	nōluisse	māluisse

	PARTICIPLE	
Pres. volēns	nōlēns	——

666. ferō, *bear, carry, endure*

Principal Parts: **ferō, ferre, tulī, lātus**

Pres. Stem **fer-**   *Perf. Stem* **tul-**   *Part. Stem* **lāt-**

INDICATIVE

Active		Passive	
Pres. ferō	ferimus	feror	ferimur
fers	fertis	ferris	feriminī
fert	ferunt	fertur	feruntur
Impf. ferēbam		ferēbar	
Fut. feram		ferar	
Perf. tulī		lātus sum	
Plup. tuleram		lātus eram	
F.P. tulerō		lātus erō	

SUBJUNCTIVE

Pres. feram	ferar
Impf. ferrem	ferrer
Perf. tulerim	lātus sim
Plup. tulissem	lātus essem

IMPERATIVE

Active		Passive	
Pres. fer	ferte	ferre	feriminī
Fut. fertō	fertōte	fertor	
fertō	feruntō	fertor	feruntor

INFINITIVE

Pres. ferre	ferrī
Perf. tulisse	lātus esse
Fut. lātūrus esse	[lātum īrī]

PARTICIPLES

Pres.	ferēns	*Pres.*	——
Fut.	lātūrus	*Ger.*	ferendus
Perf.	——	*Perf.*	lātus

GERUND

SUPINE

Gen. ferendī
Dat. ferendō
Acc. ferendum [lātum]
Abl. ferendō [lātū]

667. eŏ, *go*

Principal Parts: **eŏ, īre, iī (īvī), itūrus**

Pres. stem ĭ- *Perf. stem* ĭ- (īv-) *Part. stem* it-

	INDICATIVE		SUBJUNCTIVE	IMPERATIVE	
Pres.	eō	īmus	eam	ī	īte
	īs	ītis			
	it	eunt			
Impf.	ībam		īrem		
Fut.	ībō		——	ītō	ītōte
Perf.	iī		ierim	īto	euntō
Plup.	ieram		īssem		
F. P.	ierō		——		

INFINITIVE

PARTICIPLES

Pres. īre iēns, euntis (645)
Perf. īsse itum
Fut. itūrus esse itūrus

GERUND

SUPINE

Gen. eundī
Dat. eundō
Acc. eundum [itum]
Abl. eundō [itū]

APPENDIX II

668.   **fīō**, *be made, become, happen*

PRINCIPAL PARTS: **fīō, fierī, factus sum**

	INDICATIVE		SUBJUNCTIVE	IMPERATIVE	
PRES.	fīō	—	fīam	fī	fīte
	fīs	—			
	fit	fīunt			
IMPF.	fīēbam		fierem		
FUT.	fīam		—		
PERF.	factus sum		factus sim		
PLUP.	factus eram		factus essem		
F. P.	factus erō		—		

	INFINITIVE		PARTICIPLES
PRES.	fierī	GER.	faciendus
PERF.	factus esse	PERF.	factus
FUT.	[factum īrī]		

669.   DEPONENT VERBS

PRINCIPAL PARTS:
 I. **hortor, hortārī, hortātus sum,** *urge*
 II. **vereor, verērī, veritus sum,** *fear*
 III. **sequor, sequī, secūtus sum,** *follow*
 IV. **potior, potīrī, potītus sum,** *get possession of*

INDICATIVE

PRES.	hortor	vereor	sequor	potior
	hortāris	verēris	sequeris	potīris
	hortātur	verētur	sequitur	potītur
	hortāmur	verēmur	sequimur	potīmur
	hortāminī	verēminī	sequiminī	potīminī
	hortantur	verentur	sequuntur	potiuntur
IMPF.	hortābar	verēbar	sequēbar	potiēbar
FUT.	hortābor	verēbor	sequar	potiar
PERF.	hortātus sum	veritus sum	secūtus sum	potītus sum
PLUP.	hortātus eram	veritus eram	secūtus eram	potītus eram
F. P.	hortātus erō	veritus erō	secūtus erō	potītus erō

SUBJUNCTIVE

Pres.	horter	verear	sequar	potiar
Impf.	hortārer	verērer	sequerer	potīrer
Perf.	hortātus sim	veritus sim	secūtus sim	potītus sim
Plup.	hortātus essem	veritus essem	secūtus essem	potītus essem

IMPERATIVE

Pres.	hortāre	verēre	sequere	potīre
Fut.	hortātor	verētor	sequitor	potītor

INFINITIVE

Pres.	hortārī	verērī	sequī	potīrī
Perf.	hortātus esse	veritus esse	secūtus esse	potītus esse
Fut.	hortātūrus esse	veritūrus esse	secūtūrus esse	potītūrus esse

PARTICIPLES

Pres.	hortāns	verēns	sequēns	potiēns
Fut.	hortātūrus	veritūrus	secūtūrus	potītūrus
Perf.	hortātus	veritus	secūtus	potītus
Ger.	hortandus	verendus	sequendus	potiendus

GERUND

hortandī, etc.   verendī, etc.   sequendī, etc.   potiendī, etc.

SUPINE

[hortātum, -tū]   [veritum, -tū]   [secūtum, -tū]   [potītum, -tū]

670.   PASSIVE PERIPHRASTIC CONJUGATION

INDICATIVE

Pres. amandus sum, *I am to be, must be, loved*
Impf. amandus eram, *I was to be, had to be, loved*
Fut. amandus erō, *I shall have to be loved*
Perf. amandus fuī, *I was to be, had to be, loved*
Plup. amandus fueram, *I had had to be loved*
F. P. amandus fuerō, *I shall have had to be loved*

SUBJUNCTIVE

Pres. amandus sim
Impf. amandus essem
Perf. amandus fuerim
Plup. amandus fuissem

INFINITIVE

PRES. amandus esse, *to have to be loved*
PERF. amandus fuisse, *to have had to be loved*

So in the other conjugations:

monendus sum, *I am to be, must be, advised*
regendus sum, *I am to be, must be, ruled*
capiendus sum, *I am to be, must be, taken*
audiendus sum, *I am to be, must be, heard*
etc.

671.   SYNOPSIS OF THE VERB

The synopsis of a verb is a summary of the conjugation of that verb made by stating in succession the forms for some particular person and number.

The following is a synopsis of **amō** in the third person singular, arranged by stems. The infinitives, participles, etc. are added to complete each system.

PRINCIPAL PARTS: **amō, amāre, amāvī, amātus**

Pres. Stem **amā-**   *Perf. Stem* **amāv-**   *Part. Stem* **amāt-**

PRESENT SYSTEM, BASED ON THE PRESENT STEM

	ACTIVE		PASSIVE
		INDICATIVE	
PRES.	amā-t		amā-tur
IMPF.	amā-bat		amā-bātur
FUT.	amā-bit		amā-bitur
		SUBJUNCTIVE	
PRES.	ame-t		amē-tur
IMPF.	amā-ret		amā-rētur
		INFINITIVE	
PRES.	amā-re		amā-rī
		PARTICIPLE	
PRES.	amā-ns		GER. ama-ndus
		GERUND	
		ama-ndī	

PERFECT SYSTEM, BASED ON THE PERFECT STEM

INDICATIVE	SUBJUNCTIVE
PERF. amāv-it	amāv-erit
PLUP. amāv-erat	amāv-isset
F. P. amāv-erit	

INFINITIVE

PERF. amāv-isse

PARTICIPIAL SYSTEM, BASED ON THE PARTICIPIAL STEM

INDICATIVE	SUBJUNCTIVE
PERF. amāt-us est	amāt-us sit
PLUP. amāt-us erat	amāt-us esset
F. P. amāt-us erit	

INFINITIVE

PERF. ———	amāt-us esse
FUT. amāt-ūrus esse	[amāt-um īrī]

PARTICIPLE

FUT. amāt-ūrus   PERF. amāt-us

SUPINE

[amāt-um]
[amāt-ū]

LATIN-ENGLISH VOCABULARY

In this vocabulary words inclosed in brackets (except in the case of compounds with one or both parts changed in form) are sometimes primitives, sometimes cognates.

Translations inclosed within parentheses are not intended to be used as such. They are inserted to show literal meanings.

Abbreviations are generally self-explanatory. Cf. (*confer*) = compare; irr. = irregular.

Words printed in SMALL CAPITALS are at once derivatives and definitions: as, ABDUCT, under **abdūcō**. Many other more or less remotely derived words, not definitions, are added in *italic* in parentheses: as, (*Accident*), under **accidō**.

It will be seen that comparisons of words in reference to meaning are much more frequent than is usual in special vocabularies. This has been done from the conviction that the pupils should make such comparisons frequently from the outset.

ā (ab), *prep. with abl.*, from, by, off

ab-dō, abdere, abdidī, abditus [-*dō*, put], hide, conceal

ab-dūcō, abdūcere, abdūxī, abductus, lead away, take off; ABDUCT

ab-eō, abīre, abiī, abitūrus, go from, go off, go away

ab-iciō, abicere, abiēcī, abiectus [-*iaciō*], throw off, throw down, cast away. (*Abject*)

ab-ripiō, abripere, abripuī, abreptus [-*rapiō*], snatch away, carry off

abs-cīdō, abscīdere, abscīdī, abscīsus [*ab(s)-caedō*], cut off

abs-trahō, abstrahere, abstrāxī, abstrāctus [*ab(s)-*], drag away, draw off. (*Abstract*)

ab-sum, abesse, āfuī, āfutūrus, be away, be ABSENT, be distant, be off; *with* ā *and abl.*

ac, *conj., see* atque

ac-cēdō, accēdere, accessī, accessūrus [*ad-*], go *or* come near, approach. (*Accession.*) *Cf.* adeō *and* appropinquō

ac-cendō, accendere, accendī, accēnsus [*ad-candeō*, shine], kindle, set fire to, light; inflame

ac-cidō, accidere, accidī, —— [*ad-cadō*, fall], fall upon, fall out, happen. (*Accident.*) *Cf.* ēveniō *and* fīō

ac-cipiō, accipere, accēpī, acceptus [*ad-capiō*], (take to), receive, ACCEPT

287

ac-currō, accurrere, accurrī (accucurrī), accursūrus [ad-], run up, run toward

ācer, ācris, ācre, *adj.*, sharp, keen; active, EAGER. (*Acrid*)

acervus, -ī, *m.*, pile, heap, mass

aciēs, -ēī, *f.* [*ācer*], edge; line, line of battle, battle array·

Ācrisius, Ācrisī, *m.*, ACRISIUS, grandfather of Perseus

ācriter, *adv.* [*ācer*], sharply, EAGERly, spiritedly, fiercely

ad, *prep. with acc.*, to, toward, near, up to; *with gerund or gerundive*, to, for; ad hunc modum, after this manner; *as adv.*, about

ad-aequō, adaequāre, adaequāvī, adaequātus, become EQUAL to, EQUAL. (*Adequate*)

adclīvis, -e, *adj.*, sloping toward, rising, ascending. (*Acclivity*)

ad-dūcō, addūcere, addūxī, adductus, lead to, influence. (*Adduce*)

ad-eō, adīre, adiī, aditus, go to, approach, visit. *Cf.* accēdō *and* appropinquō

ad-ferō, adferre, attulī, adlātus, bear to, bring, render

ad-ficiō, adficere, adfēcī, adfectus [-*faciō*], AFFECT, influence; afflict, oppress

ad-gredior, adgredī, adgressus sum [-*gradior*, go], approach, attack. (*Aggressive*)

ad-hibeō, adhibēre, adhibuī, adhibitus [-*habeō*], apply, employ, use

ad-hūc, *adv.*, hitherto, as yet, still

ad-iciō, adicere, adiēcī, adiectus [-*iaciō*], add. (*Adjective*)

aditus, -ūs, *m.* [*adeō*], approach, way of access. *Cf.* adventus

ad-iungō, adiungere, adiūnxī, adiūnctus, join to. (*Adjunct*)

ad-ligō, adligāre, adligāvī, adligātus, bind to, bind

admīrātiō, -ōnis, *f.* [*admīror*], ADMIRATION, astonishment, wonder

ad-mīror, admīrārī, admīrātus sum [*admīrātiō*], wonder at, ADMIRE

ad-mittō, admittere, admīsī, admissus, permit, allow; give rein to. (*Admit*)

admōtus, *see* admoveō

ad-moveō, admovēre, admōvī, admōtus, (move to), apply, employ

ad-nectō, adnectere, adnexuī (adnexī), adnexus, tie to, fasten to, attach. (*Annex*)

ad-olēscō, adolēscere, adolēvī, adultus, grow up. (*Adult*)

ad-ōrō, adōrāre, adōrāvī, adōrātus, pray to, worship, ADORE

ad-spiciō, adspicere, adspexī, adspectus [-*speciō*, look], look at, look upon, behold. (*Aspect*)

ad-stō, adstāre, adstitī, ——, stand near

ad-sum, adesse, adfuī, adfutūrus, be present, be here; *with dat.*

Aduatucī, -ōrum, *m. plur.*, the ADUATUCI, a Gallic tribe

adulēscēns, -entis, *m. and f.* [*adolēscō*], youth, young person. (*Adolescence.*) *Cf.* iuvenis

adultus, *see* adolēscō

advectus, *see* advehō

ad-vehō, advehere, advexī, advectus, carry to, bring on, bring

adventus, -ūs, *m.,* approach, arrival. (*Advent.*) *Cf.* **aditus**
adversus, -a, -um, *adj.,* turned toward, opposite, in front, AD-VERSE
adversus, *prep. with acc.,* against
aedēs (aedis), -is, *f.,* building, temple; *plur.,* house
aedificium, aedificī, *n.* [*aedificō*], building. (*Edifice*)
aedificō, aedificāre, aedificāvī, aedificātus [*aedēs-faciō*], build. (*Edify*)
aeger, aegra, aegrum, *adj.,* sick, weak, feeble
aequus, -a, -um, *adj.,* EQUAL
āēr, āeris, *m.* (*acc.* āera), AIR
aes, aeris, *n.,* copper, bronze
aestās, -ātis, *f.,* summer
aetās, -ātis, *f.,* life, AGE
Aethiopēs, -um, *m. plur.,* the ETHIOPIANS
Aetna, -ae, *f.,* ÆTNA, a mountain in Sicily
Āfrica, -ae, *f.,* AFRICA
Āfricānus, -ī, *m.,* AFRICANUS
ager, agrī, *m.,* field, territory, land
agger, -eris, *m.,* mound, rampart
Āgis, -idis, *m.,* AGIS, a king of Sparta
agmen, -inis, *n.* [*agō*], (the thing led), army, host, column
agō, agere, ēgī, āctus, drive, lead, bring up; ACT, do; treat; celebrate; pass (life)
agricola, -ae, *m.* [*ager-colō*], farmer, husbandman
āla, -ae, *f.,* wing
Alba, -ae, *f.,* ALBA, an ancient city of Italy

Albānus, -a, -um, *adj.,* ALBAN; *as noun,* an ALBAN, inhabitant of Alba
albus, -a, -um, *adj.,* white
Alcmēna, -ae, *f.,* ALCMENA, the mother of Hercules
aliās, *adv.* [*alius*], elsewhere, at another time
aliēnus, -a, -um, *adj.* [*alius*], another's; unfavorable. (*Alien*)
ali-quandō, *adv.* [*alius*], at some time; formerly, once. *Cf.* **ōlim**
aliquis (-quī), -qua, -quid (-quod), *indef. pron. and adj.,* some one, some, any
alius, -a, -ud, *adj. and pron.,* another, other, else; alius ... alius, one ... another. (*Alias.*) *Cf.* **cēterī**
Allobrogēs, -um, *m. plur.,* the ALLOBROGES, a tribe of Gaul
Alpēs, -ium, *f. plur.,* the ALPS
altāria, -ium, *n. plur.,* ALTAR
alter, -era, -erum, *adj. and pron.,* the one, the other (of two); second; alter ... alter, the one ... the other. (*Alternative*)
altitūdō, -inis, *f.* [*altus*], height
altum, -ī, *n.* [*altus*], the sea
altus, -a, -um, *adj.,* high, deep
alveus, -ī, *m.,* hollow vessel, tub, trough
Ambarrī, -ōrum, *m. plur.,* the AMBARRI, a tribe of Gaul, near the Hædui
ambulō, ambulāre, ambulāvī, ambulātūrus, walk, take a walk. (*Perambulate*)
āmentia, -ae, *f.,* want of reason, madness

amīcitia, -ae, *f.* [*amīcus*], friendship

amīcus, -a, -um, *adj.* [*amō*], friendly; *as noun*, friend. (*Amiable*)

ā-mittō, āmittere, āmīsī, āmissus, send away; lose

amō, amāre, amāvī, amātus [*amor*], love, like, be fond of

amor, -ōris, *f.* [*amō*], love

ā-moveō, āmovēre, āmōvī, āmōtus, move away, put aside

ampliō, ampliāre, ampliāvī, ampliātus [*amplus*], increase, extend. (*Ampliative*)

amplus, -a, -um, *adj.* [*ampliō*], large, wide; honorable. (*Ample, Amplify*)

Amūlius, Amūlī, *m.*, AMULIUS, father of Rhea Silvia

an, *conj.*, or

ancilla, -ae, *f.*, maidservant

ancora, -ae, *f.*, ANCHOR

Ancus Mārcius, Ancī Mārcī, *m.*, ANCUS MARCIUS, one of the seven kings of Rome

Andromeda, -ae, *f.*, ANDROMEDA

anguis, -is, *m. and f.*, serpent, snake

angustus, -a, -um, *adj.*, narrow. (*Anguish*)

anima, -ae, *f.* [*animus*], breath, soul, life. (*Animate*)

anim-advertō, animadvertere, animadvertī, animadversus [*animus-*], turn the mind to, notice

animus, -ī, *m.* [*anima*], mind, soul, spirit, disposition. *Cf.* mēns

annōna, -ae, *f.* [*annus*], (the year's supply), provisions; price (of provisions), market; scarcity

annus, -ī, *m.*, year. (*Annual*)

ante, *adv., and prep. with acc.*, before

anteā, *adv.* [*ante*], before

ante-cēdō, antecēdere, antecessī, antecessūrus, go before. (*Antecedent*)

Antemnātēs, -ium, *m. plur.*, the inhabitants of Antemnæ

ante-quam, *conj.*, sooner than, before

antīquus, -a, -um, *adj.* [*ante*], old, ancient. (*Antiquity*)

antrum, -ī, *n.*, cave

anxius, -a, -um, *adj.*, troubled, ANXIOUS

aperiō, aperīre, aperuī, apertus, open

Apollō, -inis, *m.*, APOLLO, a god of the Greeks

appellō, appellāre, appellāvī, appellātus [*ad-*], address, call, name. (*Appeal*.) *Cf.* vocō

ap-pellō, appellere, appulī, appulsus [*ad-*], (drive to); nāvem appellere, land, put in

ap-prehendō, apprehendere, apprehendī, apprehēnsus [*ad-*], seize. (*Apprehend*)

ap-propinquō, appropinquāre, appropinquāvī, appropinquātūrus [*ad-*], approach, come near to. *Cf.* adeō *and* accēdō

aptō, aptāre, aptāvī, aptātus, fit. (*Adapt*)

apud, *prep. with acc.*, with, by, near, among

aqua, -ae, *f.*, water. (*Aquatic*)

Aquilēia, -ae, *f.*, AQUILEIA, a city at the head of the Adriatic

Aquītānī, -ōrum, *m. plur.*, the AQUITANI, a tribe of Gaul

āra, -ae, f., altar

Arar, -aris, m., the Saône, a river of Gaul, flowing into the Rhone

arbitror, arbitrārī, arbitrātus sum, think, suppose. (*Arbitrator.*) Cf. exīstimō *and* putō

arbor, -oris, f., tree

arca, -ae, f., box, chest, ARK

arcus, -ūs, m., bow. (*Arc*)

Ardea, -ae, f., ARDEA, a city of Italy

arduus, -a, -um, adj., steep; difficult, ARDUOUS

Argī, -ōrum, m. plur., ARGOS, a city of Greece

Aristotelēs, -is, m., ARISTOTLE, a Greek philosopher

arma, -ōrum, n. plur. [armō], ARMS, weapons, ARMOR

armō, armāre, armāvī, armātus [arma], ARM, equip

ar-ripiō, arripere, arripuī, arreptus [ad-rapiō], seize, snatch

Arrūns, Arruntis, m., ARRUNS, a son of Tarquinius Superbus

ars, artis, f., ART, skill

a-scendō, ascendere, ascendī, ascēnsus [ad-scandō, climb], climb to, mount, ASCEND

ascēnsus, -ūs, m. [ascendō], a going up, ASCENT

at, conj., but. Cf. sed *and* autem

Athēnae, -ārum, f. plur., ATHENS

Atlās, -antis, m., ATLAS, one of the Titans

at-que, conj., *used before vowels and consonants*, ac *before consonants only* [ad-], and also, and especially, and; as. Cf. et *and* -que

atrōx, -ōcis, adj., savage, fierce, severe. (*Atrocious.*) Cf. saevus *and* trux

at-tonitus, -a, -um, adj. [ad-], thunderstruck, astounded, awestruck

auctōritās, -ātis, f., power, AUTHORITY, influence

audācia, -ae, f. [audāx], daring, boldness, AUDACITY

audāx, -ācis, adj., daring, bold. (*Audacious*)

audiō, audīre, audīvī (audiī), audītus, hear, listen. (*Audience*)

au-ferō, auferre, abstulī, ablātus [ab(s)-], bear off, carry away, take away. (*Ablative*)

augeō, augēre, auxī, auctus [auxilium], increase, enlarge. (*Augment*)

aureus, -a, -um, adj. [aurum], of gold, golden

aurum, -ī, n., gold

aut, conj., or; aut . . . aut, either . . . or. Cf. vel

autem, conj. (*never used as the first word*), but, however, moreover, now. Cf. sed

auxilior, auxiliārī, auxiliātus sum [auxilium], give help, aid, assist, succor

auxilium, auxilī, n. [augeō], help, aid, support. (*Auxiliary*)

Aventīnus, -a, -um, adj., AVENTINE, of the AVENTINE (one of the hills of Rome)

ā-vertō, āvertere, āvertī, āversus, turn away, turn aside, AVERT, remove

avus, -ī, m., grandfather

barbarus, -ī, *m.*, BARBARIAN
Belgae, -ārum, *m. plur.*, the BELGIANS *or* BELGÆ, a Gallic tribe
bellum, -ī, *n.*, war. (*Belligerent*)
bēlua, -ae, *f.*, beast, monster
bene, *adv.* [*bonus*], well
beneficium, beneficī, *n.* [*bene-faciō*], kindness, service, BENEFIT
bibō, bibere, bibī, ——, drink. (*Imbibe*)
bis, *adv.*, twice
bonitās, -ātis, *f.* [*bonus*], fertility, goodness
bonus, -a, -um, *adj.*, good, kind
brevis, -e, *adj.*, short, BRIEF
Britannia, -ae, *f.*, BRITAIN
Britannus, -ī, *m.*, a BRITON, inhabitant of Britannia
Bruttiī *or* Brittiī, -ōrum, *m. plur.*, the BRUTTII, a people of southern Italy
Brūtus, -ī, *m.*, BRUTUS, a Roman surname

C., *abbreviation for* Gāius, Caius
caecus, -a, -um, *adj.*, blind
caedō, caedere, cecīdī, caesus, cut; kill. (*Suicide*)
Caelius, -a, -um, *adj.*, CÆLIAN
caelum, -ī, *n.*, sky, heaven, heavens
Caenīnēnsēs, -ium, *m. plur.*, the inhabitants of Cænina
Caesar, -aris, *m.*, Caius Julius CÆSAR, a famous Roman
cale-faciō, calefacere, calefēcī, calefactus [*caleō*-, be hot], make hot, heat
Campānia, -ae, *f.*, CAMPANIA, a district of Italy

canis, -is, *m. and f.*, dog. (*Canine*)
Cannae, -ārum, *f. plur.*, CANNÆ, a town of southern Italy
cantō, cantāre, cantāvī, cantātus, sing. (*Chant*)
capiō, capere, cēpī, captus, take, seize, CAPTURE; form
Capitōlium, Capitōlī, *n.*, the CAPITOL, temple of Jupiter at Rome; the CAPITOLINE Hill
captīva, -ae, *f.* [*capiō*], CAPTIVE, prisoner
captīvus, -ī, *m.* [*capiō*], CAPTIVE, prisoner
Capua, -ae, *f.*, CAPUA, a city in Italy
caput, -itis, *n.*, head; person. (*Capital*)
careō, carēre, caruī, caritūrus, be in want of, lack, want; *with abl.* (*Caret*)
carō, carnis, *f.*, flesh. (*Carnal*)
carrus, -ī, *m.*, wagon, CART, CAR
cārus, -a, -um, *adj.*, dear, precious
casa, -ae, *f.*, hut, cottage
Cassivellaunus, -ī, *m.*, CASSIVELLAUNUS, a British chief
castellum, -ī, *n.* [*diminutive of castrum*, fortress], redoubt, stronghold. (*Castle*)
Casticus, -ī, *m.*, CASTICUS, a Gallic chief
castra, -ōrum, *n. plur.*, camp. (*Chester*)
cāsus, -ūs, *m.*, a falling; chance; misfortune, loss. (*Case*)
cauda, -ae, *f.*, tail.
causa, -ae, *f.*, CAUSE, reason; causā, *after a genitive*, for the sake

LATIN-ENGLISH VOCABULARY

cēdō, cēdere, cessī, cessūrus, give way, retire. (*Secede*)
celeber, -bris, -bre, *adj.* [*celebrō*], frequented, visited; renowned, CELEBRated
celebrō, celebrāre, celebrāvī, celebrātus [*celeber*], frequent, throng. (*Celebrate*)
celer, -eris, -ere, *adj.*, swift, quick
celeritās, -ātis, *f.* [*celer*], swiftness, speed, quickness, CELERITY
celeriter, *adv.* [*celer*], swiftly, quickly
cēlō, cēlāre, cēlāvī, cēlātus, conCEAL
cēna, -ae, *f.* [*cēnō*], dinner, meal
Cēnaeum, -ī, *n.*, CENÆUM, a promontory on the island of Eubœa
cēnō, cēnāre, cēnāvī, cēnātus [*cēna*], dine, take a meal
cēnsus, -ūs, *m.*, a CENSUS
centaurus, -ī, *m.*, CENTAUR, a fabled monster, half man, half horse
centum, *adj.*, *indecl.*, hundred. (*Cent*)
centuriō, -ōnis, *m.*, CENTURION, an underofficer in the Roman army
Cēpheus, -ī, *m.*, CEPHEUS, father of Andromeda
cēra, -ae, *f.*, wax. (*Cerate*)
certāmen, -inis, *n.*, strife, contest
certē, *adv.* [*certus*], really, surely, CERTAINly
certus, -a, -um, *adj.*, fixed, determined, CERTAIN, sure; certiōrem faciō, (make more certain), inform
cēterī, -ae, -a, *adj.*, *plur.*, the rest, the remaining, the others. *Cf.* alius
cibus, -ī, *m.*, food
Cicerō, -ōnis, *m.*, CICERO, a famous Roman orator

Cīneās, -ae, *m.*, CINEAS, a friend of Pyrrhus
cingō, cingere, cīnxī, cīnctus, surround, encircle, gird
circiter, *adv.*, about
circuitus, -ūs, *m.* [*circum-eō*], (a going round), circumference, CIRCUIT
circum, *prep. with acc.*, around
circum-arō, circumarāre, circumarāvī, ———, plough around
circum-dō, circumdare, circumdedī, circumdatus, place around, surround, inclose
circum-mūniō, circummūnīre, circummūnīvī, circummūnītus, wall around, surround, fortify, blockade
circum-stō, circumstāre, circumstetī (circumstitī), ———, stand around, surround. (*Circumstance*)
circum-veniō, circumvenīre, circumvēnī, circumventus, surround, CIRCUMVENT
circus, -ī, *m.*, the CIRCUS at Rome, in which chariot races and other contests were held
Cisalpīnus, -a, -um, *adj.*, (this side the Alps), CISALPINE
citerior, -ius, *adj.*, *comp.*, hither, nearer
cithara, -ae, *f.*, lyre
citrā, *prep. with acc.*, this side of
cīvis, -is, *m.* and *f.*, citizen. (*Civil*)
cīvitās, -ātis, *f.* [*cīvis*], (body of citizens), state; citizenship. (*City*)
clāmor, -ōris, *m.*, cry, shout; barking. (*Clamor*)
clārus, -a, -um, *adj.*, CLEAR, loud; renowned, famous. (*Clarion*)

RE

claudō, claudere, clausī, clausus, shut, CLOSE. (*Clause*)

cloāca, -ae, *f.*, sewer

Cloelia, -ae, *f.*, CLŒLIA, a noble Roman maiden

Cocles, -itis, *m.*, (blind in one eye), COCLES, surname of Horatius

coepī, coepisse, coeptus (*defective; tenses from present stem wanting*), began

co-erceō, coercēre, coercuī, coercitus [*co(m)-arceō*, keep off], keep back, check, restrain. (*Coerce*)

cōgitō, cōgitāre, cōgitāvī, cōgitātus, consider thoroughly, reflect. (*Cogitation*)

cognōmen, -inis, *n.* [*co(m)-(g)nōmen*], surname, COGNOMEN

co-gnōscō, cognōscere, cognōvī, cognitus [*co(m)-(g)nōscō*, know], learn, RECOGNIZE, know, understand

cōgō, cōgere, coēgī, coāctus [*co(m)-agō*], (drive together), collect, drive, compel

cohors, -hortis, *f.*, COHORT, a division of the Roman army

Collātīnus, -ī, *m.*, COLLATINUS, a Roman

col-ligō, colligere, collēgī, collēctus [*com-legō*], COLLECT, gather together

collis, -is, *m.*, hill. *Cf.* **mōns**

collum, -ī, *n.*, neck. (*Collar*)

colō, colere, coluī, cultus, care for, CULTIVATE, till; honor. *Cf.* **agricola** *and* **incola**

com- (col-, con-, cor-, co-, cō-), *primitive form of* **cum,** *a prefix denoting completeness or union; sometimes intensive*

comes, -itis, *m. and f.* [*com-eō*], comrade, companion

comitium, comitī, *n.* [*com-eō*], (place of assembling), the COMITIUM, a part of the Roman Forum

commeātus, -ūs, *m.*, supplies, provisions

com-mittō, committere, commīsī, commissus, intrust, COMMIT; **proelium committere,** join battle, engage. (*Commission*)

com-moveō, commovēre, commōvī, commōtus, (put in violent motion), shake, disturb, agitate, move. (*Commotion*)

commūnis, -e, *adj.*, COMMON, general. (*Community*)

com-pāreō, compārēre, compāruī, ——, apPEAR

com-pellō, compellere, compulī, compulsus, (drive together), force, COMPEL. (*Compulsion*)

com-periō, comperīre, comperī, compertus [*-pariō*, bring forth], find out, learn

com-plector, complectī, complexus sum, embrace

com-pleō, complēre, complēvī, complētus, fill out, fill up, cover. (*Complete*)

com-plūrēs, -a (-ia), *adj., plur.*, very many, many, a number

com-primō, comprimere, compressī, compressus [*-premō*, press], PRESS together, grasp; check, supPRESS. (*Compress*)

compulsus, *see* **compellō**

con-, *see* com-

cōnātus, -ūs, *m.* [*cōnor*], attempt

con-cēdō, concēdere, concessī, concessus, allow, grant, permit. (*Concede*)

concilium, concilī, *n.*, COUNCIL, assembly

con-citō, concitāre, concitāvī, concitātus, rouse up, rouse, spur on

con-currō, concurrere, concurrī, concursūrus, run together, rush together, rally, gather. (*Concourse*)

condiciō, -ōnis, *f.* [*con-dīcō*], (a talking together); agreement, CONDITION, terms

con-dō, condere, condidī, conditus [*-dō*, put], conceal, hide; found, establish. *Cf.* cēlō

con-dōnō, condōnāre, condōnāvī, condōnātus, give up, surrender; forgive, pardon, CONDONE

cō-nectō, cōnectere, cōnexuī, cōnexus [*co(m)-*], bind together; join, tie. (*Connect*)

cōn-ferō, cōnferre, contulī, conlātus, bring together, collect; sē cōnferre, betake one's self

cōnfertus, -a, -um, *adj.*, crowded, thick, dense

cōn-ficiō, cōnficere, cōnfēcī, cōnfectus [*-faciō*], make, accomplish, carry out, finish; weaken, wear out

cōn-firmō, cōnfirmāre, cōnfirmāvī, cōnfirmātus, make FIRM, strengthen, steady. (*Confirm*)

cōn-fugiō, cōnfugere, cōnfūgī, ——, flee for refuge, flee

con-iciō, conicere, coniēcī, coniectus [*-iaciō*], throw together; throw, put, hurl, cast. (*Conjecture*)

con-iungō, coniungere, coniūnxī, coniūnctus, join together, unite. (*Conjunction*)

coniūnx, -iugis, *m. and f.* [*coniungō*], husband, wife. (*Conjugal*)

coniūrātiō, -ōnis, *f.* [*coniūrō*], conspiracy

con-iūrō, coniūrāre, coniūrāvī, coniūrātus, unite by oath, conspire. (*Conjure*)

con-locō, conlocāre, conlocāvī, conlocātus, place, station. *Cf.* pōnō

conloquium, conloquī, *n.* [*con-loquor*], (a talking together), conversation, conference, COLLOQUY

cōnor, cōnārī, cōnātus sum, endeavor, attempt, try. (*Conative*)

cōn-scendō, cōnscendere, cōnscendī, cōnscēnsus [*-scandō*, climb], climb up, mount, go on board

cōn-scrībō, cōnscrībere, cōnscrīpsī, cōnscrīptus, enlist, enrol, levy. (*Conscription*)

cōn-secrō, cōnsecrāre, cōnsecrāvī, cōnsecrātus [*-sacrō*, make sacred], deify, CONSECRATE

cōn-sequor, cōnsequī, cōnsecūtus sum, overtake. (*Consecutive*)

cōn-servō, cōnservāre, cōnservāvī, cōnservātus, preSERVE, save. (*Conserve*)

Cōnsidius, Cōnsidī, *m.*, CONSIDIUS, an officer of Cæsar

cōnsilium, cōnsilī, *n.* [*cōnsulō*], advice, COUNSEL, prudence, wisdom; plan, design

cōn-sistō, cōnsistere, cōnstitī, ———, stand firm, take one's stand, halt; depend, rest. (*Consist*)

cōnspectus, -ūs, *m.*, look, view, sight

cōn-stituō, cōnstituere, cōnstituī, cōnstitūtus [-*statuō*, set up], establish, determine, fix, decide, resolve. (*Constitution*)

cōn-suēscō, cōnsuēscere, cōnsuēvī, cōnsuētus, accustom; become accustomed; *perf.*, be accustomed, be wont

cōnsuētūdō, -inis, *f.* [*cōnsuēscō*], custom, habit

cōnsul, -ulis, *m.*, CONSUL

cōnsulātus, -ūs, *m.* [*cōnsul*], CONSULship

cōnsulō, cōnsulere, cōnsuluī, cōnsultus [*cōnsilium*], take counsel, CONSULT

cōn-sūmō, cōnsūmere, cōnsūmpsī, cōnsūmptus, use up, spend, pass, CONSUME

con-tegō, contegere, contēxī, contēctus, cover

con-temnō, contemnere, contempsī, contemptus, despise, CONTEMN. (*Contempt*)

con-tendō, contendere, contendī, contentus, strain, struggle, strive, hasten. (*Contend.*) *Cf.* mātūrō and properō

contentiō, -ōnis, *f.* [*contendō*], struggle, exertion. (*Contention*)

continēns, -entis, *f.* [*contineō*], mainland, CONTINENT

continenter, *adv.* [*contineō*], continuously

con-tineō, continēre, continuī, contentus [-*teneō*], hold together, keep together, hold, CONTAIN. (*Contents*)

con-tingō, contingere, contigī, contāctus [-*tangō*, touch], fall to one's lot. (*Contact*)

continuus, -a, -um, *adj.* [*contineō*], CONTINUOUS, successive

contrā, *prep. with acc.*, against, CONTRARY to

con-veniō, convenīre, convēnī, conventūrus, come together, assemble, meet; CONVENE. (*Convention*)

conventus, -ūs, *m.* [*conveniō*], gathering, assembly, meeting

con-vocō, convocāre, convocāvī, convocātus, call together, summon, CONVOKE

cōpia, -ae, *f.* [*co(m)-ops*], abundance, wealth, plenty; *plur.*, troops, forces. (*Copious*)

cōram, *adv.*, face to face, in person

Corinthus, -ī, *f.*, CORINTH

Coriolānus, -ī, *m.*, CORIOLANUS, a famous Roman warrior

Coriolī, -ōrum, *m. plur.*, CORIOLI, an ancient town in Italy

Cornēlia, -ae, *f.*, CORNELIA, a Roman name

cornū, -ūs, *n.*, horn

corōna, -ae, *f.*, CROWN. (*Coronet*)

corpus, -oris, *n.*, body. (*Corpse*)

cor-ripiō, corripere, corripuī, correptus [*com-rapiō*], seize, take hold of

cotīdiānus, -a, -um, *adj.* [*cotīdiē*], daily

cotīdiē, *adv.* [*quot-diēs*], daily

crātēra, -ae, *f.*, mixing bowl, bowl

crēber, -bra, -brum, *adj.*, thick, numerous, frequent

crēdibilis, -e, *adj.*, to be believed, CREDIBLE

crēdō, crēdere, crēdidī, crēditus, believe, think, suppose. (*Credit*)

creō, creāre, creāvī, creātus, make, CREATE; choose, elect

Crēta, -ae, *f.*, CRETE, an island southeast of Greece

cruciātus, -ūs, *m.*, torture

Crustumīnī, -ōrum, *m. plur.*, the inhabitants of Crustumerium

cubiculum,-ī, *n.* [*cubō*, lie], bedchamber

cum, *conj.*, when

cum, *prep. with abl.*, with

cūnae, -ārum, *f. plur.*, cradle

cūnctus, -a, -um, *adj.*, all together, all. *Cf.* omnis, tōtus, *and* ūniversus

cupidē, *adv.* [*cupidus*], eagerly

cupiditās, -ātis, *f.* [*cupidus*], longing, desire. (*Cupidity*)

cupidius, *adv.* [*cupidē*], too eagerly

cupidus, -a, -um, *adj.* [*cupiō*], desirous, fond

cupiō, cupere, cupīvī (cupiī), cupītus, desire, be eager for. *Cf.* volō

cūr, *adv.*, why, wherefore

cūra, -ae, *f.* [*cūrō*], care, anxiety

Curius, Curī, *m.*, CURIUS, a Roman name

cūrō, cūrāre, cūrāvī, cūrātus [*cūra*], care for, take care; *with gerundive*, have (a thing done)

currō, currere, cucurrī, cursūrus [*cursus*], run

cursus, -ūs, *m.* [*currō*], COURSE, raceCOURSE

custōdiō, custōdīre, custōdīvī (custōdiī), custōdītus [*custōs*], guard, protect, defend

custōs, -ōdis, *m. and f.* [*custōdiō*], guardian, keeper. (*Custodian*)

Cyclōps, -ōpis, *m.*, (round eye), a CYCLOPS, one of a fabulous race of giants on the coast of Sicily

Daedalus, -ī, *m.*, DÆDALUS, father of Icarus

damnō, damnāre, damnāvī, damnātus [*damnum*], conDEMN, sentence, doom

damnum, -ī, *n.* [*damnō*], hurt, harm, damage, loss

Danaē, -ēs, *f.*, DANAE, mother of Perseus

dē, *prep. with abl.*, down from, from; about, concerning, of; *of time*, in, during, for

dea, -ae, *f.* [*deus*], goddess

dēbeō, dēbēre, dēbuī, dēbitus [*dēhabeō*], owe, ought, must, should

dēbitus, -a, -um, *adj.* [*dēbeō*], owed; due, appropriate. (*Debit, Debt*)

decem, *adj.*, *indecl.*, ten

dē-cidō, dēcidere, dēcidī, —— [-*cadō*, fall], fall down, fall off

decimus, -a, -um, *adj.* [*decem*], tenth. (*Decimal*)

dē-cipiō, dēcipere, dēcēpī, dēceptus [-*capiō*], DECEIVE

Decius, Decī, *m.*, DECIUS, a Roman name

dēditīcius, -a, -um, *adj.* [*dēdō*], surrendered; *masc. plur. as noun*, prisoners of war, subjects

dēditiō, -ōnis, *f.* [*dēdō*], (a giving up), surrender

dē-dō, dēdere, dēdidī, dēditus [-*dō*, put], give up, surrender dē-dūcō, dēdūcere, dēdūxī, dēductus, lead down, lead off, escort, bring to. (*Deduct*)

dē-fendō, dēfendere, dēfendī, dēfēnsus, (strike off from), DEFEND, protect

dē-ferō, dēferre, dētulī, dēlātus, (bring down), report

dēfessus, -a, -um, *adj.*, tired out, weary, very tired

Dēianīra, -ae, *f.*, DEIANIRA, wife of Hercules

dē-iciō, dēicere, dēiēcī, dēiectus [*-iaciō*], throw down, let fall; disappoint; *pass.*, slip, stumble. (*Dejected*)

dēiectus, *see* dēiciō

de-inde, *adv.*, (from thence), then, afterwards, next

dēlectō, dēlectāre, dēlectāvī, dēlectātus, DELIGHT, please. (*Delectable*)

dē-ligō, dēligere, dēlēgī, dēlēctus [*-legō*], pick out, choose, sELECT

Delphī, -ōrum, *m. plur.*, DELPHI, a town in Greece

Delphicus, -a, -um, *adj.*, of DELPHI, DELPHIC

dē-migrō, dēmigrāre, dēmigrāvī, dēmigrātūrus, MIGRATE from; remove, go away. *Cf.* abeō

dē-mittō, dēmittere, dēmīsī, dēmissus, (send down), let down, let go, lose

dē-mōnstrō, dēmōnstrāre, dēmōnstrāvī, dēmōnstrātus, point out, show, describe. (*Demonstrate*)

dēmum, *adv.*, at length, at last; tum dēmum, not till then

dēnique, *adv.*, at last, finally; in short, in fact

dēnsus, -a, -um, *adj.*, thick, DENSE

Dentātus, -ī, *m.*, DENTATUS, a Roman name

dē-pellō, dēpellere, dēpulī, dēpulsus, drive out, drive away, remove, banish

dē-plōrō, dēplōrāre, dēplōrāvī, dēplōrātus, lament, DEPLORE

dē-pōnō, dēpōnere, dēposuī, dēpositus, put down, lay aside, abandon. (*Deposit*)

dēpositus, *see* dēpōnō

dēpulsus, *see* dēpellō

dē-scendō, dēscendere, dēscendī, dēscēnsūrus [*-scandō*, climb], (climb down), come down, DESCEND

dē-scrībō, dēscrībere, dēscrīpsī, dēscrīptus, mark off, divide. (*Describe*)

dē-serō, dēserere, dēseruī, dēsertus, abandon, DESERT

dēsertus, *see* dēserō

dē-siliō, dēsilīre, dēsiluī, dēsultūrus [*-saliō*, jump], jump down, leap down

dē-sistō, dēsistere, dēstitī, dēstitūrus, (stand off *or* apart), leave off, cease; DESIST

dēspectus, -ūs, *m.*, (a looking down upon), view, PROSPECT

dē-spērō, dēspērāre, dēspērāvī, dēspērātus, be hopeless, DESPAIR

dē-spoliō, dēspoliāre, dēspoliāvī, dēspoliātus, rob, deprive, DESPOIL

dē-sum, deesse, dēfuī, dēfutūrus, be from, be wanting, lack; *with dat.*

dē-super, *adv.*, down from above

dē-trahō, dētrahere, dētrāxī, dētractus, draw off, throw off, remove. (*Detract*)

deus, -ī, *m.*, god. (*Deity*)

dē-vorō, dēvorāre, dēvorāvī, dēvorātus, swallow up, DEVOUR, gulp down

dexter, -tra, -trum, *adj.*, right (hand). (*Dexterous*)

dextra, -ae, *f.* [*dexter*], right hand

dī-, *see* dis-

dīcō, dīcere, dīxī, dictus, say, tell, speak; appoint. (*Dictum*)

diēs, -ēī, *m.*, day

dif-ficilis, -e, *adj.* [*dis-facilis*], hard, DIFFICULT

difficultās, -ātis, *f.* [*difficilis*], DIFFICULTY

dignitās, -ātis, *f.*, rank. (*Dignity*)

dīligenter, *adv.* [*dīligentia*], DILIGENTly, industriously

dīligentia, -ae, *f.* [*dīligenter*], DILIGENCE, carefulness, industry

dīmicō, dīmicāre, dīmicāvī, dīmicātūrus, fight, contend. *Cf.* pugnō

dī-mittō, dīmittere, dīmīsī, dīmissus, send off, DISMISS; let slip, let go by

dis- (dī-), *a prefix denoting separation*, asunder, apart, in different directions. *Cf.* dīmittō, discēdō, dissimilis, dīvellō

dis-cēdō, discēdere, discessī, discessūrus, depart, withdraw, go off. *Cf.* abeō

discō, discere, didicī, discitūrus, learn. (*Disciple*)

discrīmen, -inis, *n.*, risk, danger, crisis. *Cf.* perīculum

dis-pliceō, displicēre, displicuī, displicitūrus [*-placeō*], DISPLEASE

dis-similis, -e, *adj.*, unlike, DISSIMILAR

diū, *adv.*, for a long time, long

diūturnitās, -ātis, *f.* [*diū*], length, duration

dī-vellō, dīvellere, dīvellī, dīvulsus, tear asunder, tear apart

dīversus, -a, -um, *adj.*, (turned away), separate, different, DIVERSE

Dīvicō, -ōnis, *m.*, DIVICO, a chief of the Helvetians

dīvidō, dīvidere, dīvīsī, dīvīsus, DIVIDE, apportion. (*Division*)

dīvīnus, -a, -um, *adj.*, of the gods, DIVINE

dīvulsus, *see* dīvellō

dō, dare, dedī, datus, give, offer; put. *Cf.* dōnō

doceō, docēre, docuī, doctus, teach, show. (*Docile, Doctor*)

doleō, dolēre, doluī, dolitūrus [*dolor*], grieve, be sorry. (*Condole*)

dolor, -ōris, *m.* [*doleō*], pain, grief. (*Dolorous*)

dolus, -ī, *m.*, deceit, trick, fraud, cunning

domesticus, -a, -um, *adj.* [*domus*], DOMESTIC

domī, *see* domus

domina, -ae, *f.* [*dominus*], mistress, lady

dominus, -ī, *m.* [*domus*], lord, master, owner. (*Dominate*)

domus, -ūs, *f.*, house, home; domī, at home. (*Domestic*)

dōnō, dōnāre, dōnāvī, dōnātus [*dōnum*], give, present. (*Donate.*) *Cf.* dō

dōnum, -ī, *n.* [*dō*], gift, present
dormiō, dormīre, dormīvī (dormiī), dormītus, sleep. (*Dormitory*)
dracō, -ōnis, *m.*, serpent, DRAGON
ducentī, -ae, -a, *adj.*, two hundred
dūcō, dūcere, dūxī, ductus [*dux*], lead, draw; derive. (*Duct*)
dum, *conj.*, while, as long as; until
Dumnorīx, -īgis, *m.*, DUMNORIX, a leader of the Hædui
duo, duae, duo, *adj.*, two. (*Dual*)
duo-decim [*-decem*], *adj., indecl.*, twelve
duplex, -icis, *adj.* [*duo*], twofold, double
duplicō, duplicāre, duplicāvī, duplicātus [*duplex*], double. (*Duplicate*)
dux, ducis, *m. and f.* [*dūcō*], leader, general. (*Duke.*) *Cf.* imperātor

ē, *see* ex
ē-dō, ēdere, ēdidī, ēditus [*-dō*, put], put forth, raise, utter. (*Edit*)
ēducō, ēducāre, ēducāvī, ēducātus, bring up, train, EDUCATE
ē-dūcō, ēdūcere, ēdūxī, ēductus, lead out, lead forth, bring away; draw
ef-ficiō, efficere, effēcī, effectus [*ex-faciō*], bring about, EFFECT, accomplish
ef-flō, efflāre, efflāvī, efflātus [*ex-*], (blow out), breathe out
ef-fundō, effundere, effūdī, effūsus [*ex-*], pour forth, pour out, shed. (*Effusion*)
effūsus, *see* effundō.
ego, *pers. pron.*, I; *plur.* nōs, we. (*Egotist*)

ē-gredior, ēgredī, ēgressus sum [*-gradior*, go], go out, go forth; in terram ēgressus, having gone ashore. (*Egress.*) *Cf.* exeō
ēgregiē, *adv.*, remarkably, excellently
ēgressus, *see* ēgredior
elephantus, -ī, *m.*, ELEPHANT
ē-ligō, ēligere, ēlēgī, ēlēctus [*-legō*], pick out, choose, seLECT. (*Elect*)
ē-mittō, ēmittere, ēmīsī, ēmissus, send forth, let loose, let out. (*Emit*)
emō, emere, ēmī, ēmptus, (take), buy
enim, *conj.* (*never the first word*), for; indeed, in fact. *Cf.* nam
Ennius, Ennī, *m.*, ENNIUS, an early Latin poet
ē-nūntiō, ēnūntiāre, ēnūntiāvī, ēnūntiātus, proclaim, anNOUNCE, reveal, utter. (*Enunciate*)
eō, īre, iī (īvī), itūrus, go
eō, *adv.* [*is*], to that place, thither, there
Ēpīrus, -ī, *f.*, EPIRUS, a division of Greece
epistula, -ae, *f.*, letter, EPISTLE
eques, -itis, *m.* [*equus*], horseman, knight
equester, -tris, -tre, *adj.* [*eques*], (of horsemen), EQUESTRIan
equitātus, -ūs, *m.* [*eques*], (body of horsemen), cavalry
equus, -ī, *m.*, horse. (*Equine*)
ergō, *adv.*, therefore
errō, errāre, errāvī, errātūrus, wander, ERR
ērudiō, ērudīre, ērudīvī (ērudiī), ēruditus, instruct. (*Erudite*)

ēruptiō, -ōnis, *f.*, (a bursting forth), sally. (*Eruption*)

Ēsquilīnus, -ī, *m.*, the ESQUILINE, one of the hills of Rome

et, *conj.*, and, also; et ... et, both ... and. *Cf.* atque (ac) *and* -que

etiam, *adv. and conj.* [*et-iam*], (and now), also, even. *Cf.* quoque

Etrūscī, -ōrum, *m. plur.*, the ETRUSCANS, people of Etruria, in Italy

et-sī, *conj.*, although

Eunomus, -ī, *m.*, EUNOMUS, a boy who was killed by Hercules

Eurōpa, -ae, *f.*, EUROPE

Eurystheus, -ī, *m.*, EURYSTHEUS, king of Tiryns, in Greece

Eurytus, -ī, *m.*, EURYTUS, father of Iole

ē-vādō, ēvādere, ēvāsī, ēvāsūrus, (go out), get away, escape. (*Evade*)

ē-veniō, ēvenīre, ēvēnī, ēventūrus, (come out), fall out, happen, turn out. (*Event.*) *Cf.* accidō *and* fīō

ex (ē), *prep. with abl.*, out of, from, of, off, on; in accordance with

exanimātus, -a, -um, *adj.* [*anima*], breathless, out of breath, exhausted

ex-cēdō, excēdere, excessī, excessūrus, go out, go forth, depart. (*Exceed*)

ex-citō, excitāre, excitāvī, excitātus, (call out), rouse, arouse, wake. (*Excite*)

ex-clāmō, exclāmāre, exclāmāvī, exclāmātus, cry out, EXCLAIM

excursiō, -ōnis, *f.*, (a running out), sally, sortie. (*Excursion*)

exemplum, -ī, *n.*, sample, EXAMPLE, warning

ex-eō, exīre, exiī, exitūrus, go out, go forth, come out. (*Exit.*) *Cf.* ēgredior

exerceō, exercēre, exercuī, exercitus, EXERCISE, train

exercitātiō, -ōnis, *f.* [*exerceō*], exercise, training

exercitus, -ūs, *m.* [*exerceō*], (the thing trained), army

ex-igō, exigere, exēgī, exāctus [-*agō*], drive out, expel. (*Exact*)

exīstimō, exīstimāre, exīstimāvī, exīstimātus, think, judge, consider, suppose. *Cf.* arbitror *and* putō

exitium, exitī, *n.* [*exeō*], ruin, destruction

ex-pellō, expellere, expulī, expulsus, drive out, EXPEL. (*Expulsion*)

ex-perior, experīrī, expertus sum [*perīculum*], try, test; EXPERIENCE. *Cf.* tentō

expertus, *see* experior

ex-piō, expiāre, expiāvī, expiātus, make amends for, EXPIATE

explōrātor, -ōris, *m.* [*explōrō*], scout, spy

ex-plōrō, explōrāre, explōrāvī, explōrātus [*explōrātor*], examine, EXPLORE, investigate

ex-pōnō, expōnere, exposuī, expositus, set forth, explain, relate; EXPOSE

expositus, *see* expōnō

ex-pugnō, expugnāre, expugnāvī, expugnātus, take by storm, take, capture. *Cf.* oppugnō

expulsus, *see* expellō
ex-spectō, exspectāre, exspectāvī, exspectātus, (look out for), await, wait for, wait, EXPECT
ex-struō, exstruere, exstrūxī, exstrūctus, (heap up), build, erect, CONSTRUCT
extrā, *prep. with acc.*, outside, beyond
ex-trahō, extrahere, extrāxī, extrāctus, draw out, drag out. (*Extract*)
extrēmus, -a, -um, *adj., superl.*, outermost, last, farthest; end of; EXTREME
exuō, exuere, exuī, exūtus, take off, put off

faber, -brī, *m.*, workman, artisan, smith
Fabricius, Fabricī, *m.*, FABRICIUS, a famous Roman general
fābula, -ae, *f.*, story, tale, FABLE
facile, *adv.* [*facilis*], easily
facilis, -e, *adj.* [*faciō*], (that can be done), easy to do, easy. (*Facility*)
faciō, facere, fēcī, factus, do, make; form, perform
factum, -ī, *n.* [*faciō*], act, deed, action. (*Fact*)
facultās, -ātis, *f.* [*facilis*], power, opportunity, chance. (*Faculty*)
falx, falcis, *f.*, curved sword
fāma, -ae, *f.*, rumor, report; FAME, renown
famēs, -is, *f.*, hunger, FAMINE
fātum, -ī, *n.*, FATE
Faustulus, -ī, *m.*, FAUSTULUS, a shepherd

faveō, favēre, fāvī, fautūrus, be favorable to, FAVOR, befriend; *with dat.*
fēlēs, -is, *f.*, cat. (*Feline*)
fēlīciter, *adv.* [*fēlīx*], luckily, fortunately, successfully
fēlīx, -īcis, *adj.*, lucky, fortunate, happy. (*Felicity*)
fēmina, -ae, *f.*, woman. (*Feminine.*) *Cf.* mulier
ferē, *adv.*, nearly, for the most part, almost, about
ferō, ferre, tulī, lātus, bear, bring; report, say. *Cf.* portō *and* tolerō
ferrum, -ī, *n.*, iron; sword. *Cf.* gladius
Fīdēnātēs, -ium, *m. plur.*, the inhabitants of Fidenæ
fidēs, -eī, *f.*, trust, confidence. (*Fidelity*)
figūra, -ae, *f.* [*fi(n)gō*], shape, form, FIGURE
filia, -ae, *f.* [*fīlius*], daughter
fīlius, fīlī, *m.* [*fīlia*], son. (*Filial*)
fingō, fingere, finxī, fictus, fashion, devise. (*Feign, Fiction*)
fīnis, -is, *m.*, end, border; *plur.*, territories. (*Final*)
finitimus, -a, -um, *adj.* [*fīnis*], bordering on; *masc. plur. as noun*, neighbors
fīō, fierī, factus sum (*supplies pass. to* faciō), be made, be done, become, happen. *Cf.* accidō *and* ēveniō
firmus, -a, -um, *adj.*, strong, FIRM
flagrāns, -antis, *adj.*, flaming, blazing, burning. (*Flagrant*)

flūmen, -inis, *n.* [*fluō*], (that which flows), river, stream
fluō, fluere, flūxī, fluxūrus, flow
foculus, -ī, *m.* [*focus*], sacrificial hearth, fire pan, brazier
focus, -ī, *m.,* hearth. (*Focus, Fuel*)
foedus, -eris, *n.,* league, treaty, alliance. (*Federal*)
fore, *for* **futūrum esse**
fors, fortis, *f.,* chance, luck
forte, *adv.* [*fors*], by chance, perhaps
fortis, -e, *adj.,* strong, brave, courageous. (*Fortitude.*) *Cf.* **validus**
fortiter, *adv.* [*fortis*], bravely, courageously
fortūna, -ae, *f.* [*fors*], FORTUNE, good FORTUNE
fossa, -ae, *f.,* ditch, trench, FOSSE; canal
frāter, -tris, *m.,* brother. (*Fraternal*)
fremitus, -ūs, *m.,* noise, roaring, roar
frōns, frontis, *f.,* forehead, brow. (*Front*)
frūmentārius, -a, -um, *adj.* [*frūmentum*], of grain
frūmentum, -ī, *n.,* corn, grain
frūstrā, *adv.,* in vain. (*Frustrate*)
fuga, -ae, *f.* [*fugiō*], flight
fugiō, fugere, fūgī, fugitūrus [*fugō, fuga*], run away, flee; flee from. (*Fugitive*)
fugō, fugāre, fugāvī, fugātus [*fuga, fugiō*], put to flight, rout
fūmus, -ī, *m.,* smoke. (*Fumes*)
furor, -ōris, *m.,* madness, frenzy, FUROR

Gabiī, -ōrum, *m. plur.,* GABII, a city of Italy
Galba, -ae, *m.,* GALBA
galea, -ae, *f.,* helmet
Gallia, -ae, *f.,* GAUL
Gallicus, -a, -um, *adj.,* GALLIC
Gallus, -ī, *m.,* a GAUL
gaudeō, gaudēre, gāvīsus sum (*semideponent*)[*gaudium*], be glad, rejoice
gaudium, gaudī, *n.* [*gaudeō*], JOY, gladness. *Cf.* **laetitia**
gāvīsus, *see* **gaudeō**
geminus, -a, -um, *adj.,* twin-born, twin-
Genāva, -ae, *f.,* GENEVA
gēns, gentis, *f.* [*genus*], race, tribe, house, family. (*Gentile, Gentle*)
genus, -eris, *n.* [*gēns*], race, lineage; kind, class. (*Generous*)
Germānia, -ae, *f.,* GERMANY
Germānus, -a, -um, *adj.,* GERMAN; *as noun,* a GERMAN
gerō, gerere, gessī, gestus, bear, carry on, wage (war); manage, do; wear; **sē gerere,** act, behave; *pass.,* go on, take place
gigās, -antis, *m.,* GIANT
gladius, gladī, *m.,* sword. (*Gladiator.*) *Cf.* **ferrum**
glōria, -ae, *f.,* GLORY, reputation
Gorgō, -onis, *f.,* a GORGON
Graeae, -ārum, *f. plur.,* the GRÆÆ
Graecia, -ae, *f.,* GREECE
Graecus, -ī, *m.,* a GREEK
grāmen, -inis, *n.,* grass
grātia, -ae, *f.* [*grātus*], favor, kindness; *plur.,* thanks, GRATitude
grātus, -a, -um, *adj.* [*grātia*], acceptable, pleasing; GRATEful
gravis, -e, *adj.,* heavy, severe, serious. (*Grave*)

graviter, *adv.* [*gravis*], heavily, severely, vehemently, greatly

gravō, gravāre, gravāvī, gravātus [*gravis*], oppress, burden, overcome. (*Aggravate*)

gustō, gustāre, gustāvī, gustātus, taste, eat. (*Gustatory*)

habeō, habēre, habuī, habitus, have, hold, keep; *with* ōrātiōnem, make, deliver. (*Habit*)

habitō, habitāre, habitāvī, habitātus [*frequentative of habeō*], inHABIT; dwell, live. *Cf.* incolō

Haeduus, -a, -um, *adj.*, HAEDUAN; *masc. plur. as noun*, the HAEDUI, a tribe of Gaul

haereō, haerēre, haesī, haesūrus, stick, cling, be fixed; be perplexed, HESitate. (*Adhere*)

Hammōn, -ōnis, *m.*, HAMMON, an Egyptian god, identified by the Romans with Jupiter

Hannibal, -alis, *m.*, HANNIBAL, a famous Carthaginian general

harēna, -ae, *f.*, sand, shore. (*Arena*)

hasta, -ae, *f.*, spear

haud, *adv.*, not. *Cf.* nōn

hauriō, haurīre, hausī, haustus, drink, drain. (*Exhaust*)

Helvētiī, -ōrum, *m. plur.*, the HELVETII, a tribe of Gaul

Herculēs, -is, *m.*, HERCULES, son of Jupiter and Alcmena, famous for his strength

Hesperidēs, -um, *f. plur.*, the HESPERIDES, daughters of Atlas and Hesperis, and guardians of the golden apples

hesternus, -a, -um, *adj.*, of yesterday, yester-

hīberna, -ōrum, *n. plur.* [*hiems*], winter quarters. (*Hibernate*)

hic, haec, hoc, *dem. adj. and pron.*, this, this of mine; *as pers. pron.*, he, she, it

hīc, *adv.* [*hic*], here, hereupon

hiemō, hiemāre, hiemāvī, hiemātūrus [*hiems*], spend the winter

hiems, hiemis, *f.* [*hiemō*], winter; storm

hinc, *adv.* [*hic*], hence, from here

Hispānia, -ae, *f.*, SPAIN

Hispānus, -ī, *m.*, a SPANIARD

ho-diē, *adv.* [*hōc-diē*], to-day

homō, -inis, *m. and f.* [*hūmānus*], (human being), man. *Cf.* vir

honestās, -ātis, *f.* [*honor*], honorable character, integrity, uprightness, HONESTY

honor, -ōris, *m.*, HONOR

hōra, -ae, *f.*, HOUR; in hōrās, from hour to hour, hourly

Horātius, Horātī, *m.*, HORATIUS (Cocles)

horribilis, -e, *adj.*, terrible, dreadful, HORRIBLE. *Cf.* terribilis

hortor, hortārī, hortātus sum, urge, entreat, exHORT

hortus, -ī, *m.*, garden. (*Horticulture*)

hospitium, hospitī, *n.*, HOSPITALity

hostis, -is, *m. and f.*, enemy. (*Hostile.*) *Cf.* inimīcus

hūc, *adv.* [*hic*], hither

hūmānus, -a, -um, *adj.* [*homō*], (pertaining to man), man's, HUMAN

humī, *locative*, on the ground. (*Exhume*)

iaceō, iacēre, iacuī, —— [*iaciō*], (be thrown), lie, lie dead. (*Adjacent*)

iaciō, iacere, iēcī, iactus [*iaceō*], throw, cast, hurl

iam, *adv.*, already, now, at last; nōn iam, no longer. *Cf.* nunc

Iāniculum, -ī, *n.*, the JANICULUM, one of the hills of Rome

ibi, *adv.* [*is*], in that place, there

Īcarus, -ī, *m.*, ICARUS

ictus, -ūs, *m.*, stroke, blow

īdem, eadem, idem, *dem. adj. and pron.* [*is*], same; īdem quī, same as. (*Identical*)

idōneus, -a, -um, *adj.*, fit, suitable

igitur, *conj.* (*seldom the first word*), therefore, then. *Cf.* itaque

ignis, -is, *m.*, fire. (*Ignite*)

ignōrō, ignōrāre, ignōrāvī, ignōrātus, not know, be ignorant of. (*Ignore*)

i-gnōtus, -a, -um, *adj.* [*in-(g)nōtus*, known], unknown, unfamiliar, strange

ille, -a, -ud, *dem. adj. and pron.*, that (yonder); *as pers. pron.*, he, she, it

illīc, *adv.* [*ille*], there

illūc, *adv.* [*ille*], thither

immānitās, -ātis, *f.*, savageness, cruelty, barbarity

im-mineō, imminēre, imminuī, —— [*in-*], hang over, impend. (*Imminent*)

impedīmentum, -ī, *n.* [*impediō*], hindrance; *plur.*, baggage. (*Impediment*)

impediō, impedīre, impedīvī (impediī), impedītus [*in-pēs*], entangle, hamper, IMPEDE

im-pellō, impellere, impulī, impulsus [*in-*], move, induce, drive, IMPEL. (*Impulse*)

im-pendeō, impendēre, ——, —— [*in-*], overhang, IMPEND

imperātor, -ōris, *m.* [*imperō*], commander, general. (*Emperor*)

imperātum, -ī, *n.* [*imperō*], order, command. *Cf.* iussum

imperium, imperī, *n.* [*imperō*], command, rule, power. (*Empire*)

imperō, imperāre, imperāvī, imperātus [*imperium*], order, command, demand; rule; *with dat. of person.* (*Imperative.*) *Cf.* iubeō

impetus, -ūs, *m.*, attack, assault. (*Impetuous*)

im-pleō, implēre, implēvī, implētus [*in-*], fill up, cover, fill

im-pōnō, impōnere, imposuī, impositus [*in-*], put in *or* on, place in *or* on; mount; IMPOSE; *with dat. of person or place*

impositus, *see* impōnō

impudēns, -entis, *adj.*, shameless, IMPUDENT

impulsus, *see* impellō

īmus, -a, -um, *adj.*, *superl. of* īnferus

in, *prep. with acc.*, into, to, against, on, toward, for; *with abl.*, IN, on, in case of

in-, *prefix*, into, on, toward, etc.; *also in composition with nouns, adjectives, and participles, often having negative sense. Cf. Eng.* un-, in-, not

in-cendō, incendere, incendī, incēnsus [*-candeō*, shine], set fire to, burn. (*Incendiary*) incēnsus, -a, -um, *adj.* [*incendō*], inflamed, hot, fiery. (*Incense*)

in-certus, -a, -um, *adj.*, UNCERTain, doubtful

in-cidō, incidere, incidī, —— [*-cadō*, fall], fall into; in īnsāniam incidere, become insane. (*Incident*)

in-cipiō, incipere, incēpī, inceptus [*-capiō*], (take in hand), begin. (*Incipient*)

in-citō, incitāre, incitāvī, incitātus, arouse, stir, INCITE

in-clūdō, inclūdere, inclūsī, inclūsus [*-claudō*], shut in, confine. (*Include*)

in-cognitus, -a, -um, *adj.*, unknown

incohō, incohāre, incohāvī, incohātus, begin. (*Inchoate*)

incola, -ae, *m. and f.* [*incolō*], inhabitant

in-colō, incolere, incoluī, —— [*incola*], dwell in, inhabit; live, dwell. *Cf.* habitō

incolumis, -e, *adj.*, unharmed, safe

increpitō, increpitāre, ——, ——, upbraid, taunt, abuse

inde, *adv.* [*is*], thence, thereupon

indicō, indicāre, indicāvī, indicātus, inform, disclose, make known. (*Indicate*)

in-dīcō, indīcere, indīxī, indictus, proclaim, declare, appoint. (*Indict*)

in-dūcō, indūcere, indūxī, inductus, lead to, draw to, INDUCE, persuade

induō, induere, induī, indūtus, put on, clothe one's self in, clothe, wrap

in-eō, inīre, iniī (inīvī), initus, go in, enter; begin, form

īn-fāns, -antis, *adj.*, (not speaking); *as noun*, INFANT, baby

īn-fēlīx, -īcis, *adj.*, unfortunate, unlucky, unhappy. (*Infelicitous*)

īnferior, -ius, *adj.*, *comp. of* īnferus. (*Inferior*)

īn-ferō, īnferre, intulī, inlātus, (bear in *or* against), cause, bring on, inflict. (*Infer*)

(īnferus), -a, -um, *adj.*, low, below, underneath

īnfestus, -a, -um, *adj.*, hostile; *as noun*, enemy. (*Infest*)

īn-ficiō, īnficere, īnfēcī, īnfectus [*-faciō*], soak, imbue, stain. (*Infect*)

īnfīnītus, -a, -um, *adj.*, many, countless. (*Infinite*)

ingēns, -entis, *adj.*, huge, great. *Cf.* magnus

in-iciō, inicere, iniēcī, iniectus [*-iaciō*], throw on, cast on, put on. (*Inject*)

iniectus, *see* iniciō

in-imīcus, -a, -um, *adj.* [*-amīcus*], unfriendly, hostile; *as noun*, ENEMY. (*Inimical.*) *Cf.* hostis

in-īquus, -a, -um, *adj.* [*-aequus*], unEQUAL; uneven, unfavorable

initium, initī, *n.* [*ineō*], beginning. (*Initial*)

iniūria, -ae, *f.* [*in-iūs*], wrong, harm, insult, INJURY

inopia, -ae, *f.*, want, poverty, lack, need

in-rīdeō, inrīdēre, inrīsī, inrīsus, laugh at, mock, ridicule īnsānia, -ae, *f.*, INSANity, madness

īn-sideō, īnsidēre, īnsēdī, īnsessūrus [*-sedeō*], sit on

īnsolēns, -entis, *adj.*, arrogant, overbearing. (*Insolent*)

īn-spiciō, īnspicere, īnspexī, īnspectus [*-speciō*, look], look into, look on, INSPECT

īn-stituō, īnstituere, īnstituī, īnstitūtus [*-statuō*, set up], set up, fix, arrange. (*Institute*)

īnstrūctus, *see* īnstruō

īn-struō, īnstruere, īnstrūxī, īnstrūctus, build in, form; INSTRUCT, train; prepare, provide

īnsula, -ae, *f.*, island. (*Peninsula*)

intel-legō, intellegere, intellēxī, intellēctus [*inter-legō*], (choose between), learn, know, perceive, understand. (*Intellect*.) *Cf.* cognōscō

in-tendō, intendere, intendī, intentus, (stretch out towards), bend, aim. (*Intend*)

inter, *prep. with acc.*, between, among, amid, during, while; inter sē, among themselves, together

inter-clūdō, interclūdere, interclūsī, interclūsus [*-claudō*], shut off, cut off

inter-dum, *adv.*, sometimes

inter-eā, *adv.*, meanwhile

interfectus, *see* interficiō

inter-ficiō, interficere, interfēcī, interfectus [*-faciō*], kill, slay, put to death. *Cf.* necō *and* occīdō

inter-iciō, intericere, interiēcī, interiectus [*-iaciō*], place between; *pass.*, intervene. (*Interjection*)

interim, *adv.*, meanwhile, in the meantime. (*Interim*)

interior, -ius, *adj.*, *comp.*, inner, INTERIOR

inter-mittō, intermittere, intermīsī, intermissus, (send between), leave off; *pass.*, intervene, pass. (*Intermittent*)

inter-rogō, interrogāre, interrogāvī, interrogātus, ask, question. (*Interrogate*)

inter-rumpō, interrumpere, interrūpī, interruptus, break down. (*Interrupt*)

inter-sum, interesse, interfuī, interfutūrus, be between

intervāllum, -ī, *n.*, space, INTERVAL

intrō, intrāre, intrāvī, intrātus, go into, ENTER

introitus, -ūs, *m.* [*introeō*, go in], ENTRance

intrō-mittō, intrōmittere, intrōmīsī, intrōmissus, (send in), let in, adMIT

in-vādō, invādere, invāsī, invāsus, come upon, attack, INVADE, take possession of

in-veniō, invenīre, invēnī, inventus, come upon, find, discover. (*Invent*.) *Cf.* reperiō

in-vicem, *adv.*, in turn, mutually

in-videō, invidēre, invīdī, invīsūrus (look toward), be jealous of, ENVY

invītō, invītāre, invītāvī, invītātus, INVITE

Iolē, -ēs, *f.*, IOLE, daughter of Eurytus

Īphiclēs, -is, *m.*, IPHICLES, brother of Hercules

ipse, -a, -um, *dem. adj. and pron.*, self, very
īra, -ae, *f.*, anger, wrath, IRE
is, ea, id, *dem. adj. and pron.*, that; *as pers. pron.*, he, she, it
iste, -a, -ud, *dem. adj. and pron.* [*is*], that (of yours)
ita, *adv.*, so, thus. *Cf.* **sīc** *and* **tam**
Italia, -ae, *f.*, ITALY
ita-que, *conj.*, and so, therefore. *Cf.* **igitur**
item, *adv.* [*ita*], also, likewise
iter, itineris, *n.* [*eō*, go], way, journey, march, line of march. (*Itinerary*)
iterum, *adv.*, a second time, again. (*Iteration*)
iubeō, iubēre, iussī, iussus, bid, order, command. *Cf.* **imperō**
iugum, -ī, *n.* [*iungō*], yoke; ridge
Iūlia, -ae, *f.*, JULIA, a Roman name
iūnctus, *see* **iungō**
iungō, iungere, iūnxī, iūnctus, unite, JOIN, span, cross. (*Junction*)
Iūnius, Iūnī, *m.*, JUNIUS, a Roman name
Iūnō, -ōnis, *f.*, JUNO, queen of the gods and wife of Jupiter
Iuppiter, Iovis, *m.*, JUPITER, the supreme deity of the Romans
Iūra, -ae, *m.*, JURA, a chain of mountains in Gaul
iūrō, iūrāre, iūrāvī, iūrātūrus [*iūs*], swear, take an oath. (*Abjure*)
iūs, iūris, *n.*, right, JUSTICE
iussū, *adv.* [*iubeō*], by order, by command of
iussum, -ī, *n.* [*iubeō*], order, command. *Cf.* **imperātum**
iussus, *see* **iubeō**

iūstus, -a, -um, *adj.* [*iūs*], JUST
iuvenis, -e, *adj.*, young; *as noun*, young man, youth. (*Juvenile.*) *Cf.* **adulēscēns**
iuvō, iuvāre, iūvī, iūtus, help, aid

L., *abbreviation for* **Lūcius**
Labiēnus, -ī, *m.*, LABIENUS, a lieutenant in Cæsar's army
labor, -ōris, *m.* [*labōrō*], LABOR, toil. *Cf.* **opus** *and* **opera**
labōrō, labōrāre, labōrāvī, labōrātūrus [*labor*], work, toil; suffer. (*Elaborate*)
lac, lactis, *n.*, milk. (*Lacteal*)
Lacaena, -ae, *f.*, a Laconian woman, a woman of Sparta
lacrima, -ae, *f.*, tear. (*Lachrymal*)
lacus, -ūs, *m.*, LAKE, pool
laetitia, -ae, *f.* [*laetus*], joy, gladness
laetus, -a, -um, *adj.*, glad, merry, pleasant, joyful
Laevīnus, -ī, *m.*, LÆVINUS, a Roman consul
lambō, lambere, ——, ——, lick, lap
lāmenta, -ōrum, *n. plur.* [*lāmentor*], wailing, LAMENTS, LAMENTation
lāmentor, lāmentārī, lāmentātus sum [*lāmenta*], wail, LAMENT
lapis, -idis, *m.*, stone, milestone. (*Lapidary*)
lateō, latēre, latuī, ——, lurk, lie hid, be concealed. (*Latent*)
Latīnus, -a, -um, *adj.*, LATIN; *masc. plur. as noun*, the LATINS
lātitūdō, -inis, *f.* [*lātus*], breadth, width. (*Latitude*)
latrō, -ōnis, *m.*, robber, brigand
lātus, -a, -um, *adj.*, broad, wide

laudō, laudāre, laudāvī, laudātus, praise, LAUD. (*Laudatory*)

lēctus, *see* legō

lēgātiō, -ōnis, *f.* [*lēgātus*], embassy, LEGATION

lēgātus, -ī, *m.* [*lēgātiō*], ambassador, deputy, lieutenant, LEGATUS. (*Legate*)

legiō, -ōnis, *f.* [*legō*], (a gathering), LEGION

legō, legere, lēgī, lēctus, gather; seLECT; read

Lemannus, -ī, *m.*, the Lake of Geneva

lēnis, -e, *adj.* [*lēniter*], soft, smooth, gentle, mild. (*Lenient*)

lēniter, *adv.* [*lēnis*], gently, moderately

Lentulus, -ī, *m.*, LENTULUS, a Roman name

Leōnidās, -ae, *m.*, LEONIDAS, commander of the Greeks at Thermopylæ

lēx, lēgis, *f.*, law. (*Legal*)

libenter, *adv.*, willingly, gladly

liber, -brī, *m.*, book. (*Library*)

līber, -era, -erum, *adj.*, free. (*Liberal*)

līberī, -ōrum, *m. plur.* [*līber*], children

līberō, līberāre, līberāvī, līberātus [*līber*], set free, free, LIBERATE; *with abl. of separation*

lībertās, -ātis, *f.* [*līber*], freedom, LIBERTY

Lichās, -ae, *m.*, LICHAS, an attendant of Hercules

ligneus, -a, -um, *adj.*, wooden

lignum, -ī, *n.*, wood; stake, stick

Lingonēs, -um, *m. plur.*, the LINGONES, a tribe in Gaul

lingua, -ae, *f.*, tongue, LANGUAGE

Linus, -ī, *m.*, LINUS, teacher of Hercules in music

littera, -ae, *f.*, a LETTER (of the alphabet); *plur.*, LETTER, epistle. (*Literature*)

lītus, -oris, *n.*, shore. (*Littoral*)

locō, locāre, locāvī, locātus [*locus*], place, put, set. (*Locate*)

locus, -ī, *m.* (*plur.* locī, *m.*, *and* loca, *n.*), place, position, situation; chance, opportunity. (*Local*)

locūtus, *see* loquor

longē, *adv.* [*longus*], far, far off, by far

longinquus, -a, -um, *adj.* [*longus*], distant, remote, far away

longitūdō, -inis, *f.*, length. (*Longitude*)

longus, -a, -um, *adj.*, long, tedious

loquor, loquī, locūtus sum, speak, talk, say. (*Elocution*, *Eloquent*)

Lūcānī, -ōrum, *m. plur.*, the LUCANIANS, a people of southern Italy

lūdus, -ī, *m.*, game, sport

lūgeō, lūgēre, lūxī, ———, mourn, mourn for

lūmen, -inis, *n.* [*lūx*], light. (*Luminous*)

lupa, -ae, *f.*, she-wolf

lūx, lūcis, *f.*, light. (*Lucid*)

M., *abbreviation for* Mārcus

māchinātiō, -ōnis, *f.*, contrivance, MACHINE, engine

magicus, -a, -um, *adj.*, MAGIC

magis, *adv.* [*mag(nus)*], more, rather

magister, -trī, *m.* [*magis*], MASTER, teacher. (*Magistrate*)

magnificus, -a, -um, *adj.* [*magnus-faciō*], splendid, MAGNIFICENT

magnitūdō, -inis, *f.* [*magnus*], greatness, size, MAGNITUDE

magnopere, *adv.* [*abl. of magnum opus*], greatly, exceedingly, heartily

magnus, -a, -um, *adj.*, great, large; loud. (*Magnify*)

maior, -ius, *adj.*, *comp. of* magnus. (*Major*)

male, *adv.* [*malus*], badly, ill. (*Malevolent*)

mālō, mālle, māluī, —— [*magis-volō*], be more willing, prefer, would rather

malum, -ī, *n.* [*malus*], bad thing, evil

malus, -a, -um, *adj.*, bad, evil

mandō, mandāre, mandāvī, mandātus [*manus-dō*], (put in hand), charge, comMAND, intrust. (*Mandate*)

maneō, manēre, mānsī, mānsūrus, stay, reMAIN, wait. (*Permanent*)

manus, -ūs, *f.*, hand; grappling hook; force, band. (*Manual*)

Mārcius, Mārcī, *m.*, MARCIUS, a Roman name

Mārcus, -ī, *m.*, MARCUS, a Roman first name

mare, -is, *n.*, sea. (*Marine*)

marītus, -ī, *m.*, husband. (*Marital*)

Mārs, Mārtis, *m.*, MARS, the god of war. (*Martial*)

māter, -tris, *f.*, mother. (*Maternal*)

mātrimōnium, mātrimōnī, *n.* [*māter*], MATRIMONY, marriage; in mātrimōnium dūcere, marry

mātrōna, -ae, *f.* [*māter*], MATRON, woman

mātūrō, mātūrāre, mātūrāvī, mātūrātus, hasten. (*Mature*.) Cf. properō *and* contendō

maximē, *adv.* [*maximus*], most, especially, greatly. Cf. praecipuē

maximus, -a, -um, *adj.*, *superl. of* magnus. (*Maximum*)

mē, *see* ego

medicus, -ī, *m.*, doctor, physician. (*Medicine*)

medius, -a, -um, *adj.*, middle, middle of; in mediō, between (them); in medium, to the center. (*Medium*)

Medūsa, -ae, *f.*, MEDUSA, one of the Gorgons, slain by Perseus

melior, -ius, *adj.*, *comp. of* bonus, better. (*Ameliorate*)

membrum, -ī, *n.*, limb. (*Member*)

memoria, -ae, *f.* [*memorō*], MEMORY

memorō, memorāre, memorāvī, memorātus [*memoria*], mention, relate, state. (*Commemorate*)

mēns, mentis, *f.*, mind. Cf. animus

mēnsa, -ae, *f.*, table

mēnsis, -is, *m.*, month

mercātor, -ōris, *m.*, trader, MERchant

Mercurius, Mercurī, *m.*, MERCURY, the messenger of the gods

mergō, mergere, mersī, mersus, sink. (*Merge*)

meritum, -ī, *n.*, thing deserved, deserts, MERIT

mersus, *see* mergō

meus, -a, -um, *possess. adj. and pron.*, my, mine

migrō, migrāre, migrāvī, migrātūrus, depart. (*Migrate*)

mihi, *see* ego

mīles, -itis, *m.*, soldier. (*Military*)

mīlitāris, -e, *adj.* [*mīles*], MILITARY

mīlle, *adj., indecl. in sing.; in plur.*, mīlia, -ium, thousand; *also* (*supply* passuum), MILES

Minerva, -ae, *f.*, MINERVA, the goddess of wisdom

minimē, *adv.* [*minimus*], least, not at all, by no means

minimus, -a, -um, *adj.*, *superl. of* parvus, least, very little. (*Minimum*)

minor, -us, *adj.*, *comp. of* parvus, smaller, lesser. (*Minor*, *Minus*)

minus, *adv.* [*minor*], less

mīrāculum, -ī, *n.* [*mīror*], wonder, marvel, MIRACLE

mīror, mīrārī, mīrātus sum [*mīrus*], wonder, wonder at, adMIRE

mīrus, -a, -um, *adj.* [*mīror*], wonderful, extraordinary

miser, -era, -erum, *adj.*, wretched, unhappy, MISERable

miserē, *adv.* [*miser*], wretchedly, MISERably

misericordia, -ae, *f.*, pity, compassion

mittō, mittere, mīsī, missus, send. (*Mission*)

modo, *adv.* [*modus*], only; nōn modo ... sed etiam, not only ... but also

modus, -ī, *m.*, way, manner. (*Mood*)

moenia, -ium, *n. plur.* [*mūniō*], walls (of a city). *Cf.* mūrus

moneō, monēre, monuī, monitus, remind, advise, warn. (*Monitor*)

mōns, montis, *m.*, MOUNTain, hill. *Cf.* collis

mōnstrō, mōnstrāre, mōnstrāvī, mōnstrātus, show, point out. (*Demonstrate*)

mōnstrum, -ī, *n.*, MONSTER

mora, -ae, *f.* [*moror*], delay

morior, morī, mortuus sum (*fut. part.* moritūrus) [*mors*], die. (*Mortuary*)

moror, morārī, morātus sum [*mora*], retard, hinder, delay. (*Moratorium*)

mors, mortis, *f.* [*morior*], death. (*Mortal.*) *Cf.* nex

mortuus, -a, -um, *adj.* [*morior*], dead

mōs, mōris, *m.*, manner, habit, custom. (*Moral*)

moveō, movēre, mōvī, mōtus, MOVE

mox, *adv.*, soon, presently

Mūcius, Mūcī, *m.*, MUCIUS, a Roman name

mulier, -eris, *f.*, woman. *Cf.* fēmina

multitūdō, -inis, *f.* [*multus*], great number, MULTITUDE, quantity

multō, *adv.* [*multus*], by much, much

multum, *adv.* [*multus*], much

multus, -a, -um, *adj.*, much; *plur.*, many. (*Multiply*)

mūniō, mūnīre, mūnīvī (mūniī), mūnītus [*moenia*], fortify, defend

mūnītiō, -ōnis, *f.* [*mūniō*], fortification, defense. (*Munitions*)

mūnus, -eris, *n.*, duty, office

mūrus, -ī, *m.*, wall. (*Mural, Immure.*) *Cf.* moenia

mūs, mūris, *m. and f.*, mouse

Mūs, Mūris, *m.*, MUS, a Roman surname

mūsica, -ae, *f.*, MUSIC
mūtō, mūtāre, mūtāvī, mūtātus, change, alter. (*Mutation*)

nam, *conj.*, for. *Cf.* enim
nārrō, nārrāre, nārrāvī, nārrātus, tell, relate, NARRATE
nāscor, nāscī, nātus sum, be born. (*Native*)
Nāsīca, -ae, *m.*, NASICA, a Roman surname
nātiō, -ōnis, *f.*, tribe, people, NATION
natō, natāre, natāvī, natātūrus [*frequentative of nō*], swim, float. (*Natatorial*)
nātūra, -ae, *f.* [*nāscor*], (birth), NATURE, character
nātus, *see* nāscor
nauta, -ae, *m.* [*for nāvita*; *nāvis*], sailor. (*Nautical*)
nāvigium, nāvigī, *n.* [*nāvigō*], boat
nāvigō, nāvigāre, nāvigāvī, nāvigātus [*nāvis-agō*], sail, cruise, NAVIGATE
nāvis, -is, *f.* (*acc.* -em, -im; *abl.* -ī, -e), ship. (*Naval*)
-ne, *interrog. adv.*, enclitic, *sign of a question*
nē, *conj.*, that not, that; lest; nē . . . quidem, not even
nec, *see* neque
necesse, *neut. adj.*, *indecl.*, unavoidable, NECESSARY
necessitās, -ātis, *f.* [*necesse*], need, NECESSITY
necō, necāre, necāvī, necātus [*nex*], kill, slay. *Cf.* interficiō *and* occīdō
negōtium, negōtī, *n.*, business, labor. (*Negotiate*)

nēmō, -inī (*dat.; no gen. or abl.*), *m.* and *f.* [*nē-homō*], no one, nobody, no man
Neptūnus, -ī, *m.*, NEPTUNE, the god of the sea
ne-que *or* nec, *conj.*, and not, nor; neque . . . neque, neither . . . nor
Nerviī, -ōrum, *m. plur.*, the NERVII, a tribe of northeastern Gaul
Nessus, -ī, *m.*, NESSUS, a centaur slain by Hercules
neuter, -tra, -trum, *adj. and pron.* [*nē-uter*], neither (of two). (*Neutral*)
nex, necis, *f.* [*necō*], death, slaughter, murder. *Cf.* mors
nihil, *n.*, *indecl.*, nothing; nihil cibī, no food. (*Nihilist*)
ni-si, *conj.*, if not, unless, except
nix, nivis, *f.*, snow
nō, nāre, nāvī, ——, swim
nōbilis, -e, *adj.* [*nōscō*, know], well known, celebrated; of high birth; NOBLE
nōbilitās, -ātis, *f.* [*nōbilis*], rank, NOBILITY
noceō, nocēre, nocuī, nocitūrus, do harm to, hurt, injure; *with dat.* (*Noxious*)
noctū, *adv.* [*nox*], by night
nōlō, nōlle, nōluī, —— [*nē-volō*], be unwilling, will not, not wish
nōmen, -inis, *n.* [*nōscō*, know], (that by which a thing is known), name. (*Nominal*)
nōminō, nōmināre, nōmināvī, nōminātus [*nōmen*], name, call. (*Nominate*)

nōn, *adv.* [*nē-ūnum*], not; nōn iam, no longer; nōn sōlum . . . sed etiam, not only . . . but also. (*Nonentity.*) *Cf.* haud

nōn-dum, *adv.*, not yet

nōn-nūllus, -a, -um, *adj. and pron.*, (not none), some, several

nōs, *see* ego

noster, -tra, -trum, *possess. adj. and pron.* [*nōs*], our, ours; nostrī, our men. (*Nostrum*)

novem, *adj., indecl.*, nine

novus, -a, -um, *adj.*, new. (*Novelty*)

nox, noctis, *f.*, night. (*Nocturnal*)

nūbēs, -is, *f.*, cloud

nūllus, -a, -um, *adj. and pron.* [*nē-ūllus*], no, none, no one. (*Nullity*)

num, *interrog. adv.*, *in an indir. question*, whether

Numa Pompilius, Numae Pompilī, *m.*, NUMA POMPILIUS, the second king of Rome

numerus, -ī, *m.*, NUMBER. (*Numeral*)

numquam, *adv.* [*nē-umquam*], never

nunc, *adv.*, now. (*Quidnunc.*) *Cf.* iam

nūntiō, nūntiāre, nūntiāvī, nūntiātus [*nūntius*], report, anNOUNCE. (*Annunciation*)

nūntius, nūntī, *m.* [*nūntiō*], bearer of news, messenger. (*Nuncio*)

nūper, *adv.* [*for noviper; novus*], recently, lately

nympha, -ae, *f.*, NYMPH

ob, *prep. with acc.*, on account of

ob-, *prefix*, against, opposite

ob-iciō, obicere, obiēcī, obiectus [*-iaciō*], (throw in the way), throw between, interpose. (*Object*)

obiectus, *see* obiciō

oblātus, *see* offerō

obnoxius, -a, -um, *adj.*, liable to, exposed to. (*Obnoxious*)

obscūrō, obscūrāre, obscūrāvī, obscūrātus, darken, conceal. (*Obscure*)

obses, -idis, *m. and f.* [*ob-sedeō*], (one who sits or remains as a pledge), hostage

ob-sideō, obsidēre, obsēdī, obsessus [*-sedeō*], (sit down against), beSIEGE, beset, blockade. (*Obsess.*) *Cf.* oppugnō

obsolētus, -a, -um, *adj.*, old. (*Obsolete*)

ob-struō, obstruere, obstrūxī, obstrūctus, (build up against), block up, bar, barricade, OBSTRUCT

ob-stupefaciō, obstupefacere, obstupefēcī, obstupefactus, astonish, amaze, astound

ob-tineō, obtinēre, obtinuī, obtentus [*-teneō*], (hold against), possess, occupy, hold. (*Obtain*)

occāsiō, -ōnis, *f.*, chance, opportunity. (*Occasion.*) *Cf.* potestās

occāsus, -ūs, *m.*, setting (of the sun)

oc-cīdō, occīdere, occīdī, occīsus [*ob-caedō*], cut down, slay, kill. *Cf.* interficiō *and* necō

occupō, occupāre, occupāvī, occupātus [*ob-capiō*], take possession of, seize; OCCUPY

oc-currō, occurrere, occurrī, occursūrus [*ob-*], run toward; meet, fall in with. (*Occur*)

ōceanus, -ī, *m.*, OCEAN
Ocelum, -ī, *n.*, OCELUM, a town in Cisalpine Gaul
octingentī, -ae, -a, *adj.* [*octō-centum*], eight hundred
octō, *adj.*, *indecl.*, eight. (*Octave*)
octōgintā, *adj.*, *indecl.*, eighty
oculus, -ī, *m.*, eye. (*Ocular*)
odium, odī, *n.*, hatred, enmity. (*Odium*)
Oeneus, -ī, *m.*, ŒNEUS, father of Deianira
Oeta, -ae, *f.*, ŒTA, a mountain in Greece
of-fendō, offendere, offendī, offēnsus [*ob-*], strike against; come on, find. (*Offend*)
of-ferō, offerre, obtulī, oblātus [*ob-*], OFFER, present
officīna, -ae, *f.*, workshop, laboratory
officium, officī, *n.*, duty, task. (*Office*)
ōlim, *adv.* [*olle*, *old form of ille*], (at that time); formerly, once; once upon a time. *Cf.* aliquandō
Olympus, -ī, *m.*, OLYMPUS, a mountain in Greece, the abode of the gods
o-mittō, omittere, omīsī, omissus [*ob-*], let go by, disregard, neglect, OMIT
omnīnō, *adv.* [*omnis*], wholly, altogether, entirely
omnis, -e, *adj.*, whole, all, every. (*Omnipresent.*) *Cf.* cūnctus, tōtus, *and* ūniversus
opera, -ae, *f.* [*opus*], labor, care, work. (*Opera.*) *Cf.* labor *and* opus
oppidānus, -ī, *m.* [*oppidum*], townsman
oppidum, -ī, *n.*, town, stronghold

op-primō, opprimere, oppressī, oppressus [*ob-premō*, press], overcome, crush, OPPRESS
op-pugnō, oppugnāre, oppugnāvī, oppugnātus [*ob-*], attack, assault, besiege. *Cf.* expugnō *and* obsideō
(ops), opis, *f.*, aid, help. *Cf.* auxilium
optimus, -a, -um, *adj.*, *superl. of* bonus, best. (*Optimist*)
opus, -eris, *n.*, work, labor. (*Operate.*) *Cf.* labor
ōrāculum, -ī, *n.* [*ōrō*], ORACLE
ōrātiō, -ōnis, *f.* [*ōrō*], speech, plea; ORATION
orbis, -is, *m.*, circle, ORB, world; orbis terrārum, earth, world. (*Orbit*)
orbō, orbāre, orbāvī, orbātus, deprive, bereave
ōrdinō, ōrdināre, ōrdināvī, ōrdinātus [*ōrdō*], plan, arrange. (*Coördinate*, *Ordain*)
ōrdō, -inis, *m.*, rank, ORDER; ex ōrdine, in succession, one after another; extrā ōrdinem, out of the ranks. (*Extraordinary*)
Orgetorīx, -īgis, *m.*, ORGETORIX, a Helvetian chief
orior, orīrī, ortus sum, arise, spring, descend (from); ortā lūce, at daybreak
ōrnō, ōrnāre, ōrnāvī, ōrnātus, adORN, ORNAMent, deck
ōrō, ōrāre, ōrāvī, ōrātus, (speak), beg, pray, entreat, plead. (*Oratory*)
ortus, *see* orior
os-tendō, ostendere, ostendī, ostentus [*ob(s)-*], stretch out; show, display. (*Ostensible*)

ōstium, ōstī, *n.*, mouth
ovis, -is, *f.*, sheep

P., *abbreviation for* Pūblius
pācō, pācāre, pācāvī, pācātus, subdue, PACify
paene, *adv.*, nearly, almost
palaestra, -ae, *f.*, wrestling school, gymnasium
Palātīnus, -a, -um, *adj.*, PALATINE, of the PALATINE (one of the hills of Rome)
pālus, -ī, *m.*, stake, PALE
palūs, -ūdis, *f.*, swamp, marsh
parēns, -entis, *m. and f.*, PARENT
pāreō, pārēre, pāruī, ——, (come forth, apPEAR), be obedient to, obey; *with dat.*
pariter, *adv.*, equally; pariter ac, equally with, as well as
parō, parāre, parāvī, parātus, make ready, prePARE for, prePARE
pars, partis, *f.*, PART, share; direction, side. (*Partial*)
parum, *adv.*, too little, not enough
parvulus, -a, -um, *adj.* [*diminutive of parvus*], very small, slight, insignificant
parvus, -a, -um, *adj.*, small, little
passus, *see* patior
passus, -ūs, *m.* [*pateō*], (a stretching out of the feet in walking), step, PACE; mīlle passuum, MILE
pāstor, -ōris, *m.*, (feeder), shepherd. (*Pastor*)
pate-faciō, patefacere, patefēcī, patefactus [*pateō*], (make open), open, throw open

pateō, patēre, patuī, ——, lie open, be open, be exposed; extend. (*Patent*)
pater, -tris, *m.*, father. (*Paternal*)
patior, patī, passus sum, bear, suffer, allow, permit. (*Patient, Passive*)
patria, -ae, *f.* [*pater*], native land, country. (*Patriotism*)
patrimōnium, patrimōnī, *n.* [*pater*], property. (*Patrimony*)
paucus, -a, -um, *adj.* (*generally plur.*), few, little. (*Paucity*)
paulō, *adv.*, by a little, little
paululum, *adv.* [*diminutive of paulum*], a very little, somewhat
paulum, *adv.*, a little, somewhat
pauper, pauperis, *adj.*, POOR. (*Pauper*)
paupertās, -ātis, *f.* [*pauper*], want, POVERTY
pavor, -ōris, *m.*, fear, dread, alarm. *Cf.* terror *and* timor
pāx, pācis, *f.*, PEACE. (*Pacify*)
pectus, -oris, *n.*, breast. (*Pectoral*)
pecūnia, -ae, *f.* [*pecus*], money. (*Pecuniary*)
pecus, -oris, *n.*, cattle, flock
pedes, -itis, *m.* [*pēs*], foot soldier
peditātus, -ūs, *m.* [*pedes*], infantry
peior, -ius, *adj.*, *comp. of* malus, worse
pellō, pellere, pepulī, pulsus, beat, drive, defeat. (*Expel, Pulse*)
per, *prep. with acc.*, through, by, by means of, on account of. (*Percentage*)
peragrō, peragrāre, peragrāvī, peragrātus [*per agrum*], wander through, pass over, traverse. *Cf.* perlūstrō

per-cipiō, percipere, percēpī, perceptus [-capiō], PERCEIVE, feel. (Perception.) Cf. sentiō

percussus, see percutiō

per-cutiō, percutere, percussī, percussus [-quatiō, strike], hit, strike, run through. (Percussion)

per-dō, perdere, perdidī, perditus [-dō, put], lose. (Perdition.) Cf. āmittō

per-dūcō, perdūcere, perdūxī, perductus, lead through, conDUCT, bring; construct

per-ficiō, perficere, perfēcī, perfectus [-faciō], accomplish; PERFECT

perfrāctus, see perfringō

per-fringō, perfringere, perfrēgī, perfrāctus [-frangō, break], break to pieces, shatter, completely wreck

pergō, pergere, perrēxī, perrēctūrus [per-regō], go on, proceed, hasten. Cf. prōcēdō and prōgredior

perīculum, -ī, n. [experior], trial, attempt; risk, danger, PERIL

per-lūstrō, perlūstrāre, perlūstrāvī, perlūstrātus, wander through, view all over, examine, survey. Cf. peragrō

per-maneō, permanēre, permānsī, permānsūrus, reMAIN

per-mittō, permittere, permīsī, permissus, allow, grant, suffer, PERMIT; yield, give up; with dat. of person. (Permission)

per-moveō, permovēre, permōvī, permōtus, excite

per-scrībō, perscrībere, perscrīpsī, perscrīptus, write at length, deSCRIBE fully

Persēs, -ae, m., a PERSIAN

Perseus, -ī, m., PERSEUS, a hero of Greek mythology

perspectus, see perspiciō

per-spiciō, perspicere, perspexī, perspectus [-speciō, look], (see through), see clearly, ascertain. (Perspective)

per-suādeō, persuādēre, persuāsī, persuāsus, PERSUADE; with dat. of person. (Persuasion)

per-terreō, perterrēre, perterruī, perterritus, thoroughly frighten, alarm

pertinācia, -ae, f., perseverance; obstinacy, PERTINACITY

per-tineō, pertinēre, pertinuī, —— [-teneō], extend, PERTAIN to

pertrāctus, see pertrahō

per-trahō, pertrahere, pertrāxī, pertrāctus, (drag through), drag, drag along

per-turbō, perturbāre, perturbāvī, perturbātus, disTURB, arouse. (Perturbation)

per-veniō, pervenīre, pervēnī, perventūrus, come up, arrive, reach

pēs, pedis, m., foot; pedem referre, retreat, fall back. (Pedal)

pessimus, -a, -um, adj., superl. of malus, worst. (Pessimist)

petō, petere, petīvī (petiī), petītus, seek, demand, ask for, ask, beg; attack. (Petition.) Cf. postulō, quaerō, and rogō

pīlum, -ī, n., javelin. (Pile-driver)

pinguis, -e, adj., fat, heavy

pīrāta, -ae, m., PIRATE

piscātor, -ōris, m., fisherman. (Piscatorial)

placeō, placēre, placuī, placitūrus, PLEASE; *with dat.* (*Placid*)
plānitiēs, -ēī, *f.*, (a flatness), level ground, PLAIN
plēbs, plēbis, *f.*, the common people, PLEBeians
plōrō, plōrāre, plōrāvī, plōrātus, bewail, lament, grieve. (*Deplore*)
plūrimus, -a, -um, *adj., superl. of* multus, most, very many; plūrimum posse, be very powerful, have most influence
plūs, plūris, *adj., comp. of* multus, more; *plur.*, more, many. (*Plural*)
poena, -ae, *f.* [*pūniō*], fine, punishment; poenās dare, suffer punishment. (*Penalty, Subpœna*)
Poenus, -ī, *m.*, a Carthaginian
poēta, -ae, *m.*, POET
polliceor, pollicērī, pollicitus sum, promise; *rarely as pass.*, be promised
Polydectēs, -is, *m.*, POLYDECTES, a king of Seriphos
Polyphēmus, -ī, *m.*, POLYPHEMUS, a Cyclops
pōmum, -ī, *n.*, apple. (*Pomology*)
pondus, -eris, *n.*, weight, bulk. (*Ponderous*)
pōnō, pōnere, posuī, positus, put, place, set, set up, pitch (camp); *pass.*, lie. (*Position, Postpone*)
pōns, pontis, *m.*, bridge. (*Pontoon*)
populor, populārī, populātus sum, lay waste, devastate, plunder, pillage. (*Depopulate*)
populus, -ī, *m.*, PEOPLE. (*Populous*)
Porsena, -ae, *m.*, PORSENA, a king of Clusium, in Etruria

porta, -ae, *f.*, gate, door. (*Portal*)
portō, portāre, portāvī, portātus, carry, bring. (*Import.*) *Cf.* ferō
portus, -ūs, *m.*, harbor, PORT
poscō, poscere, poposcī, ——, demand. *Cf.* postulō
positus, *see* pōnō
possum, posse, potuī, ——, be able, can; plūrimum posse, be very powerful, have most influence. (*Possible*)
post, *prep. with acc.*, after, behind; *adv.*, afterwards. (*Postscript*)
post-eā, *adv.*, afterwards
(posterus), -a, -um, *adj.* [*post*], following, next. (*Postern, Posterity*)
post-quam, *conj.*, after
postrīdiē, *adv.* [*posterō diē*], on the next day
postulō, postulāre, postulāvī, postulātus, ask, request, demand. (*Postulate.*) *Cf.* petō, quaerō, *and* rogō
potestās, -ātis, *f.* [*possum*], power, authority; opportunity, permission
prae-, *prefix*, before, very
prae-acūtus, -a, -um, *adj.*, sharpened at the end, pointed
praebeō, praebēre, praebuī, praebitus [*prae-habeō*], hold forth, offer, furnish; cause, render
praecipuē, *adv.* [*praecipuus*], chiefly, especially, particularly. *Cf.* maximē
praecipuus, -a, -um, *adj.*, particular; of high rank
prae-clārus, -a, -um, *adj.*, very splendid, glorious
praeda, -ae, *f.* [*praedor*], booty, spoil, PREY. (*Predatory*)

praedor, praedārī, praedātus sum [*praeda*], rob, plunder. (*Depredation*)

prae-ficiō, praeficere, praefēcī, praefectus [*-faciō*], put in command. (*Prefect*)

prae-mittō, praemittere, praemīsī, praemissus, send ahead

praemium, praemī, *n.*, reward, prize. (*Premium*)

Praeneste, -is, *n. and f.*, PRÆNESTE, a town of Italy

praesēns, -entis, *adj.*, instant, immediate, PRESENT

praeses, -idis, *m. and f.* [*prae-sedeō*], (one who sits before), protector, guardian

praesidium, praesidī, *n.* [*praesideō*, sit before], defense, help, protection, support, guard. *Cf.* **auxilium** *and* **subsidium**

prae-stō, praestāre, praestitī, praestitus, stand out, surpass, be superior to, be preferable; perform, furnish. *Cf.* **superō** *and* **vincō**

prae-sum, praeesse, praefuī, praefutūrus, be before, be at the head of, command; *with dat.*

praeter-eā, *adv.*, besides, moreover

praeter-eō, praeterīre, praeterīī, praeteritus, go by, pass by. (*Preterit*)

prehendō, prehendere, prehendī, prehēnsus, grasp, seize. (*Comprehend*)

pretiōsus, -a, -um, *adj.* [*pretium*], costly, valuable, PRECIOUS

pretium, pretī, *n.*, PRICE, value; reward, ransom. (*Appreciate*)

prex, precis, *f.*, PRAYER, entreaty. (*Imprecate*)

prīmō, *adv.* [*prīmus*], at first, first, in the first place

prīmum, *adv.* [*prīmus*], first, at first

prīmus, -a, -um, *adj.*, first, foremost. (*Prime, Primal*)

prīnceps, -cipis, *m.* [*prīmus-capiō*], (taking the first place), chief, leader. (*Prince, Principal.*) *Cf.* **dux**

Prīscus, -ī, *m.*, Tarquinius PRISCUS, one of the seven kings of Rome

prius, *adv.*, before, sooner, previously

prius-quam, *conj.*, sooner than, before

prīvātus, -a, -um, *adj.* [*prīvō*], PRIVATE

prīvō, prīvāre, prīvāvī, prīvātus, dePRIVE; *with abl.*

prō, *prep. with abl.*, before, in behalf of, for, instead of; considering; in accordance with

probō, probāre, probāvī, probātus, PROVE, apPROVE

prō-cēdō, prōcēdere, prōcessī, prōcessūrus, come forward, go forward, advance, PROCEED. *Cf.* **prōgredior** *and* **pergō**

procul, *adv.*, far, afar off

prō-dūcō, prōdūcere, prōdūxī, prōductus, lead forth, bring forth. (*Produce*)

proelium, proelī, *n.*, battle, combat, skirmish. *Cf.* **pugna**

profectus, *see* **proficīscor**

proficīscor, proficīscī, profectus sum, set out, march, go. *Cf.* **exeō** *and* **ēgredior**

prō-gredior, prōgredī, prōgressus sum [-gradior, go], go forward, advance, PROGRESS. Cf. prōcēdō

prōgressus, see prōgredior

pro-hibeō, prohibēre, prohibuī, prohibitus [-habeō], prevent, keep from, PROHIBIT

prō-iciō, prōicere, prōiēcī, prōiectus [-iaciō], throw, cast. (Projectile)

prō-mittō, prōmittere, prōmīsī, prōmissus, put forth, PROMISE

prōmō, prōmere, prōmpsī, prōmptus [prō-emō], take out, bring forth. (Prompt)

prō-moveō, prōmovēre, prōmōvī, prōmōtus, MOVE forward, advance. (Promote)

prōmunturium, prōmunturī, n., PROMONTORY

prope, prep. with acc., near, near to; adv., close at hand, nearly, almost

properō, properāre, properāvī, prōperātūrus, hasten. Cf. mātūrō and contendō

propinquus, -a, -um, adj. [prope], near. (Propinquity)

propior, -ius, adj., comp. [prope], nearer, close

propius, adv. [propior], nearer

prō-pōnō, prōpōnere, prōposuī, prōpositus, put before, set forth; make known, declare, PROPOSE. (Proposition)

propter, prep. with acc., on account of

prō-sternō, prōsternere, prōstrāvī, prōstrātus, strike down, knock down

prōstrātus, -a, -um, adj. [prōsternō], thrown down, PROSTRATE

prō-sum, prōdesse, prōfuī, prōfutūrus, be before, be useful to, benefit, avail; with dat.

prōvectus, see prōvehō

prō-vehō, prōvehere, prōvexī, prōvectus, carry forward, carry off; pass., advance, proceed

prōvincia, -ae, f., PROVINCE

prō-vocō, prōvocāre, prōvocāvī, prōvocātus, call forth, challenge, invite. (Provoke)

proximus, -a, -um, adj., superl. of propior, nearest, next. (Proximity)

pūblicē, adv., in the name of the state, PUBLICly

Pūblicola, -ae, m., PUBLICOLA, a Roman surname

puella, -ae, f. [diminutive of puer], girl, maiden

puer, -erī, m., boy, child. (Puerile)

pugna, -ae, f. [pugnō], battle, contest, fight. Cf. proelium. (Pugnacious)

pugnō, pugnāre, pugnāvī, pugnātūrus [pugna], fight. Cf. dīmicō

pulcher, -chra, -chrum, adj., beautiful, fair, pretty. (Pulchritude)

pūniō, pūnīre, pūnīvī (pūniī), pūnītus [poena], PUNISH

putō, putāre, putāvī, putātus, think, believe, reckon. (Compute.) Cf. arbitror and exīstimō

Pyrrhus, -ī, m., PYRRHUS, a king of Epirus

Pȳthia, -ae, f., the PYTHIA, the inspired prophetess of Apollo at Delphi

quā, *adv.* [*quī*], where
quadrāgintā, *adj., indecl.*, forty
quaerō, quaerere, quaesīvī (quaesiī), quaesītus, seek, ask, INQUIRE. *Cf.* petō *and* rogō
quālis, -e, *interrog. and rel. adj.*, what sort of. (*Quality*)
quam, *adv.* [*quī*], than, how
quam-quam, *conj.*, though, although
quandō, *adv.*, at any time
quantus, -a, -um, *interrog. and rel. adj.* [*quam*], how great, how much; as great as, as much as. (*Quantity*)
quā-rē, *adv.*, for which reason, wherefore, therefore
quārtus, -a, -um, *adj.* [*quattuor*], fourth. (*Quart*)
qua-si, *adv.*, as if
quattuor, *adj., indecl.*, four
quattuor-decim, *adj., indecl.* [*-decem*], fourteen
-que, *conj., enclitic*, and. *Cf.* et *and* atque (ac)
quī, quae, quod, *rel. pron. and adj.*, who, which, what, that
quīdam, quaedam, quoddam (quiddam), *indef. pron. and adj.*, a certain one, certain, a
quidem, *adv.* (*never the first word*), indeed, certainly, in truth; nē . . . quidem, not . . . even
quiēs, -ētis, *f.*, QUIET, rest; repose
quīnquāgintā, *adj., indecl.* [*quīnque*], fifty
quīnque, *adj., indecl.*, five. (*Quinquennial*)
quīntus, -a, -um, *adj.* [*quīnque*], fifth

Quirīnālis, -is, *m.*, the QUIRINAL, one of the hills of Rome
quis (quī), quae, quid (quod), *interrog. pron. and adj.*, who? which? what?
quisquam, ———, quidquam, *indef. pron. and adj.* (*no plur.*), any one, anything (at all), any
quisque, quaeque, quidque (quodque), *indef. pron. and adj.*, each one, each, every
quī-vīs, quaevīs, quodvīs (quidvīs), *indef. pron. and adj.*, any one, anything (you wish), any whatever
quō, *interrog. and rel. adv.* [*quis, quī*], whither, where
quod, *conj.* [*quī*], because, in that
quoque, *conj.* (*after an emphatic word*), also, too. *Cf.* etiam
quot, *interrog. and rel. adj., indecl.*, how many? as many as

rapīna, -ae, *f.* [*rapiō*], robbery, plundering. (*Rapine*)
rapiō, rapere, rapuī, raptus, seize; snatch, drag. (*Rapt, Rapture*)
rārō, *adv.*, seldom, RAREly
ratiō, -ōnis, *f.*, (a reckoning), reason, method, plan, way, conduct. (*Ratio*)
re- (red-), *prefix*, back, again
re-cēdō, recēdere, recessī, recessūrus, withdraw. (*Recede, Recess*)
re-cipiō, recipere, recēpī, receptus [*-capiō*], take back, RECEIVE, recover; sē recipere, withdraw, retreat, betake one's self. (*Reception*)

rēctus, -a, -um, *adj.* [*regō*], straight, diRECT, right

re-cumbō, recumbere, recubuī, ———, lie down, sink down. (*Recumbent*)

re-currō, recurrere, recurrī, ———, (run back), retire, return. (*Recur*)

re-cūsō, recūsāre, recūsāvī, recūsātus [*causa*], decline, refuse

red-dō, reddere, reddidī, redditus [*re(d)-dō*, put], give back, return, RENDER, make

red-eō, redīre, rediī, reditūrus [*re(d)-*], go back, return

red-imō, redimere, redēmī, redēmptus [*re(d)-emō*], buy back, purchase, REDEEM, ransom. (*Redemption*)

reditus, -ūs, *m.* [*redeō*], return

re-dūcō, redūcere, redūxī, reductus, lead back, bring back. (*Reduce*)

re-ferō, referre, rettulī, relātus, bring back; return, repay; report, announce; **pedem referre**, withdraw, retreat, fall back. (*Refer, Relate*)

refrāctus, *see* refringō

re-fringō, refringere, refrēgī, refrāctus [*-frangō*], break down, break open. (*Refraction*)

re-fugiō, refugere, refūgī, ———, flee for safety, flee, take to flight. (*Refuge*)

rēgīna, -ae, *f.* [*regō*], (the ruling one), queen

regiō, -ōnis, *f.*, place, REGION, country

rēgius, -a, -um, *adj.* [*rēx*], the king's, of the king, royal

rēgnō, rēgnāre, rēgnāvī, rēgnātūrus [*rēgnum*], rule, REIGN

rēgnum, -ī, *n.* [*rēx*], kingdom

regō, regere, rēxī, rēctus [*rēx*], rule

re-iciō, reicere, reiēcī, reiectus [*-iaciō*], throw back, drive back, hurl back. (*Reject*)

re-lābor, relābī, relāpsus sum, (slide back), flow back, subside. (*Relapse*)

re-linquō, relinquere, relīquī, relictus, leave behind, leave, abandon. (*Relinquish*)

reliquus, -a, -um, *adj.*, remaining, rest of; *plur. as noun*, the rest. (*Relic.*) *Cf.* cēterī

re-mandō, remandāre, remandāvī, remandātus, send back word. (*Remand*)

re-moveō, removēre, remōvī, remōtus, (move back), REMOVE. (*Remote*)

re-mūneror, remūnerārī, remūnerātus sum, repay, reward. (*Remunerate*)

Remus, -ī, *m.*, REMUS, brother of Romulus

rēmus, -ī, *m.*, oar

re-nūntiō, renūntiāre, renūntiāvī, renūntiātus, report, anNOUNCE. (*Renunciation*)

re-parō, reparāre, reparāvī, reparātus, renew, revive. (*Repair*)

re-pellō, repellere, reppulī, repulsus, drive away, cast down, deprive; REPULSE, REPEL

repentīnō, *adv.* [*repentīnus*], suddenly, unexpectedly

repentīnus, -a, -um, *adj.*, sudden

re-periō, reperīre, repperī, repertus [*-pariō*, bring forth], find, discover, ascertain. *Cf.* inveniō

repertor, -ōris, *m.* [*reperiō*], discoverer, inventor

re-pleō, replēre, replēvī, replētus, fill up again. (*Replete*)

re-pōnō, repōnere, reposuī, repositus, put away, store, keep

re-portō, reportāre, reportāvī, reportātus, bring back, win, gain. (*Report.*) *Cf.* referō

re-poscō, reposcere, ——, ——, demand back, ask for, claim

repositus, *see* repōnō

re-prehendō, reprehendere, reprehendī, reprehēnsus, find fault with, blame. (*Reprehend*)

re-prōmittō, reprōmittere, reprōmīsī, reprōmissus, promise in return

repulsus, *see* repellō

rēs, reī, *f.*, thing, event, circumstance, affair, scheme, cause, matter, fact; rēs pūblica, REPUBLIC, state, commonwealth; rēs frūmentāria, grain supply, provisions; quā rē, wherefore. (*Real, Rebus*)

re-scindō, rescindere, rescidī, rescissus, cut off, break down, demolish. (*Rescind*)

rescissus, *see* rescindō

re-sistō, resistere, restitī, ——, RESIST, oppose; *with dat.*

re-spondeō, respondēre, respondī, respōnsus, (promise in return), answer, reply, RESPOND

respōnsum, -ī, *n.* [*respondeō*], reply, RESPONSE

re-stituō, restituere, restituī, restitūtus [*-statuō*, set up], replace, restore. (*Restitution*)

re-tineō, retinēre, retinuī, retentus [*-teneō*], keep back, reserve. (*Retain*)

reversus, *see* revertō

re-vertō, revertere, revertī, reversus (*or, in the present system, commonly* revertor, *etc.*, *deponent*), turn back, return. (*Revert*)

rēx, rēgis, *m.* [*regō*], (ruler), king. (*Regal*)

Rhēa Silvia, Rhēae Silviae, *f.*, RHEA SILVIA, a priestess of Vesta, and mother of Romulus and Remus

Rhēnus, -ī, *m.*, the RHINE

Rhodanus, -ī, *m.*, the RHONE

rīdeō, rīdēre, rīsī, rīsus, smile, laugh at, laugh. (*Deride*)

rīpa, -ae, *f.*, bank. (*Riparian*)

rogō, rogāre, rogāvī, rogātus, ask, question. *Cf.* quaerō, petō, *and* postulō

rogus, -ī, *m.*, funeral pile, pyre

Rōma, -ae, *f.*, ROME

Rōmānus, -a, -um, *adj.* [*Rōma*], ROMAN; *masc. as noun*, a ROMAN

Rōmulus, -ī, *m.*, ROMULUS, first king of Rome

rūpēs, -is, *f.*, steep rock, cliff. *Cf.* saxum

rūrsus, *adv.* [*for reversus*], (turned back), again

Sabīnī, -ōrum, *m.*, the SABINES, a tribe of Italy

sacer, -cra, -crum, *adj.*, SACRED

sacerdōs, -ōtis, *m. and f.* [*sacer*], priest, priestess. (*Sacerdotal*)

sacrificium, sacrificī, *n.* [*sacrificō*], SACRIFICE

sacrificō, sacrificāre, sacrificāvī, sacrificātus [*sacer-faciō*], SACRIFICE

sacrum, -ī, *n.* [*sacer*], shrine

LATIN-ENGLISH VOCABULARY

saepe, *adv.*, often, frequently
saepiō, saepīre, saepsī, saeptus, (hedge in), surround, fortify, guard
saevus, -a, -um, *adj.*, cruel, savage, fierce. *Cf.* atrōx *and* trux
sagitta, -ae, *f.*, arrow. (*Sagittarius*)
saltus, -ūs, *m.*, forest, glade, thicket
salūs, -ūtis, *f.*, SAFEty, welfare; greeting
Samnītēs, -ium, *m. plur.*, the SAMNITES, a tribe of Italy
sanguis, -inis, *m.*, blood. (*Sanguinary*)
Santonēs, -um, *m. plur.*, the SANTONES, a tribe of Gaul
satis, *adv.*, enough, sufficiently. (*Satisfy*)
saxum, -ī, *n.*, stone, rock. *Cf.* rūpēs
scelus, -eris, *n.*, wickedness, crime
sciō, scīre, scīvī (sciī), scītus, know, know how. (*Science*.) *Cf.* cognōscō
Scīpiō, -ōnis, *m.*, SCIPIO, a famous Roman general
scrība, -ae, *m.* [*scrībō*], writer, clerk, secretary. (*Scribe*)
scrībō, scrībere, scrīpsī, scrīptus, write. (*Scripture*)
scūtum, -ī, *n.*, shield
sē, sēsē, *see* suī
sectiō, -ōnis, *f.*, (a cutting), sale of confiscated goods, booty. (*Section*)
secundus, -a, -um, *adj.* [*sequor*], following, next; SECOND
sed, *conj.*, but. *Cf.* autem
sēdecim, *adj.*, *indecl.* [*sex-decem*], sixteen
sedeō, sedēre, sēdī, sessūrus [*sēdēs*], sit. (*Sedentary*)
sēdēs, -is, *f.* [*sedeō*], seat, dwelling, perch. (*See of a bishop*)

sēditiō, -ōnis, *f.*, discord, revolt, SEDITION
Segusiāvī, -ōrum, *m. plur.*, the SEGUSIAVI, a tribe of Gaul
semper, *adv.*, always, ever
senātor, -ōris, *m.* [*senātus*], SENATOR
senātus, -ūs, *m.* [*senātor*], council of elders, SENATE
senectūs, -ūtis, *f.* [*senex*, old], old age
senior, -ōris, *m.* [*comp. of senex*, old], elder. (*Senior*)
sentiō, sentīre, sēnsī, sēnsus, feel, know (by the senses), see, perceive. (*Sense*.) *Cf.* percipiō
sepeliō, sepelīre, sepelīvī (sepeliī), sepultus, bury, inter. (*Sepulture*)
septem, *adj.*, *indecl.*, seven
septimus, -a, -um, *adj.* [*septem*], seventh
Sēquanī, -ōrum, *m. plur.*, the SEQUANI, a tribe of Gaul
sequor, sequī, secūtus sum, follow. (*Prosecute*)
Serīphus, -ī, *f.*, SERIPHOS, a small island east of Greece
serpēns, -entis, *m.*, SERPENT, snake
servitūs, -ūtis, *f.* [*servus*], slavery, SERVITUDE
Servius Tullius, Servī Tullī, *m.*, SERVIUS TULLIUS, one of the kings of Rome
servō, servāre, servāvī, servātus, save, keep, preSERVE
servus, -ī, *m.*, slave, SERVant
sex, *adj.*, *indecl.*, six
sī, *conj.*, if, whether
sīc, *adv.*, so, thus, in this way. *Cf.* ita *and* tam

siccus, -a, -um, *adj.*, dry; in siccō, on dry ground. (*Desiccate*)

Sicilia, -ae, *f.*, SICILY, an island off the coast of Italy

signum, -ī, *n.*, mark, SIGN, enSIGN, SIGNal

silva, -ae, *f.*, wood, forest. (*Silvan*)

similis, -e, *adj.* [*simul*], like, resembling, SIMILar

simul, *adv.* [*similis*], at the same time; simul ac, as soon as

sine, *prep. with abl.*, without. (*Sinecure*)

sinister, -tra, -trum, *adj.*, left (hand). (*Sinister*)

sinus, -ūs, *m.*, lap, bosom

situs, -a, -um, *adj.*, placed, set, lying, SITUated

socius, sociī, *m.*, comrade, companion, ally. (*Social*)

sōl, sōlis, *m.*, sun. (*Solar*)

sollicitō, sollicitāre, sollicitāvī, sollicitātus, stir, arouse, tempt. (*Solicit*)

sōlus, -a, -um, *adj.*, alone, single; SOLE

solvō, solvere, solvī, solūtus, loose, loosen; melt; break; pay. (*Solve*)

somnus, -ī, *m.*, sleep. (*Somnolent*)

sonitus, -ūs, *m.*, SOUND, noise, din, clash

soror, -ōris, *f.*, sister. (*Sorority*)

Sparta, -ae, *f.*, SPARTA, a city of Greece

Spartānus, -ī, *m.*, a SPARTAN

spatium, spatī, *n.*, room, SPACE, distance, time

speciēs, (-ēī), *f.* [*spectō*], sight, appearance, pretense. (*Species*)

spectāculum, -ī, *n.* [*spectō*], a show, exhibition. (*Spectacle*)

spectō, spectāre, spectāvī, spectātus, look at, behold, witness. (*Spectator*)

speculum, -ī, *n.* [*spectō*], mirror

spēlunca, -ae, *f.*, cave, cavern, den

spernō, spernere, sprēvī, sprētus, despise, reject, scorn, spurn

spērō, spērāre, spērāvī, spērātus [*spēs*], hope, hope for

spēs, speī, *f.* [*spērō*], hope; in spem venīre, to entertain hopes

spondeō, spondēre, spopondī, spōnsus, pledge, promise. (*Spouse*)

sponte (suā), *only abl.*, of (one's own) accord. (*Spontaneous*)

statim, *adv.* [*stō*], (standing there), on the spot, immediately, at once. *Cf.* subitō

statua, -ae, *f.* [*statuō*, set up], (the thing set up), STATUE

stella, -ae, *f.*, star. (*Constellation, Stellar*)

stīpendium, stīpendī, *n.*, wages, pay; military service. (*Stipend*)

stō, stāre, stetī, statūrus, stand

studeō, studēre, studuī, —— [*studium*], desire, be eager for; *with dat.* (*Student*)

studiōsus, -a, -um, *adj.* [*studium*], eager, desirous, STUDIOUS

studium, studī, *n.* [*studeō*], zeal, eagerness; STUDY

stupeō, stupēre, stupuī, ——, be astonished, be amazed. (*Stupefy*)

suādeō, suādēre, suāsī, suāsus, advise, urge; *with dat. of person.* (*Suasion*)

sub, *prep. with acc. and abl.*, under, up to; sub vesperum, toward evening. (*Subway*) sub-dō, subdere, subdidī, subditus [-*dō*, put], put under, set to

sub-eō, subīre, subiī, subitus, go under, go up to, enter; undergo

sub-iciō, subicere, subiēcī, subiectus [-*iaciō*], put under, place under; *with dat. of the object under which*. (*Subject*)

sub-igō, subigere, subēgī, subāctus [-*agō*], bring under, subdue

subitō, *adv*., SUDDenly, unexpectedly. *Cf.* statim

sublātus, *see* tollō

sublicius, -a, -um, *adj*., resting on piles; pōns Sublicius, the Sublician bridge, the pile bridge

subsidium, subsidī, *n*., help, aid, relief. (*Subsidy*.) *Cf.* auxilium *and* praesidium

suc-cēdō, succēdere, successī, successūrus [*sub*-], come up, approach, follow. (*Succeed*)

Suessa Pōmētia, Suessae Pōmētiae, *f*., SUESSA POMETIA, a city of Italy

suī, *reflex. pron.*, of himself (herself, itself, themselves). (*Suicide*)

Sulpicius, Sulpicī, *m*., a Roman name

sum, esse, fuī, futūrus, be, exist. (*Essence, Future*)

summus, -a, -um, *adj*., *superl. of* superus, highest, greatest, extreme. (*Sum, Consummate*)

sūmō, sūmere, sūmpsī, sūmptus, take, take up; ASSUME

super, *prep. with acc. and abl*., over, above, upon. (*Superhuman*)

super-incidō, superincidere, ——, ——, fall on from above

superior, -ius, *adj., comp. of* superus, higher, SUPERIOR

superō, superāre, superāvī, superātus [*super*], pass over; surpass, outdo, overcome, conquer. (*Insuperable*.) *Cf.* praestō *and* vincō

super-sum, superesse, superfuī, superfutūrus, be over, be left over; survive; *with dat.*

(superus), -a, -um, *adj*. [*super*], above

supplicium, supplicī, *n*., punishment, torture

suprā, *adv*. [*superus*], above, before

suprēmus, -a, -um, *adj., superl. of* superus, last. (*Supreme*)

sus-cipiō, suscipere, suscēpī, susceptus [*sub(s)-capiō*], take up, undertake, receive. (*Susceptible*)

suspīciō, -ōnis, *f*. [*suspicor*], SUSPICION

suspicor, suspicārī, suspicātus sum [*suspīciō*], SUSpect, mistrust

sus-tineō, sustinēre, sustinuī, sustentus [*sub(s)-teneō*], hold up, bear, endure; support; withstand, SUSTAIN

suus, -a, -um, *possess. and reflex. adj. and pron*. [*suī*], his, her, hers, its, their, theirs

tālāria, -ium, *n. plur*., winged shoes

tālis, -e, *adj*., such

tam, *adv*., so, so much. *Cf.* ita *and* sīc

tamen, *adv*., yet, but, however, nevertheless

tandem, *adv*. [*tam-*], (just so far), at length, finally

tantulus, -a, -um, *adj.* [*diminutive of tantus*], so small
tantum, *adv.* [*tantus*], only
tantus, -a, -um, *adj.* [*tam*], so great, so much, such. (*Tantamount*)
Tarentīnus, -a, -um, *adj.*, of Tarentum, a city of southern Italy; *masc. plur. as noun*, the TARENTINES
Tarentum, -ī, *n.*, TARENTUM, a city of southern Italy
Tarquinius, Tarquinī, *m.*, TARQUIN, name of two kings of Rome, Tarquinius Priscus and Tarquinius Superbus
tēlum, -ī, *n.*, weapon
temperō, temperāre, temperāvī, temperātus, refrain from, keep from. (*Temperate*)
tempestās, -ātis, *f.* [*tempus*], storm, TEMPEST, weather
templum, -ī, *n.*, TEMPLE
tempus, -oris, *n.*, time. (*Temporal*)
teneō, tenēre, tenuī, ——, hold, keep, have. (*Tenacious, Retain*)
tentō, tentāre, tentāvī, tentātus, try, atTEMPT. *Cf.* **experior**
tergum, -ī, *n.*, back; **ā tergō,** behind, in the rear. (*Tergiversation*)
terra, -ae, *f.*, earth, land; region. (*Terrace*)
terreō, terrēre, terruī, territus [*terror*], frighten, alarm, TERRIfy
terribilis, -e, *adj.* [*terreō*], dreadful, frightful, TERRIBLE. *Cf.* **horribilis**
territōrium, territōrī, *n.* [*terra*], lands. (*Territory*)
terror, -ōris, *m.* [*terreō*], TERROR, alarm, fear. *Cf.* **pavor** *and* **timor**

tertium, *adv.* [*tertius*], the third time
tertius, -a, -um, *adj.* [*trēs*], third. (*Tertiary*)
Thalēs, -is, *m.*, THALES, a Greek philosopher
Thēbae, -ārum, *f. plur.*, THEBES, a city of Greece
Tiberis, -is, *m.* (*acc.* -im), the TIBER, a river of Italy
Ticīnus, -ī, *m.*, the TICINUS, a river of Italy
timeō, timēre, timuī, —— [*timor*], fear, be afraid of. *Cf.* **vereor**
timidus, -a, -um, *adj.* [*timeō*], fainthearted, TIMID
Tīmōn, -ōnis, *m.*, TIMON, an Athenian
timor, -ōris, *m.* [*timeō*], fear. *Cf.* **pavor** *and* **terror.** (*Timorous*)
tintinnābulum, -ī, *n.*, bell. (*Tintinnabulation*)
Tīryns, -nthis (-os) (*acc.* **Tīryntha**), *f.*, TIRYNS, a city of Greece
tolerō, tolerāre, tolerāvī, tolerātus, bear, endure. (*Tolerate*.) *Cf.* **ferō**
tollō, tollere, sustulī, sublātus, raise, pick up, take. (*Extol*)
Tolōsātēs, -ium, *m. plur.*, the TOLOSATES, inhabitants of Tolosa, a city in Gaul
tōtus, -a, -um, *adj.*, whole, all, entire. (*Total*.) *Cf.* **omnis, ūniversus,** *and* **cūnctus**
trabs, trabis, *f.*, beam, timber, log
tractō, tractāre, tractāvī, tractātus [*trahō*], handle, feel of. (*Tractate*)
trā-dō, trādere, trādidī, trāditus [*trāns-dō*], put], give over, give up, surrender, deliver; **trādunt,** they say. (*Tradition*)

trā-dūcō, trādūcere, trādūxī, trāductus [*trāns-*], lead over, lead across. *Often with a secondary object, as,* flūmen cōpiās trādūcere, lead the troops across the river. (*Traduce*)

trahō, trahere, trāxī, trāctus, draw, drag, lead. (*Traction*)

trā-iciō, trāicere, trāiēcī, trāiectus [*trāns-iaciō*], throw across, cross; pierce. (*Trajectory*)

trā-nō, trānāre, trānāvī, —— [*trāns-*], swim across

tranquillus, -a, -um, *adj.*, calm, TRANQUIL

trāns, *prep. with acc.*, across, beyond, over, the other side of. (*Transatlantic*)

trāns-eō, trānsīre, trānsiī, trānsitus, go over, cross. (*Transit*)

trāns-fīgō, trānsfīgere, trānsfīxī, trānsfīxus, pierce through, stab. (*Transfix*)

trānsfīxus, *see* trānsfīgō

trāns-fodiō, trānsfodere, trānsfōdī, trānsfossus, run through, pierce through, stab

trāns-fugiō, trānsfugere, trānsfūgī, ——, go over (to the enemy), desert

trāns-marīnus, -a, -um, *adj.* [*mare*], foreign

trāns-portō, trānsportāre, trānsportāvī, trānsportātus, carry across. (*Transport*)

trecentī, -ae, -a, *adj.* [*trēs-centum*], three hundred

trepidō, trepidāre, trepidāvī, trepidātūrus, be in alarm, be in confusion. (*Trepidation*)

trēs, tria, *adj.*, three. (*Trefoil*)

tribūnal, -ālis, *n.* [*tribūnus*], judgment seat, TRIBUNAL

tribūnus, -ī, *m.*, TRIBUNE, a Roman officer

trīcēnsimus, -a, -um, *adj.*, thirtieth

trīduum, -ī, *n.*, three days

trīstis, -e, *adj.*, sad, gloomy

triumphō, triumphāre, triumphāvī, triumphātūrus, celebrate a TRIUMPH

Trōia, -ae, *f.*, TROY, an ancient city of Asia Minor

trux, trucis, *adj.*, wild, harsh, savage, fierce, TRUCulent. *Cf.* atrōx *and* saevus

tū, *pers. pron.*, thou, you

tuba, -ae, *f.*, trumpet

Tullus Hostīlius, Tullī Hostīlī, *m.*, TULLUS HOSTILIUS, the third king of Rome

tum, *adv.*, at that time, then

tunc, *adv.* [*tum*], at that time, then

turba, -ae, *f.* [*turbō*], crowd, throng; turmoil

turbō, turbāre, turbāvī, turbātus [*turba*], disTURB, confuse, trouble

turris, -is, *f.*, TOWER. (*Turret*)

Tuscī, -ōrum, *m. plur.*, the Etruscans, people of Etruria, in Italy

Tuscia, -ae, *f.*, Etruria, a district of Italy

Tusculum, -ī, *n.*, TUSCULUM, a town near Rome

tūtēla, -ae, *f.*, guardianship, charge, care. (*Tutelary*)

tūtus, -a, -um, *adj.*, safe

tuus, -a, -um, *possess. adj. and pron.*, thy, thine; your, yours (*of only one person*)

ubi, *interrog. and rel. adv.,* where, when
ulcīscor, ulcīscī, ultus sum, avenge
Ulixēs, -is, *m.,* ULYSSES, a Greek hero
ūllus, -a, -um, *adj. and pron.* [*for ūnulus, diminutive of* **ūnus**], any, any one, anybody
ulterior, -ius, *adj., comp.,* farther, more remote. (*Ulterior*)
ultimus, -a, -um, *adj., superl. of* **ulterior,** farthest, last. (*Ultimate*)
umbra, -ae, *f.,* shade, shadow. (*Umbrage, Umbrella*)
umerus, -ī, *m.,* shoulder. (*Humerus*)
umquam, *adv.,* at any time, ever
unda, -ae, *f.,* wave
unde, *interrog. and rel. adv.,* whence
ūndecimus, -a, -um, *adj.,* eleventh
undique, *adv.,* from all parts, on all sides, everywhere
ūniversus, -a, -um, *adj.* [*ūnus-versus*], (turned into one), whole, all, in a mass. (*Universal, Universe, University.*) *Cf.* **cūnctus, omnis,** *and* **tōtus**
ūnus, -a, -um, *adj.,* one; alone. (*Union*)
urbs, -is, *f.,* city. (*Suburb*)
ūsus, -ūs, *m.* [*ūtor*], USE, benefit, advantage
ut (utī), *adv. and conj.,* how, as, when; that, in order that, so that, to
uter, -tra, -trum, *interrog. pron. and adj.,* which (of two)? **uter ... utrī,** which ... to the other
ūter, -tris, *m.,* leather bottle, skin (of wine)

uterque, utraque, utrumque, *indef. pron. and adj.,* each (of two), both
ūtilis, -e, *adj.* [*ūtor*], useful, advantageous. (*Utility*)
ūtor, ūtī, ūsus sum [*ūsus*], USE, employ, enjoy, maintain; *with abl.*
uxor, -ōris, *f.,* wife. (*Uxorious*)

vacō, vacāre, vacāvī, ——, be unoccupied. (*Vacant*)
vadum, -ī, *n.,* shoal, ford
vāgītus, -ūs, *m.,* a crying
valeō, valēre, valuī, valitūrus, be strong, be in good health; **valē,** farewell, good-by. (*Valiant, Value*)
Valerius, Valerī, *m.,* VALERIUS, a Roman name
valētūdō, -inis, *f.* [*valeō*], health, state of health. (*Valetudinarian*)
validus, -a, -um, *adj.* [*valeō*], strong, stout, sturdy. (*Valid.*) *Cf.* **fortis**
vāllum, -ī, *n.,* earthworks, rampart. (*Circumvallation*)
vās, vāsis (*plur.* **vāsa, -ōrum**), *n.,* VASE, pot
vāstō, vāstāre, vāstāvī, vāstātus, lay WASTE, ravage
-ve, *conj., enclitic,* or
vehementer, *adv.,* eagerly, earnestly, very much, VEHEMENTly
Vēientēs, -ium, *m. plur.,* the inhabitants of Veii
vel, *conj.* [*volō,* wish], or; **vel ... vel,** either ... or. *Cf.* **aut**
vēlō, vēlāre, vēlāvī, vēlātus, cover, encircle, envelop, VEIL
vel-ut, *adv.,* just as, as if, like

vendō, vendere, vendidī, venditus, sell, VEND

venēnum, -ī, *n.*, poison. (*Venom*)

venia, -ae, *f.*, indulgence, favor. (*Venial*)

veniō, venīre, vēnī, ventūrus, come. (*Convene*)

vēnor, vēnārī, vēnātus sum, hunt, chase. (*Venison*)

venter, -tris, *m.*, belly, stomach. (*Ventriloquist*)

ventus, -ī, *m.*, wind. (*Ventilate*)

verbum, -ī, *n.*, word. (*Verb*)

vereor, verērī, veritus sum, fear, revERence, respect. *Cf.* timeō

veritus, *see* vereor

vērō, *adv.* [*vērum*], in truth, but

versus, *see* vertō

vertō, vertere, vertī, versus, turn, change. (*Convert, Verse*)

vērum, *conj.* [*vērō*], but

vesper, -erī, *m.*, evening, nightfall. (*Vespers*)

Vesta, -ae, *f.*, VESTA, the goddess of the hearth

vester, -tra, -trum, *possess. adj. and pron.*, your, yours (*of more than one person*)

vestis, -is, *f.*, garment, robe, clothing

Vesuvius, Vesuvī, *m.*, VESUVIUS, a volcano near Naples

Veturia, -ae, *f.*, VETURIA, mother of Coriolanus

via, -ae, *f.*, way, road, street; gap. (*Via, Viaduct*)

viātor, -ōris, *m.* [*via*], traveler

vīcīnus, -a, -um, *adj.* [*vīcus*], near, neighboring; *masc. as noun*, neighbor. (*Vicinity*)

victor, -ōris, *m.* [*vincō*], conqueror, VICTOR; *as adj.*, VICTORious

victōria, -ae, *f.* [*victor*], VICTORY

vīcus, -ī, *m.*, village, district, street

videō, vidēre, vīdī, vīsus, see, perceive; *pass.*, be seen, seem. (*Vision*)

vigilia, -ae, *f.*, watch, night watch. (*Vigil*)

vīgintī, *adj., indecl.*, twenty

vīmen, -inis, *n.*, pliant twig, withe, osier

Vīminālis, -is, *m.*, the VIMINAL, one of the hills of Rome

vinciō, vincīre, vīnxī, vīnctus, bind

vincō, vincere, vīcī, victus, conquer, defeat. (*Invincible.*) *Cf.* superō

vinculum, -ī, *n.* [*vinciō*], chain, bond; in vincula, into prison, into chains

vīnea, -ae, *f.*, covered shed, movable shelter, VINEA

vīnum, -ī, *n.*, WINE. (*Vine*)

vir, virī, *m.*, man, hero. (*Virile.*) *Cf.* homō

vireō, virēre, viruī, ——, be green

virgō, -inis, *f.*, maiden, VIRGIN

virtūs, -ūtis, *f.* [*vir*], manliness, courage, bravery, valor; VIRTUE

vīs, *see* volō, wish

vīs, vīs, *f.*, strength, power, force, violence. (*Vim*)

vīta, -ae, *f.*, life. (*Vital*)

vix, *adv.*, hardly, with difficulty

vocō, vocāre, vocāvī, vocātus [*vōx*], call. (*Vocation.*) *Cf.* appellō

Vocontiī, -ōrum, *m. plur.*, the VOCONTII, a tribe in the Roman province in southeastern Gaul

volō, velle, voluī, ——, wish, be willing, desire, intend. (*Volition*)
volō, volāre, volāvī, volātūrus, fly. (*Volatile*)
Volscī, -ōrum, *m. plur.*, the VOLSCIANS, a people of Italy
Volumnia, -ae, *f.*, VOLUMNIA, wife of Coriolanus
voluntās, -ātis, *f.* [*volō*, wish], will, good will, consent. (*Voluntary*)
voluptās, -ātis, *f.* [*volō*, wish], pleasure, enjoyment. (*Voluptuous*)

vōx, vōcis, *f.* [*vocō*], VOICE, word, remark. (*Vocal*)
Vulcānus, -ī, *m.*, VULCAN, the god of fire
vulnerō, vulnerāre, vulnerāvī, vulnerātus [*vulnus*], wound, hurt, injure. (*Vulnerable*)
vulnus, -eris, *n.* [*vulnerō*], wound
vultus, -ūs, *m.*, countenance, looks, features

Zama, -ae, *f.*, ZAMA, a town in Africa

ENGLISH-LATIN VOCABULARY

For the principal parts of verbs, and for other details not given here, reference may be made to the Latin-English Vocabulary or to the special vocabularies. The figures 1, 2, 3, 4 after verbs indicate the conjugation.

about, dē, *with abl.*
across, trāns, *with acc.*
act, agō, 3
advance, prōgredior, 3
advise, moneō, 2
after, post, *with acc.*; *implied in a participle*
afterwards, posteā
against, contrā *or* ad, *with acc.*
aid, auxilium, auxilī, *n.*
all, omnis, -e; tōtus, -a, -um
ally, socius, socī, *m.*
alone, sōlus, -a, -um; ūnus, -a, -um
also, etiam
although, *implied in a participle*
among, inter, *with acc.*; in, *with abl.*
ample, amplus, -a, -um
and, et, -que; **and also**, atque; **and so**, itaque
announce, nūntiō, 1
another, alius, -a, -ud
any, ūllus, -a, -um; aliquī, aliqua, aliquod; **any at all**, quisquam, ———, quidquam; **any one**, aliquis
anything, aliquid
approach, appropinquō, 1
approve, probō, 1
arm, armō, 1
arms, arma, -ōrum, *n. plur.*

army, exercitus, -ūs, *m.*
arouse, incitō, 1; commoveō, 2
arrival, adventus, -ūs, *m.*
arrow, sagitta, -ae, *f.*
ask, rogō, 1; petō, 3
assistance, auxilium, auxilī, *n.*
at, **in**, *with acc. or abl.*; *abl. of cause*; *abl. of time*; **at last**, tandem; **at once**, statim
Athens, Athēnae, -ārum, *f. plur.*
attack, *v.*, oppugnō, 1; impetum faciō, 3
attack, *n.*, impetus, -ūs, *m.*
attempt, cōnor, 1
await, exspectō, 1
away from, ā *or* ab, *with abl.*

baggage, impedīmenta, -ōrum, *n. plur.*
band, manus, -ūs, *f.*
bank, rīpa, -ae, *f.*
barbarian, barbarus, -ī, *m.*
battle, pugna, -ae, *f.*; proelium, proelī, *n.*
be, sum, *irr.*; **be able**, possum, *irr.*; **be made**, fīō, *irr.*; **be unwilling**, nōlō, *irr.*; **be wanting**, dēsum, *irr.*; **be willing**, volō, *irr.*
bear, ferō, *irr.*

331

because, quod; **because of,** ob *or* propter, *with acc.*; *abl. of cause*
become, fīō, *irr.*
began, coepī, *defective*
best, optimus, -a, -um
better, melior, melius
between, inter, *with acc.*
boat, nāvigium, nāvigī, *n.*
body, corpus, -oris, *n.*
bold, audāx, -ācis; fortis, -e
book, liber, -brī, *m.*
booty, praeda, -ae, *f.*
both ... and, et ... et
boy, puer, -erī, *m.*
brave, fortis, -e
bravely, fortiter; cum virtūte
bravery, virtūs, -ūtis, *f.*
bring, portō, 1
Britain, Britannia, -ae, *f.*
broad, lātus, -a, -um
brother, frāter, -tris, *m.*
build, aedificō, 1
building, aedificium, aedificī, *n.*
but, sed
buy, emō, 3
by, ā *or* ab, *with abl.*; *abl. of means or instrument*

Cæsar, Caesar, -aris, *m.*
call together, convocō, 1
camp, castra, -ōrum, *n. plur.*
can, possum, *irr.*
captive, captīvus, -ī, *m.*
capture, capiō, 3
care, cūra, -ae, *f.*
carry, portō, 1; **carry on war,** bellum gerō, 3
cart, carrus, -ī, *m.*

cause, causa, -ae, *f.*
cavalry, equitātus, -ūs, *m.*
centurion, centuriō, -ōnis, *m.*
certain, quīdam, quaedam, quoddam (quiddam)
certainly, certē
chief, prīnceps, -cipis, *m.*
children, līberī, -ōrum, *m. plur.*
citizen, cīvis, -is, *m.*
city, urbs, urbis, *f.*
clan, cīvitās, -ātis, *f.*
cohort, cohors, cohortis, *f.*
come, veniō, 4; **come near,** accēdō, 3; appropinquō, 1
coming, adventus, -ūs, *m.*
command, *v.*, iubeō, 2; imperō, 1, *with dat.*
command, *n.*, imperium, imperī, *n.*
comrade, socius, socī, *m.*
concerning, dē, *with abl.*
conference, conloquium, conloquī, *n.*
confidence, fidēs, -eī, *f.*
confuse, perturbō, 1
conquer, superō, 1; vincō, 3
contend, pugnō, 1
Corinth, Corinthus, -ī, *f.*
Cornelia, Cornēlia, -ae, *f.*
country, patria, -ae, *f.*
courage, virtūs, -ūtis, *f.*
cut off, interclūdō, 3

daily, cotīdiē
danger, perīculum, -ī, *n.*
daughter, fīlia, -ae, *f.*
dawn (at), prīmā lūce
day, diēs, -ēī, *m.*
daybreak (at), prīmā lūce
death, mors, mortis, *f.*

ENGLISH-LATIN VOCABULARY

decide, cōnstituō, 3
deep, altus, -a, -um
defend, dēfendō, 3
delay, *v.*, moror, 1
delay, *n.*, mora, -ae, *f.*
delight, dēlectō, 1
Delphi, Delphī, -ōrum, *m. plur.*
demand, postulō, 1
depart, discēdō, 3
deprive, prīvō, 1
desire, cupiō, 3; studeō, 2, *with dat.*
desist, dēsistō, 3
difficulty, difficultās, -ātis, *f.*
diligence, dīligentia, -ae, *f.*
dismiss, dīmittō, 3
disturb, commoveō, 2
do, faciō, 3; agō, 3
down from, dē, *with abl.*
draw up, īnstruō, 3
dwell, habitō, 1; incolō, 3

each, each one, quisque; each of two, uterque, utraque, utrumque
eager, ācer, ācris, ācre
easy, facilis, -e
embassy, lēgātiō, -ōnis, *f.*
enemy, hostis, -is, *m.*
enough, satis
every one, quisque; omnēs, -ium, *m. plur.*
exhort, hortor, 1
extend, pateō, 2

fact, rēs, reī, *f.*; the fact that, quod, *with a clause of fact*
fail, dēsum, *irr., with dat.*
farmer, agricola, -ae, *m.*
father, pater, -tris, *m.*
fear, *v.*, timeō, 2; vereor, 2

fear, *n.*, timor, -ōris, *m.*
few, paucī, -ae, -a, *plur.*
field, ager, agrī, *m.*
fight, *v.*, pugnō, 1
fight, *n.*, pugna, -ae, *f.*
fill, compleō, 2
find, reperiō, 4
fire, ignis, -is, *m.*
first, prīmus, -a, -um
fit, idōneus, -a, -um
five, quīnque
flank, cornū, -ūs, *n.*
flee, fugiō, 3
follow, sequor, 3
food, cibus, -ī, *m.*
foot, pēs, pedis, *m.*; foot soldier, pedes, peditis, *m.*
for, *sign of the dative*; prō, *with abl.*; for the purpose of, ad, *with gerundive or gerund*; ut, *with subjunctive*
force, vīs, vīs, *f.*
forest, silva, -ae, *f.*
formerly, ōlim
fortify, mūniō, 4
fortune, fortūna, -ae, *f.*
free, *v.*, līberō, 1
free, *adj.*, līber, -era, -erum
friend, amīcus, -ī, *m.*
friendly, amīcus, -a, -um
frighten, terreō, 2
from, dē, *with abl.*; away from, ā *or* ab, *with abl.*; out from, ē *or* ex, *with abl.*; *abl. of separation*

Galba, Galba, -ae, *m.*
garden, hortus, -ī, *m.*
gate, porta, -ae, *f.*
gather together, cōgō, 3

Gaul, Gallia, -ae, *f.*; a Gaul, Gallus, -ī, *m.*
general, dux, ducis, *m.*
Germans, Germānī, -ōrum, *m. plur.*
Germany, Germānia, -ae, *f.*
gift, dōnum, -ī, *n.*
girl, puella, -ae, *f.*
give, dō, 1; dōnō, 1
go, eō, *irr.*; go away, discēdō, 3; go forward, prōgredior, 3; go out, ēgredior, 3
god, deus, -ī, *m.*
good, bonus, -a, -um
grain, frūmentum, -ī, *n.*
great, magnus, -a, -um; great number, multitūdō, -inis, *f.*
greatly, magnopere
Greece, Graecia, -ae, *f.*
grieve, doleō, 2

hand, manus, -ūs, *f.*
happen, fīō, *irr.*
harbor, portus, -ūs, *m.*
hardship, labor, -ōris, *m.*
harm, noceō, 2, *with dat.*
hasten, properō, 1
have, habeō, 2
he, is, hic, ille
head, caput, -itis, *n.*
hear, audiō, 4
heavy, gravis, -e
help, auxilium, auxilī, *n.*; subsidium, subsidī, *n.*
Helvetians, Helvētiī, -ōrum, *m. plur.*
her, (*objective*) eam, hanc, illam; (*possessive*) eius, huius, illīus; (*reflexive possessive*) suus, -a, -um
herself, suī

high, altus, -a, -um; superus, -a, -um
hill, collis, -is, *m.*
him, eum, hunc, illum
himself, suī
hinder, impediō, 4
his, eius, huius, illīus; (*reflexive*) suus, -a, -um
hold, habeō, 2; teneō, 2; hold in check, sustineō, 2
home, domus, -ūs, *f.*
hope, spēs, speī, *f.*
horn, cornū, -ūs, *n.*
horse, equus, -ī, *m.*
horseman, eques, -itis, *m.*
hostage, obses, -idis, *m.*
hour, hōra, -ae, *f.*
house, domus, -ūs, *f.*
how many, quot
however, tamen
hundred, centum
hurl, iaciō, 3
hurry, properō, 1

I, ego
if, *implied in a participle*
impel, incitō, 1
in, in, *with abl.*; abl. of specification; in defense of, prō, *with abl.*; in front of, prō, *with abl.*; in order to, ut, *with subjunctive*; in such a way, ita; in vain, frūstrā
increase, augeō, 2
infantry, peditātus, -ūs, *m.*
inform, certiōrem faciō, 3
inhabitant, incola, -ae, *m.*
injure, noceō, 2, *with dat.*
into, in, *with acc.*
island, īnsula, -ae, *f.*

ENGLISH-LATIN VOCABULARY

it, id, hoc, illud
Italy, Italia, -ae, *f.*

javelin, pīlum, -ī, *n.*
journey, iter, itineris, *n.*
Julia, Iūlia, -ae, *f.*

kill, interficiō, 3
king, rēx, rēgis, *m.*
know, sciō, 4; cognōscō, 3, *in perf. tenses*

Labienus, Labiēnus, -ī, *m.*
labor, labōrō, 1
lack, *v.*, careō, 2, *with abl.*; dēsum, *irr., with dat.*
lack, *n.*, inopia, -ae, *f.*
lady, domina, -ae, *f.*
lake, lacus, -ūs, *m.*
land, terra, -ae, *f.*
large, magnus, -a, -um
last, proximus, -a, -um
lay waste, vāstō, 1
lead, dūcō, 3; lead back, redūcō, 3; lead out, ēdūcō, 3
leader, dux, ducis, *m.*
learn, cognōscō, 3
least, minimus, -a, -um
leave behind, relinquō, 3
left, sinister, -tra, -trum
legion, legiō, -ōnis, *f.*
lest, nē, *with subjunctive*
letter, litterae, -ārum, *f. plur.*
liberate, līberō, 1
lieutenant, lēgātus, -ī, *m.*
like, similis, -e
line of battle, aciēs, -ēī, *f.*
little, parvus, -a, -um
live, habitō, 1

long, longus, -a, -um; for a long time, diū
look at, spectō, 1
love, amō, 1

make, faciō, 3
man, vir, virī, *m.*; homō, -inis, *m.*
many, multī, -ae, -a, *plur.*
march, *v.*, iter faciō, 3
march, *n.*, iter, itineris, *n.*
Marcus, Mārcus, -ī, *m.*
marsh, palūs, palūdis, *f.*
master, dominus, -ī, *m.*
meanwhile, interim
messenger, nūntius, nūntī, *m.*
mile, mīlle passuum
mine, meus, -a, -um
money, pecūnia, -ae, *f.*
more, plūs, plūris
most, plūrimus, -a, -um
mother, māter, -tris, *f.*
mountain, mōns, montis, *m.*
move, moveō, 2
much, *adj.*, multus, -a, -um
much, *adv.*, multum; multō
must, *passive periphrastic conjugation*
my, meus, -a, -um

nation, nātiō, -ōnis, *f.*
native land, patria, -ae, *f.*
near, *adj.*, fīnitimus, -a, -um; propinquus, -a, -um
near, *prep.*, apud, *with acc.*
neighboring, fīnitimus, -a, -um
neighbors, fīnitimī, -ōrum, *m. plur.*
neither . . . nor, neque . . . neque
never, numquam
new, novus, -a, -um

night, nox, noctis, *f.*
no, nūllus, -a, -um; **no longer**, nōn iam
nor, neque
not, nōn; **not even**, nē ... quidem
nothing, nihil
now, iam, nunc
number, numerus, -ī, *m.*

ocean, ōceanus, -ī, *m.*
of, *sign of the genitive*; dē, *with abl.*; **out of**, ē *or* ex, *with abl.*
offer, dō, 1
often, saepe
on, in, *with abl.*; *abl. of time*; **on account of**, ob *or* propter, *with acc.*
once (upon a time), ōlim
one, ūnus, -a, -um
order, *v.*, iubeō, 2; imperō, 1, *with dat.*
order (in order that), ut, *with subjunctive*
other, alius, -a, -ud; **other of two**, alter, -era, -erum
ought, dēbeō, 2; *passive periphrastic conjugation*
our, noster, -tra, -trum; **our men**, nostrī, -ōrum, *m. plur.*
ourselves, nōs; ipsī, -ae
out of, ē *or* ex, *with abl.*
overcome, superō, 1; vincō, 3
own, (his, her, its, their) suus, -a, -um; **(my)** meus, -a, -um; **(our)** noster, -tra, -trum; **(your,** *sing.***)** tuus, -a, -um; **(your,** *plur.***)** vester, -tra, -trum

part, pars, partis, *f.*
peace, pāx, pācis, *f.*
people, populus, -ī, *m.*; nātiō, -ōnis, *f.*

personal enemy, inimīcus, -ī, *m.*
persuade, persuādeō, 2, *with dat.*
pirate, pīrāta, -ae, *m.*
pitch camp, castra pōnō, 3
place, *v.*, pōnō, 3; conlocō, 1; **place in command**, praeficiō, 3, *with dat. of the object over which*
place, *n.*, locus, -ī (*plur.* loca *and rarely* locī), *m.*
plan, cōnsilium, cōnsilī, *n.*
plead, ōrō, 1
please, placeō, 2, *with dat.*
pleasing, grātus, -a, -um
plenty, cōpia, -ae, *f.*
poet, poēta, -ae, *m.*
point out, dēmōnstrō, 1
poor, miser, -era, -erum
power, potestās, -ātis, *f.*; vīs, vīs, *f.*
praise, laudō, 1
prefer, mālō, *irr.*
prisoner, captīvus, -ī, *m.*
promise, polliceor, 2
protection, subsidium, subsidī, *n.*
province, prōvincia, -ae, *f.*
purpose (for the purpose of), ut (*neg.* nē), *with subjunctive*; ad, *with gerund or gerundive*; causā, *following a gerund or gerundive*
put in command, praeficiō, 3, *with dat. of the object over which*; **put to flight**, fugō, 1

queen, rēgīna, -ae, *f.*

receive, capiō, 3; recipiō, 3
relate, nārrō, 1
remain, maneō, 2
remember, memoriā teneō, 2

ENGLISH-LATIN VOCABULARY

reply, respondeō, 2
report, nūntiō, 1
resist, resistō, 3, *with dat.*
rest, reliquī, -ōrum, *m. plur.*; rest of, reliquus, -a, -um
return, revertō, 3; *commonly deponent in the present system*
reward, praemium, praemī, *n.*
right, dexter, -tra, -trum
river, flūmen, -inis, *n.*
road, via, -ae, *f.*
Roman, *adj.*, Rōmānus, -a, -um
Roman, *n.*, Rōmānus, -ī, *m.*
Rome, Rōma, -ae, *f.*
rule, regō, 3

sail, nāvigō, 1
sailor, nauta, -ae, *m.*
sake (for the sake of), causā, *following a genitive*
same, īdem, eadem, idem
say, dīcō, 3
scare, terreō, 2
scout, explōrātor, -ōris, *m.*
sea, mare, -is, *n.*
second, secundus, -a, -um
see, videō, 2
seek, petō, 3
self, ipse, -a, -um; suī
senate, senātus, -ūs, *m.*
send, mittō, 3; send ahead, praemittō, 3
servant, servus, -ī, *m.*
set free, līberō, 1; set out, proficīscor, 3
severe, gravis, -e
she, ea, haec, illa
shield, scūtum, -ī, *n.*
ship, nāvis, -is, *f.*

shore, lītus, -oris, *n.*
short, brevis, -e
show, dēmōnstrō, 1; praebeō, 2; doceō, 2
shut off, interclūdō, 3
sick, aeger, -gra, -grum
signal, signum, -ī, *n.*
since, *implied in a participle*
sing, cantō, 1
sister, soror, -ōris, *f.*
six, sex
slave, servus, -ī, *m.*
slight, parvus, -a, -um
small, parvus, -a, -um
so, tam, ita; so as not to, nē, *with subjunctive*; so great, tantus, -a, -um; so that, ut, *with subjunctive*
soldier, mīles, -itis, *m.*
some . . . others, aliī . . . aliī
somebody, some one, aliquis
something, aliquid
sometimes, interdum
son, fīlius, fīlī, *m.*
sortie, ēruptiō, -ōnis, *f.*
spear, hasta, -ae, *f.*
speed, celeritās, -ātis, *f.*
spend the winter, hiemō, 1
state, cīvitās, -ātis, *f.*
station, conlocō, 1
stay, maneō, 2
story, fābula, -ae, *f.*
street, via, -ae, *f.*
strength, vīs, vīs, *f.*
summer, aestās, -ātis, *f.*
sun, sōl, sōlis, *m.*
sunset, sōlis occāsus
supplies, commeātus, -ūs, *m.*
surpass, superō, 1
surrender, dēditiō, -ōnis, *f.*

survive, supersum, *irr., with dat.*
swamp, palūs, palūdis, *f.*
swim, natō, 1
sword, gladius, gladī, *m.*

take, capiō, 3
tall, altus, -a, -um
teach, doceō, 2
tell, nārrō, 1 ; dīcō, 3
ten, decem
tenth, decimus, -a, -um
terms, condiciō, -ōnis, *f.*
territory, fīnēs, -ium, *m. plur.*
than, quam
that, *dem. pron.*, is, ea, id ; ille, illa, illud ; **that of yours**, iste, -a, -ud
that, *rel. pron.*, quī, quae, quod
that, *conj., in purpose or result clauses*, ut, *with subjunctive*; *not expressed after a verb of saying*; **that not**, nē, ut nōn, *with subjunctive*
their, eōrum, eārum, eōrum ; (*reflexive*) suus, -a, -um
them, eōs, eās, ea
themselves, sē (sēsē); ipsī, -ae, -a
then, tum
there, ibi; *not translated in such expressions as* **there is**
therefore, itaque
they, eī, eae, ea ; hī, hae, haec ; illī, illae, illa
thing, rēs, reī. *f.*; *sometimes omitted*
think, putō, 1
third, tertius, -a, -um
this, is, ea, id ; hic, haec, hoc
though, *implied in a participle*
thousand, mīlle
three, trēs, tria

through, per, *with acc.*
throw, iaciō, 3
time, tempus, -oris, *n.*
tired, tired out, dēfessus, -a, -um
to, *sign of the dative*; ad *or* in, *with acc.*; *expressing purpose*, ut, *with subjunctive*; ad, *with gerund or gerundive*; causā, *following a gerund or gerundive*
to-day, hodiē
toward, ad, *with acc.*
tower, turris, -is, *f.*
town, oppidum, -ī, *n.*
trader, mercātor, -ōris, *m.*
tree, arbor, -oris, *f.*
tribune, tribūnus, -ī, *m.*
troops, cōpiae, -ārum, *f. plur.*
trumpet, tuba, -ae, *f.*
turret, turris, -is, *f.*
two, duo, -ae, -o ; **which of two**, uter, utra, utrum ; **each of two**, uterque, utraque, utrumque

unfriendly, inimīcus, -a, -um
unhappy, miser, -era, -erum
unwilling (be), nōlō, *irr.*
urge, hortor, 1

valor, virtūs, -ūtis, *f.*
very, *superlative degree*; maximē; ipse, -a, -um
victory, victōria, -ae, *f.*
village, vīcus, -ī, *m.*

wage, gerō, 3
wagon, carrus, -ī, *m.*
wait, wait for, exspectō, 1
walk, ambulō, 1
wall, mūrus, -ī, *m.*

ENGLISH-LATIN VOCABULARY

war, bellum, -ī, *n.*
warn, moneō, 2
water, aqua, -ae, *f.*
way, via, -ae, *f.*; iter, itineris, *n.*
weapon, tēlum, -ī, *n.*
welcome, *v.*, recipiō, 3
welcome, *adj.*, grātus, -a, -um
well, bene
what, quis (quī), quae, quid (quod)
when, cum; *ablative absolute*; *implied in a participle*
whence, unde
where, ubi
whether, num
which, quī, quae, quod; **which of two**, uter, utra, utrum
while, cum; *implied in a participle*
whither, quō
who, *(rel.)* quī, quae; *(interrog.)* quis
whole, tōtus, -a, -um; omnis, -e
why, cūr
wide, lātus, -a, -um
width, lātitūdō, -inis, *f.*

wind, ventus, -ī, *m.*
winter, hiems, hiemis, *f.*; **winter quarters**, hīberna, -ōrum, *n. plur.*
wish, volō, *irr.*; cupiō, 3
with, cum, *with abl.*; *sometimes abl. alone*
without, sine, *with abl.*
woman, fēmina, -ae, *f.*
woods, silva, -ae, *f.*
word, verbum, -ī, *n.*
work, labōrō, 1
wound, *v.*, vulnerō, 1
wound, *n.*, vulnus, -eris, *n.*
wretched, miser, -era, -erum

year, annus, -ī, *m.*
yet, tamen
you, *(sing.)* tū; *(plur.)* vōs
young man, adulēscēns, -entis, *m.*
your, *(sing.)* tuus, -a, -um; *(plur.)* vester, -tra, -trum

zeal, studium, studī, *n.*

INDEX

References are to sections unless otherwise indicated

ā or ab with ablative of agent, 242, 243
ablative, XXIV, *b*
   of adjectives of third declension, 208, *c*
   absolute, 452-455
   of accompaniment, 142, 143
   of agent, 242, 243
   of cause, 184, 185
   of degree of difference, 320, 321
   of manner, 128, 129
   of means, 121, 122
   of place from which, 177, 229, 230
   of place where, 58, 59
   of separation, 281, 282
   of specification, 480, 481
   of time, 218, 219
   with ex, equivalent to partitive genitive, 309, *a*
   with prepositions, 194
accent, 20-22
accusative, XXIV, *b*
   in indirect statements, 400, 401
   object of transitive verbs, 32, 33
   of extent, 332, 333
   of place to which, 179, 229, 230
   subject of the infinitive, 398, 399
   with prepositions, 193
ācer, declension, 644
   comparison, 306, 647
adjectives, definition, III, *a*
   kinds and definitions, III, *b-f*
   of first and second declensions, 78, 79, 643; in -er, 103, 643; with genitive in -īus and dative in -ī, 385-387, 646
   of third declension, 208, 644; of one, two, and three terminations, 208
   agreement, 79
   comparison, 296, 306, 307, 317, 319, 647, 649; irregular, 307, 317, 319, 649; by adverbs, XXVI, *c*

declension of comparatives, 297, 648
meaning of comparative and superlative, 296, *c*
interrogative, 152, 154
possessive, 278; distinction in use: between suus and eius, 279; between tuus and vester, 278; omission of suus, 280
predicate, XV, *a*; 86, 88; with complementary infinitive, 394, *b*
used as nouns, III, *f*; 196
adverbial clauses with quā and ut, 497
adverbs, definition, V, *a*
   kinds and definitions, V, *b-f*
   formation, 325, 326; of the comparative and superlative, 327, *a*
   comparison, 327, 650
agent, expressed by the ablative with ā or ab, 242, 243
ager, declension, 97, 637
agreement, of adjectives, 79; after a complementary infinitive, 394, *b*
   of appositives, 93, 94
   of predicate nouns, XV, *c*; 87
   of relative pronouns, 247, 248
   of verb with its subject, 29
aliquis, 420, *c*; 657
alius, declension, 646
   alius ... alius, 387
alphabet, 1
alter ... alter, 387
amāns, declension, 645
amō, conjugation, 658
antecedent, definition, II, *b*
antepenult, 11
   when accented, 21
apposition, 93, 94
article, not used in Latin, 27, *a*
audāx, declension, 644
   comparison, 296, 647
audiō, conjugation, 662

base, 63, *a*
bonus, declension, 643
    comparison, 317, 649
brevis, declension, 644
    comparison, 296, 647

capiō, conjugation, 661
caput, declension, 171, 638
cardinals, definition, III, *c*
    declension, 378, 646
    indeclinable forms, 378
    table of, 651
case, definition, XXIV
    of relative pronoun, 247
case endings, 25, *a*; 63, 73, 171, 189, 292, 331
cases, names of English, XXIV, *a*
    names of Latin, XXIV, *b*. See under **nominative, genitive**, etc.
    uses, 512
causā with gerund, 461, *a*
    with gerundive, 472
causal clauses with **quod**, 50, 51
cause, expressed by the ablative, 184, 185
    expressed by a prepositional phrase, 186, 195, *b*
characteristic vowels of the four conjugations, 38
clauses, definitions, XX, *a–f*
    indirect questions, 372, 373
    of cause, with **quod**, 50, 51
    of purpose, with **ut** and **nē**, 343, 344; substantive, 355, 356
    of result, with **ut** and **ut nōn**, 357, 358
    temporal, with **cum**, 487, 488
cohors, declension, 189, 639
comparative, declined, 297, 648
    formation, 296, *a*
    meaning *too*, etc., 296, *c*
comparison, definition, XXVI, *a*
    methods of, in English and in Latin, XXVI, *b, c*
    of adjectives, 296, 306, 307, 317, 319, 647, 649; of adjectives in -lis, 307; irregular, 307, 317, 319, 649
    of adverbs, 327, 650
complement of verb, XV, *b*
complementary infinitive, 394

conjugation, definition, XXVII, *a*. See **verbs**
    in English and Latin verbs, XXVII, *b, c*
conjunctions, definition, VII, *a*
    kinds and definitions, VII, *b, c*
consonant-i, 3
consonants, how pronounced, 6
contraction in genitive of nouns in -ium and -ius, 98
coördinate clauses, XX, *f*
copula, XV, *b*
cornū, declension, 292, 640
cum (conj.) in temporal clauses, 487, 488
cum (prep.), with ablative of accompaniment, 142, 143
    with ablative of manner, 128, 129
    joined to ablative of personal, reflexive, relative, and interrogative pronouns, p. 109, note 1

dative, XXIV, *a*, 4; *b*
    double, 426, *a*
    of indirect object, 56, 57
    of purpose, 426, 427
    of reference, 426, 428
    with adjectives, 110, 111
    with compound verbs, 424, 425
    with special intransitive verbs, 432, 433
declension, definition, XXII. See **nouns, pronouns, adjectives**, and **comparatives**
degree of difference, expressed by the ablative, 320, 321
demonstrative adjectives and pronouns, definition, II, *f*; III, *e*. See **pronouns**; also **hic, īdem, ille, ipse, is, iste**
dependent clause, XIX, note; XX, *a–e*
deponent verbs, 482, 483, 669
deus, declension, 642
diēs, declension, 331, 641
    gender, 331
diphthongs, how pronounced, 5
direct statements, 400
domō, used of place from which, 229, 230, *a*
domum, used of place to which, 229, 230, *b*

# INDEX

domus, declension, 642
  gender, 292, *b*
dōnum, declension, 73, 637
dum with present indicative, p. 133, note 4
duo, declension, 646

ego, declension, 652
eius compared with **suus**, 279
enclitics, 22
eō, conjugation, 667
Eutropius, selections from, 547–551
exercitus, declension, 292, 640
extent of time or space, how expressed, 332, 333

ferō, conjugation, 666
fifth declension, 331, 641
filius, declension, 98, 637
fīō, conjugation, 668
first declension, 63, 636
fourth declension, 292, 640
future active participle, XXXIV, *b*
  formation, 441, *a*
  in principal parts, p. 63, note 1
  use, 444
future perfect tense, formation of, active, 223, *a*; passive, 286, *b*

gender, in English and in Latin, XXV, *a*, *b*; 64
  in first declension, 64, *a*
  in second declension, 99
  in third declension, 171, *b*
  in fourth declension, 292 and *b*
  in fifth declension, 331
genitive, XXIV, *a*, 2; *b*
  objective, 380, 381
  of material, p. 79, note 1
  partitive, 308, 309
  possessive, 43, 44
gerund, a verbal noun, XXXII, *c*; 459, 460
  uses, 461
gerundive, a verbal adjective, 471
  agreement of, 471
  used with **ad** and **causā** to express purpose, 472
  used with **sum** to form the passive periphrastic conjugation, 473;
  expresses necessary action, 473, *a*

Helvetians, campaign against the, 440, 451, 479, 494, 514–523
hic, declension, 654
  uses, 228, 263
hortor, conjugation, 669
hortus, declension, 73, 637
hostis, declension, 189, 639

i with force of a consonant before a vowel, 3
i-stems, 189, 639
īdem, declension, 654
  use, 410, *a*
iēns, declension, 645
ille, declension, 654
  uses, 228, 263
in with accusative and ablative, 193, 194
indefinite pronouns and adjectives, definition, II, *g*; III, *e*. See pronouns
independent clause. XVIII, note
indirect object, definition, XIV, *b*
  case of, 56, 57
indirect questions, 372, 373
indirect statements, 400–402
infinitive, definition and English uses, XXXII, *a*, *b*
  formation, 38, 392; omission of **esse** in compound forms, p. 190, note 1
  as object, 398
  as subject, 393
  complementary, 394
  in indirect statements, 400–402; tenses in, 402
  not used to express purpose, 343, *b*
  takes a subject accusative, 398, 399
inflection, definition, XXI
interjection, definition, VIII
interrogative adjective, 152, 154
interrogative pronoun, 152, 153
intransitive verb, definition, IV, *c*
  followed by dative, 432, 433
-iō, verbs in, of the third conjugation, 175, 661
ipse, declension, 654
  distinguished from **suī**, 410, *c*
  used for emphasis, 410, *c*

irregular adjectives (genitives in -īus), 385-387, 646
irregular comparison, 307, 317, 319, 649
irregular verbs: eō, 667; ferō, 666; fīō, 668; possum, 664; sum, 663; volō, nōlō, and mālō, 665
is, declension, 147, 654
　relation to hic and ille, 148
　uses as a demonstrative pronoun and adjective, 148
　used as a personal pronoun, 263
iste, declension, 654
　uses, 410, *a*, *b*
iter, declension, 642
Iuppiter, declension, 642

lātior, declension, 297, 648
lātus, comparison, 296, 647
līber, declension, 643
locative case, XXIV, *b*

magnus, comparison, 317, 649
mālō, conjugation, 665
malus, comparison, 317, 649
manner, how expressed, 128, 129
manus, gender, 292, *b*
mare, declension, 189, 639
means, expressed by the ablative, 121, 122
mīles, declension, 171, 638
mille, declension, 378, 646
　use, 379
miser, comparison, 306, 647
moneō, conjugation, 659
mōns, declension, 189, 639
moods, kinds and definitions, XXIX-XXXI
multus, comparison, 317, 649

-ne, enclitic, 22, 27, *d*
nē, *that not* (*lest*), introducing negative clauses of purpose, 343, 344
nōlō, conjugation, 665
nominative, XXIV, *a*, 1; *b*
　as subject of a finite verb, 28
　of pronouns expressed only for emphasis or contrast, 39, *b*; 264
　predicate, 86-88
nōs, declension, 652
noster, declension, 643

nouns, definition, 1, *a*
　kinds and definitions, 1, *b-f*
　first declension, 63, 636
　second declension, 73, 97, 98, 637
　third declension, 171, 189, 638, 639
　fourth declension, 292, 640
　fifth declension, 331, 641
　predicate, 87
　rules of gender, 64, *a*; 99, 171, *b*; 292 and *b*, 331
number, singular and plural, XXIII
numerals, definition, III, *c*
　declension, 378
　table of, 651

object, definition, XIV, *a*
　direct and indirect, XIV, *b*
　of a transitive verb, 33
on account of, how expressed in Latin, 195
order of words, 35, 60, 81, 89, 228, 386, *b*
ordinals, definition, III, *c*
　declined like bonus, 378
　table of, 651

participles, definition and uses, XXXIV, *a-c*
　agreement, 443
　declension, 442, 645
　formation, 441, *a*
　in deponent verbs, 483; perfect, 483, *a*
　no past and perfect active and no present passive, in Latin, XXXIV, *b*
　often best rendered as a clause, 445
　tenses, 444
partitive genitive, 308, 309
parvus, comparison, 317, 649
passive voice, XXVIII, 237
　formation, 238, *a*; 239, 286, *a*, *c*
　agent expressed by the ablative with ā or ab, 242, 243
penult, definition, 11
　when accented, 21
perfect tense, formation of, active, 134 and *b*; passive, 286, *a*, *c*
　definite and indefinite, 134, *a*
periphrastic conjugation, passive, 473
　synopsis of, 670

INDEX

person, distinctions, II, c
personal pronouns, see pronouns
phrase, definition and kinds, XVI, a–c
place to which and from which, 229, 230
pluperfect tense, formation of, active, 223, a; passive, 286, b
plūs, declension, 648
portus, irregular dative and ablative plural, 292, a
possessive adjectives, see adjectives
possum, how compounded, 411
  conjugation, 664
potior, conjugation, 669
predicate, definition, XI, c
  complete, XIII
  simple, XII
predicate adjective, agreement, 88
  definition, XV
predicate nominative, XV, c
predicate noun, agreement, 87
  definition, XV
prefixes, 630
prepositions, definition, VI
  with the ablative, 194
  with the accusative, 193
primary tenses, 349
principal parts of verbs, 132
proelium, declension, 98, 637
pronouns, definition, II, a
  kinds and definitions, II, c–h
  demonstrative, definition, II, f; declension, 654; hic and ille, uses, 228; is, uses, 228; relation of is to hic and ille, 148; iste, idem, ipse, 410
  indefinite, definition, II, g; declension, 657; uses, 420; quid forms used as pronouns, quod forms as adjectives, 420, e
  interrogative, definition, II, e; declension, 153, 656; followed by cum, p. 109, note 1
  personal, definition, II, c; declension, 652; nominative expressed only for emphasis or contrast, 264; third person supplied by is, sometimes by hic or ille, 263; followed by cum, p. 109, note 1
  possessive, see possessive adjectives

  reflexive, definition, II, h; declension, 653; use, 266; followed by cum, p. 109, note 1
  relative, definition, II, d; agreement, 247, 248; declension, 246, 655; followed by cum, p. 109, note 1; referring to a personal pronoun, 267
pronunciation, sounds of letters, 4–6
puer, declension, 97, 637
purpose, dative of, 426, 427
  expressed by the accusative of the gerund or gerundive with ad, 461, 472
  expressed by the genitive of the gerund or gerundive with causā, 461, 472
  expressed by the subjunctive with ut and nē, 343, 344
  not expressed by the infinitive, 343, b
  substantive clauses of, 355, 356

quā in adverbial clauses, 497
-que, enclitic, 22
questions, indirect, 372, 373
quī, declension, 246, 655
quīdam, 420, d; 657
quis, declension, 153, 656
quisquam, 420, 657
quisque, 420, 657
quod clause of fact, 495, 496

reflexive pronouns, see pronouns
regō, conjugation, 660
relative pronouns, see pronouns
rēs, declension, 331, 641
result, expressed by the subjunctive with ut and ut nōn, 357, 358
rēx, declension, 171, 638

sē, distinguished from ipse, 410, c
second declension, 73, 97, 98, 637
secondary tenses, 349
sentences, definition, IX
  kinds and definitions, X, a–d
separation, expressed by the ablative, 281, 282
sequence of tenses, 348–352
sequor, conjugation, 669
space, extent of, 332, 333

specification, ablative of, 480, 481
stems of verbs, 132, 133
Stories from Roman History, 552–555
Stories of Hercules, 529–538
Stories of Perseus, 277, 291, 316, 339, 370, 391, 408
Stories of Ulysses, 539–546
Story of the Aduatuci, 524–528
subject, definition, xi, *b*
  complete, xiii
  simple, xii
  agreement of verb with, 29
  not expressed, 264
  of an infinitive, 399
  of a verb, 28
subjunctive, definition, xxx
  formation, of present, 342; of imperfect, 347; of perfect and pluperfect, 371
  in indirect questions, 372, 373
  in purpose clauses, 343, 344, 355, 356
  in result clauses, 357, 358
  in temporal clauses with **cum**, 487, 488
  tenses, 341; sequence of, 348–352
subordinate clauses in indirect statements, 501, 502
substantive clauses, of fact with **quod**, 495, 496
  of purpose, 355, 356
suffixes, 632
suī, declension, 653
  distinguished from **ipse**, 410, *c*
sum, conjugation, 663
summary of uses, of nouns, 512
  of verbs, 513
suus, 278, 279
  compared with **eius**, 279
  omission of, 280
syllables, number of, 8
  division of, 9, 10; in compound words, 10
  how named, 11
  long and short, 17–19
synopsis of the verb, 671

temporal clauses introduced by **cum**, 487, 488
tense, xxxiii, *a, b*

tenses, distinction in use between the perfect and the imperfect, 134, *a*
  of the infinitive in indirect statements, 402
  primary and secondary, 349
  sequence of, 348–352
  sign of the future, 126, *a*
  sign of the imperfect, 120, *b*
terminations, of first declension, 63
  of second declension, 73
  of third declension, 171, 189
  of fourth declension, 292
  of fifth declension, 331
third declension, 171, 638
  i-stems, 189, 639
time, at which and within which, 218, 219
  extent of, 332, 333
to, how expressed in Latin, 195
towns, names of, expressing place to which and from which, 229, 230
transitive verb, iv, *b*
trēs, declension, 646
tū, declension, 652
tuus, compared with **vester**, 278

-ubus, in irregular dative and ablative plural, 292, *a*
ultima, 11
ūnus, declension, 646
ut, in adverbial clauses, 497
  in clauses of purpose, 343, 344, 355, 356
  in clauses of result, 357, 358
  translations, 343, 1 and *b*

verbs, definition, iv, *a*
  kinds and definitions, iv, *b–f*
  agreement, 29; in relative clauses, 267
  case, of subject, 28; of object, 33
  conjugations, how distinguished, 38
  deponent, form, meaning, how distinguished, 482; active forms, 483; participles of both voices, 483; perfect participle, active in meaning, 483, *a*; conjugation, 669
  intransitive, which are transitive in English, 432, 433
  irregular, see **eō, ferō, fīō, mālō, nōlō, possum, sum**, and **volō**

of first conjugation, 658
of second conjugation, 659
of third conjugation, 660, 661
of fourth conjugation, 662
passive periphrastic conjugation, 473; synopsis of, 670
personal endings, 25, *a*; 39, 134
principal parts, 132
vereor, conjugation, 669
vester, compared with **tuus**, 278
vir, declension, 97, 637

virtūs, declension, 171, 638
vīs, declension, 642
vocative case, XXIV, *b*
voice, XXVIII
volō, conjugation, 665
vōs, declension, 652
vowels, how pronounced, 4
 long, 14, 15
 short, 12, 13

with, how expressed in Latin, 195